Arguing Sainthood

Arguing Sainthood

Modernity, Psychoanalysis, and Islam

Katherine Pratt Ewing

Duke University Press   Durham and London 1997

© 1997 Duke University Press
All rights reserved
Printed in the United States of America
on acid-free paper ∞
Typeset in Sabon by Keystone Typesetting, Inc.
Library of Congress Cataloging-in-Publication Data
appear on the last printed page of this book.
All photographs are by the author.

I dedicate this book to my parents,

Edith Pratt Ewing and Scott Ewing

Contents

Illustrations

Preface

In Pakistan the Muslim *pīr* is a teacher of Sufi (mystical) wisdom, spiritual guide, healer, worker of miracles, hidden governor, and the object of devotion at shrines. In many areas, practicing pīrs and active shrines can be found in nearly every neighborhood, and the pīr continues to play a significant role in the constitution of identity and subjectivity in the Muslim world. My interest in the Sufi pīr developed after I arrived in Pakistan for my first fieldwork. What struck me most when I got to Pakistan and began to work in the complex urban environment of Lahore were the arguments I encountered. Whenever anyone made a statement about religious practice, and especially about pīrs and Sufism, there always seemed to be someone else around to disagree — even within the confines of a single family. Furthermore, people were intensely interested in the topic, as if something crucial were at stake in my coming to *the* proper understanding of where Sufism and pīrs fit (or why they did *not* fit) into their lives and into a broader picture of Islam and of Pakistan. It was this conflictual aspect of the phenomenon — at both personal and political levels — that pushed me into a focus on culture as a process by which individuals negotiate ambiguity and inconsistency (see Ewing 1988, 1990a). This book is based on observations of practices surrounding these Sufi pīrs that I made over the course of two years of anthropological fieldwork in Lahore.[1]

I also came to know Sufis who deeply impressed me with their wisdom and with their successful negotiation and resolution of personal conflicts involving the relationship between Sufi practice and a "scientific" orientation. Gradually, I began to take seriously the challenges they put to me concerning the foundation of my own beliefs and practices: my own positioning came into question. I had found that the interpretive strategy of "bracketing" the truth value of Sufi doctrines set me firmly apart from the people I most wanted to know and understand. As time went on, I allowed my own beliefs and values to be challenged; I allowed Sufi insights about human nature and the world to speak to me as truth. Oddly, it was my anthropological training — specifically, the taboo against "going native" — that placed the strongest barrier to this process (Ewing 1994). The whole experience was intensely challenging, both intellectually and emotionally.

In order to develop new tools for investigating the negotiation of identity and the phenomenon of conflict within the context of subjective experience that had impressed me so much in my first fieldwork, I spent several years engaged in psychoanalytic training at the Chicago Institute for Psychoanalysis. I was concerned with acquiring a knowledge of psychoanalytic theory and an experience of clinical practice in order to tackle the problem of how to look at identity as both a psychological and a political/cultural phenomenon. But perhaps the most valuable aspect of my training was learning to use myself more effectively as an observational tool — learning to focus on my own relationships with the people I worked with, reading my own conflicts and reactions as a key source of information about the other person's concerns and intentions (see Ewing 1987). Of course, I also learned a lot about myself — my immaturities, unresolved conflicts, desires, and peculiarities — and my feelings about Sufism. I found that at the end of the psychoanalytic process, a process that is in many respects the epitome of the Enlightenment project of replacing the forces of instinct and tradition with the powers of observation and reason, Sufism continued to offer a powerful perspective, almost a temptation, that I could not fully reconcile with a psychoanalytic perspective and the interpretive constraints it imposed on my subjectivity.[2]

Much of my work over the next few years went toward seeking to transcend or at least reduce the gulf that has long existed between studies of the individual and psyche on the one hand and, on the other hand, anthropological studies of culture and society — most of which are founded on unexamined and, therefore, oversimplified theories of human nature and the psyche. Fortunately, many others have also been involved in this effort, both from within anthropology, and from other disciplines. In recent years, for instance, Lacan's recasting of psychoanalytic theory has been taken up by a number of social theorists — primarily within the areas of gender theory and political/cultural theories (such as Laclau and Mouffe 1985; Žižek 1989). Many have struggled with a theoretical tension between the positing of a discursively constituted subject and the problem of agency.[3] Harshly critical of Lacan and Freud, yet inspired by them, Deleuze and Guattari (1983, 1987) have brought to this endeavor a Nietzschean perspective that radically decenters the subject.

This book, then, addresses what I see as a crucial question about how to theorize the place of the individual as a subject operating in a complex social field of conflicting ideologies and cross-cutting interests. But at the same time, I seek to resolve the difficult issue for myself of how to live at the nexus of conflicting discourses — psychoanalysis, anthropology, and Sufism — all of which compete for my own loyalty and identity. I have employed two basic strategies to resolve this tension. First, I have focused on comparable (if not the same) conflicts among the people I came to know in Pakistan, recasting both psychoanalytic theory and anthropology in my efforts to develop a satisfactory model of their experience. Second, I have brought Sufi views of the nature of culture, reality, and the psyche directly into the theoretical conversation, not only as phenomena to be explained and interpreted but as explanatory models. These models facilitate the effort to move beyond Eurocentric theories and histories by undermining the barriers created by Orientalist discursive strategies.

Field research in Pakistan was funded by two grants from the American Institute of Pakistan Studies (in 1975–77 and 1984–85). Duke University has been generous in its support of my research, providing funds for research assistance as I worked to prepare this manuscript for publication.

In Pakistan I thank those friends, neighbors, and strangers who were willing to spend time with me, helping me to feel welcome, answering my many questions, putting up with what at times must have been my inconvenient presence. Thanks go especially to the family of Malik Abdul Hamid for their support of many aspects of my research while I was in Pakistan. Perhaps most trying for them was that period when I brought my then two-year-old daughter Julia to live with them for several weeks; I apologize again for the broken china. William Das was an invaluable associate, who enriched me with his insights and knowledge and enthusiastically helped me to contact a diverse array of people in Lahore. I thank also members of the sociology and psychology departments at Punjab University, who served as the local sponsors of my research and were generous in their offers of help and facilities.

I would like to thank my colleagues in the Cultural Anthropology Department at Duke University for their support, stimulating company, and insightful suggestions all along the way. I am also grateful to the following people, who have given me comments and suggestions on this manuscript at various stages in its preparation: Anne Allison, Art Buehler, Carl Ernst, Jan French, Müge Galin, David Gilmartin, Bruce Lawrence, Gananath Obeyesekere, Charlie Piot, Naomi Quinn, John Richards, Orin Starn, Ken Surin, Tony Stewart, Jim Wilce, Rick Collier, Ayşe Gül Karayazgan, Omid Safi, Scott Kugle, and members of the Triangle South Asia Colloquium and the Carolina Islamic Studies Seminar. Clare Talwalker, in addition to giving me her scholarly reactions to the manuscript, also devoted hours to the painstaking task of helping me get my references right.

Special thanks go to Ken Wissoker at Duke University Press, who gave me just the right guidance in the final stages of "massaging" the manuscript into shape and who facilitated the process of publication. He has been a pleasure to work with. I thank also two anonymous readers, whose suggestions for revision were knowledgeable and insightful.

I want to express my enduring appreciation and gratitude to my husband, Thomas DiPrete, for his scholarly advice, unflagging support, patience, and, perhaps most crucial, his flexibility in the negotiation of the joint and enormous task of running a household filled with small children while managing two academic careers. And, finally, my love and my thanks go to my daughters, Julia, Bethany, and Justine, who have deepened my understanding of what life is all about in ways that I hope have made this a better book than it might otherwise have been.

1

Hegemony, Consciousness, and
the Postcolonial Subject

Sufi Ghulam Rasul was a pīr, a Sufi "saint" and healer, who now lies
buried in a tomb in the Miānī Sahib Graveyard in the Pakistani city of
Lahore, a modest contribution to Lahore's architectural and historical
riches. When I first met him in 1976, he lived in a middle-income
neighborhood that borders the graveyard. He was receiving visitors in
a large reception room (*baithak*) built for the purpose. At our first
meeting, unexpected for each of us,[1] his wife ushered me through an
interior courtyard to a doorway. Scattered beside the doorway were
seven pairs of shoes. We stopped to add our shoes to the pile and then
entered a large, dim room. It had no furniture, but there were straw
mats on the floor. Sufi Sahib, as he was ordinarily called, was seated
facing the doors, cross-legged on a fine Bokhara carpet, his telephone
beside him[2] and several large cushions behind him. Four women were
sitting in a semicircle around him, and two men sat off to one side,
apart from the women.

Sufi Sahib's wife introduced me and the young Pakistani woman with
me as students who were interested in studying pīrs and Islam. Sufi
Sahib invited us to join the small circle around him, and his wife left the
room. I asked if he would mind if we sat there for a few minutes to
watch him with his followers.

Sufi Sahib's appearance was impressive and conformed to my expectations of the Sufi pīr. He was dressed in white and wore a white turban.
His white beard was long but neatly trimmed. He sat in a meditative

pose, gently smiling, eyes half-closed when he wasn't staring intently into the eyes of the person before him. In front of him was a tray on which were arranged a small pile of newspaper, rock salt, and a tiny hammer. As he sat before his followers, he would gently, almost abstractedly, tap the salt with the hammer while muttering prayers under his breath.

He dealt with his followers one by one, handing each of them a small packet of salt. Finally, I asked him what the salt was for. He explained that sick people come to him and that this is their medicine: "I read prayers over it all night. Whenever I blow over the salt, my followers, wherever they are, feel better." One of the women went up to him, sat before him, and told him that her son was sick. As she spoke, he quickly licked a piece of the salt, wrapped it in paper, and handed it to her, giving her instructions on how to use it. She thanked him, rose, and backed out of the room.

I asked some of his followers where they lived. Though this pīr worked in very unassuming quarters (the entry to his home was just a doorway like any other doorway along an unpaved street in a lower-middle-class neighborhood) and was but one out of a couple of dozen pīrs in this part of town, he drew a socially and geographically diverse following: one man present that day had come from another city, and the others were from all over Lahore, including the wealthiest part of town. One man was a brigadier general. Another had recently returned from study in England.

The presence of followers such as these illustrates how modernity, whatever it may be, has not created a population of the sort of secularized, rational subjects envisioned by many nation-builders and policymakers in the early days of Pakistan's independence. The Lahore District Census Report for 1961, for instance, described pīrs in the following terms:

> *Pirs* are held in great esteem and respect by villagers who pay quarterly, half-yearly or annual visits to their *Mureeds* [disciples] and get *Nazranas* [offerings] in the form of cash, or clothes according to the economic status of the follower. Besides the living *Pirs,* the people have great faith in the *Pirs* who died centuries ago and attend their shrines at the time of their annual *Urs* [death anniversary festival]. The hold of the *Pirs* is gradually dying away. (*Population Census of Pakistan: Lahore District* 1961:22)

This passage is a manifestation of a modernizing discourse that has pervaded most public policy within the "developing" countries in the postcolonial period. It sets up a series of dichotomies in what today appears a naive celebration of modernization: tradition versus modernity, rural versus urban, and (implicitly) wasted economic resources versus economic rationality. These dichotomies formed the basis for the construction of a range of ideologies that articulated what administrators and politicians saw as the task ahead for the consolidation of Pakistan as a modern nation. In this particular passage from the census, the pīrs were depicted as a part of the dying "traditional" that still stood between the population and the modern development of Pakistan. The passage expresses, apparently unselfconsciously, the Enlightenment view of human history as a single trajectory of Progress. More specifically, it is a manifestation of the Orientalist discourse sketched out by Said (1979), in which an imagined passive, traditional Oriental stands unfavorably contrasted with the active, modern, rational Western self. It is also a vision of the future that has since crumbled into the uncertainties of what has been called postmodernity or late capitalism (Harvey 1989), a time when the premises of this modernizing discourse and the Eurocentric notion of history that such premises presuppose have been exposed and challenged.

When modernization is assumed to be an unstoppable force shaping the future in a predetermined way, it is likely that contemporary Sufi practice will be interpreted in either of two ways: (1) as a watered-down version of liberal democracy dressed up in local symbols that have been propagated in state ideological formations to modernize the general population (see chapter 3 below), or (2) as a form of resistance to the hegemony of a secularized Western discourse, a Sufism therefore thoroughly penetrated by the hegemonic order that it stands against.[3] These two interpretations do describe two ideologies that have been constructed out of signs drawn from Sufism and from other aspects of Islam: they are positions that are publicly articulated in Pakistan and play a role in the politics of Sufism. Nevertheless, they do not adequately capture the ways in which aspects of the modern have been taken up into Sufi practice.

Both of these interpretations of Sufi practice presume that the force of Western-invented technologies, Western epistemologies, Western political ideologies such as liberal democracy, and Western modes of domination — industrial capitalism and colonial empire — have been so utterly transforming of an entity that we have constructed and labeled "traditional" society as to create a fundamental rupture with the past. It implies, in other words, that this master narrative of the project of modernization within the historical period of modernity has been hegemonic, that it forms the basis of the subjective experience of the postcolonial, even when resisted. This argument has been made even by scholars who have sought to disrupt the presumed equation of modernity with progress. My argument is organized in reaction to this presumption of hegemony.

One source of distortion in our perception of the power of modernity and the processes of modernization is the way modernity is seen as a single entity that bears an overwhelming discursive and material force. In order to avoid exaggerating its power, it is important to recognize that modernity itself is not a single force but rather the temporary conjunction of practices and ideologies that have diverse sources and divergent trajectories (see Reddy 1987, 1993). Current technologies are, of course, taken up into Sufi practice, but they are transformed and encompassed in local circles of meaning. Sufism, itself a diverse phenomenon, thus has a historical trajectory that has been affected but not determined by the composite of forces that we call modernity. An example of the transformation of a fragment of "modernity" in the context of Sufi practice is Sufi Sahib's placement of his telephone alongside his rock salt: it enables him to listen to the problems of his more distant followers and to blow them blessings through the phone line, but it does not in itself transform the discourse through which he operates. I use evidence from Sufi practice in Pakistan to demonstrate that in most aspects of social life, the practices associated with modernity contribute fragments to individual experience. But these fragments are taken up and rearticulated in ways quite different from the discursive monolith that has figured so prominently in theories focused on deconstructing it, so that they come to bear meanings not predictable from a modernizing, secularist, or other Western discourse. These fragments also leave diverse traces in individuals, who themselves are historically specific conjunctions shaped by multiple others, of which the Western other is only one.

Using the pīr as a focus of inquiry, this study realigns a triad of concepts — hegemony, consciousness, and the subject — that have appeared in a number of recent writings on the postcolonial subject. I challenge the premise that a hegemonic discourse is naturalized as

"consciousness" by distinguishing the experiencing subject as a historically located, embodied, and psychologically organized individual
from the discursive subject positions that such an individual may occupy. Breaking with the tendency of many recent writers to assume a
determined relationship between hegemonic discourse and consciousness, I return to an older usage of the concept of hegemony as a control
over public discursive space, a phenomenon that must be distinguished
from consciousness. Discourses constitute subject positions, but the
experiencing subject is a nonunitary agent (perhaps better described as
a bundle of agencies) who — in part through the experience of competing ideologies and alternative discourses — operates with a potential for
critical distance from any one discourse or subject position, including a
discourse of modernity. I thereby create a theoretical space for a desiring, experiencing subjectivity that stands at a nexus of discourses. It is
this space, which enables a critically conscious center of experience,
that I demonstrate and explore in this book.

From this perspective, I examine the way in which competing ideologies that have emerged in the process of nation-building in Pakistan
are played out in individual experience among ordinary Pakistanis.
Secularism, versions of Islamic modernism, Islamic reform, fundamentalism, and "traditionalism" are all platforms on which political leaders
have sought to mobilize a following and shape government policy. The
pīr, or Sufi saint, has been a target of much of this ideological conflict
about the place of Islam in the Pakistani nation-state. But the pīr also
plays an important role in the lives of individuals, who often turn to the
pīr for healing in times of personal crisis and conflict. I, therefore, focus
on the pīr as a kind of nodal point where these political and personal
processes come together. At this intersection, I observe closely the extent to which ordinary people are shaped or determined by a discourse
of modernity and by the ideologies that arise out of and in reaction to
this discourse.

Two places where the operations of the complex individual subject
can be seen are in everyday interpersonal arguments and in the telling
of personal narratives. Through each of these phenomena, it is possible
to highlight the ways in which the experiencing subject, the individual,
moves among discourses, taking different stances, expressing different
realities, shifting from moment to moment. The book, therefore, includes a series of arguments and stories: middle-class women, for instance, disagree about whether a neighborhood pīr is a fraud. A univer-

sity student suggests to a wandering beggar ascetic that he should move into a housing project. A pīr with a questionable past tells me several versions of his life story, as do various followers, neighbors, and relatives. A psychiatrist who worked for years in England speaks with longing about his own search for a pīr who will be a guide and teacher. I find myself in the presence of a Sufi who forces me to confront my own desire and fear. Through arguments and narratives we can observe a series of ideological positionings, which are like snapshots that capture the subject in frozen moments. But narratives in which a subject accounts for its past activities, as in a life history, also display conflicts and inconsistencies as the individual as experiencing subject claims or denies identity with past positionings. Through narratives the subject visibly works to cover over the gaps created by these slippages, thereby indicating its presence while evading capture.

I examine this evidence for the organization of subjectivity to determine (1) to what extent or in what ways modernity has come to be experienced as a set of discursive practices that constitute a commonsense, everyday reality, the focus of parts 1 and 2, and (2) to what extent there is evidence of "other" spaces that are not organized according to the logic of the modern and retain their radical otherness, based on a foundation in one or more alternative discourses, which I explore in part 3. I seek to preserve and develop a theoretical space for this alterity that does not simply locate it as the unchanging traditional, an essence to be preserved or destroyed in the face of external pressure and change, as happens in essentializing nativist ideologies or in the theoretical stance of cultural relativism. I find this "otherness" in the self as well as in the other: I presume that there is no Cartesian subject that knows itself, but rather a decentered, inconstant agent that often does not recognize its own productions.

Furthermore, I argue, with theorists from Hegel to Lacan, that the constituting experience at the heart of human subjectivity is recognition by another. But I reexamine and recast the phenomenon of recognition. The concept of recognition that lies at the heart of virtually all current theories of the subject is itself a manifestation of a specific Western ideology of progress that must be deconstructed. It is based on the assumption that recognition is won only through competitive struggle with another who is unwilling to give it, a view that is epitomized in Hegel's myth of the encounter between the master and the slave. Drawing on my own observations of people in action as they negotiate the contested realities surrounding pīrs and on insights from Sufi discourse itself, I recast the concept of recognition so that struggle and competition, while still very much present in subjective experience and still constitutive of political hegemony, are located in relationship to mutuality and accommodation in the organization of subjective experience.

To put my position more directly: there is always a potential distance between the individual and his or her beliefs, including those that appear taken for granted and self-constitutive. Or, to put the matter even more starkly in what may for the moment appear to be a non sequitur but is particularly relevant in the context of the Sufi discourse which is the focus of this book: even the most unsophisticated, provincial subject evades but is always aware of the truth of death, which undercuts all human projects and the apparent reality of all ideologies and hegemonies. The knowledge of death forces us to stand in a space between discourses. In the face of death, it is mutuality and connectedness rather than ideology and status that make us human.

Sufism, Modernity, and the Postcolonial Intellectual

Responses to a complex ever-changing social world and their implications for a theory of subjectivity are particularly significant within the context of a postcolonial society, since in theories that posit the past hegemony of an overarching colonial discourse and the ever-tightening hegemony of modernity, the postcolonial has been identified as the ruptured subject par excellence, survivor of a political domination and supposedly hegemonic order in which the subject was interpellated as a radically subordinate "other" to the Western "self." Such postcolonial subjects — for whom "tradition" has been devalued and frozen — would seem to face a rupture with the past and a slide into a condition of rootless modernity. This postcolonial subject has been characterized as a new, distinctly modern phenomenon, severed from its cultural roots by the behemoth of a global capitalist system, its consciousness sundered by the persuasive power of European, Orientalizing ideologies and hegemonies (Said 1979; Inden 1990), its present goals and identities shaped by a divisive discourse of nationalism that generates newly imagined communities based on supposedly primordial ties of language, religion, and ethnicity (Anderson 1991; Van der Veer 1994).

This characterization of the postcolonial as a subject ruptured by the process of modernization and colonialism has emerged primarily from the study of textual sources, specifically, literary productions generated by elites who occupy and articulate a narrow range of subject positions vis-à-vis postcolonial discourse. And much of the theorizing about the postcolonial has itself been developed by expatriate postcolonial academics who now occupy Western academic positions.[4] It is not surprising that, reflecting their own subjective experiences, such writers and similarly positioned elites would highlight the ruptures and regard their cultural heritage as an irretrievably lost object, overwhelmed by the forces of modernity. But we must be careful to keep in mind the positionality of these intellectuals before generalizing from their experience and reflections to postcolonial experience more broadly and to the Pakistani as modern subject in particular. For instance, looking back to Fanon in order to rekindle a flame of resistance, the transplanted Indian intellectual Homi Bhabha has written: "It is a painful re-membering, a putting together of the dismembered past to make sense of the trauma of the present" (Bhabha 1986b:121). Bhabha is here alluding to the specific trauma of the postcolonial intellectual and is positioning the postcolonial writer as a revolutionary at the doors of the canon of English literature. While this has been an important move in disrupting established literary canons, it should be kept in mind that the writings of an intellectual such as Bhabha reflect his specific, material positioning in the Western academic and literary worlds. Those working within the discipline of literature tend to overemphasize the role of the Western gaze and resistance to it in the constitution of the subject because they work primarily with texts. Dirlik (1994), in a critique of the concept of postcolonial, has articulated how use of the term has obscured an important distinction between this "diffuse group of intellectuals and their concerns" on the one hand and a global condition on the other (Dirlik 1994: 330). One effect of this blurring has been a tendency to equate the subjectivity of these highly visible postcolonial intellectuals—with their radical rethinking of social identities into forms such as "hybridity" (Bhabha 1994) or "catachresis" (Spivak 1988)—and that of a nation and its population. As Dirlik points out, not all postcolonials repudiate modernization and nationalism. Nor, I argue, do they all necessarily seek to recapture the local as an act of resistance to these discourses. For some, local practices continue unselfconsciously even when they coexist with new technologies, new practices, and foreign influences.[5] The new is experienced not as a "modernity" that stands against tradition but as a part of the everyday, where changes of all sorts are a part of life.

Within the context of poststructuralist and (even more saliently) postmodernist theories, the rupture experienced by the postcolonial subject is conceptualized as a severance of signifiers from that which had traditionally been signified. This rupture was produced by the insertion of the gaze and discursive practices of the Western other. This kind of insertion has certainly happened within specific contexts. But it cannot be assumed that basically local narratives such as stories about a cure by a neighborhood pīr or even about a hospital established next to a shrine are constructed in response to something experienced as a grand narrative that must be accommodated or resisted.[6] Nor have such local narratives passed through the gaze of a Western other. The assumption that the local has been uniquely disrupted by modernity in this manner oversimplifies and ultimately distorts our perception of the nature of local culture.

These writers, however, do describe an important discursive process that should not be ignored, as anthropologists tended to do in the past. What does it mean to say that local narratives have passed through a Western gaze? In the self-conscious stance of many postcolonial writers, the local has first been distanced as frozen tradition through the mediation of the Western gaze and then reclaimed as an identity rooted in difference from the West. As represented by writers such as Prakash (1990, 1992), Bhabha, and Spivak (1988a), postcolonial discourse is, first and foremost, concerned with repudiating the master narratives of modernization and nationalism. Such writers see the postcolonial subject as having been discursively constituted in relationship to a colonial discourse, and therefore they seek to transform this subject by reconstituting it in relationship to another discourse. One strategy for doing this is to construct locally inspired narratives, claiming the power to write history by drawing on local representations in new ways. In Raymond Williams's terms, this use of the local has already passed through the "crucible" of modernity (Williams 1989).[7]

The subject of this discourse speaks from three positions simultaneously: the devalued subject of tradition, the internalized Western other, and the negation of the devaluation as resistance through reappropriation of that which has been devalued. The positioning of the postcolonial intellectual thus sets up a specific relationship to tradition as a source of material to be discovered, reworked, and presented to a broader audience. These reworkings are transparently a kind of "play" with signifiers detached from their moorings, so that they slide with a postmodern fluidity like that celebrated by Clifford in the *Predicament of Culture* (1988), a fluidity that itself is grounded in rupture with an imagined past. But, as Fanon argued from his own experience as a "third world" intellectual, the bits and pieces of custom that such intellectuals claim as a banner of resistance may be dead, inert remnants that have been evacuated by the people, who have moved on to other things. He argued that these remnants mark the separation of the intellectual from the general population (Fanon 1968:222–224). Sign use by intellectuals, then, may not reflect local uses of the local.[8]

Like other local phenomena, Sufism has been taken up into this intellectual project of resistance, passed through a modernist filter, broken apart, and reappropriated into literary genres such as the novel and play. The three subject positions listed above can be identified, for instance, in the work of the early-twentieth-century Pakistani writer Muhammad Iqbal (see chapter 9), or more recently in the use of *qalandar* imagery in the work of the Pakistani poet Sarmad Sehbai.

By his own account, Sarmad Sehbai was in the 1960s one of a group of self-labeled modernist writers who sought to "find themselves" in a new social order by embracing the antiestablishment mood and avant-garde forms then fashionable in Europe. Sufism had no place in these writers' efforts to eliminate the colonial traditions that had given rise to the horrors of World War II and the Partition of India and Pakistan in 1947. These modernists picked up Europe's discourse of resistance to entrenched traditions and tried to make it their own. But more recently, these writers, Sehbai among them, have experienced a self-conscious return to their roots, across the rupture associated with modernity. Sehbai's efforts echo the intellectual struggle of many other intellectuals in the "developing" world.

In a 1984 interview for the Pakistani English-language magazine the *Herald,* Sehbai articulated his own relationship to modernism and a turn toward Sufism in a manner that echoes the theorizing of writers such as Williams. Reflecting on his own youthful poetry and theatrical productions of the early 1970s, he said:

> It was the poetic anarchy of a disinherited youth, termed as 'modernism.' . . . Some of us looked towards post World War Europe to seek our 'dadaist' roots without realizing the latent energy of indigenous cultures, and without sharing our predicament with the Afro-Asian world. . . . It's a much later realization that the alienation of this generation was confused with the alienation of the

individual in the West. . . . If absurdity was born in the West out of affluence, in Asia it rose out of scarcity. Here, it is the alienation of man from his heritage and productivity. (Khan 1984:78)

With this realization of alienation from the past has come an aesthetic that self-consciously draws on local tradition, and Sufism in particular, for its power. As he says, "I think it is time that the prodigal son came home."

He does not reject a modernist stance, but redefines it: "*Kafi* [a genre of Sufi folk poetry] and modernism are not in conflict with one another. . . . It is misleading to think that 'modernism' implies 'westernization' or 'industrialization' of literary diction. There can be no modernism without an awareness of your past and living traditions." And then he adds, "It will be just like driving without a back mirror, which could be suicidal" (Khan 1984:79).[9] Sehbai has reached across what is in his experience a modern divide. He seeks to reconstitute his roots in an imagined reconstruction of "Sufism."

In one of his plays, *Panjwan Chirāgh*, written in the local language of Punjabi,[10] Sehbai explicitly foregrounded the thirteenth-century Sufi saint Lāl Shahbāz Qalandar as a signifier that expressed Sehbai's own modernist rejection of fixed tradition:

> It [the play] is an attempt to reinterpret the legend of Lal Shahbaz Qalandar, the great sufi of Sind, in purely contemporary terms. Qalandar is the one who breaks all inhibitions to chant the truth. Legend has it that once the great Qalandar was captured by the king and put into chains. One night he started dancing in ecstasy and as he danced the chains melted and he was free.[11] I have juxtaposed the two images of the ecstatic dancers and the paralysed grave worshippers. The conflict is heightened by this tension between movement and fixity; between dance and paralysis. There is this grotesque spectacle depicting the historical role of the sufis and the degeneration of this order into *mujawari* [the office of caretaker of a shrine]. They have lost the will to dance, and to dance is to be free. (Kahn 1984:80)

Sehbai objected to the fixity of tradition, of folk Islam and devotion to pīrs. This is a theme around which views of Muslims of a variety of orientations — modernist, reformist, fundamentalist — as well as colonial theories of progress and postcolonial technocratic modernization theories have converged.[12] Throughout the struggle for independence from Britain, Muslims of these otherwise diverse persuasions shared the view that the colonial powers were able to dominate the Muslim world only because Muslims had corrupted Islam through popular practices such as devotion to Sufi saints and worship at shrines, a view consistent with the colonial image of enlightened progress, which cast local practices as manifestations of ignorant tradition. Sehbai thus retained the notion of static "tradition" that is one of the concepts underlying a modernist discourse.

Sehbai's Qalandar emerges as a secular humanist in a world that displays characteristics of postmodernity. But this double move of rupture with and recapture of local tradition, though consistent with Raymond Williams's view of modernity as a force that recasts tradition, is in this instance a manifestation of an evolving literary discourse with direct roots in European modernism. Here we can clearly see the observer and observed shaping each other, with Sehbai having read theorists such as Williams himself, having imagined himself in the alienated shoes of Sartre or Camus, and now discovering roots that are also mediated through a process of Western theorizing that has moved through and beyond Orientalism to a doubly reflexive postmodernism.

At the same time, however, Sehbai did not develop a play about Lāl Shahbāz Qalandar in a cultural vacuum, responsive only to global intellectual currents. His turn toward Sufism occurred in the midst of a broader, local Sufi "revival" (*Herald* 1984a) that became particularly visible in reaction to the threat of a more stringent imposition of Islamic law throughout Pakistan. Reporters writing for the Pakistani English weekly, the *Herald,* who themselves inhabit Sehbai's modernist world, have stressed the gulf that separates many participants from the local festivals they attend at Sufi shrines. One *Herald* reporter, also writing in 1984 (the date of the Sehbai interview), characterized the attendance at the 'urs (death anniversary) of the Punjabi poet and Sufi Wāris Shāh as bifurcated into two "streams, the rural one still sustained by the indigenous culture and the urban one lost in the pursuit of colonial objectives" (*Herald* 1984b:57). These urban attendees were characterized by these journalists as "small pockets of visitors from the cities, who have convinced themselves that they are actively striving to assert their cultural identity," who voiced their concerns in "speeches and poetry recitals full of rhetoric about the revival of Punjab's identity, which a committed commentator described as 'chauvinistic' " (*Herald*

1984b:58). The gulf that separated the reporter from the proceedings actively organized his perception of the festival. It is through the gaze of these intellectuals that the activities at the shrines are what Fanon (1968) called remnants of custom.

But the practice of Sufism goes far beyond this Sufi revival. Furthermore, it is not simply a vestige of a peripheral, traditional society not yet fully penetrated by modernity, though the reporter at Wāris Shāh's shrine would have us think of the larger half of the crowd at the festival in these terms. Not all of the elite and not all of the urban attendees (many of whom were, of course, not elite) at this festival or at many of the other festivals at Sufi shrines in Pakistan are concerned with reasserting Punjabi local identity or with bringing a political message to a large audience.

Far from stepping into a postmodern hall of mirrors in their Sufi practice, many practicing Sufis who are also professionals or businessmen have simply highlighted and allowed themselves to articulate one of their own practices that had never been totally submerged in the dominant discourse of modernity (see Ewing 1990b, 1993). Is their practice, like that of modernist intellectuals, an ongoing colonized structure of desire, impelled by a search for recognition by the Western other?

As I will show in subsequent chapters, the interpretive lens through which practices are labeled either "modern" or "traditional" and aligned with the dichotomy Western and Eastern did have a powerful impact on the ideological formation of Pakistan and on the assessment of many of the practices associated with Sufism. British assessments of the evils associated with "traditional" religious practices—the wandering holy men and the prominent pīrs whom the British saw as little more than powerful landowners—were in many respects retained in these ideological formulations. But these views, though highly visible and propagated through the media, the courts, and through administrative practices, were not absolutely hegemonic. As Certeau has recognized, beneath the dominant technologies of modernity, there survives a "'polytheism' of scattered practices . . . dominated but not erased by the triumphal success of one of their number" (Certeau 1984:48). We must not exaggerate the extent of this "triumphal success." Not all such practices necessarily pass through the Western gaze, even when they are materially affected by an array of technological changes and even new ideas coming in from elsewhere, and even when the Western-trained intellectual may interpret it so. They constitute what Deleuze and Guattari (1987) have called "lines of flight," or potentials for change that escape apparently dominant classifications and technologies.

Given what appear from the perspective of a hegemonic discourse as "scattered practices," how are we to understand the role of these practices in shaping or constituting the subject? Do these practices take on particular roles in a postcolonial society? To what extent do they escape the imposition of a discursive formation that subsumes all practice under the dichotomy "tradition-modernity"? To what extent are they the basis for alternative histories — histories in which the West is not constituted as a demonized or even dominating other (Prakash 1990, 1992)?

Clearly, the technological impact of the West on colonial societies such as Pakistan and India has been immense, and the penetration of Western ideas of political order and the relationship of the individual to the state is evident in contemporary Sufi discourse. But the West is not the only other present. When we look at the histories Pakistani Sufis claim for themselves, we see them constructed out of a complex set of resistances and identifications with others who are not necessarily constituted out of and in reaction to a hegemonic master narrative of modernity, progress, and Orientalism.[13]

The extent to which discourses of modernity actually bear a relationship to the "ordinary" postcolonial's subjective experience is thus a question that must be addressed. I will argue that only those in certain social positions have experienced such a discourse as a master narrative. The evidence for the ruptured postcolonial subject gathered from the growing literature produced by intellectuals in postcolonial societies should not be assumed to be representative of the experience of ordinary people in such societies but rather of the experience of these intellectuals. We must consider whether the discursive practices of such an intellectual elite within the postcolonial nation-state are hegemonic and have shaped the ordinary person's subjective experience. We must do the same for the ideologies and policies generated by politicians and the state bureaucracy.

Before turning to evidence drawn from Sufi practice in Pakistan that will permit a characterization of the subjective experience of a range of persons within a postcolonial milieu, I must first address the question of how to theorize the individual as experiencing subject within a complex social field while taking into account increasingly sophisticated understandings of how signs operate to generate structures of meaning that play a central role in organizing experience. This project requires disentangling and rearticulating a triad of concepts: the "subject," "consciousness," and "hegemony." These terms, though used freely in an array of social theories, are actually quite variable in meaning and often subject to considerable conceptual slippage as they are taken up in diverse theoretical approaches. Since I contend with much of this diversity — a consequence of positioning this study at the intersection of the social and the individual — I have felt it necessary to articulate in detail this conceptual slippage. The rest of this chapter provides the grounding required to build a theory of the experiencing subject embedded in a social and political field.

Hegemony

What does "hegemony" mean when we focus on the shaping of individual consciousness and subjectivity? As the term has been taken up in anthropology and cultural studies, "hegemony" is generally understood to be a historically particular set of premises about the nature of reality, often expressed through habitual practices that have come to appear natural to those who enact them.[14] In other words, for the subject of a hegemonic discourse, arbitrary conventions and signs are mistaken for an essential reality. For the young Pakistani man who unquestioningly calls his grandmother superstitious because she visits pīrs, a modernist discourse has presumably become hegemonic. He believes what he says, and his beliefs may even be consistent with a practice of avoiding pīrs (though, as we shall see in subsequent chapters, it may very likely not be). The historical subject is itself constituted through this process. Such statements about superstition and (implicitly) rationality constitute the young man and his grandmother as positioned subjects within a discourse of modernity and, perhaps, give the man power over his grandmother within a specific sociopolitical order.

For anthropologists trained to think in terms of a concept of culture, particularly for the hermeneutic, interpretivist school that developed out of the work of Clifford Geertz, the supposed naturalness generated by a hegemonic discourse has been a congenial and therefore unchallenged concept. In Geertz's influential *Interpretation of Cultures* (1973a), culture — defined as a shared system of symbols and meanings — was the proper object of anthropological study. Culture shaped individual experience by creating meaningful "reality" from what Geertz assumed would otherwise be an inchoate mass of disconnected sensations. It made that reality seem natural and inevitable, though one culture's reality was quite different from another's. The result was a deterministic model of culture that focused exclusively on public meaning and artificially severed an unknowable private psyche from the public "self," which was collapsed into the symbolically constituted "person." This position was taken to its logical extreme in relativist theories that argued for the cultural shaping of emotion as a public phenomenon, appropriating for cultural analysis more and more of what had been considered psychological, minimizing any theoretical space for agency, motivation, or differential positionings within a socioeconomic order.

This concept of culture has been challenged as attention has shifted to contested, rather than shared, meanings. Some scholars have even argued that the term "culture" should be replaced by "hegemony," because the latter better encompasses an emphasis on the power relations through which meanings are imposed on others and made to seem natural (e.g., Fox 1989; Lears 1985; Williams 1977). Nevertheless, the assumption that a system of signs operates to constitute a seemingly natural order has been retained in recent uses of the concept of hegemony by anthropologists.

Among social theorists, the concept of hegemony has been a useful device for deconstructing and disrupting Eurocentric histories — "grand narratives" organized around the signifiers of modernity and progress. Calling attention to how such histories have been instances of a hegemonic discourse that maintains and justifies the domination of the West is a way of undercutting this discourse's claims to truth: it shows that this particular organization of knowledge is arbitrary and serves the interests of a dominant power. Considerable energy has been focused on the deconstruction and disruption of this presumption of progress and the grand narrative of Western history that underlies it, particularly by the French poststructuralists and by theorists inspired by them,[15] including participants in the Subaltern Studies group (Guha 1982–89), whose work has played a prominent role in current academic theorizing about South Asia.[16]

Despite the efforts of these scholars to deconstruct the totalizing grand narrative and to highlight its arbitrary and illusory structure, the

totalizing narrative reappears at another level: they, too, privilege Western capitalism and colonization as a uniquely transformative force.
Those who write of the colonizers' discourse or of the colonized mind
portray the discursive construction of the Orient as a force that has
irrevocably sundered the postcolonial subject from a past that can only
be imagined across the divide of colonialism: this subject is split by the
gaze and constituted by the discursive practices of the colonizer; it is
mediated, silenced and discernible only through aporias in a dominant
discourse.[17] Though such scholars recognize the structure of Western
discourse to be arbitrary, they write as though this discourse, through
its control of practice (including knowledge as practice), nevertheless
"imposes a total milieu, institutional as well as intellectual, to whose
hegemonic sway its subjects must inevitably succumb" (O'Hanlon
1988:216).[18]

The tendency to overprivilege a Western discourse may arise in part
out of a fear of falling into what Young disparaged as a "more conventional political topos," in which "a native otherness is constituted in a
space outside the boundaries of colonial discourse" (Young 1990:149).
This topos, however, is conventional only within the context of a discourse that already constructs this native otherness as "traditional" or
pristine, a position that reproduces the decontextualized, static notions
of culture characteristic of cultural relativism.

Another reason for the tendency of poststructuralist theories to posit
a dominant discourse and a subject constituted out of this is their roots
in structuralism. Such theories are, like Lévi-Strauss's structuralism,
explicitly antihumanistic. The subject is posited, not as a specific historical individual embedded in a complex web of material forces, interests,
and conflicting meanings but as a construct, a determined "position"
within the discourse itself.[19] This antihumanism is intended to disrupt
the Enlightenment notion of a free and autonomous agent's movement
toward liberation from tradition and oppression, one of the premises
on which a Eurocentric discourse of progress is founded. But in making
this theoretical move, poststructuralists who focus on discourse have
removed the space for a subject's critical distance and reflexivity (see
Young 1990). There is no way to locate subjectivity or resistance as
anything other than a consequence of contradictions within the discourse itself and, hence, determined by it.[20] Consciousness itself is reduced to the hegemonic. In this antihumanism, the individual is replaced by structure. As a result, even among poststructuralists who

have criticized the Lévi-Straussian version of structure, it continues to reside in their theories as a locus of agency.[21] When poststructuralists took up the concept of hegemony, they developed a peculiar amalgam of historical materialism and a primacy given to the systematicity of signs that transcends the specific historical, material circumstances in which they appear — characterized as a "structure" (from Lévi-Strauss), as a "Symbolic Order" (Lacan), a "discursive formation" or "discourse" (Foucault), or simply "language" (Derrida). With this theoretical move the term "hegemony" has been subject to slippage toward the assumption of an overarching order that cannot be escaped, creating a discursively constituted subject imprisoned within meaning.

Inspired by poststructuralist critiques of the premises of Eurocentric historiographies, the writers identified with the Subaltern Studies group also smuggle in elements of the Eurocentric "grand narrative," though in a different way, with different implications for a concept of hegemony. The central project of these scholars is the recovery for subalterns — the underclass — of their "own" history, in contrast to a history that is given to the subaltern by elites. The focus is thus on acts of resistance to domination and to the hegemonic discourse of the elite. Instead of granting excessive power to a Western-inspired discursive formation that constitutes a subaltern subject,[22] these theories for the most part posit quite a different relationship between the dominant discourse and the subject. The resistant subaltern subject is posited as self-originating and in possession of sovereign, free consciousness based on reason. This subject, then, operates in a space outside of the hegemonic discourse, and it is from this space that resistance is possible.[23] But this theoretical move also re-creates a premise of the Enlightenment humanism that these scholars seek to dismantle: the priority of the free, autonomous subject (a point made by O'Hanlon in her review of the place of the subject in Subaltern Studies [1988:191]).[24]

The difficulties posed by each of these theoretical approaches point to the need to reexamine not only the space from which resistance to a hegemonic discourse operates, but also the notion of hegemony itself. In particular, we must closely scrutinize the assumption that hegemony operates to support a dominant group by convincing people that the domination is legitimate because it is "natural." This assumption results in a subject that is either determined by a discourse (i.e., reduced to the discursive subject) or totally outside of that discourse (i.e., essentially and statically "traditional" or unproblematically free, autonomous, and rational). These theories are inadequate to capture subjective experience in the face of the clash of discourses and the competition of ideologies characteristic of postcolonial societies.

Hegemony defined in terms of an experience of arbitrary signs as a naturalized, everyday reality is a theory of perception and consciousness. It presumes that there is a direct, causal relationship between a system of signs and the consciousness or experience of the individual, and that reality can be experienced only through a grid of signs. A theory of consciousness necessarily rests on a theory of the experiencing individual, however implicit that theory may be in the writings of particular scholars. For a discourse to be hegemonic in this sense, there must be individuals whose reality is determined by this naturalized experience of arbitrary signs. This notion of hegemony creates unresolvable theoretical difficulties, such as those I have already described. These difficulties become evident when the experiencing individual is seriously considered.

Positing the hegemonic as the dominant signifying order that unconsciously determines the experience of the individual entails the existence of a unitary subject. Foucault recognized this entailment. Though his project was to identify and describe the properties of a discourse that was generated by historically specific social practices and technologies, his theoretically entailed subject did not necessarily have any counterpart in the lived world: it was a discursive "subject position." Foucault's subject is not an individual or even a particular aspect of the psyche; it is merely a property of a discourse. The subject is reduced to an effect of a nonsubjective process, and individuals are seen only to the extent that they assume subject positions within a specific historical formation. By focusing on a discourse that is abstracted from specific social relations and by talking of the subject of that discourse rather than of multifaceted individuals, theorists in the Foucauldian tradition avoid addressing the question of whether the experience of the naturalness of a discourse is a property of concrete social situations. This reduction thereby avoids the problem of individual consciousness altogether.

The problems that arise when the hegemonic is assumed to shape consciousness have also been obscured by the use of the concept "consciousness" by scholars influenced by Marxism. In this theoretical milieu, consciousness is a property attributed to groups and not to individuals, as in the ideal of "class consciousness." Recognizing that consciousness has rarely been treated as a problem in studies of the hegemonic, the Comaroffs, for instance, have focused on what they identify as a crucial moment in the formation of the consciousness of the colonial subject. Developing and systematizing a Gramscian-inspired notion of hegemony as a theory of consciousness within the context of colonial South Africa, they have convincingly demonstrated disjunctions between local resistance to the content of Western ideas and a more fundamental acceptance of the terms of Western argument. They conclude that the colonial experience produced a new kind of consciousness vis-à-vis local practice that had not previously been present in the subjects of their study (despite a history of continuous contact with other peoples in precolonial Africa). They argue that this new consciousness involved a growing objectification and systematization of local practice that developed as Africans struggled to argue with colonial missionaries. They attributed a newly emergent stance of cultural relativism and self-consciousness to these Africans (Comaroff and Comaroff 1991:243–245). This argument for a change in self-consciousness—the development of reflexive, systematized awareness of one's habitual practices—presumes the prior existence of an unreflexive plenitude in which tradition is hegemonic and simply reproduced (as in Bourdieu's [1977] concept of *habitus*), a presumption that itself reproduces the tradition-modernity dichotomy that deconstructions of Western discourse so decisively undercut.

It is precisely this assumption of premodern consciousness as nonreflexive that I question. In the Muslim world, at least, the kind of objectification arising out of disputations similar to those identified by the Comaroffs is nothing new. The history of Islam could be told as a chronicle of sectarian debate and dispute. It can certainly be argued that the particular challenges of colonialism, which involved new forms of bureaucratic administration and control, may have led to the objectification of certain everyday practices that had never before come under scrutiny. This is the type of argument made by Cohn (1987), for instance, about Indian caste. Similar arguments have been made about other aspects of existing practice—such as the self-conscious development of local languages (Chatterjee 1986; Prakash 1973). I suggest, however, that the whole notion of the increasing objectification of practices rests on the shaky ground of the dichotomy between tradition and modernity. It assumes, once again, a traditional subject who inhabits everyday practices with an unexamined plenitude—a manifestation of Bourdieu's habitus.[25]

Arguments about consciousness such as those made by the Co-maroffs rest on an implicit but undeveloped theory of the subject. Their use of the term "consciousness" comes, like Gramsci's, from the Marx-ist tradition and is not accompanied by an elaborated theory of the individual, the mind, or subjectivity, beyond noting (following Gram-sci) the human capacity to tolerate cognitive dissonance as the basis of "contradictory consciousness."

I have devoted considerable attention in part 3 to this problem of the so-called traditional subject, focusing particularly on what to Western eyes is the exotic figure of the qalandar, the wandering beggar ascetic. I do this because the qalandar, "traditionally" — from the tenth century at least — disrupts all tradition, dramatically drawing people's attention to the arbitrariness of social order. The presence of the qalandar and his controversial but highly visible place in Muslim societies suggests to me that our notion of the unexamined life of the traditional subject is another rationalist fantasy, by which we separate civilized from primi-tive, West from Orient, and rational, reflexive consciousness from the unquestioning habits of the masses.

Ultimately, I take the position that there is not a fundamental trans-formation of consciousness that takes place with the rise of capitalism and Western domination. The image of the pre-Contact native who lacked self-consciousness about the arbitrariness of his own means of representation is a vestige of a nineteenth-century fantasy, reinforced by anthropologists of a previous generation and their tendency to ig-nore the presence of self-reflexivity or to downplay the significance of continuous contact among culturally diverse precolonial peoples. My goal is to deconstruct the premises that lead to the conclusion that modernity gives rise to a distinctively new form of consciousness.

Turning to the work of Gramsci himself, we find a concept of hege-mony that avoids many of the difficulties that the positing of a hege-monic discursive formation in either a structuralist or culturally rela-tivist fashion presents. Gramsci's theory, which views both hegemonies and the individual who is subject to them as fragmentary, allows us to begin to conceptualize the postcolonial subject in a way that transcends the dichotomy of a subject either reduced to discourse or positioned outside of it. Though Gramsci retained a Marxist version of the grand narrative of the progressive development of consciousness, his formu-lation of how hegemonies operate within individuals offers a useful

starting point for the development of a theory of the postcolonial subject that does not posit a rupture with the past or a locus outside of the
present discourse.

Gramsci applied the concept of hegemony within a Marxist framework as a way of characterizing the power of a group to shape public
discourse. Hegemony was in most circumstances experienced as a fragmentary phenomenon: as the individual moves from one social context
to another, different and mutually inconsistent background understandings and habits would come into play, understandings that the
individual might or might not be self-consciously aware of (Gramsci
1971). It is from this usage of Gramsci's that the association of hegemony with unconscious habit has developed in later theories. But in
Gramsci, the association of hegemony with that which is unconscious
actually breaks down, since the goal of praxis theory is the establishment of modernity as the hegemony of a critical consciousness (Gramsci 1971:417), that is, a class consciousness that is the antithesis of
unreflexive habit (324). In Gramsci's usage (at least in certain contexts),
"consciousness" is a state of awareness characteristic only of the intellectual who knows himself as a product of historical circumstances and
has a critical and coherent conception of the world (324). It is thus a
specific type of reflexive activity.

Gramsci took this formation of reflexive, coherent consciousness
to be a new phenomenon. When hegemony was experienced as a coherent order, it would no longer be unconscious. Though he recognized
the ever-present potential for a more critical, reflexive consciousness
through history by seeing the philosopher in everyman, he also in my
opinion unjustifiably identified the emergence of a "new" kind of critical consciousness and overrated the potential of modern institutions to
create such a consciousness by putting too much faith in the rational,
critically conscious subject.

Despite his active and highly political involvement with the grand
narrative of progress, Gramsci, in my opinion, had a remarkably clear
view of people as they are: he saw them for the most part caught
unreflexively in the fragmentary hegemonies of everyday life, getting by
on snippets of received wisdom. When we turn to the individual as a
locus of subjectivity in specific contexts, inconsistency and fragments
are more salient than a coherent structure of signs. According to Gramsci, one of the manifestations of hegemony is the phenomenon of "common sense" (see also Mouffe 1979; Eagleton 1991). For Gramsci, com-

mon sense (which can reasonably be taken as an equivalent to the anthropological "culture") was fragmentary and episodic because the individual is a part of many social groups simultaneously (Gramsci 1971:323). The disjoined conceptions that constitute common sense are context-specific; their particular content has its source in ideological forces of the past that have become "hegemonic," that is, taken for granted and assumed to be true, in a manner similar to Geertz's notion of culture but far more fragmentary. They are taken for granted only insofar as they have not been specifically challenged in the context in which they occur.

For many people, even an explicitly labeled sectarian identity can be fluid and contextually specific. In one conversation, for instance, I was talking with a man, a government servant, who had been a neighbor of Sufi Sahib. This man knew that I had visited Sufi Sahib and made it quite clear to me that he himself viewed at least this particular pīr as corrupt. As we settled into our conversation, I asked him what his own sect was, and he responded "Ahl-i Sunnat ul-Jamaʿat." He went on to describe four sects, including his own. Perhaps because of the similarity of his characterization of the Wahhabi sect to the stance he himself had taken when criticizing his pīr-neighbor, I asked him, "What are you?" basically repeating my earlier question about sectarian identity. He responded "I'm a Wahhabi," thereby changing his identity. When I asked if there was anyone else in his family who is Wahhabi, his wife added the rather snide comment: "He is the only one — from today." He countered with the claim that he had gotten the idea twenty years ago, from books.

For my benefit, this man had constructed what was to his wife, at least, a new narrative. Its purpose within the context of our conversation was to position himself explicitly against the pīr and against his "traditional" neighbors who are the pīr's followers, taking for himself the moral high ground through his claim to a purer Islam. But this objectification of his own religious identity would seem to be a contextually specific phenomenon and did not bear a close relationship to his religious practice in other situations.

Just how contextually bounded and fragmentary an ideological, self-conscious challenge to hegemonic practices — accepted ways of doing things — often is can be seen by turning one of Geertz's ethnographic descriptions to my own purposes. This episode describes a phenomenon that is also common in debates surrounding proper Islamic practice in Pakistan with regard to Sufism, local ritual, and Islamist reform. It illustrates how self-reflexivity does not necessarily result even when modern ideologies would seem to have brought local practice to political consciousness. In an article originally written in 1957, Geertz described the breakdown of a funeral conducted for a boy who died unexpectedly while staying with his uncle. It was suddenly the uncle's responsibility to oversee the funeral. To this uncle's dismay, the Muslim official whose job it was to conduct the funeral refused to do so because of the uncle's involvement with a political party that advocated a rejection of Muslim practices and a return to indigenous traditions and rituals, in a society where events such as funerals and marriages are conducted by Muslim officials. Almost as an aside, Geertz offered an impressionistic statement concerning the actions of the bereaved uncle: "It had evidently never occurred to him that the anti-Muslim funeral agitation of the party would ever appear as a concrete problem" (Geertz 1973c:155).

How could it not have occurred to him? What kind of theory of the subject, consciousness, and hegemony do we need to explain this disjunction? Like those of Pakistanis who talk of pīrs and are involved in practices associated with pīrs, this man's practices and understandings were contextualized and fragmentary, even though in certain contexts he was involved in a self-conscious ideological movement that explicitly challenged many routine practices. Gramsci's model of a fragmented composite subject or personality that is constituted as an "inventory of traces" of unconscious hegemonies (Gramsci 1971:324) would seem to be a particularly apt way of beginning to characterize this Javanese uncle.

Given Foucault's exclusive focus on the subject of discourse and deliberate avoidance of any consideration of the individual, it is perhaps surprising that he, nevertheless, presents us with a sketch of the individual that is consistent in certain respects with Gramsci's model of the individual. In one of his last works, *The History of Sexuality,* Foucault came close to addressing the problem of the relationship between the individual and competing discourses in a paragraph about the "plurality of resistances" to power: "One is dealing with mobile and transitory points of resistance, producing cleavages in a society that shift about, fracturing unities and effecting regroupings, furrowing across individuals themselves, cutting them up and remolding them, marking off irreducible regions in them, in their bodies and minds" (Foucault

1990a:98). Though himself focused relentlessly on an abstract network of power relations and on the logic of a hegemonic discourse that is crystallized out of them, his brief sketch of the individual also suggests that with respect to the social, the individual is not a unitary being. We harbor within ourselves "irreconcilable regions," marked off by shifting points of resistance to a hegemonic discourse.[26]

These formulations of Gramsci and Foucault offer only a starting point. What is lacking in either Gramsci's suggestive comments about the individual as a composite or in Foucault's brief comment on the transsected individual is a theory of how these fragments coexist within the individual and, thus, a coherent theory of how "hegemonies" and ideologies shape belief and action. Gramsci's use of the term "consciousness" is very different from the notion of consciousness in a psychological sense, particularly as this has been developed in psychodynamic, psychoanalytic theories. As a result, Gramsci offered no theory of how the individual negotiates the diverse contexts and fragmentary hegemonies of daily life. For Gramsci, "unconsciousness" is a state one is in when one is not reflexively self-conscious and thus aware of one's history. It is merely a term for characterizing the fragmentary quality of the subject's perceptions; a state in which one's (psychically conscious) conceptions of the world are disjointed, episodic, and passively received from the social groups of which one is a part. He does not theorize a state in which conflictual thoughts and memories are kept from awareness by, for example, dynamic repression, as in classical psychoanalytic theory.

I argue that hegemony as a political phenomenon must not be confused with individual consciousness. Rather, it can be more adequately understood in two distinct senses: (1) the fragmentary practices and ideas that shape and constitute narrowly delimited, uncontested situations of everyday life, and (2) the control of public discursive space — a control that may itself be limited to specific contexts while other contexts may be organized according to different principles. This control of discourse does not create "consciousness" and must certainly not be equated with the ability to be self-reflexive.

The Decentered Subject

It is from outside of anthropology that we see serious efforts to draw together social and political processes and issues of motivation and agency that are useful for examining the nature of hegemony, consciousness, and the constitution of the postcolonial subject. While retaining Gramsci's idea of the fragmentary subject, I turn in the direction of psychoanalytic theory and critiques of psychoanalytic theory for considerations of a decentered subject that (1) escape the dual pitfalls of positing either a free autonomous subject or a discursively determined subject and (2) more closely articulate the vicissitudes of individual, subjective experience. Aside from the work of the Frankfurt School, which sought to draw together Marxism and Freudian theory,[27] it is for the most part theorists who have directly addressed Lacan's poststructuralist reworking of Freud who have found new strategies for locating a decentered subject within sociopolitical processes. Yet those whose work builds directly on Lacan have been weakened by the poststructuralist overemphasis on a dominant "Symbolic Order" (Lacan's term) or hegemonic discourse. The result has been a basic difficulty in theorizing resistance or phenomena unstructured by such a discourse.

Freudian psychoanalytic theory, particularly in its earlier focus on libido and repression, was revolutionary in its decentering of the subject. Freudian-based theories avoid the Cartesian subject by decentering the subject away from a rational consciousness motivated by free will to unconscious processes as the locus of an agency that is not aware of itself: an unreflexive, unobjectified agency. But as Lacan and even more radically Deleuze and Guattari have argued, the Western ideal of the autonomous ego crept back into Freud's later theorizing and has gradually become the cornerstone of most current psychoanalytic practice, particularly that associated with ego psychology.[28] Most modern interpretations of Freud see the center of experience and agency located in the ego, which fights off incursions from the id and constraints from the civilizing force of the superego. But Lacan argued that this autonomous ego is merely a reproduction of the Cartesian subject, a manifestation of the ideology of individualism, what Lacan would call an Imaginary fantasy.

One of the reasons for this move away from the decentered subject was Freud's handling of the issue of recognition. Freud's early drive model, in which the locus of agency is the drive itself, ignored the role of social recognition and relationship in the constitution of the subject. Early efforts at psychoanalytic anthropology were unsatisfactory because they trained attention on the drives but made them an acultural force to be uncovered beneath the trappings of culture. Culture was reduced to a defense against sexuality and aggression, and the complexities of social process and relationship disappeared. When Freud himself turned to the issue of narcissism (1957a, 1957b), he conceptualized it in terms of the sexual drive, which he envisioned as a pseudopod that reaches out but then turns back on itself to create a narcissistic state. This was a convoluted model that was difficult to apply to issues of recognition and social relationship, except by reintroducing the ego as the locus of agency, as later thinkers such as Winnicott and Kohut have done. Lacan tackled this problem head on and developed a theory that both addressed the social issue of recognition and maintained the decentered subject. I have, therefore, found it essential to engage Lacanian theory in order to problematize (rather than assuming) the place of the subject in the social world.

For Lacan, splits in the subject, whether they be splits that separate consciousness from unconscious processes or splits that divide the self or ego, are not historically contingent, not a product of the peculiar conditions of modernity in a late capitalist society, as Adorno and Marcuse of the Frankfurt School suggested, nor of the peculiar conditions of postcoloniality, as postcolonial theorists have argued. Rather, the subject is split by something more fundamental to the human condition: language. It is the acquisition of language that plays a formative role in the constitution of the Lacanian subject as a gap or "lack," as something always "other" to itself. Language creates a self-image that is at variance with the unstable flux of desire that is the experiencing subject.

Lacan's theory of the subject emerged from a blend of a Freudian unconscious, the Hegelian other, and the Saussurean signifier. He privileged a certain modality of human experience — the Hegelian struggle for recognition — and articulated it in terms of a Freudian desire for the mother (in Lacan's terms, desire for recognition by the mother), through which the child develops an illusory ego in the presence of the mother's gaze and operates in terms of an "Imaginary Order" of fantasy.

According to Lacan, the subject's experience of wholeness, selfhood, or identity rests on an illusion, a negativity. The ego, the reflexive "I" (the Cartesian subject) is a fantasy. It does not exist as a cohesive entity, an essence, but is rather an internalization of a specular or mirror image, an illusion that constitutes the foundation of what Lacan calls an Imaginary Order. In order to maintain the conscious illusion of autonomy, we imagine ourselves in terms of representations that alienate ourselves from our own subjectivity (Lacan 1977:19). Structures of knowledge organize the ego and its objects and attribute to them permanence, identity, and substantiality (17), thereby alienating the flux of subjectivity as locus of intentionality, creating an ideology of a self. This "self" or "ego" can be understood as multiple layers of narcissistic identifications with significant others.

The subject as locus of intentionality and "truth" always threatens to escape these Imaginary identifications. From a developmental perspective, the subject rests initially on archaic, fragmentary imagos, bodily experiences founded on the gratifying presence and subsequent absence of the mother. These are fragmentary images that have not been captured and taken up by the ego or self (Lacan 1977:14) into the Imaginary Order of fantasy. With the entry into language, the subject is constituted by a Symbolic Order—a structure of signs in which meaning is based on difference, in the Saussurean sense. This Symbolic Order organizes unconscious desire and structures the unconscious. Desire is mediated through the oedipal father, and the individual is positioned with regard to a social discourse. This father is understood not as the embodied "real" person but as a representation of social order: the Phallus is a signifier representing the Law. In contrast to the Imaginary Order of fantasy, the Symbolic Order is experienced as fundamentally Other, as an externally imposed Law. With this positioning in the Symbolic Order comes also the alienation of the subject, an inchoate awareness that something has been left behind, an experience of being somehow split, of not being fully recognized in the subject position where one has been fixed. This experience is the source of an impossible desire. Desire is first, and beneath all, a desire for wholeness and plenitude—an imaginary unity based on an unremembered experience of merger with the mother. The subject is founded on an impossible desire, oriented toward an object that cannot be grasped, a goal that cannot be attained, a totality or plenitude of being that does not exist. Upon entry into the Symbolic Order, this desire is transmuted into the desire to be recognized by the Other (a Hegelian formulation), to be the object of another's desire.

The subject avoids full determination by the Symbolic Order only by holding onto this ultimately impossible desire. By doing so, the subject cannot be fully captured. The object of this impossible desire, what Lacan labeled the "other," or "objet petit a" to distinguish it from the

Other of the Symbolic Order (Lacan 1977:xi, 308), is described by Lacan as a lack, a negativity. It refers to those primordial images that were formed prior to the child's acquisition of language and even prior to the totalized self-image of the mirror stage — that is, physiological experiences and parts of the body that fail to be mirrored or symbolized (a gaze, lips, voice, imaginary phallus). These images play a constituting role in the structuration of the psyche (Elliott 1992:129), but they always escape the knowledge of the subject; they lack meaning. They are the surplus of the "Real" over any symbolization (Žižek 1989:3). Desire thus follows a trajectory in human relationships in which imaginary fantasies of a relationship between the ego and an other cover over or "suture" the gap between, on the one hand, the rigid structure of the subject's unconscious, linguistic constitution within the Symbolic Order and, on the other hand, the fragmentary "remainder" of the primordial subject. The desire for recognition by an Other is thus linked through a metonymic chain of signifiers to the unattainable fragmentary imago that the desire for recognition has covered over. This unrecognized desire for the impossible object creates in the subject an unresolvable tension. But it also makes the subject ultimately ungraspable within the Symbolic Order, not reducible to an object of scientific scrutiny, and not reducible to the discursively constituted subject associated with the poststructuralist notion of hegemony. Desire, though conjoined with proximate ends such as sexual satisfaction, is an opening into a rift that cannot be breached. It is this opening that differentiates Lacan's theory of the subject from those that reduce the subject to a position within a discourse.

Lacan offers one foundation for a theory of the desiring subject and its relationship to a discursive order. With its emphasis on the entry into language creating a split in the subject that is a fundamental aspect of the human condition and not simply a product of a specific historical condition, the theory avoids a tenet of the totalizing grand narrative of Western progress: that capitalism has created a uniquely modern form of consciousness.

But Lacan's theory, with its roots in Saussurean structural linguistics and its exclusive focus on the European subject, shares with other poststructuralist theories the weakness of presuming a single overarching Symbolic Order with specific semantic content, namely, that power is located in the "Name of the Father" (the father as signifier within the Symbolic Order), and that Phallus signifies Law. This assumption does not transport well to a postcolonial setting, where it becomes difficult to locate a single Symbolic Order without presuming the total hegemony of Western colonial discourse. On the other hand, positing multiple Symbolic Orders disrupts Lacan's developmental theory of the subject by leaving totally unspecified how the constitution of the subject might be affected by the awareness that there is not a single Law of the Father, a single judging Gaze.

Despite its limitations, Lacanian theory has offered new perspectives on issues of ideology and hegemony in the shaping of the subject because of its focus on the discursive structure of desire. Inspired by Lacan, Althusser sought to develop a psychoanalytic theory of hegemony (Althusser 1971, 1984; Silverman 1992:23). In Althusser's work the idea of hegemony is expressed in terms of a dominant ideology that is accepted as true, not because of an act of rational consciousness, or because it is received wisdom, or because it emerges out of habitual action, but because of the ideology's successful appeal to an unconscious, unrealizable desire that locates the subject within a system of representations, the Lacanian Symbolic Order. Althusser thus addressed directly the problem of how ideologies come to be believed and to motivate action. Althusser sought to bring together the two very different ways in which consciousness has been used in the intellectual traditions stemming from Marx and Freud, drawing an equivalence between the absence of class consciousness and the unconscious in a psychodynamic sense. But Althusser's position, like Lacan's, is weakened by the positing of a single hegemonic order of signs. Althusser's theory identified the Symbolic Order with a dominant ideology that reflected the class-based interests of a dominant group. This identification creates a tension in Althusser's theory, since seeing the source of hegemony in historical materialist terms (i.e., relations of production and the interests of a dominant class) is not readily reconcilable with seeing its source in terms of a Lacanian Symbolic Order that equates the Phallus with the Law, a system of signs based on difference that is not limited to the articulation of the interests of a specific class or even to current relations of production. The result in Althusser's work is a subtle shift from a class-based analysis of hegemony (which in Gramsci's work might be one of many hegemonies, all operating on the individual simultaneously) to the positing of a Symbolic Order as a signifying system that is exterior and prior to all present class ideologies. The individual and the subject were confounded, giving rise to notions of interpellation and a determined subject position that have created conceptual difficulties for scholars seeking to create a theoretical space for resistance or agency in a subject/individual.[29]

Deleuze and Guattari also theorize the desiring subject. Like Althusser, they are concerned with the way a totalizing economic and political order constitutes the subject and shapes consciousness by imposing repressions and recasting desires through the generation of new needs and wants. But they avoid Althusser's confounding of the universal and the historically contingent by criticizing Lacan's positing of a universal Symbolic Order. Like Foucault, they identify psychoanalysis itself as a tool that furthers a repressive social order, rather than accepting that psychoanalysis reveals the "truth" of the subject. But they nevertheless retain a focus on that which escapes discursive formation. According to Deleuze and Guattari, there is no single Symbolic Order, but rather an ongoing tension between specific structures of domination and their ideological formations (what they call the "molar") on the one hand and "lines of flight" (what they call the "molecular") on the other hand — desires that escape these hegemonic formations and bear the seeds of change. Rather than attempt the impossible task of trying to identify possible sources of resistance from a discursively determined subject, they articulate a theory of nondiscursive desire that places the subject and identity at the periphery, as a passive effect of action that is not discursively mediated.[30]

They counter Lacan's developmental model with one of their own. The difficulty with psychoanalysis from Freud on is that it focuses exclusively on the parent-child relationship as a model for the development of the psyche. Freud himself overemphasized the triadic relationship mother-father-child, in which all desire is mediated through the Oedipus complex. Subsequent developments in psychoanalytic theory led to more focus on preoedipal issues involving the negotiation of a merged relationship between mother and infant and issues of separation, as if the emerging social individual experienced the world only in terms of demands focused on the mother. It is possible, in my opinion, to retain many of Freud's insights about intrapsychic conflict while recognizing that the individual retains a direct, unmediated experience of the world.[31]

Deleuze and Guattari criticize this exclusive focus on the parent-child relationship and Lacan's elaboration of it in terms of the Symbolic Order and the Law of the Father. They opt instead for a Nietzschean view of the decentered subject. In Lacan's theory, the subject is alienated by its entry into the Symbolic Order, where its desire is perpetually deferred through a chain of signifiers and can never be satisfied because it is aimed at a primordial experience of merger that can never be recaptured. The subject who desires is founded on a lack. The apparent solidity of the ego, the image with which the subject identifies, is illusory. Deleuze and Guattari (1983: 24) contrast this view of what they call "desire as acquisition" with their materialist view of "desire as production." In contrast to the post-Freudian ego psychologists, they agree with Lacan that there is no centered subject. But in contrast to Lacan's assumption that desire is necessarily lack, they see instead a flux of desires that create their own objects: "Desire does not lack anything; it does not lack its object. It is, rather, the *subject* that is missing in desire, or desire that lacks a fixed subject; there is no fixed subject unless there is repression. . . . The objective being of desire is the Real in and of itself" (26).[32] The individual[33] thus has at least the potential for an unmediated relationship with the world. The "perversion" of that relationship into an experience of desire as lack is a historical and political process: it is a social production of needs and wants and of a fixed subject through the process of repression. This view of the enunciating subject as a productive flow of desires subject to repression is consistent with my emphasis on the elusive, multivocal shifting subject.

But where does language come into this approach? In disrupting the centrality of Lacan's Symbolic Order, Deleuze and Guattari turn away from a structuralist theory of language to one that focuses on breaking down the structuralist distinction between speech and language, seeing enunciation as a pragmatic act through which "the individual repeatedly passes from language to language" during the course of a day (Deleuze and Guattari 1987:94).

Given this view of language, the Lacanian Symbolic Order loses its privileged position. Nevertheless, the phenomenon of a fixed structure of signs remains — as an ideological formation, one of several that may coexist, which when enunciated fixes subjects as "identities," or subject positions in relations of power. Even when operating in terms of such an ideological structure, the enunciating subject slips away, along lines of flight, passing into other languages, other ideologies, realizing other desires.

Deleuze and Guattari take an important step with their evacuation of the subject. But what are these dispersed desires that they highlight?

Their approach draws heavily on Nietzsche, who himself identified the content of desire as a will to power (Nietzsche 1968) and saw this will pervading life itself. Life is a competitive struggle, a theme common to Hegel and Nietzsche, and a premise of most Western philosophical discourse, including Lacan. Nevertheless, there are significant differences between the Hegelian power structure that underlies the Lacanian model and the Nietzschean will to power that inspired Deleuze and Guattari.

Lacan bases his theory of recognition on Hegel's model of competitive struggle for recognition as exemplified in the master-slave relationship (Hegel 1979:111–19). For Hegel the founding moment of self-consciousness was a dialectical struggle for recognition by the other. This theory has roots in a competitive fantasy: "When the "first" two men confront one another for the first time, the one sees in the other only an animal (and a dangerous and hostile one at that) that is to be destroyed, and not a self-conscious being representing an autonomous value" (Kojève 1969:10). It is a theory of love as a limited good. It assumes that for me to respond to your desire by recognizing you somehow diminishes or destroys me just as an apple is destroyed by being the object of your desire.[34]

The result in Lacan's theory and in any other theory that posits a competitive power struggle as the basic motive of human action is a blindness to other possible modalities of interaction that might also serve to constitute the subject. When this emphasis on competitive struggle is transported to considerations of postcolonial societies, the exaggerated emphasis on interactions involving competition and struggle obscures other possible modalities of relationship that constitute subjectivity in other ways. This emphasis is unfortunate, since in current views of the constitution of the postcolonial subject that highlight the unjust domination of the European colonizers to the exclusion of any other mode of interaction, the possibility of other modalities is already nearly invisible.[35] Like the notion of the autonomous self, which has been explicitly criticized as Eurocentric by poststructuralists, the positing of a competitive struggle for recognition as the foundation of the subject is remarkably congruent with the competitive operation of a capitalist system. Lacan has transformed a particular form of Hegelian desire into a theory of human nature.

The reduction of human interaction and desire to a single modality has been most explicitly questioned by theorists who have addressed gender issues. Lorraine (1990) has demonstrated how this competitive focus reveals a pervasive male bias in the Western philosophical tradition that recent gender theorists have cogently deconstructed. Julia Kristeva (1986b) has also sought to articulate how the subject operates in modalities other than competitive struggle. She sees the prediscursive (involving what she calls "semiotic" processes) as a source of creativity and a potential locus of subversion of the Symbolic Order and its categories of meaning. Kristeva, like Deleuze and Guattari, regards the enunciating subject as moving between discursive and prediscursive modalities. In the prediscursive modality, the subject follows a different desire — for connectedness, for contact, fusion, where the boundary between self and other breaks down into an experience of pleasure rather than an impossible search for recognition. This is a contact that is not perpetually deferred through the signifying chain of a Symbolic Order but rather escapes the discursive altogether and is experienced immediately and bodily.[36] But she avoids the biological essentialism of certain feminist writers such as Irigaray, who assigns to the feminine privileged access to this modality.

Object relations theorists, such as Winnicott (1971), Flax (1990), and Benjamin (1988), also argue for the possibility of a prediscursive subject that is more than a developmental stage to be outgrown and repressed. They reject Lacan's developmental sequence and the proposition that the discursively constituted subject is separated by a bar from its primordial matrix. For Winnicott, Lacan's characterization of the subject as founded on a lack through an act of self-alienation describes only a pathological condition that Winnicott calls a "false self" (Winnicott 1965). The development of a false self results from the parents' failure to form an adequate reciprocal relationship with the young child and is not a human universal. Flax (a gender theorist who has chosen Winnicott over Lacan), argues that Lacan's model is distorted because Lacan assumes that the preoedipal period is asocial, resting on a merged experience of the mother as an extension of the child's own body. Lacan assumes no innate impulse toward separation, so that language and culture are imposed over and against the child, creating a "rupture" not only in the relationship with the mother but also between the speaking child and its preoedipal desires and (asocial) experiences, which were all focused on the mother. Winnicott focuses on "good enough mothering" as a social relationship that begins at birth and enables the child to creatively use language and other objects in the environment.[37] The Hegelian struggle for recognition is rather different from the child's experience of recognition and self-consciousness that arises from the gaze of the parent within the context of unconditional love.

Though these solutions to the difficulties raised by theories that posit a discursively constituted subject are useful, the theorists I have considered have addressed the issue of the marginalized "other" — the woman, the homosexual — only within the context of Western discourse and popular culture. It will be necessary to extend the issues raised by these theories to the rather different problematic raised by postcoloniality, a setting where the historical diversity of competing discourses is the most salient feature of the political landscape within which individuals seek to constitute themselves as subjects. But the problem of the constitution of the subject has also occupied scholars in the Muslim world over the centuries, particularly within the intellectual tradition now most commonly glossed as "Sufism." Subsequent chapters focus on this tradition and its contemporary practice within the setting of postcolonial Pakistan. Sufism is both my object of study — an alternative discourse that stands in juxtaposition to modernity as a discursive formation — and a theoretical stance in its own right, through which modernity and the human subjects it creates may themselves be constituted as an object of study.

Conclusion

My argument thus far has developed several strands that can now be drawn together. The individual is a complex site of conflicting desires and multiple subjective modalities (what I elsewhere [Ewing 1990a] have called "shifting selves") whose experience of wholeness is illusory and contextually specific. This contextual subject is not constituted solely out of the gaze of the Other (by which Lacan means the Father as sign that emerges as the outcome of the competitive oedipal struggle) but out of multiple others that form through different types of relationships or subjective modalities. The individual takes on a history or histories through the construction of narratives in conversation with an interlocutor, aligns itself with ideologies, becomes the "subject" of an ideology. But, like the Javanese uncle that Geertz encountered, the subject is inconstant in its loyalties and usually oblivious to its own inconsistencies.

This view accords well with the Gramscian view of competing hegemonies: these hegemonies are unexamined ideologies and habits that are contextually specific. They may shape the subject's self-perception within a specific context, but they do not determine all contexts in which the subject operates. In contrast to Althusser's equation of an overarching Symbolic Order with the interests of a specific class or social group or Foucault's focus on the discursive constitution of the subject by a historically specific discursive formation, both of which eliminate any kind of critical distance between the subject and this overarching order, my view restricts the role of the hegemonic in shaping consciousness and the perception of reality. With Gramsci, I see the possibility of a critical distance, from which the subject — the "organic intellectual" — may recognize the conditions of its own constitution. I argue, however, that such critical distance is not a unique product of modernity or the capitalist system but is a consequence of the existence of competing discourses in any historical period. In fact, a theory that posits a traditional subject characterized by an unreflexive consciousness and thus no awareness of the arbitrariness of its conventions and habitual practices is itself a manifestation of a Western discursive structure that separates the Western self from the traditional other.

The possibility of plenitude (i.e., an unreflective experience of a culturally constructed truth as simply "real") that the Western notion of the traditional or primitive subject projects onto this traditional other and that is associated with an unreflexive consciousness is what Lacan recognized as the subject's impossible desire. I take from Lacan the idea of a subject that may be split by its entry into language, but language of a particular sort — the signifiers of an ideology that are fixed through the process of domination. This subject may be activated by a desire for recognition that passes through a Symbolic Order, constituted out of a linguistic structure of difference. Coherent ideologies offer the illusory promise of experiencing plenitude, and the individual temporarily adopts shifting subject positions vis-à-vis various ideological discourses. But this Symbolic Order is not, in my view, the overarching deterministic structure that Lacan assumes it to be. I agree with Silverman (and Lévi-Strauss [1963]) that the unconscious has no specific content, and that any specific linking of a signifier with meaning, such as Phallus = Law, is an ideology, one of many possible ideologies out of which the ego may construct a fantasy of identity. But I disagree with Silverman's and ultimately Lacan's structuralist view of the unconscious, in terms of which a linguistic structure of differences inevitably inserts itself between the experiencing subject and reality, the theoretical move that results in a theory of the discursive subject. With Deleuze and Guattari and, ultimately, Freud, I take a materialist view of language: it is a tool by means of which we expand our world and ourselves; it is not a prison that makes the other unknowable. Furthermore, it is not the only means by which we know our world and each other, as both Winnicott and Deleuze and Guattari have recognized.

The individual as subject can never fully avoid the ultimate contradiction at the heart of all human projects: that signs are human constructions, that no social order is ever permanent, and that death brings an end to all projects and obliterates the subject. This awareness of the arbitrariness of ideologies and the class-based interests that are represented by the hegemonic discourses that dominate public talk is particularly acute in historical situations in which alternative discourses confront one another, producing a reflexive consciousness; yet it is not an exclusively modern phenomenon. Conversely, even "modern" individuals, subjected to an escalating bombardment by diverse discourses, fulfill their desires productively as they move (like their predecessors) among taken-for-granted habitual activities. They also make reflexive ideological commentaries on these activities. Their overt articulation of desires and of a movement among subject positions in speech and action, however, is constrained by the power of those who hegemonically control the various public spaces in which individuals act. In Pakistan engagement with Sufi pīrs occurs in ways ranging from unquestioned habitual activity to intense ideological argument. This book depicts the interplay of these habits and arguments, demonstrating the movements and articulations of the desiring subject.

I

The Tradition-Modernity Dichotomy

as a Hegemonic Discourse

2

Sādhus and *Faqīrs*: The Sufi *Pīr*

as a Colonial Construct

To a foreign eye on the eve of Partition, Sufi saints and shrines were one of the most visible elements of the South Asian landscape. Flora Davidson wrote from Peshawar in 1946: "No one can live long on the North West frontier of India without hearing of *ziarats,* or shrines. Some of these are in villages, some by the roadside, or even in the streets of the towns. . . . The fluttering flags and the collection of different colored rags soon tell the traveler how celebrated it is" (Davidson 1946:170). But for Flora Davidson, the presence of the shrines and the respect they inspired in the local population were not simply interesting phenomena to be recorded. Taking the position of an objective and knowing observer, Davidson, in a brief article published shortly before Indian Independence, constructed a descriptive account of local practices, most of which was devoted to documenting stories about the origins of local shrines. She concluded her account with an act of rhetorical violence cloaked in a veil of compassion:

> It goes to one's heart to see poor women who have trudged wearily miles and miles, with an ailing and perhaps dying baby in their arms, prostrating themselves at one of these shrines. They mutter long prayers, brush themselves down, present little oil lamps or a bit of cloth or food, at the grave of "who-knows-who," while the living Christ, the great Healer, His heart throbbing with love and compassion, stands by unknown and unrecognized.

Islam, a religion founded on a Prophet now dead and buried, on obsolete laws, sterile precepts, customs and practices of the Dark Ages, maintains and even fosters a belief in superstitions and the efficacy of graves and dead men's bones. (172)

Knowing nothing more about Flora Davidson than what she reveals in her essay, we see her establishing a subject position grounded in a "throbbing" fantasy of otherness. Davidson's heart and gaze merge with the heart and gaze of Christ, encompassing the "poor woman" she constructs through her prose. The woman's subjectivity has been fully encapsulated, interpellated by Davidson's compassion and her knowledge both of Christ and of the histories of the shrines of the area.

The "poor woman" captured in such a portrait has been subjected to the power of what Said (1979) has identified as an Orientalizing discourse, fixed in the "Dark Ages" as a demeaned "other," cut off by her own blindness from a modern Christ. This fantasy freezes both observer and observed in a chain of signifiers, a series of stereotypes. These signifiers have been aligned in a set of dichotomies that fixes the Muslim with regard to Christ: Christ is living, modern, socially progressive, and powerfully efficacious. Muhammad and the Sufi saints are dead, medieval, associated with an array of superstitious practices, and tied to an archaic "sterile" social order, which is, therefore, weak and helpless. As Bhabha (1986a) has suggested, such a stereotype fixes the subjectivity of the colonizer in an Imaginary Order in which the subject finds or recognizes itself through an image that is simultaneously alienating. Articulating the structure of desire expressed in Davidson's fantasy, we can see that Davidson identifies fully with Christ (alienating herself in the process as she merges with Christ as an ideal ego), just as a little white girl described by Fanon experiences a total, narcissistic identification with her "white" mother when she gazes at Fanon and says, "Look, a Negro. . . . Mama, see the Negro! I'm frightened" (Fanon 1968:112). The "poor woman" or the "Negro" becomes absolutely other and functions as a support for the colonizer's narcissistic identification as "not" other.[1]

What happens when the "poor woman," the silenced subaltern par excellence, looks back? Fanon, writing back, described this moment of colonial stereotyping as a primal scene, in which he, as the colonial subject, was fixed, "amputated." In Bhabha's words, "the black child turns away from himself, his race, in his total identification with the positivity of whiteness which is at once colour and no colour" (Bhabha

1986a:163). Fanon wrote as a postcolonial, who having already been interpellated or fixed in this ideological order, deconstructed it while acknowledging its pervasive power. The colonial subject is split between "contradictory beliefs, one official and one secret" (Bhabha 1986a:168). This view, then, does not suggest that colonial discourse is hegemonic in any simple sense — that this Imaginary Order of signifiers succeeded in fully naturalizing colonial authority and institutions, since the colonized subject maintains a kind of split consciousness.

Postcolonial studies emerging from India and the Indian diaspora have highlighted these processes of subjectification that are made possible through stereotypical discourse (Bhabha 1986a:149). Postcolonial intellectuals have been particularly acute spokespersons for the plight of the split subject, stressing at the same time the pervasive power of colonial discourse. But these writers, in their very positioning as postcolonial intellectuals, have themselves been situated most directly in the colonial/postcolonial gaze. Writers in such a position are most likely to identify Flora Davidson's Orientalism as hegemonic, as constitutive of the colonial subject. From this assumption, the "poor woman" is left with only two possible subject positions: acceptance of a colonized subjectivity or resistance. Either she accepts that she has been worshiping "old bones" and gives it up in favor of some form of modernity or she clings to her "tradition" (or, by extension, her "ethnicity"). But if she resists in this fashion, hers becomes a practice that has passed through the Western Imaginary and has been reconstituted as an ideological position in the modern world — it has become "tradition" (as Fox [1989] argues).

Suleri has written of an uncertainty that characterized British authority, an uncertainty that "manifests itself as a continual anxiety that India is actually indifferent to imperialism and may be uncannily equipped to absorb and contain invasion" (Suleri 1992: front flap of cover).[2] It is, perhaps, the fear of this indifference that stimulated Davidson's violent outburst against Islam. The "poor woman" she conjures up in her imagination, blinded by Islam and the false promise of the saints, cannot see the Christ who gazes at her. She is oblivious, too, of Davidson's gaze. If the poor woman does remain oblivious, this colonized subject has not been "split" at all, and the void at the heart of Davidson's ideology, the discontinuity with reality that her discourse imposes, threatens to reveal itself, shattering the Imaginary forms that maintain Davidson's subject position as a "civilized" self.

Within the framework of a colonial ideology, the Sufi *faqīr* (mendi-

cant) represented the epitome of this indifference, a refusal to be captured by the "naturalness," the hegemony of the colonial order.[3] The
more threatening the presence of the faqīr, the more demeaning were
the images used to "capture" him, images that continue to circulate in
postcolonial discourse as versions of modernity, Islam, and secularism
vie for dominance in the political arena. The Sufi saint occupies a contested position in these contemporary debates, which have inevitably
been molded by the colonial experience out of which Pakistan emerged
as a nation.

Broadly speaking, the terms in which Islam was and is discussed were
forged in a public discourse shaped by a dichotomy of tradition and
modernity that organized much of the colonizers' experiences. The
ideological positions articulated in the alignment of Islam with various
political stances attempted to locate or fix certain practices with respect
to an Islam that stood in a particular relationship to modernity.

Davidson located the Sufi shrine in the Dark Ages, but the fixed
chains of signifiers that her text embodied refused to remain firmly
linked, even for the colonizers themselves. For the British to have succeeded in imposing a hegemonic cultural order on their colonial subjects, it would have been necessary for them to effectively break down
indigenous behaviors into categories explainable and locatable within
a British colonial discourse and to articulate an effective critique of the
activities that fell into these categories in terms that ultimately reinforced the authority of the colonial power. Cultural domination and
the constitution of a "colonial subject" — in a psychological as well as a
political sense — requires an effective critique of the dominated culture,
a critique that is convincing to both dominator and dominated.

Theories that argue for a rupture with the past assume that this
cultural penetration and colonial hegemony were successfully accomplished. But the colonizers were not the agents of a monolithic process.
They were themselves caught in conflict, with competing interests and
at times dramatically differing visions of colonialism (see Comaroff
1989; Comaroff and Comaroff 1991). They also had inconsistent images of the holy man, some of which they absorbed from their colonized subjects, and some of which they struggled to impose on them.

Through the late nineteenth century and into the twentieth century,
the content of the "Islam" that was being defended as an identity for
Muslims became an increasingly important issue as politics moved toward mass representation and the practices and attitudes of the general

population became a focus of debate. Sufi practice was a part of this debate. To the extent that Sufi practice is articulated in terms of the dichotomy between tradition and modernity, a Sufi identity is a colonized identity. The contrast between tradition and modernity forms one component of the discourse of Orientalism, which, as Said (1979) has argued, was taken up by "Orientals" themselves as the British imposed their views on their subjects. But there was not a simple Orientalized image of spirituality or the mystical holy man for South Asian activists, either Hindu or Muslim, to reproduce or to resist.

In tracing how today's ideologies and identities emerge out of, or rather in relation to, the discursive formation of modernity and the stereotypes of colonial ideologies, I begin with an examination of the ways in which the Sufi saint was constructed through colonial discourse. I do this to show that, ultimately, there is an excess of meaning embodied in Sufi practice and expressed in Sufi identities. It is an excess that escaped colonial gaze(s) and is not fully captured by modernity as a discourse or a practice.

Sufism as "Religion"

Recent scholarship in the social sciences, reflecting back on its own history, has become self-conscious about how the very notion of "tradition" arises out of the discursive formation of "modernity." To colonial administrators, Orientalists, and anthropologists in particular, phenomena such as religion, ethnicity, and caste appeared traditional and timeless, the static background for the dramatic changes that Western-inspired modernity would produce. Challenging this notion of tradition, scholars such as Cohn (1987) and Dirks (1987) have emphasized the ways in which such apparently "traditional" phenomena were constructed or at least shaped, often unintentionally, by the colonial project and its administrative practices.[4] Within the Western analytic categories that were deployed to understand South Asian social life, Sufi practice fell into the domain of "religion" and was, therefore, something that Muslims, as opposed to Hindus and Christians, do. Though an apparently straightforward act of classification, it had implications for administrative policy and for the place of the Sufi in colonial discourse.

The colonial project operated within an Enlightenment paradigm in which "freedom" was a key and particularly problematic signifier. One of the arenas in which the British could point to their own enactment of this principle was with respect to this category of religion. In India, they developed a hands-off policy that recognized separate state and sacred realms. This policy was explicitly manifested in a series of government acts, beginning in 1863, when an act to enable the Government to divest itself of the management of Religious Endowments (*Calcutta Gazette* 1863) was passed. The government was moving to get out of the business of directly administering shrines, which it had been involved in earlier.

But this hands-off policy did not mean that religious practice was unaffected by the colonial presence. Just as census-taking and the codification of law produced a consolidation of castes and new arenas for playing out status competitions, policies toward religion had multiple intended and unintended consequences for the developing colonial state. These policies altered the nature of existing religious institutions. The effort to allocate and even preserve "native custom" created profound changes in the significance of temples, shrines, and religious functionaries (see Cohn 1987; Dirks 1987; Fox 1989).[5]

The British courts used their interpretations of "Muhammadan Law" (*sharī'at*) to transform the nature of sharī'at from a flexible system in which individual religious scholars treated each question that came before them as unique into a codified system based on precedent. This was a conscious effort at transformation. The British judge Frank Beaman, for instance, stated explicitly that Muhammadan law was the creation of the Anglo-Indian courts (Kozlowski 1985:152). This transformation occurred through the claim that the courts were simply applying a code of law that was centuries old.[6] It conceptually identified religious practice as timeless and traditional—thereby severing its links to the political process. At the same time, it located religion in the domain of the personal, the spiritual, the otherworldly, which is another strategy for finding a place for religion in a modern world. When "religious practice" seeped beyond this conceptual boundary, it reinforced views of the South Asian Oriental as excessively religious—an other to the dynamic, progressive, modern Westerner.[7]

This contrast between a dynamic Western self and a passive otherworldly other is, of course, the foundational dichotomy of Orientalism. The otherworldly holy man as an embodiment of the ancient wisdom of the spiritual Orient is a figment of the Western imagination embedded in a dichotomy of West and East. The progressive rationality of the Western scientist confronts the tradition-bound mysticism of the Muslim faqīr or the Hindu *sādhu*.[8] This discourse captures a whole range of institutions and activities, fixing them in a position of otherness with respect to modernity and the West.

The Splitting of the Holy Man

The simple label "religion" is but one of the ways in which colonial discourse located the Sufi saint in the colonial order imposed on South Asia. In Western writings during the colonial period, the Indian holy man was also the object of a peculiar split that effectively created a barrier between him and the European observer. The holy man as represented in and by old texts was sharply distinguished from any living representatives. This split was part of a rhetorical strategy, grounded in a modernist ideology, that encompassed and, in principle at least, disempowered a threatening other.[9] The object of yearning—the Oriental sage—was safely unreachable, while the other who was immediately present was denigrated, abjected.

The Orientalists, who were European scholars and poets removed from the rigors of daily administration and the politics of domination, were engaged in a project of appropriating as knowledge the "sacred books of the East,"[10] obtaining manuscripts, translating texts,[11] creating university chairs for Oriental scholarship, even making texts newly available to Sufis themselves.[12] There was a bifurcation in nineteenth-century writings, then, between those generated by the Orientalists whose skills were linguistic and who focused on the reproduction and interpretation of texts that greatly expanded European awareness of a common cultural heritage (with Sanskrit being recognized as closer to the Indo-European roots of the European languages than was English itself) and the administrators, travelers, and emerging social scientists, who reported on a geographically distant and alien place. The Oriental was either common in spirit but distant in time or of a common era but distant in space and culture, in either case denied the status of "modern." Romanticism constituted the Orient as a repository for the spirituality and traditional values that had in the West been sacrificed to modernity. Orientalist scholars had relegated the positive image of the powerful holy man as a source of wisdom to the timeless, distant past.

Holy men also existed in the present, but their significance was severed from the texts of the tradition.[13] An image of Indian spirituality

was not the stereotype that prevailed in colonial administrative discourse focused on the living religious ascetic of the urban streets and
countryside and on the powerful landowning families of hereditary
saints. This living holy man was either mired in corruption or trapped
in superstition.[14]

This discursive structure, which projects all spirituality and truth
into the past, created a specific problematic for scholars who, coming
from textually based Orientalist scholarship, turned their attention to
the modern world. The negative stereotypes and their foundation in the
discursive formation of "modernity" appeared in scholarly Orientalist writings themselves when such scholars ventured into the domain
of the living or recently deceased. Their theoretical arguments have
sought to reconcile the romanticized spirituality of the ancient tradition
with the depreciated, colonized other of the present by constructing an
array of explanatory devices.

The temporal splitting is particularly clear in scholarly volumes such
as Trimingham's history of Sufism, first published in 1971. In this study,
which served as an introduction to Sufism for many scholars of my
generation, Trimingham (1971) turned a social scientist's eye to the
history of Sufism, focusing on its institutional structure. He defined
Sufism in opposition to legalistic "orthodoxy." He regarded early Sufism as a "*natural* expression of personal religion," in contrast to orthodoxy, which he characterized as "institutionalized religion based on
authority, a one-way Master-slave relationship, with its emphasis upon
ritual observance and a legalistic morality" (2). He characterized the
development of the genealogy of spiritual descent (*silsila*) within Sufism
as "the beginning of the process whereby the creative freedom of the
mystic was to be channelled into an institution," giving rise to a hierarchical structure and modes of spiritual outlook and worship "foreign
to its essential genius" (11). Aspects of popular focus on the personality
of the Sufi teacher (*shaikh*) were used as examples of how Sufi ideas
were "vulgarized" (165). Dividing the development of Sufism into three
stages, he characterized the first as "surrender to God" and the "golden
age of mysticism," the second as "surrender to a rule," and the third as
"surrender to a person," in which the seeker had been transformed into
a spiritual slave, and the mystical content of the orders had been weakened. This organization "carried within itself the seeds of its own decay" (103). Trimingham's condemnation was explicit: "The orders had
now attained their final forms of organization and spiritual exercises.

Innovations had become fully integrated and their spirit and aims were stereotyped. No further development was possible and no further work of mystical insight which could mark a new point of departure in either doctrine or practice was to make its appearance" (104).

Trimingham obviously thought that the system deserved to be overthrown by Western thought, which, like his construction of early Sufism, celebrates the autonomous creativity of the individual. In Trimingham's work, as in many others, a series of signifiers was fixed vis-à-vis the dichotomy of modernity versus tradition. Tradition was aligned with superstition, error, stasis, and corruption. When the institutional components of Islam were criticized and delegitimated in terms borrowed from Christian Protestantism, particular activities could be labeled as corrupt and separated from religion proper.

For the most part, colonial administrators confined their concerns to the institutionalized practices of living holy men in their writings. In their efforts to impose a hegemonic cultural order, they attempted to locate the practices of these people in a social space articulated in categories meaningful back home. With respect to Muslims, people and practices that could have been broadly associated under the rubric of Sufism were broken apart. The wandering ascetic was condemned for being shiftless. The hereditary saint (*sajjāda nishīn*), who might control large areas of land and people, was recognized as an important figure within a patronage system and treated like any other local "chief." His Sufi affiliation became a caste or tribe designation in colonial parlance, analogous to a family title (Talbot 1988). The phenomenon of the pīr was perceived as sharply distinct from Sufism as a "pure" religious practice.[15] The hereditary saints were seen primarily in terms of their economic power. British policy, especially in the Punjab and Sind, was to treat them in essentially the same way that landlords and tribal leaders were treated. The British continued the policy of their Muslim predecessors with respect to the shrines, making further grants to influential pīrs. They tried to maintain the traditional social structure intact, securing the loyalty of the pīrs, landlords, and chiefs by reinforcing their economic positions and educating them in the British tradition (Gilmartin 1979).

Their treatment of the sajjāda nishīns of Pir Pagaro was an instance of this policy. Pir Pagaro had a large following in Sind and surrounding areas. Among the disciples of the pīr were the Hurs, who were willing to lay down their lives as his followers. The Hurs staged two rebellions

against the British, in the 1890s and again in the 1940s. Pir Sabgha-
tullah held the title Pir Pagaro during the second rebellion. The British
saw him as a threat to their administration and executed him in 1943.
They educated his son in England with the intention of having him
become a successor who would keep the Hurs in line (Lambrick 1972;
Ansari 1992). That is, they would secularize the pīr, then use him to
control the superstitious impulses of the natives. Though following in
Muslim footsteps in making grants to the shrines, the ideological significance of such grants was thus quite different.

The wandering ascetic, in contrast, was the object of a harshly negative Orientalism that reinforced the barrier between colonizer and colonized. Administrators highlighted various activities associated with
these ascetics — specifically, drug use, wandering, and begging — that
had been the target of vigorous social agendas in Europe. They then
argued for a starkly negative evaluation of these categories that supported the moral authority of the colonial order. The prevalence of
religious mendicants was proof of the gullibility of the Indian and his
incapacity to deal with the rigors of the real world of commerce, administration, and self-rule.

In the colonial period, the British articulated what constituted resistance in their eyes and acted accordingly, attempting to control specific aspects of the behavior of wandering ascetics. Though the sādhus
and faqīrs were not so numerous that they constituted a direct threat to
colonial operations,[16] they represented in both ideology and practice an
alternative source of authority that the British sought to combat both
ideologically and through administrative control of their practice. The
colonizers focused particularly on the activities of drug use, wandering,
and begging, which they perceived as a threat to social order.

DRUG USE

The drugs primarily associated with wandering ascetics were marijuana and hashish, indigenous products that had been in widespread
use in India long before the arrival of the British. The colonial government was concerned with controlling and regulating international
trade in opium; but wandering religious mendicants did not at that time
seem to have been associated with this trade, at least in the eyes of
administrators. Efforts at regulating the use of hashish and marijuana
seem to have been limited to establishing a controlled system of distribution that made consumption more expensive.[17]

A turn-of-the-century "Dream of Hashish" (from Somerville 1929)

Prominent in the literature of this period, however, is the rhetorical focus on drug consumption in a religious setting as evidence supporting the cultural superiority of the British and the "degeneracy" of the Oriental. In 1929, a time when the subcontinent had become a pressure cooker of anticolonial Indian nationalism, in a book called *Crime and Religious Beliefs in India* (1929), Augustus Somerville wrote:

> No Indian — I refer to the ignorant masses mainly — considers the smoking of opium, ganga or bhang anything but a virtuous occupation. If his holy men — yogis, rishis and fakirs smoke it, why should not he? I can imagine the consternation in any English parish in which the Pastor indulged in a little public opium smoking, and yet in India, in the shade of the sacred "pepul" tree, on the steps of some old-world temple, sits the Yogi and smokes his "Ganja" and the reverent masses pass him by, wondering greatly what glorious visions have been vouchsafed to their holy man. (Somerville 1929:41)

Somerville included a drawing entitled "A Dream of Hashish," which foregrounds a sensual woman with voluptuous curls flowing into her lap, surrounded by curling smoke and demon-like faces (Somerville 1929: facing p. 16).

The rhetorical intention of this illustration is, from today's vantage

point, transparent: how can Indians expect to govern themselves when
their role models are lost in narcotic dreams of voluptuous sensuality?
The contradiction embedded within the first sentence — "No Indian,"
immediately contained by the qualifier "ignorant masses" — simultaneously denies and suggests the possibility of rational enlightenment for
the few Indians who have been penetrated by Christian morality.

Eighty years earlier Richard Burton, the noted adventurer, saw the
use of intoxicants in a similar light — as constituting a divide between
the European and the Indian, despite his own "occasional" indulgence.
Hired in 1844 by the governor of Sind as a surveyor, Burton spent some
of his time traveling through Sind disguised as "Mirza Abdullah of
Bushire," claiming to be half Arab, half Persian. He gathered information on the Sindhis that was first published as official government reports. One of the reports, *Remarks on the Division of Time, and the
Modes of Intoxication in Sind,* included extensive information on the
use of hemp,[18] which he associated with Sindhi degeneracy: "The lower
orders of the Moslems are extraordinarily addicted to the use of Indian
hemp, and take it to such an extent that, like the Guzerattee opium
eaters, they find it necessary to existence. The general use of this delete-
rious preparation has doubtlessly done much towards causing physical
and mental degeneracy in the Sindhi: it produces madness, catalepsy
and a multitude of other disorders" (Burton 1973:168). He specifically associated hemp with "Fakirs and religious mendicants" (171),
particularly those whom he calls "Jelali pirs,"[19] by which he meant the
antinomian ascetic, as opposed to the more respectable settled pīr.
From Burton's perspective, the *jalālī* pīr is "permitted to make earth as
pleasant a place as he can, by the liberal use of hemp or spirits, and the
pursuit of the most degrading sensuality" (209). Such stories of the
opium and hemp smoker stressed that those who indulge in such practices were not good for any productive activity and, therefore, account
for the degenerate state of India. By the same token, however, such
people were not dangerous, and, therefore, were not usually a direct
threat to colonial authority.

WANDERING

Though drug consumption was not perceived to be a direct threat
to government authority, wandering was another matter. Space and
movement through space are one of the modalities through which the
wandering ascetic expresses and constructs a social position and rela-

tionship to social order. When that order changes, so does the significance of the ascetic's movement. For the Muslim of the Mughal period, the wandering ascetic could also be a problem and a danger, but his habit of wandering was not his most salient feature. (Aurangzeb, the powerful Mughal ruler known for his efforts to purify Muslim practice in India, himself wandered about from one encampment to the next for twenty-five years of his rule.) For the nomadic Mongols and other central Asians who invaded and dominated much of the Muslim world, the ability to move across great distances while maintaining dispersed personal networks signified control and power. Scholars, religious leaders, and Sufis also traveled frequently and for extended periods of time. In this environment, ascetics like the qalandar were more notable for their violation of aspects of religious law governing dress and personal grooming, ritual behavior, and sexuality and, above all, for the alternative model of saintliness and religious authority they represented than for their propensity to hit the road or their lack of fixed abode.

To the British, the faqīr was someone whose roots could not be traced — who could, therefore, deceive. "Faqīrs and sādhus" were as likely to be bands of criminals as not. Their religious practice was irrelevant. In the late eighteenth and early nineteenth centuries, when the British were gradually extending their influence and control over India, there were what Freitag has characterized as "powerful wandering and/or predatory groups [that] exercised hegemony through plunder or collecting tribute" (Freitag 1985:14). British images of wandering ascetics were colored by the existence of these bands. In the late eighteenth century some of these large bands were armed *sanyāsīs* who fought as mercenaries for Hindus, Muslims, and the British (Lorenzen 1978:74). The British focused considerable attention on the organization and activities of such criminal bands but found it extremely difficult to control their movements.

In this environment, the British indiscriminantly lumped the various ascetic wanderers together with other "bandits" and engaged in frequent military activities against them. Warren Hastings, working at a difficult time to establish British administrative control over Bengal, characterized the ascetics as "a set of lawless Bandette [who have] infested these countries and under the pretence of religious pilgrimage have been accustomed to traverse the chief part of Bengal, begging, stealing and plundering wherever they go" (Cohn 1964:176).[20]

Hastings wrote this during the period of what was commonly labeled the "Sanyasi Rebellion." According to one analysis (Lorenzen 1974; 1978), the British read "rebellion" into what was actually a complex set of phenomena. A combination of famine and heavy taxes imposed by the British had forced a group of peaceful Muslim wandering ascetics, the Madari faqīrs,[21] into direct competition for contributions from local landowners, who had been part of their traditional begging circuit. A particular branch of Hindu sanyāsīs, the Dasnami Naga Sanyasis, also became involved in antagonistic relations with the British and joined with the faqīrs to resist the new order (Lorenzen 1978:74).[22] Destitute farmers may also have joined the ranks of the faqīrs, swelling their numbers.

The association between wandering and criminal activity was strong in the discourse of British colonial administrators and seems to have shaped the behavior of the wanderers themselves. What the British described as raiding had been a part of a regular pilgrimage cycle.[23] In a letter to one powerful landowner, a leader of the faqīrs explained how British assaults on their members had forced a change in their behavior: "Formerly the fakirs begged in separate and detached parties but now we are all collected and beg together. Displeased at this method they (the British) obstruct us in visiting the shrines and other places" (Ghosh 1930:47). With the pressures of severe famine, the ascetics had come into direct conflict with the British over the right to collections from landowners (Lorenzen 1978:73), a right which had officially been granted to the Madari faqīrs by Prince Shah Shuja in 1629 (Ghosh 1930:22). Joined by landowners who had also been forced into destitution through excessive taxation in a time of famine, these wandering ascetics did play a role of active, armed resistance to the colonial order, but not because they were inherently or "essentially" militant wandering bandits.

Freitag has traced the history of the colonial administration's handling of what they labeled "criminal tribes" from a perspective that highlights a gradual change in public discourse about these bands, grounded in changing evaluations of the practice of wandering. The signifying system that emerged out of British efforts to establish their authority in India evolved as an amalgam of British values and the values of the sedentary elites through whom the British had established its land-revenue-based state (Freitag 1985:3). In the early colonial period, "thugs" were seen as admirable and awesome opponents by sedentary local populations and British alike. By the second half of the nineteenth century, the indigenous agrarian elite as well as the British colonizers defined the behavior of wandering groups as outside the norm. Collective crime had become equated with "criminal tribes or castes." Martial valor was replaced by the ability to operate in a court of law (Freitag 1985:14–18). Wandering groups were increasingly marginalized and criminalized. Government policy was to enforce settlement, often through coercive confinement.

It is against this background that we can see the changing significance, specifically the criminalization, of the wandering ascetic. Administrators saw faqīrs and other ascetics in the context of the activities of what they had designated criminal tribes, and they were preoccupied with controlling their movements, especially during times of civil disturbance. Even in my cursory survey of historical sources, mendicants appear in the colonial records of this period:

> In order to facilitate the process of identification of those who had taken part in the rioting, a regulation (*Martial Law Notices, p. 55) (no. 9) was issued on April 25th forbidding any persons to leave Kasur and announcing that measures would be taken against the property of all persons not returning by a certain date. In view of the belief first held that religious mendicants had largely been concerned in fomenting disorder, a regulation was also issued (no. 10) for the registration of all religious mendicants and for a daily roll-call of them. (*Report on the Punjabi Disturbances, April 1919* 1919:86)

This British act of registering and administering a roll call of "religious mendicants" is one that was remembered and continued to be significant for qalandars in the 1970s (see Ewing 1984b).

With the categories of tribe and caste as basic administrative units, and with the assumption that those who wander are probably criminal, administrators made rather awkward efforts to assimilate various wandering ascetics such as qalandars and faqīrs to the categories of tribe and caste. The difficulties they had in doing so demonstrate the distorting objectifications that this administrative practice generated in social science discourse of the period. In 1881 Sir Denzil Ibbetson, for instance, struggled to categorize members of "Ascetic and Mendicant Orders" in an official report based on census data:

> I now turn to the consideration of that section of the community which is commonly included under the generic term of Faqir. I must first point out that our [census] figures, though representing

with fair accuracy the total numbers of this class, are wholly im-
perfect so far as the details are concerned. . . . [T]he real reason
of the failure of our figures to show details is, that the great mass
of these Faqirs entered the name of their order not under "tribe"
but under "sect"; and as we were forbidden to tabulate any sects
except Shiah, Sunni, Wahabi, and Farazi, the details were not
worked out at all. (Ibbetson 1974:169)

Having discussed the lack of fit among census categories, people's self-
designations, and census tabulations, Ibbetson went on to characterize
the faqīrs:

I have said that many of the members of these orders are pious,
respectable men whose influence is wholly for the good. But this is
far from being the case with all the orders. Many of them are
notoriously profligate debauchers, who wander about the country
seducing women, extorting alms by threat of curses, and relying
on their saintly character for protection. Still even these men are
members of an order which they have deliberately entered and
have some right to the title which they bear. But a very large
portion of the class who are included under the name Faqir are
ignorant men of low caste, without any acquaintance with even
the general outlines of the religion they profess, still less with the
special tenets of any particular sect, who borrow the garb of the
regular orders and wander about the country living on the alms of
the credulous, often hardly knowing the names of the orders to
which the external signs they wear would show them to belong.
Such men are mere beggars, not ascetics; and though their numbers are unfortunately large, we have no means of separating
them. (169)

Ibbetson did not even include the qalandars among the ascetic and
mendicant orders. He instead categorized qalandars as a Gypsy tribe:

The gipsy tribes are hardly to be distinguished from those whom I
have called the wandering and criminal tribes. . . . But I have
classed as Gipsies, for want of a better distinction, those tribes
who perform in any way, who practice tumbling or rope-dancing,
lead about bears and monkeys, and so forth. (212–13)

The Qalandari is the Kalender of the *Arabian Nights*. He is properly a holy Mahomedan ascetic who abandons the world and

wanders about with shaven head and beard. But the word is generally used in the Punjab for a monkey-man; and I have classed him
here instead of with faqirs. I believe that some of them have a sort
of pretence to a religious character. (215–16)

Ibbetson was obviously struggling with the arbitrariness of his catego-
rizations. But ultimately, the qalandars fell for practical purposes under
the shadow of the label "criminal castes," despite his inability to separate them from the faqīrs, a religious designation.

   This shadow was deepened by deliberate British indifference to the
significance of Sufi practice. British efforts to leave a community's religious and other cultural affairs to itself,[24] coupled with their concern
to establish a sedentary population of identifiable tribes and castes for
administrative purposes, meant that to them the most significant feature of the wandering faqīrs was not their possible lack of religious
orthodoxy but rather their inclination to wander. Wandering was associated with criminal activity, and it was detached from its spiritual
significance in Sufi doctrine, this being something that did not directly
concern colonial administrators. On the issue of wandering, then, the
British (and perhaps sedentary Indian elites) succeeded in making their
values hegemonic in public discourse: by the late nineteenth century,
ascetic wandering had become an act of resistance, criminalized to the
extent that it did not even constitute a moral challenge to the foundations of order, being beyond the pale of admirable behavior. Nevertheless, the qalandar and faqīr could not easily or convincingly be fully
subsumed under this category.

BEGGING AND THE WORK ETHIC

It was through the act of begging in the name of spirituality that the
ascetic touched a raw nerve amongst the upholders of the Raj, manifesting a form of activity that could not be neutralized into the disreputable as readily as wandering and drug use had been. European
responses to both wandering and begging reflect a strategy of contain-
ment and confinement in the name of order that Foucault (1973, 1977)
has traced in European history. As with its treatment of the insane, how
a society handles its indigent is an instance of the conceptual and political order of that historical era (Foucault 1973:40).[25] Wandering became increasingly criminalized over the course of the nineteenth and
early twentieth centuries, and even when administrative strategies for

handling "criminal tribes" came under scrutiny, the glorification of a sedentary existence itself remained unquestioned (except perhaps in the lore of the American frontier). The criminalization of drug use came somewhat later, so that in the nineteenth century drug use fell principally into the category of moral failing, analogous to (and linked with) sexual promiscuity. Attitudes toward begging, in contrast, shifted in the opposite direction, to the extent that today it is not fashionable, at least among self-styled liberals, to blame the beggar for his or her woes. Modern social theories interpret begging as an index of flaws in the socioeconomic order.

Begging confronted the nineteenth-century English as they negotiated the streets of India. As is the case with today's global discourse on homelessness, begging was both an immediate physical confrontation and a highly charged signifier. For the British, the visibility of the Indian beggar was another of the grounds, along with drug use, on which a firm line could be drawn between a fantasy of England's tidy moral order and India's lack of civilization.

Confrontations with the phenomenon of begging were not new to the Europeans who arrived in India. On the contrary, European ideologists and policymakers had for two centuries been struggling with the existence of a large class of European beggars and other poor that had been spawned by economic dislocations. Foucault has identified a new conceptual and social order, which suddenly emerged in the middle of the seventeenth century and replaced other strategies for handling the poor in earlier eras. This newly established social sensibility focused on the idea of "confinement" (Foucault 1973:45). It was manifested in a system of workhouses that rapidly became established all over Europe. In England a series of Poor Laws were enacted: beggars, vagabonds, and "those who live in idleness and will not work for reasonable wages or who spend what they have in taverns" were to be punished and placed in houses of correction (Foucault 1973:50). Foucault linked these developments to a new "dream of a city where moral obligation was joined to civil law, within the authoritarian forms of constraint" (Foucault 1973:46).

In the complex of ideas associated with these institutions, begging was linked with the moral sins of idleness and sloth. As Weber's classic analysis of the link between the Protestant ethic as articulated in Calvinist doctrine and the spirit of capitalism suggested (Weber 1958), labor for its own sake had taken on a transcendental value beyond any particular material reward that labor might offer, and conversely, mendicity was regarded as a refusal to labor, a form of willful idleness. Idleness was interpreted as a manifestation of sinful pride, the ultimate rebellion against God. Mendicity and idleness were seen as the sources of all disorder (Foucault 1973:57). The punishment was confinement and enforced labor.

The begging ascetic of India was drawn up into this existing European discourse on mendicity. The writings of J. Campbell Oman, the son of a colonial planter born in Calcutta in 1841,[26] provide a remarkably articulate example of this discourse as it was played out in India at the turn of the twentieth century. A member of the Royal Asiatic Society, Oman wrote in his later years a number of books based on his extensive experience and observations of daily life in Bengal and the Punjab. Taking the empiricist stance of the British social scientist/administrator of that period, he wrote in the "Peculiar Customs of the Natives" genre, focusing particularly on what he called "customs and superstitions" and paying particular attention to the religious practices of the lower social strata.

Though all of his books are similar in content, one of his later books, *The Mystics, Ascetics, and Saints of India* (1905), reveals a shift in attitude when compared to his earliest book, *Indian Life, Religious and Social* (1889),[27] a shift that is suggestive of the changes that were occurring more broadly in the British Raj. Many of his statements in the earlier book exactly parallel the discourse on the poor that developed in Europe in the middle of the seventeenth century. But in the otherwise similar work written sixteen years later (1905), Oman exposed the deep cracks that had developed in British understandings of moral and social order. He challenged the foundations of the capitalist system itself. The immediate stimulus for Oman's challenge was the practice of the begging ascetic and his place in the Indian social order.

European strategies for handling the insane and beggars and the significance of these strategies for the notion of order are transparent in Oman's earlier (1889) discussion of mendicancy in India. "In all civilizations an essential characteristic is the keeping up of appearances, and the more complete and perfect the civilizations the more marked is this feature" (Oman [1889] 1908:229). He discussed, perhaps with a touch of irony, how the English of all classes regard the "mere externals" of poverty as so disreputable that even the poorest go to great lengths to hide themselves and their miseries from the public eye (230).[28] In England, "natural feeling . . . forces poverty and bodily infirmity into the background of the social world, in order to keep up appearances and to maintain what it believes to be a proper standard of national respectability" (230).

The British glorification of labor is evident in Oman's comments on the story of a faqīr, a story that he attributes to Guru Govind Singh: "A faquir lived in the jungles and never asked anything from any one; once on a time the will of God was this, that for eight days he got no food from anywhere; then the faquir thought to himself, 'As God has given me hands and feet I will go into the city and beg.' Here we have a truly Indian solution of the difficulty in which the faquir found himself. The idea of *work* would never occur to him, he was a faquir, and labour of any kind was out of the question" (231).

Oman saw in India the rise of a middle class that shared the English work ethic and was beginning to condemn begging: "With the modern apotheosis of wealth in India, which necessarily involves an increase of selfishness, the support of a large mendicant community is becoming irksome to the classes whose unstinted generosity could in former years always be fully relied upon by the poor, the needy, and the religious" (242).

In contrast to his earlier books, which simply wind down with one more "peculiar" fact or story, Oman's later book (1905) includes a thoughtful conclusion that, in its stance toward the assumption of "progress" that lies at the heart of the capitalist colonial project, is remarkably reminiscent of Max Weber's famous lament about the "iron cage" of capitalism.[29]

The colonial administration was not only losing confidence in its ability to shape India according to its own goals and values; some people were also beginning to question those very goals and values as a guiding theme for themselves at home. The faqīr, a wandering, begging ascetic, was for Oman the focal point of this shift in attitude. The beggar ascetic became for Oman the representation of the Orientalist ideal of Indian spirituality, thus bringing together into one image what was usually split and ejected into the past. There is in his writing a change from his focus on beggar-ascetics as the antithesis of British ideals of action, respectability, sedentariness, and industriousness to their being a repository of the values of democracy, equality, and spirituality. He recognized in the ascetic an alternative route to the achievement of many of the social ideals to which the British at least paid lip service:

Holding as I do that happiness, virtue, dignity, *personal* freedom, and reasonable comfort are quite compatible with modes of life, political institutions, industrial systems, and religious creeds which are not those of England or the Western world, the present transition state of India seems to me a subject of more than passing interest.

By no means enamoured of Indian *sadhuism,* I feel at the same time no particular admiration for the *industrialism* of Europe and America, with its vulgar aggressiveness, its eternal competition, and its sordid, unscrupulous, unremitting, and cruel struggle for wealth as the supreme object of human effort. (Oman 1905:281–83)

Oman saw the beggar-ascetic as a form of resistance to the goal of capitalist accumulation. Even in 1889 he had recognized this resistance but at that time had labeled it shameful. By 1905, he seems to have changed sides.

Indian Spirituality as Resistance

Though we see hints of a respect for Indian spirituality in Oman's writing, England did not participate in the German veneration of India's superior spirituality that began with the "discovery" and translation of Sanskrit texts in the late seventeenth century. Schwab (1984) argued that this was because such veneration did not fit well with their colonial interests. We have already seen how the British confronted the phenomenon of the holy man in their administrative practice and writings. But how could this romanticized spirituality not have penetrated English consciousness earlier? The Romantic tradition was highly developed in England. The "Lake poets" drew inspiration from the Germans such as Goethe, who had been heavily influenced by the teachings of the East. But it is striking in perusing commentaries on the English Romantic writers that there is virtually no mention of India or the Orient, despite works such as Coleridge's "Kubla Khan" and "Mohamet." Romanticism in England took the form of an intense focus on Nature: the reaction of poets such as Blake and Wordsworth to the industrialization of the north of England led to a pantheistic view of nature, infused with a romanticized desire for a lost pastoralism (Ahmad 1992). When the English Romantic impulse reached India, it did so in the form of an adulation of nature, a seeking out of replicas of the Romantic sites of Europe. The people of India, particularly the beggars and ascetics, are at best quaint objects, bits of scenery (Freitag forthcoming); their subjectivity, their insights, did not penetrate English public discourse. But Oman's reassessment of the sādhu and faqīr suggests that the theme of Indian spirituality — "affirmative orientalism" (Fox 1989:106) — which had been developing in Europe and, more recently in American discourse, had by the turn of the century finally begun to penetrate even the consciousness of those Englishmen who were firmly invested in the colonial enterprise.[30]

The eventual penetration of Indian spirituality into colonial consciousness can be attributed largely to the activities of the Theosophical Society, which was influential in bringing the Romantic Orientalist tradition into direct confrontation with the negative Orientalism that was characteristic of the colonial administration.[31] Not only had the founders of the movement turned to India as a source of "ancient wisdom" (as had many other nineteenth-century intellectuals), but several of its leading figures began to take an active role in Indian politics during this period (see Campbell 1980). Annie Besant, an Englishwoman who had been prominent for her vocal advocacy of liberal causes while still in England (Campbell 1980:102), joined the Theosophical Society in 1889, traveled to India in 1893, and became a leading participant in the development of the Indian National Congress. She championed a return to Indian cultural symbols as the vehicle for Indian resistance to European domination and worked with Indian leaders who ultimately were successful in undermining colonial authority and legitimacy altogether and bringing an end to European domination.

Conclusion

Western Orientalist discourses contained and neutralized the authority of the holy man and his dangerous indifference to colonial authority by developing an ideology in which the representation of the holy man was split — polarized into positive and negative signifiers. These images were separated chronologically. The positive image of Indian spirituality, when acknowledged at all, was the domain of scholarly study: the holy man was a producer of profound texts in the safely distant past. The negative image was itself split between the landed hereditary pīr, whose authority the British attempted to replace with the status and position of a landowner, and the wandering beggar-ascetic. The negative image was highly developed in colonial administrative discourse — census and fact-finding reports, popular narratives, travel chronicles, and so on. Colonial narratives reinforced an Orientalizing discourse with dramatic descriptions, drawings, and photographs of degenerate "holy men" that would appeal to audiences back in England.

But the British failed to fully capture the faqīr, the qalandar, the sādhu, and the sanyāsī in their negative articulations. Their categories failed them: the qalandar or faqīr could not plausibly be reduced to an identity as a member of a wandering criminal tribe. More seriously, the grounds of their moral critique failed them: even in England, the discourse on mendicity had shifted: the beggar was becoming a victim of the economic system rather than a shameful criminal.

Though the British were not the first to accuse many pīrs and other holy men of corruption — Sufis have been a target of controversy in the Muslim world since they first appeared — the British also created a dichotomy between themselves and their colonial subjects, and they were often strategically blind to any Indian ability to discriminate between the corrupt opportunist and the holy man whose practice was consistent with his stated goals. At their most glaringly Orientalist, colonial writers implied that only the European was astute enough to recognize the corruption of the wandering ascetic or the money-collecting pīr at a shrine while the Indian would blindly worship the most obvious degenerate. Such gullibility and superstition was a sign of the degeneracy of Oriental culture as a whole. The colonized Indian had been fully identified with his holy men. In this move, the British misrecognized the fault lines within the society they were attempting to administer. They underestimated the moral authority of the holy man they attempted to denigrate and failed to recognize his ability to speak a kind of truth even to the "modern." The resistance of the sādhu, the faqīr, the qalandar to this discourse exposed contradictions and challenged the naturalness of the colonial order in ways that many colonizers themselves found difficult to ignore. The religious ascetic ultimately provided a signifier for the self-doubt of the colonizer. Oriental spirituality became a vehicle of colonizers' incipient critiques of the very basis of colonial order that merged well with Romantic critiques of encroaching industrialization and capitalism.

The spirituality of the holy man that emerged into public (i.e., visible to the British) discourse in the twentieth century had been present in Muslim and Hindu discourses all along, written off by the British as ignorant superstition, quaint customs, or corrupt practice. The British assessments failed to become hegemonic.[32] In the social/religious movements that developed with increasing force in the late nineteenth and early twentieth centuries, South Asians dismissed the dichotomy that the colonists thought they had imposed on them. They reclaimed connection with traditions that located the "wisdom of the East" in the present while taking into account and encompassing the scientism and materialism of the capitalist system.

Though perhaps convincing to those who had the most investment in maintaining the legitimacy of the colonial order, the colonial degradation of the holy man was, on closer analysis, highly implausible and masked the developing mutual penetration of the perspectives of colonizers and colonized and their human interaction. As the colonial order decayed, this mutual penetration emerged into a common public discourse that is visible in social movements of the twentieth century. In this process both parties retained ties of continuity to pasts that were neither timeless nor ruptured.

3

The *Pīr*, the State, and the Modern Subject

As a focus for the movement to end colonial rule in South Asia in the first half of the twentieth century, activists turned to "religion," which the British had sought to relegate to the sphere of private life, as a way of resisting the hegemony of colonial discourse. Hinduism and Islam became a major component of public discourse and took center stage as foci for ideological elaboration. The colonial subject was interpellated as "Hindu" or "Muslim" in an increasingly violent bifurcation of communities. Muslim religious leaders sought to mark the Muslim as culturally distinct, specifying and controlling bodily practice in order to give Islam a more specific and uniform content in its role of creating the Muslim. Hindu revivalist movements had similar goals. This increasingly ideological bifurcation ultimately led to the mass migrations and bloodshed of Partition.[1]

Being the sole justification for the creation of two separate nation-states, Pakistan and India, Hinduism and Islam continued to be the focus of postcolonial ideological elaboration. Initially split territorially into two widely separated wings, Pakistan could not claim to be in essence a people of shared ethnicity, language, culture, or even territorially contiguous space. What they claimed instead was a shared identity based on adherence to Islam, and many of Pakistan's leaders articulated their political goal as the establishment of "Islamic democracy." But this idea of Islam as it was articulated by many politicians was abstract. Because the range of practices to be subsumed under the label "Islam" was so great, the word functioned in political discourse (though not, of course, in the lives of individual Muslims) as virtually an empty signifier — a signifier attached to no preexisting substantive relationships or practices that all "Pakistanis" had in common.[2] In the South Asian political context, being "Muslim" had become a signifier whose meaning was based primarily on difference, that is, on being "not Hindu." A task for the consolidators of the nation-state was to give the Pakistani citizen as subject some positive content that could be pointed to as an identifiable "essence" beyond the empty difference "not Hindu." In the process of injecting a positive content, aspects of Muslim practice such as the status of women and the interpretation of sharīʿat (Islamic law) became the focus of competing interpretations. In the same way, Sufism and the pīr have been caught up in this discursive process of articulating what is and is not the true Islam that Pakistan should embody.

In this task — and the ideological storms associated with it — many of the premises underlying colonial discourse continued to play a significant role. For many of the politicians who played an active role in the constitution of this new government, the essence of an Islam that would be the foundation of an Islamic democracy echoed Western ideological views of a moral political order. In a 1974 pamphlet entitled "The Ideology of Pakistan," fairly typical of the genre, Sharif al-Mujahid, a professor of journalism at the University of Karachi, summarized the basic principles of "Islamic ideology" that the "Pakistani people" were seeking to establish as the foundation of the Pakistani state. His list included belief in God and his sovereignty, fundamental human rights and basic freedoms, human brotherhood, equality of status and opportunity, the inviolability of private property, equitable distribution of national wealth, Islamic laws of inheritance, the levying of zakāt (annual tax), and a ban on charging interest. (The last three principles, he explained, are intended to prevent the capitalist concentration of wealth in a few hands.) He also emphasized the values of righteousness, charity, tolerance, justice, and morality. He acknowledged the point that "most of these values . . . are also professed by other nations on earth," but he argued that to Pakistanis they are Islamic values "because they have been received through the agency of Islam" (Mujahid 1974:27): a difference without a difference. The idea of a distinctive "Pakistani Islam," the principle of difference that is the rationale for the founding of a nation-state separate from other nation-states, was inconsistent with the universality of Islam at the ideological level and with the reality of diversity amongst the practitioners of Islam who were to be subsumed under the signifier "Pakistani."

That the ideology of Pakistani identity was founded on a signifier whose specific content could not be agreed upon was difficult to hide, even for those deeply committed to the idea of Pakistan. The development of an ideological process, with the signifier "Islam" as an unspecified object of desire that mobilizes a population (Žižek 1989), can be seen in Mujahid's account of the beginnings of the movement for Pakistan: "Rising bewildered, and reclaimed from their psychological wilderness, they searched their inner social consciousness in an attempt to find coherent and meaningful articulation to their cherished but undefined yearnings" (Mujahid 1974:13). His account of the ideological process involves a remarkable but typical inversion of cause and effect, as if the essence of a common Muslim identity had finally given rise to the signifiers that would express this identity. This inversion is characteristic of ideologies. Islam was unifying only as long as it remained an empty container. Specifying its contents inevitably created splits amongst the population that were to be encompassed under the umbrella of Islamic democracy in Pakistan.

The Sufi pīrs were drawn up into this ideological process, stripped of much of their specific content, their significance and legitimacy assessed in terms of the values of liberal democracy that had been subsumed under the signifier Islam.[3] The traditional-modern dichotomy was pervasive; the goal was to create a "modern" Pakistani citizen who would be energetic, autonomous, and free, a direct participant in the political process. The citizen would have a direct relationship to the political center, "Pakistan," unmediated by "traditional" relationships and identities. In the eleventh to fourteenth centuries, the institutionalized relationship between the Sufi pīr and his followers had been an important component of an administrative system that rested on considerable local autonomy (see Hodgson 1974). The colonial administration was viewed as having reinforced this traditional political, economic, and religious structure, which fixed landed pīrs and other landholders in positions as mediators between the government and local populations. Having persisted over the centuries, this "traditional" institutional structure was seen as an impediment to the creation of a "modern" economic and political structure resting on the principle of the nation-state.

In attempting to resist and transform the colonial administrative structures of the British, Pakistan's leaders retained other aspects of British discourse, with its blend of capitalism and Orientalism. The British had worked with the idea that "middle-class values" would gradually penetrate the Indian population, thereby causing the ultimate elimination of the wandering faqīr and even the pīr who lives off donations at an established shrine. In the meantime, by implication, the masses were shrouded in superstition and ignorance. This sentiment was echoed by Mohammed Ali Jinnah, recognized as the founder of Pakistan: "Jinnah knew that the Muslim masses were too ignorant to be fully aware of their interests and too content to follow their pirs and landlords" (Sayeed 1968:209, 210).

The ideological dichotomy of modernity and tradition that the British impressed upon South Asia was not particularly consistent or plausible when it came to religion,[4] but it did provide a moral justification for denigrating the pīrs and the practices associated with them. This justification was reinforced by the argument that "worshiping" pīrs was against Islam, stimulating an antipīr sentiment among Islamic reformists, as well as among those whose central preoccupation was modernizing Pakistan.

The linkage of pīrs with the "tradition" pole of the tradition-modernity axis — with its associated labels of ignorance, superstition, weakness, and gullibility — has persisted in contemporary Pakistani discourse. But not all of Sufism succumbed to this designation. As I suggested at the end of the last chapter, certain practices and Sufis escaped into (and were transformed by) a positive Orientalism — the discursive space that opened up when Western Romanticism became linked to Eastern spirituality. And, as I will argue in subsequent chapters, there was much of Sufi practice that simply continued to develop on its own path, as much shaping as shaped by its historical context, constituting the subjectivity of its practitioners in ways probably unimagined by the British carriers of modernity.

But one of the consequences of labeling pīrs antithetical to the project of modernity was a bifurcation of Sufism itself, so that for many Pakistanis today, the practices associated with pīrs are seen as something that has no relationship to Sufism.

Iqbal's Modernism

One of the most influential articulations of the "problem" of pīrs and of the sharp differentiation of *pīri-murīdi* (the institution of pīrs and their followers) from Sufism as a positive, modern force was the poet Muhammad Iqbal. He was also a source of inspiration for how to deal with this "problem" of pīrs and shrines.[5] Iqbal, who inspired much of the ideology for Pakistan, criticized the spiritual role of the pīr in the lives of Indian Muslims, calling the doctrines that generated the institution of pīri-murīdi "Persian mysticism." At the root of this Persian mysticism, Iqbal saw the distinction between esoteric and exoteric knowledge: "Thus Muslim democracy," he wrote, "was gradually displaced and enslaved by a sort of Spiritual Aristocracy pretending to claim knowledge and power not open to the average Muslim" (Iqbal 1964a:81). In his opinion, this claim of limited access to secret doctrine was the source of both the status of the pīr and the thralldom of the people (Iqbal 1964a:82).

But Iqbal did not associate this brand of mysticism with all forms of Sufism. On the contrary, his own poetry was inspired by Sufi literature, particularly the writings of Jalāl ud-Dīn Rūmī. He felt, for instance, that the philosophical stance expressed in his major poem, *Asrar-I-Khudi* (*Secrets of the Self* [1940]), had developed directly from the experience and speculation of earlier Muslim Sufis and thinkers (Iqbal 1964c:101). The doctrine Iqbal presented in *Asrar-I-Khudi* connects his interpretation of Sufism with the political action necessary to create a new Muslim community. The orientation he advocated was influential in the emergence of a movement for Pakistan. It also created an opening for a new relationship between Sufism and modernity, one that would be developed particularly by a postcolonial elite.[6]

After the death of Iqbal in 1938 and the creation of Pakistan in 1947, his son Javid tried to translate his father's ideas about pīrs and shrines into concrete policy measures. In his book *Ideology of Pakistan*, originally published in 1959, Javid Iqbal offered his advice with regard to the creation of a ministry of *auqāf* (religious endowments). He suggested that this ministry would take possession of and administer all religious endowments in Pakistan (Iqbal 1959:57). He quoted his father's negative views on the mysticism that "enervated the people and kept them steeped in all kinds of superstition" and concluded: "The establishment of such a ministry on the lines suggested above is the only remedy for the paralyzing influence of the Mullah and the Pir over the rural and urban masses of Islam. Unless and until the Mullah and the Pir are excluded from our religious life, there is no likelihood of the successful dissemination of enlightenment, liberalism and a meaningful and vital Faith among the people of Pakistan" (Iqbal 1959:58).

Javid Iqbal's book was enthusiastically received by Ayub Khan, then president of Pakistan, who declared that he had begun thinking along the same lines after reading the book with great interest (in a letter from Ayub Khan to J. Iqbal, July 11, 1959, shortly after the publication of his book [letter published in Iqbal 1971]).

With respect to pīrs, Ayub Khan initiated a new administrative policy in 1959, a policy that was continued and extended by Zulfikar Ali Bhutto. The West Pakistan Waqf Properties Ordinance of 1959 (*All Pakistan Legal Decisions* 1959) gave the government the power to take direct control over and to manage shrines, mosques, and other properties dedicated to religious purposes. The act was superseded by the West Pakistan Waqf Properties Ordinance of 1961 (Government of West Pakistan 1961–62) and, under Bhutto's regime, by the Auqāf (Federal Control) Act of 1976 (*All Pakistan Legal Decisions* 1976), each of which further extended the authority of the Auqāf Department. The 1959 ordinance was promulgated less than one year after Ayub's coup d'état, while he was intent on reforming what was considered to be a corrupt administration. The auqāf acts were intended to undercut the political power of both the hereditary pīr families (the sajjāda nishīns) and the 'ulamā (scholars of Islamic law). Using the state to shape the relationship between pīr families and their followers was reminiscent of British policy, though in most cases the British had worked to consolidate the power of selected families as local intermediaries.

The Ayub Khan administration thus adopted Javid Iqbal's suggestion. In addition to taking over the administration of the shrines, it worked to develop a new ideology with respect to saints and shrines. On the one hand, the Auqāf Department sought to undercut the economic relationship between the pīrs and their followers. But this strategy alone was not adequate, because to most people the sajjāda nishīns (literally, "keeper of the prayer rug") are not mere caretakers of the shrines. They are seen to possess blessing in their own right and thus to wield spiritual power over their followers directly. From the perspective of the follower, failure to follow the wishes of the sajjāda nishīn in any sphere of activity was thought to have serious consequences. The government therefore had to demonstrate simultaneously that the sajjāda nishīn was superfluous in both his religious and his caretaking functions.

As part of the direct assault on what was labeled the "traditional" meaning of the pīr, which gave him spiritual power that was branded superstitious, the Auqāf Department stressed the aspect of Sufism that Iqbal had drawn on and himself embodied: the original Sufi as poet and social reformer. The government published pamphlets describing several of the major Sufi poets of Pakistan (e.g., Khalid 1967, 1971; Sind Directorate of Public Relations 1971; Sind Information Department n.d.). These pamphlets were published on the occasion of the annual 'urs celebrations (celebrations marking the anniversary of the death of a saint) at the major shrines. They describe in detail the historical circumstances in which each saint lived, his individuality in appearance, and his social and political activities. In sharp contrast to most hagiographies, they do not give accounts of the miracles performed by the saint. Rather, they stress the saint's pious actions, actions that are within the capacity of the ordinary man, actions that do not violate a modern, scientific worldview.

The contrast that the government made between the original saint and the sajjāda nishīn is explicit in the following passage taken from a pamphlet about the shrine of Sachal Sarmast:

> The region of Sind has been under the influence of Syeds and Pirs due to the hold of mysticism over the simple and straightforward masses of the area. Sachal Sarmast, like his elderly contemporary Shah Abdul Latif of Bhit, also belonged to one of the most influential and dominant Pir families, and the shape of things in Sind would have been different had both these saintly poets indulged in the type of life which the people of their class usually lead.
>
> The personal life and character of Sachal was exemplary for he had not only studied various voluminous books on religion and philosophy but his mind was so open because of his spiritual experience in the pursuit of Truth, that he gave up all legacies, and stood for a very noble cause to foster unity among human beings without any consideration of caste, creed, and geographical factors. (Khalid 1971:14)

In addition to mentioning the corruption of the traditional pīr families, this passage stresses that Sachal Sarmast was a pīr, and yet he was not a pīr in the traditional, degenerate sense. The universalist message is presented. The mention of "caste, creed, and geographical factors" is particularly important, because it is precisely on these factors that the authority of the traditional pīr usually rested. And it was precisely these factors that the state saw as obstacles to the goal of consolidating state authority — particularly in Sind, where regional loyalties competed with central authority, which was associated with Punjab. Many castes or tribes were associated with specific shrines (see Eaton 1978). The local influence of each shrine was clearly defined by the sajjāda nishīn and other descendants, who would make regular circuits of their territories in order to collect contributions from followers.

The governments of Ayub Khan and Zulfikar Bhutto drew parallels between the social goals and reformist activities of the saints and those of the government. They identified "caste, creed, and geographical factors" as major sources of disruption in the effort to build Pakistan as a nation. By attributing such concerns to the founders of Islam in Pakistan, the modern universalist and nationalist orientation acquired a historical depth. This striving for historical continuity by constructing a long-term "memory" of the essential unities of Pakistan is particularly evident in the following passage from a *Pakistan Times* article, which commemorates the saint Data Ganj Bakhsh. The article associates "Islamic socialism," a key slogan that Bhutto used to represent his general policy, with one of the oldest and most popular saints in Pakistan: "He [Data Ganj Bakhsh] preached egalitarianism and visualized a classless society based on the concept of *Musawat-i-Muhammadi* which Allama Iqbal and Qaid-i-Azam later termed as 'Islamic Socialism'" (Shibli 1974). Bhutto's policy merely made manifest the "essence" of Pakistan, which had been embodied in its earliest Sufis.

In outlining the philosophical orientation of the Sufi saints, the government pamphlets emphasized that the saints described adhered to the philosophical doctrine of *wahdat al-wujūd* (unity of being), which was first expounded by Ibn 'Arabī (1165–1240 CE) and was vehemently denounced by some Muslim thinkers. Though later philosophers have accommodated to the doctrine and made it less controversial by carefully distinguishing it from pantheism, these pamphlets did not hesitate to label it pantheistic, apparently without deprecatory intent. Such a doctrine is congruent with the cosmological system that the government was trying to project. If these saints were pantheists, believing that God is immanent in all things, then there was no need, according to their own doctrine, for any mediator between God and man. The role and responsibility of the individual in such a system is analogous to the role he is expected to play in a Muslim democracy as an informed, voting citizen participating directly in the government: the government is "immanent" in its citizens.

The pamphlets also discussed conversion, but its significance was shifted away from emphasis on the conversion of certain tribes by a particular saint toward the idea of the saints as a collective body who worked together to convert Pakistan as a nation to Islam. In the story of Four Friends, for example, four important early Sufis were supposed to have worked together: "Under these conditions these Four Companions traveled thousands of miles to preach and propagate the message of Islam and to exemplify the godly way. They radiated their message to the lands and peoples of the Punjab, Sind, and Baluchistan" (Sind Information Department n.d.:17).[7]

In keeping with this change in emphasis was an effort to make certain shrines and 'urs celebrations national rather than regional affairs. For example, in 1974 the head of the Ministry for Information and Broadcasting, Auqaf and Haj inaugurated the 'urs of Madho Lal Hussain in Lahore. In his speech he said that this 'urs was the second largest in the country after the 'urs of Hazrat Data Ganj Bakhsh and that in years to come it would not only remain a *mēla* (fair) of the Punjab but would also become a mēla on the all-Pakistan level (*Pakistan Times* 1974b). In 1959 the 'urs of Shāh 'Abdu'l-Latīf of Bhit in Sind received extensive newspaper coverage in the Punjab (*Pakistan Times* 1959b). President Ayub Khan, a national figure, inaugurated the cultural festivities associated with the 'urs. An academic conference attended by poets and writers from various parts of the country was also held (*Pakistan Times* 1959a).

In addition to pamphlets, books, and newspaper articles presenting the perspective on the saints that the government wished to popularize, the Auqāf Department used other strategies that were more immediately visible to the common man. Under Ayub Khan, the department concentrated on shifting the focus of activities at the shrines away from those that directly involved the sajjāda nishīn. The goal was to make the shrines centers of more general social welfare by building at the shrines hospitals, schools, and other facilities for poor and rural people. The hospitals are, in a sense, in direct competition with the sajjāda nishīns, who claim as one of their spiritual powers the ability to cure their followers by writing a *ta'wīz* (amulet) for them. Though many saw the two approaches as complementary, access to a hospital provided a hitherto unavailable alternative to many rural people. Activities such as agricultural and industrial exhibitions and horse and cattle shows were scheduled at 'urs celebrations (see, e.g., Sind Directorate of

Public Relations 1971:24). An emphasis on these scientific and technological activities was consistent with Ayub Khan's overall approach to religious ideology, as revealed in his speeches:

> I humbly request that whenever in any public or private functions and ceremonies any passages from the Holy Quran are recited, they should invariably be translated into the language of the audience, followed by a clear and lucid interpretation of the mode and application to the life and conditions of today. Representative institutions like the various tiers of the basic democracies, corporations, municiple committees, etc. can play a valuable part in this mission. (Message to the nation on the occasion of Eid-us-Zuha, May 26, 1961, reproduced in Jafri 1966:85)

> I feel that during the early period of Islam the rationalists and the religious divines were not so wide apart as they are today.
> Science has made tremendous progress. . . . [O]n the other hand, religious thought has lost its original dynamism and is bogged down in a quagmire of stagnation. Actually there is no conflict between science and religion. (Speech delivered on the occasion of the founding-stone-laying ceremony of the Jamia Taleemaat-i-Islamia, Karachi, September 3, 1962, reproduced in Jafri 1966:129)

To encourage a scholarly rather than a magical approach to the shrines and Sufism, research centers and libraries were set up at or planned for several major shrines, including those of Khwāja Ghulām Farīd (*Pakistan Times* 1969), Shāh 'Abdu'l-Latīf, Bullhē Shāh in Kasur, and Lāl Shahbāz Qalandar in Sind.

In addition to developing the shrine areas as centers of social welfare, the government also made improvements on the shrines themselves, thus demonstrating that the government can satisfactorily fulfill the caretaking functions of the sajjāda nishīns. The policy of the Auqāf Department under both Ayub Khan and Zulfikar Ali Bhutto was to concentrate its attention and resources on a limited number of shrines with a large following and to let the rest gradually diminish in importance. At several of these important shrines the government made major, highly visible repairs and improvements, greater than those that the hereditary pīr families would have been willing to undertake. The government took care to stress that, in supporting and maintaining the shrines, it was also following the tradition of other Muslim rulers.

In an Auqāf Department pamphlet written in the Ayub Khan era, the author summarized the history of the construction and development of the shrine of Lāl Shahbāz Qalandar. In this summary the Auqāf Department is the last of a series of Muslim rulers who have made major repairs and additions to the shrine: "It would be difficult to say who built his tomb, for almost every pious ruler of Sind or Sehwan has contributed something to it" (Sind Information Department n.d.:22). There follows a detailed account of improvements and expenditures made by the Auqāf Department on the shrine. Guest houses and other facilities for the comfort of pilgrims were an important part of the development plans for this and other shrines. Such improvements are immediately visible to the large number of people who visit the shrines and thus, hopefully, would dispose them favorably toward the government control of the shrines. This would also serve as concrete evidence that the government, in displacing the sajjāda nishīns, was not out to destroy the shrines themselves.

The replacement of the sajjāda nishīns by the government was also symbolized ritually. Especially in Bhutto's time, the government played an active role in ritual proceedings at the shrines. Under Ayub Khan, participation in the ʿurs by government officials was generally limited to the literary and social welfare activities scheduled to occur in conjunction with the ʿurs. When, for example, Ayub Khan attended the ʿurs of Shāh ʿAbdu'l-Latīf in 1959, he did not perform the *chādar*-laying ceremony himself (*Pakistan Times* 1959a) (the chādar is a sheet that covers the saint's grave). But the policy of Bhutto was to promote direct participation in the ʿurs by government officials: in his religious ideology Bhutto placed less emphasis than Ayub Khan did on the rationalization of Islam. Bhutto also wished to project an image of himself as personally involved in the activities of the common man, including shrine activities. In 1972 the Sind Department of Public Relations published a book entitled *The Poet of the People: A Miscellany of Articles to Commemorate the 220th Anniversary of Shah Abdul Latif of Bhit* (Khalid 1972). It includes a speech given by Bhutto ten years earlier when he personally performed a ceremony at the shrine. The title of the book is reminiscent of Bhutto's self-designation as "leader of the people" and suggests that he wished to be seen in a position analogous to that of the saints, who were in touch with the common man.

During the Bhutto era, the central ceremonies of the ʿurs were performed by high government officials, and their activities were publicized in the newspapers and often filmed on television. At most shrines, the 'urs includes a washing of the grave and the laying of a new chādar, which will cover the grave for the following year. Traditionally the central ceremonies of the 'urs are performed by the sajjāda nishīn; when an 'urs at a small shrine is announced in the newspaper, for example, it is usually mentioned that the chādar-laying ceremony will be performed by the sajjāda nishīn. Under Bhutto, however, a government official performed the ceremony at most of the major shrines, and this ceremony was the main part of the 'urs to be publicized. The following account from the *Pakistan Times* is typical: "The 932nd annual urs of Data Ganj Bakhsh Hazrat Ali Hujweri is commencing in Lahore on Monday. Chief Minister Sadiq Hussain Qureshi will inaugurate the three-day celebrations by laying a 'chadar' at 9 PM. The Auqaf Department has made special arrangements to celebrate the urs in a befitting manner" (*Pakistan Times* 1977).

The announcement for the 1974 'urs of Data Ganj Bakhsh laid particular stress on the participation of government officials. Ten sessions of speeches on the life and works of the saint were conducted, various sessions being presided over by the chief justice of Pakistan, chief justice of the Lahore High Court, and three other High Court justices (*Pakistan Times* 1974a).

During General Zia ul-Haq's administration, which sought legitimacy through the active promotion of Islamization, there was considerably less overt promotion of the 'urs celebrations and activities at the shrines than there had been in Bhutto's time. Clearly, the government did not need to demonstrate its ties to Islam through its support of shrine activities, since it pushed so heavily a program of Islamization. Furthermore, establishing an ideological policy concerning shrines was at that point a tricky matter, since many of the Islamicists who supported Zia, particularly the Jama'at-i Islami, were themselves hostile to Sufism, pīrs, and shrines. The *Pakistan Times,* which in the Bhutto era included articles announcing and describing the 'urs celebrations of many saints, such as Shāh 'Abdu'l-Latīf and Mēla Chirāghān, gave them no mention at all in the Zia era.

Nevertheless, there was not a disavowal of the saints and shrines, as might have been expected from an administration so overtly concerned with reinstating the "original" Islamic social order that prevailed at the time of the Prophet Muhammad. Emphasis was instead placed on the saints as models of the pious Muslim, as devout men who observed all the laws of Islam. Because of their piety, they impressed the population and spread Islam throughout South Asia. This was clearly a continuation of the efforts at redefinition that occurred under Ayub and Bhutto. The policy of turning the shrines into multifunctional religious and social welfare centers under the control of the state, administered by the Auqāf Department, which began under Ayub Khan, continued under Zia ul-Haq. Shortly before the 'urs of Data Ganj Bakhsh in January 1980, for instance, the provincial minister of auqāf announced that the hospital associated with the shrine was to be expanded. He also announced plans to begin construction of a new mosque at the shrine, which was to be the second largest in the city (*Pakistan Times* 1980a).

The policy concerning the definition of the proper role of the saints and shrines was explicitly stated by Miyan Hayat Bakhsh, the Punjab provincial adviser for auqāf. In 1980 he conducted a seminar in conjunction with the 'urs of Data Ganj Bakhsh, the one Lahore shrine that continued to receive extensive publicity. According to him, the 'urs was meant to invite devotees to make self-appraisals and to determine whether their actions were in accordance with the teachings of Islam and the Islamic mystics. The "seats of the saints" were training centers where people were "transformed into noble human beings" (*Pakistan Times* 1980b).

Though continuing most of the auqāf policies of previous administrations, the government of Zia ul-Haq created a subtle shift of emphasis in defining the meaning of the saints. Articles describing the lives of the saints regularly listed key writings and sayings of the saint, which the ordinary person could take to heart and try to follow. The sole *Pakistan Times* article announcing the 1979 'urs of Bābā Farīd (who had previously received much more extensive coverage in the newspapers) included a list of fourteen of his sayings, which emphasized piety and obedience and made no reference to esoteric practices or understanding (Amin 1979:4). Associated with this emphasis on the writings and sayings of the saints was a stress on the fact that the saints were educated scholars, that is, 'ulamā. In a 1980 article, "Ulema and Saints of Sialkot," for instance, the two saints focused on were also 'ulamā (Sabri 1980). A 1980 article about the mission of the saint Data Ganj Bakhsh highlighted the attributes of the old saints in a modern, reformist vocabulary:

> Missionaries of today have much to learn from the old pioneers, particularly in the acquisition of proper, methodical education. Those pioneers were not miracle mongers but educated luminaries

well versed in the physical sciences and the dialects of the people
they worked amongst. Today no missionary who does not have a
perfect command over their languages can hope to succeed. . . . He
will also have to be proficient in some of the sciences or a recognized scholar on some such subject as philosophy or history or the
indispensable economics. Character and devotion to prayers are of
prime importance but the mundane arts and sciences must keep
pace with the pursuits of the spirit. Above all, the masses must not
be neglected. Mission work should be done intensively among
them, for it is the common man that controls the destiny of nations. (*Pakistan Times* 1980c)

This emphasis on the education of missionaries suggested that the
early Sufi saints were equated with those who were being trained to
serve as *imāms* in local villages, in Auqāf-controlled *madrasas* (schools
for the study of the Quran and associated subjects). The emphasis was
on minimizing the distinction between the saints and the 'ulamā, Sufism
and sharī'at.

Benazir Bhutto, daughter of Zulfikar Ali Bhutto, eventually succeeded Zia as prime minister. Her approach to the shrines followed a
reaction against the heavy-handed Islamization of the Zia years and
returned to public devotionalism in a manner similar to her father's.
Benazir Bhutto's first political move after returning from exile in 1986
was to pay her respects to several shrines in both the Punjab and Sind
(Malik 1996:78 n. 39).

Auqāf Policies and the Shrines

THE SHRINE OF SHĀH DAULA SHĀH

The government through the Auqāf Department has over the years
gradually taken over the control and administration of most income-
producing shrines in the country. One consequence of this change is
that *pīrzāda* (descended from a pīr) families scramble around, striving
to capture the donations of pilgrims and visitors before they reach the
little green collection box that the Auqāf Department has put out,
adding to the stress and discord in those extended families where there
are several descendants who must compete for the diminished income.
Many pīrzāda sons have had little interest in following in their fathers'
footsteps as the caretaker of a shrine, choosing instead to go into what
they consider "modern" professions such as engineering or business.

A microcephalic beggar associated
with the shrine of Shāh Daula Shāh
of Gujrat

The declining economic power of families who were dependent on
shrine income can be seen in the case of the shrine of Shāh Daula Shāh,
a major shrine in the city of Gujrat, approximately seventy miles northwest of Lahore. The shrine of Shāh Daula Shāh was originally built in
the latter part of the seventeenth century and rebuilt in 1867, so that
today it is a large and impressive shrine. Homes of Shāh Daula Shāh's
descendants surround the shrine. The shrine had no lands attached to
it, so that the saint's descendants were dependent on offerings and
donations for their livelihood. There were no regular rules of succession, and each member of the family had a share in it, though one was
generally known as the sajjāda nishīn. At that time, Shāh Daula's faqīrs
would visit each devotee annually soliciting offerings, conducting a
circuit of the territory under the influence of the shrine.

Though the shrine of Shāh Daula Shāh had been taken over by the
Auqāf Department a few years before my visit there in 1976,[8] faqīrs
associated with the shrine continued to travel through the Punjab. One
of the peculiarities of this particular shrine is a band of what are known
as *chūhā* (literally, "mouse," a label used for people afflicted with microcephaly). Microcephalic children were traditionally left at the shrine
and raised by caretakers associated with the shrine. Shāh Daula Shāh's
chūhās are often seen in Lahore begging from house to house, guided
by an "owner" dressed in the clothing of a wandering faqīr. On two

occasions, I talked with these faqīrs and learned that each faqīr was from a village several miles from the town of Gujrat, where the shrine is located, and had hired the chūhā from the Auqāf Department for an annual fee. The faqīrs who currently rent out these microcephalic men were not descendants of Shāh Daula Shāh. It is difficult to know what to make of the perpetuation and bureaucratization of a practice seemingly antithetical to the goals of the Auqāf Department — except to suggest that we have here the forces of free enterprise and bureaucracy at work.

The saint's descendants were very bitter about the Auqāf takeover of the shrine. I spoke with the widow of a sajjāda nishīn who had died twenty-five years earlier and with some of her younger relatives. This is a case in which the descendants of the saint fought the takeover and were completely shut out of the administration of the shrine. According to her, they went to court, and the Lahore Sessions judge ruled that the family may accept donations only when people give them to the family directly.

She explained that before the government takeover, the descendants were divided into three groups. These groups rotated responsibility for the shrine, and selected a day on which each family would get the contributions for that day. The women showed me a *shajra* (genealogical chart) on which this system was recorded. At many shrines, the history of the family has been characterized by discord over who is entitled to the revenues from the shrine. One common arrangement for ensuring a fair distribution of the proceeds is a rotation system, according to which the several lines of descendants receive the donations for specified fractions of the year, month, or week. At the shrine of Nizām ud-Dīn Auliyā near Delhi, for instance, the descendants have worked out an arrangement whereby several male descendants take turns acting as pīr and collecting donations, each being responsible for certain days of the week (see Jeffery 1979:44–50).

This woman complained that the Auqāf-appointed manager of the shrine at that time was very strict and didn't allow them to receive anything: "The beggars who sit outside get the things that people give — money, milk, but we are strictly stopped by the government from taking things." She explained that parents continue to bring the chūhās to the shrine and offer their greetings, but that the Auqāf Department doesn't allow them to stay here. "They say 'take them back home.' In our times, the rooms where the manager now sits were built for chūhās.

Food was given to them, some by us, some by visitors." She complained that there are many widows and orphans who come to the shrine for help, but now that the shrine is the government's responsibility, it doesn't help them. There have traditionally been three ʿurses held at the shrine each year. The government continues to celebrate the ʿurs, but does only the bare minimum. "They just put on the chādar; the officials come." In the past there used to be *qawwālī* (devotional singing) and speeches.

This family has been located within a particular state discourse — and dislocated economically. Though the practices of the visitors to the shrine have not dramatically changed, the state has inserted itself into the relationship between the dead saint and the devotee, attempting to cut out the sajjāda nishīn as middleman.

THE SHRINE OF MIĀN NĀSIR AHMED SUHRAWARDĪ

In other cases, the descendants of a saint whose shrine has been taken over by the Auqāf Department were not cut out completely from the administration of the shrine. The outcome typically depended on political alignments, with progovernment pīrs being allowed to retain control of their shrines. But even in these cases, members of the next generation have often been less interested in following in their fathers' footsteps, in what has become essentially a government job.

The shrine of Miān Nāsir Ahmed Suhrawardī (Miān Sahib) in Lahore has also been adversely affected by Auqāf Department takeover. The shrine was established centuries ago, and, though still the locus of considerable activity, it embodies in its architecture many of the changes that have occurred in Sufism over the past century and the tensions that are salient in belief and practice today. Beyond the shrine itself are a few rooms that are obviously used for daily activities. There are several structures in various states of decay, a phenomenon that can be attributed in part to the policies of the Auqāf Department, which took over the shrine in 1961. In 1976, fifteen years after the takeover, I talked with two men who were then in charge of the shrine, the sajjāda nishīn, a direct descendent of the founding saint, and his *khalīfa* (a term that in most Sufi circles means spiritual successor). In the opinion of the khalīfa, who is responsible for the daily maintenance of the shrine, the *mazār* (i.e., the shrine as a focus of devotion) was "ruined" after the government took it over, and now all that remains is a tomb like those of Mughal rulers, which are now maintained as tourist attractions. He lamented that there are no lamps burning in devotion around the grave of Miān Sahib. But at the time of my visit there was still considerable activity at the shrine. I noticed a Coke bottle full of water perched on the low wall that surrounded the simple graves. When I asked about it I was told that women frequently put water there after the khalīfa has read Quranic verses over it, in order to imbue it with the blessing of the saint before they use it in healing. Several of these women were sitting in a room waiting for the khalīfa as he showed me around the shrine.

Differences of opinion about the proper practice of Sufism and the honoring of saints had apparently pervaded the shrine for many years, if not throughout its history. Even the several graves at the shrine display a shift away from simplicity and asceticism to the architectural ornament that is typically associated with the honoring of a saint in this area. Beside the simple graves of the founding saint and his immediate successors are two graves covered with elaborate domes. According to the khalīfa, the saint had wanted his grave uncovered, as well as the graves of all of his successors. Some of his successors apparently did not follow the wishes of their pīr. One of the elaborate graves belongs to the great-grandfather of the present sajjāda nishīn. This man had had it built during his own lifetime, around the turn of the century.

Despite the takeover of the shrine by the Auqāf Department during the time of his father, the hereditary sajjāda nishīn was still in charge of the shrine. He explained how it happened: "For some time there was animosity among petty officials. My father dealt well with them, with what is now the Religious Purposes Committee. So he was made chairman for this shrine." He explained that there are few cases where the sajjāda nishīn has been made an employee of Auqāf. In Pakpattan at the shrine of Bābā Farīd Ganj-i Shakar, one of the major shrines of Pakistan today, the sajjāda nishīn is attached to Auqāf and retains a central role in the annual ʿurs celebration at the shrine, along with many government officials (see Gilmartin 1979). But at the shrine of Data Ganj Bakhsh, the largest shrine in Lahore, government officials run events at the shrine directly. As this sajjāda nishīn explained, in most places, the sajjāda nishīns were dependent on the income from the shrine, so they became bitter when the Auqāf Department took over, to the extent that in some cases, sajjāda nishīn families became involved in court cases against the department in the effort to fight takeover or to retain their income. But in the case of this shrine, the takeover did not cause financial hardship for the family, because their private business was kept separate from the income of the shrine.

Despite the continuity due to the retention of the sajjāda nishīn as administrator of this shrine, its takeover by the Auqāf Department was a real turning point for the shrine. This young man's father had been the sajjāda nishīn at the time. Until that point, there had been a school attached to the shrine, where about two hundred students from all over the Punjab received full religious training in the Quran and *Hadīth* (traditions describing the sayings and acts of the Prophet Muhammad). When the Auqāf Department took over, they closed the school and terminated the *langar* (a kind of soup kitchen, offering food to anyone in need). For two or three years, the school was completely shut down, but then his father argued to the Auqāf Department that the school had been in operation continuously for four hundred years and that the department should carry it on. He was successful to the extent that the school reopened with about thirty students, and the Auqāf Department provided scholarships. The Auqāf Department also supplies the school with its teachers, making it an institution directly controlled by the government. At the time of our meeting, there were only fifteen students actually living at the school, and it no longer had a full course of study. It was clearly not a vital institution.[9]

The sajjāda nishīn, though still somewhat involved in the affairs of the shrine, was less so than his father had been, at least at the time I met him. He had returned to Lahore from study in England only two years earlier, and he became the sajjāda nishīn a year later in a simple turban-tying ceremony when his father died. He admits that he himself has very little knowledge of Sufism, but mostly handles administrative matters concerning the shrine and school. He does not usually get involved in providing people with spiritual guidance, and he spends most of his days away from the shrine, involved instead in business and accounting.

But he does not feel that his activities mark a break with the past. He is not the first in his family to be involved in the management of business affairs apart from the shrine. Despite his Western education and his involvement in other enterprises, this sajjāda nishīn stressed a continuity between his life and the lives of his forefathers. He was admiring of his ancestors' foresight in providing for both the family and the shrine so that the disruption was minimal when the government stepped in. "From the beginning, our private family affairs were separate. My father's 'grandfathers' were four brothers. They created a trust for the shrine, not donated by outsiders, but by the family itself. It was created in 1896. Before that, the institution was supported by its own income. They created a trust from the property of one brother who died, Miān Muhammad Azim, in case the children would dissipate the money." He was obviously proud of his father and how he had been able to stand up to the Auqāf Department in working to retain control over the shrine and to reestablish the school. But he did not stress his father's qualities as a pīr. He was frank in admitting that there were no specialists in Sufism at the school, and said that his father had been involved in Sufism "to a certain extent," indicating by his tone of voice that neither he nor his father had been particularly concerned about Sufism. His father had been a man of means and some political influence, who sent his son off to England for an education and established him well in the world. This young man was comfortable following in his father's footsteps. The historical trajectory of this family is typical of those who were beneficiaries of the British colonial policy that cultivated hereditary pīr families as Punjab "chiefs" who were to be Westernized and left in place as landowning families.

The sajjāda nishīn also articulated a continuity that he experiences with the principles that his saintly ancestor had worked to establish: "Miān Sahib was Suhrawardī [the Sufi order]. He believed men should be as active in religious duties as in ordinary life. He did not believe in monks or an ascetic life. Students were supposed to live a normal life, even when the school was first founded. Even us administrators — we attend our lands." He maintains a reformist orientation toward Islam, which he argued was advocated by his ancestor, the founder of the school and the earliest saint buried at the shrine. He compared Suhrawardī thought to Calvinist thought, which he saw as getting back to basic religion by getting rid of extraneous practices. This attitude toward Sufism and Islam is perhaps one reason why his father was able to retain control of the shrine, for this sajjāda nishīn's orientation to his Sufi ancestor is consistent with government policies concerning the shrines (and explicitly echoes the Western Protestant view of religion that has been part of the organizing structure of Orientalist discourse), and an emphasis on the reformist or fundamentalist orientation of the early Sufis — though far from the beliefs and activities that have for centuries been associated with the shrines — has been an important agenda of the Auqāf Department.

Given this reformist orientation to Sufism, he is critical of the type of "traditional" activity that now goes on at the shrine, exemplified by the Coke bottle perched near the grave of his ancestor.[10] He felt that the beliefs of people that prompt them to come for this kind of spiritual intervention have probably crept into the system gradually over the past three hundred years and that "now the tree has died," meaning that Sufism is no longer what it once was, and that the spiritual lineage of his saintly ancestor is no longer successfully transmitting his message, a view that closely echoes Trimingham's views of Sufism. He said, "I try to dissuade from ta'wīz [amulets] — I write ta'wīz only if they really want it. But mostly I tell them to read certain verses of the Quran and follow the teachings of their religion. Ta'wīz is not a cure-all."

It was actually his khalīfa (spiritual successor) who handled the people, mostly women, that came to the shrine asking for ta'wīz and help with their daily problems. This khalīfa, who was in his early sixties when I met him, had been appointed by the present sajjāda nishīn's father long before the present sajjāda nishīn was born. The khalīfa's background was very different from that of the sajjāda nishīn. He had no blood relationship to the family of the saint, but his life was completely entwined with that of the shrine. His story of how he came to be in his present position clearly aligned him with the women who come to pray for a miracle from the saint, rather than with the ascetic Sufism of the Suhrawardī order that is espoused by the sajjāda nishīn: His mother had come to the shrine and prayed for a son. As part of her prayer, she promised to leave him at the shrine. When he was born, she left him to serve the sajjāda nishīn and the dead saint, and also to receive a religious education. He received all of his education in the school, and when he was twelve years old, he was given the *khilāfat* (the office of khalīfa). When I met him, he was handling all of what he called the "administrative" work, which included what struck me as the rather disparate tasks of writing amulets, dealing with students, and cleaning. He was very protective of his special seat (*gaddī*), which no one was allowed to sit on except the sajjāda nishīn and himself. He had been the khalīfa for fifty years and had never married.

Though he was called a khalīfa, he did not seem to be a spiritual successor in the way the term is most commonly used among Sufis, to mean someone who will eventually transmit his spiritual heritage and training to his own disciples, continuing a Sufi lineage. He did not accept disciples. At the shrine in the past, khalīfas were appointed in a manner more consistent with the Sufi model. According to the present

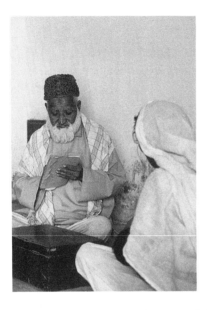

The *khalīfa* of Miān Nāsir Ahmed
Suhrawardī preparing an amulet

khalīfa, several went out to spread the teachings of Miān Sahib. He told
me that there was a book which included biographies of the khalīfas
who had gone to different areas, developed their own followings, and
appointed their own khalīfas.

Up to the time of the Auqāf takeover, four khalīfas remained at the
shrine and school to perform the duties he now performs by himself. Of
the four khalīfas who remained at the shrine, one sat on the gaddī and
wrote out taʿwīz for those who sought them, a second had the duty of
organizing the distribution of food at the langar, a third looked after
the maintenance of the shrine, and a fourth served as the imām for the
mosque attached to the shrine. The sajjāda nishīn assigned the duties.

Acutely aware of the changes instituted by the Auqāf Department,
the khalīfa did not know if there would be another khalīfa to follow
him when he dies. "It is the sajjāda nishīn's decision to make, and not
mine," he said. Though retaining the model of sajjāda nishīn and
khalīfa, these men were both salaried employees of the Auqāf Department, and the sajjāda nishīn, as chairman of the shrine, was his "boss"
in the bureaucratic hierarchy of government employees.

Like the sajjāda nishīn, the khalīfa felt a sense of decline, not only in
this particular shrine, but in Sufism more generally. But his perception
of the evidence for decline was very different from that of the sajjāda

nishīn. The sajjāda nishīn dismissed the very activities engaged in by the khalīfa, particularly the writing of amulets and the blessing of water to cure the sick, as evidence that the "tree has withered." The khalīfa was confident in his ability to help others in this manner but lamented the fact that the process of spiritual training necessary for performing these actions effectively had lost its rigor. On his tour of the shrine he showed me a cavelike underground room that had fallen to disuse, which he pointed to as an illustration of how Sufism is not as rigorous as it used to be. The room used to be used for *chillā* (a forty-day period of se- clusion for a mother and her newborn infant). The condition of this room has deteriorated because "these days people are afraid to go there. In the old days, *chillā* was stronger and more difficult. If a spir- itual guide asked a follower to do *chillā,* they could come out only twice a day for food, and they got very little food, but now there are no restrictions in *chillā.* Anyone can come and take instructions from his guide and do *chillā* by a mosque or in a graveyard."

When I saw it, this shrine retained a skeleton of its original institu- tions. Although there was a sajjāda nishīn who is a descendant from the founding saint and a pīr who continued to receive people seeking prayers and healing, the shrine's future was uncertain. There was no ongoing training in Sufi techniques, none of the master-disciple rela- tionships that form the heart of Sufi training. The sajjāda nishīn, him- self not trained as a Sufi, was not at all certain that his children will continue the tradition. When asked, he replied, "God knows. I can't predict about tomorrow. It was taken over during my lifetime. My children may feel no attachment. I hope it will be carried on." The sajjāda nishīn was nostalgic about the shrine and had managed to reconcile his own economic activities in a modern world with the be- liefs of his ancestors. He was one for whom Sufism did not present a strong personal, affective draw, at least not at this point in his life. He also had no economic incentive to establish or maintain a large follow- ing, since he had independent sources of wealth and income. If his children show no attachment to the shrine, management of the shrine will presumably pass to a government employee, whose primary con- cerns would be any income that the shrine might generate from its little green collection box, and whatever maintenance the Auqāf Depart- ment deems appropriate, which in such situations (i.e., relatively minor shrines) is typically not adequate for preventing deterioration of the shrine and its surrounding structures. With several larger and more impressive shrines nearby to draw tourists, it is unlikely that this shrine will find new life as a tourist attraction. Many shrines like it are quietly crumbling into oblivion.

DATA GANJ BAKHSH: A THRIVING SHRINE

Not all shrines are declining under the government control of the Auqāf Department. The shrine of Hazrat Data Ganj Bakhsh, (known in Sufi literature as Hujwīrī [d. ca. 1071 CE), is a centerpiece of Lahore.[11] "Data Sahib," as he is popularly known, is Lahore's most honored Sufi saint, and his shrine is a point of convergence for devotees of many backgrounds who otherwise have little in common. A large section of Lahore is transformed during his ʿurs. According to annual newspaper accounts, anywhere between 500,000 and 900,000 people attend the three-day celebration each year — "thousands of devotees from all parts of the country."

Despite the views of some, that people are gradually becoming less interested in pīrs and less involved in Sufism, the ʿurs of Data Sahib has thrived and grown. In 1968, the ʿurs was only a two-day affair, and a newspaper reporter observed that there were fewer people than in the past and that the festivities were not what they used to be. But in subsequent years, the ʿurs was extended to three days and the crowds grew, so that by 1974, larger crowds than ever were reported.

Most noticeable in newspaper accounts is the role of government officials in the ʿurs. In most years, the chādar-laying ceremony is performed by the Auqāf minister. The standard phrase that appears year after year in newspaper accounts is, "The Auqāf Department has made elaborate arrangements to celebrate the ʿurs in a befitting manner." Virtually everyone I met in Lahore visits the shrine. The shrine draws visitors from all over Pakistan. Even those who denounce the practice of visiting shrines and castigate all pīrs as frauds may find themselves drawn to Data Sahib at one time or another. His name will come up often in the chapters that follow.

Conclusion

The Sufi ideology that was formulated by the governments of Ayub Khan and Zufilkar Ali Bhutto during the course of their establishment of the Auqāf Department represented a new, relatively coherent cosmology based on the dichotomy of tradition and modernity. It was intended to replace what had been labeled the "traditional" cosmology, which prevailed among much of the population. Traditional cosmology was viewed as constituting a static, traditional subject who had no place in a modern world. And its ritual practice, which placed the common man in a position where God was inaccessible except through spiritual mediators, was congruent with the "traditional" social, political, and economic structure. The new cosmology, by contrast, was intended to give a universally acceptable content to the Islam that was the founding signifier of Pakistani nationalism. One version of this cosmology, particularly that propagated during Bhutto's administration, is grounded in certain aspects of Sufi doctrine. In this model God is not absolutely transcendent. On the contrary, he is immanent in all of his creation. Any man, if he is pious and receives the proper training, can achieve the goal of the Sufi, union with God. The Sufi poets whose shrines are venerated were pious, educated men who achieved this goal and now serve as a dynamic example for others to follow.

Political ideologies resting on the principles of democracy or socialism require for their successful implementation an educated, voting population. The relationship between the government and the people is, ideally, interactive. The Sufi model of the relationship between God and man is also interactive: the religious experience of God is open to anyone. Perhaps it is because of this congruence with the modern Western-influenced goals of a secular government, which stresses the autonomy of the individual, that Sufism, which posits a unique course of spiritual development for each individual, has become so popular among the educated elite of Pakistan.

This effort to redefine the Sufi saints and shrines — by weeding out what was regarded as "traditional" and corrupt and by locating the values of modernity and liberal democracy in the Sufis of a distant past — was one strategy for attempting to put some positive content into the empty vessel that was "Islam" as it had been articulated by a largely secular, postcolonial Western-educated political elite. Other leaders with other agendas vigorously contested the efforts of this political elite to maintain legitimacy by linking their agendas to Islam. Other versions of Islam, some of them more overtly resistant to "modernity," have been propagated in the political arena and in other channels of public discourse, institutionalized through law and the system of sharīʿat courts. Many of these other articulations of Islam reject

Sufism in any form. As a result, Sufism has become a nexus of competing ideologies and the basis for individuals and groups to articulate identities in opposition to others.

In these first chapters I have laid out the ideological formations that were shaped by the currents of colonial administrative policy, Orientalist categories, Western political values and the idea of the nation-state, and by the dichotomy "tradition-modernity" that underlies them all. The question that guides my inquiry in subsequent chapters is the extent to which these currents of public discourse have actually penetrated and constituted the postcolonial subject. Can we see the refractions that the image of the Sufi has undergone through the colonial period and the creation of the nation in the conversations and practices of the Pakistani citizen?

The Modern Subject and Conflicting Ideologies

4

Everyday Arguments

When talking with people in the neighborhood where I lived in Lahore, I needed only to turn the conversation to the subject of pīrs to see ideology in action. Even among neighbors whose relationships are close and complex and whose goals in interaction are usually quite removed from and more diverse than contests for political dominance, the pīr as a topic of conversation readily generates ideological discourse. When the topic is pīrs and shrines, the debates of policymakers and sectarian points of contention are often manifested in ordinary conversation.

Urban Pakistanis have been a target of various ideological formulations associated with colonialism, economic modernization, scientific secularism, anti-Hindu communalism, and a range of Islamisms, to name some of the most salient. Individuals' positionings vis-à-vis these ideologies locate them within the broader discourses of modernity and Islam, constitute them as subjects within a contested discursive field, and give them specific, labeled identities such as "uneducated and traditional," "Wahhabi," "modern." Many are in occupations such as government service that were directly shaped by the colonial bureaucracy and its successors. In such settings, and from other sources such as television and newspapers, the individual is exposed to competing ideologies that differ in their authority, authoritativeness, and power to convince.

Despite the recent convergence of theories emerging out of textually inspired cultural studies and those developed by anthropologists, who on occasion have also confused culture, practice, and text, there is something fundamentally different about the appearance of ideology in a self-consciously produced text such as a political tract, a pamphlet distributed at a shrine, or even a novel, and the spontaneous use of ideology in complex social situations. Furthermore, any formulation of a concept of identity, the subject, or of consciousness that rests on collectively articulated signs as they are systematized in an ideology will look very different from such a concept when it is grounded in the observation of specific practice. A shift of focus from the level of discourse, subject positions, and ideologies to the organization of the experiences of the individual prompts the question: How do competing ideologies play themselves out at the level of the individual negotiation of identity? It is obvious that individuals move among discursively constituted subject positions; but can we capture and elucidate the moments and processes of transition? Can we glimpse the maneuvers of the speaking subject?

The individual's speech is polyvocal. Despite participation in explicit, ideological debates that objectify and evaluate everyday practices, generating a self-conscious perspective, many of an individual's practices remain unobjectified, the reenactment not only of habitual activities but also of activities organized in terms of different principles, oriented toward different goals. The task before us, then, is to specify how individuals are transected by various ideological positionings and resistances, while also maintaining concerns that are orthogonal to such ideologies. Can we trace the vicissitudes of the desiring, speaking subject through this array of realities?

Today in Pakistan, after many years of reformist activity, there is a wide range of opinions about which activities fall within the boundaries of proper Islam and which fall outside, despite many efforts to articulate an Islam that would draw all Pakistanis together as a nation. A number of reform movements of various orientations had a major impact across the subcontinent during the nineteenth and twentieth centuries and continue to form a basis for individual identity. Some reformist leaders in Pakistan have taken an extreme position and attempted to weed out nearly all of what they perceive as local practices, leaving a rather austere form of Islam. Certain movements, including the Ahl-i Hadīth (also known popularly as Wahhabi, though it had no direct connections with the Middle Eastern movement of the same name),[1] the

Ahmadiyya,[2] and the political party Jamaʿat-i Islami, founded by the Islamist Maulana Maudoodi,[3] while very different in important respects, have attempted to eliminate all practices associated with Sufi pīrs and shrines, disrupting the hierarchical, mediatory relationship between the pīr and his followers that had echoed and supported the hierarchical administrative structure maintained by the British during the colonial era.

But others, such as the influential *madrasa* at Deoband in India (see Metcalf 1982), which trained many of the ʿulamā who then became influential in Pakistan, focused on carefully delimiting the relationship between pīr and disciple and eliminating certain mediatory activities at shrines while retaining basic practices associated with the transmission of Sufism within the pīr-disciple relationship. Still others, including the Barelvis (named after Maulana Ahmad Riza Khan of Bareilly [1855–1921]) and the Lahore-based Ahl-i Sunnat ul-Jamaʿat (literally, the Society of People who Follow the Traditions of Muhammad), resisted certain types of reform altogether, seeking especially to preserve the mediatory relationship between the pīr and disciples (Metcalf 1982: 296–314; Gilmartin 1988:60; Sanyal 1996). Their very labels, "Barelvi" and "Ahl-i Sunnat ul-Jamaʿat," however, indicate a systematization and objectification of practices that occurred during the late nineteenth and early twentieth centuries in reaction to the competitive pressure of the various Islamic reform movements.

Today in Lahore, "Ahl-i Sunnat ul-Jamaʿat" is the label most people will give themselves when asked to articulate a sectarian identity. The name was originally adopted by a late-nineteenth-century group of ʿulamā who established a network of schools in the Punjab that stressed the legitimacy of pīrs as mediators between the ordinary follower and God (and, especially in rural areas, often between the follower and the state). These schools, to which a number of Punjabi pīrs made generous financial donations, provided doctrinal support for a growing revival of Sufi practice in the Punjab. Though supporting what was regarded as traditional practice, the Ahl-i Sunnat ul-Jamaʿat was also affected by reformist concerns.[4] The organization of their schools, for instance, was modeled after the organization of the Deobandi schools. They also developed an ideological emphasis on sharīʿat — scripturally based Islamic norms for the conduct of everyday life — in a political climate in which the personal practice of Islam was increasingly important as an ideological basis for establishing a Muslim community within the context of colonial domination (Freitag 1988; Ewing 1988; Gilmartin 1988:61). Most pīrs in Lahore today show the effects of the Ahl-i Sunnat ul-Jamaʿat's increasing emphasis on adherence to sharīʿat, though the specific manifestations of reform may at times be idiosyncratic. One pīr I met, for instance, emphasized as evidence of his "reformist" orientation the fact that the food (lentils) offered at the annual ʿurs that he presides over is served to people on plates rather than on the "traditional" *chapātī*s (flat bread).

There is a variable cluster of practices that bear the label "traditional" or "corrupt" in modernist and reformist discourse. I often heard statements about its being "against Islam" to "worship" saints because this practice involved someone between oneself and God. So a man who acts like a miracle worker, who claims to mediate between God and his visitors, is committing *shirk* (idolatry), a boundary-setting label of difference between the proper Muslim and the other. Practices that are the target of ideological debate include activities intended to protect people from harmful forces in the environment, such as ghosts (*bhūt*) and dangerous influences from one's living neighbors. Illness and other misfortunes are often attributed to such dangerous forces, and treatment is usually sought from a pīr, either from a local living pīr or from the shrine of a deceased pīr (Ewing 1982).[5] Protection from harmful influences is sought by such means as wearing an amulet that has been prepared by a pīr (and usually consists of a small case containing a verse of the Quran which is worn around the neck), and by carefully observing rituals such as *chillā*. These are the types of practices that are severely criticized both by reformists concerned with purifying Islam and by those with a modernist, secular orientation (Ewing 1982).

I will base this examination of the tension between subject position and the vicissitudes of the speaking subject, which ranges across experiences unconstrained by discursively constituted ideologies, around a Pakistani family that I came to know quite well while I was in Pakistan. Members of this family, like many others I met in Lahore, identified themselves as practitioners of the "true" Islam, stripped of superstition, irrationality, and ignorant custom. They saw themselves as rational, pious, and modern. The family lived in a middle-class urban neighborhood dotted with new construction,[6] amongst neighbors of a wide range of backgrounds and orientations. When I first got to know the family, the parents—Zahida and Muhammad—were middle-aged, and their children ranged in age from their middle twenties to early teens.[7] Muhammad was a government servant and the co-owner of a small factory, and the children were college-educated or still in school. Zahida always wore a *burqa*ʿ (a coat and matching veil that completely hides the body and face) when she left the house, as did the eldest daughter. The younger daughters were in the process of opting for a more "modern" form of covering — the white "lady doctor's" coat. Their articulations of Islam were replete with highly ideological positionings, in terms of which, among other things, they claimed status differences that set them apart from their neighbors. But I had the opportunity to see them negotiate certain complexities and challenges of everyday life and to observe some of the ways in which they drew on the practice of Islam in such situations. I also listened to their stories, through which they often communicated the tensions that arose out of challenges to their assertions of a reformist Muslim identity. I now present a series of these situations and stories.

The Goat's Head: Managing Challenges to a Reformist Position under Stress

Among the practices that people of a wide range of reformist orientations denounce as ignorant superstition, as a Hindu-influenced corruption of Islam, is an activity known as *tauṇā*. According to the perspective of those who acknowledge the power and danger of tauṇā, it is believed that an envious person may exert a powerful influence on another by using specific ritual actions to transfer his or her "misfortune" (*balā*) to that other person. In a typical act of tauṇā, a woman who desires a son or wants to improve the health of a sickly child will throw the head of a goat down at the door of a neighbor who has a healthy son. When the neighbor's son walks over or touches the goat's head, he will sicken and die. The woman who performed the tauṇā will then be free of the trouble that prevented her from conceiving a son or caused her child to be sickly.

Zahida, the mother in this reformist family, once told me a story about tauṇā, a story that must be understood in terms of the "politics" of her neighborhood, where people tended to be very conservatively working and middle class — "traditional":

> Now the people who live near us always think that someone who says "hello" has done magic, that with this hello someone has done tauṇā. They think, "Now we will suffer some injury." But we

don't think so. No one can cause us injury. When I first moved to this neighborhood, I heard some kind of noise outside. So I thought, "Someone has done taunā to me." And I told my son about the incident and asked him to pick up the goat's head and throw it far away. My neighbor was there. She was affectionately disposed toward me. She said, "No, no child. Don't put your hand on it. Child, don't touch it." I said, "Why?" She answered, "No, someone has done taunā, someone has done *jādū* [magic]." I obeyed what she told me, but I didn't believe that there was anything in it that would come out by picking it up. But people say to be sure not to pass near it. They say, "Don't go near it, lest something happen because of it." In my opinion, this is wrong.

This was a family story of long duration: Aisha, one of Zahida's daughters had recounted essentially the same story to me ten years earlier. Aisha had told me the story in the context of a discussion of her neighbors at a time when she was feeling particularly uncomfortable in her neighborhood. Aisha described her family's relations with their neighbors:

> We and the next door people are almost equal in status. That is why we borrow things from them. The other thing is mental status. We don't believe in pīrs and false beliefs, and they don't believe in these things either. When we start to talk, our subject is almost one. Our mental level is equal. But these other people in the neighborhood sit in their houses and say, "She doesn't wear a burqaʿ; boys come and go and she goes with them." They also feel shy because they think we belong to the high class. We don't talk to them because our taste is different. Those women sit together and talk about people. They even talk about each other when they are not present.

In this description, Aisha drew together a wide range of phenomena that distinguished her family from that of most of her neighbors, marking her family as educated, modern, and moral. She also told me a story about her sister that served to demonstrate further the differences between her family and the neighbors: "The neighbors also think that a woman shouldn't go out of her house during the chillā after childbirth because she might be susceptible to harmful influences. They were amazed that my older sister went out during chillā. They think that our family has strange principles." To further emphasize the differences between her family and her neighbors, Aisha contrasted what she regarded as her own well-thought-out position on practices such as taunā with that of her ignorant neighbors. The stimulus for her anger at her neighbors was the fact that she had recently given up wearing a burqaʿ and was hearing considerable criticism from her neighbors about this, despite the approval of her own family.[8]

It was in the context of this discussion that Aisha told me of her mother's experience of taunā. The conclusion of Aisha's story of the taunā episode differed slightly from her mother's. In Aisha's version her mother did not rescind her order to her son, and he actually picked up the goat head and threw it over the wall. In her daughter's account, Zahida's order to her son to pick up the goat's head was a political act. The account highlighted the confrontational nature of the act, reflecting the daughter's own current state of confrontation with her neighbors over the issue of wearing a burqaʿ. Having the son pick up the goat's head would have been a direct refusal of the belief system of the neighbors, openly contradicting their admonishments. Zahida's account was far more conciliatory, reflecting her willingness to accommodate to her neighbors' concerns while making clear her own beliefs. But both accounts expressed an unambiguous subject position constituted by an ideology of modern reformist Islam in terms of which the neighbors are a traditional other. What Zahida did not acknowledge in her description of this personal experience was the pain that she must have felt when she realized that someone had done this to her: out of envy someone had threatened the life of her child. By focusing on the meaninglessness of the act, locating herself within a different interpretive world, Zahida placed a barrier between herself and the play of desires and fears that characterize everyday sociality. Despite her refusal of this act of taunā, it retained its communicative force, its meaning as a hostile act that marked and shaped a human relationship.

Of Goats and Reform

Given the pervasiveness of reformist and modernist teachings that have shaped the sensitivities even of those who claim the label Ahl-i Sunnat ul-Jamaʿat, it is not surprising that local pīrs are themselves confronted with a tension between inconsistent perspectives on Islam. Zahida's son, Akbar, once introduced me to a pīr who lived nearby. Akbar, of

Interviewing a *pīr*

course, was himself not a follower of pīrs, but he knew this pīr as a neighbor. With his self-described antipīr sectarian orientation, Akbar found it difficult simply to sit quietly and watch me take notes on the pīr's descriptions of how he prescribes treatments for his followers. After listening deferentially for half an hour, Akbar could not restrain himself from asking a few questions which, though respectfully framed, challenged the pīr to defend his practices from the perspective of what Akbar considered to be "proper" Islam. The pīr was suddenly in the position of having to reconcile certain inconsistencies that the younger man had pointed out between sharī'at and the pīr's practices.

Just before Akbar's intervention in the conversation, this pīr, an un-educated man who learned his techniques as the disciple of another neighborhood pīr, described the instructions he might give to a person afflicted by some "thing" (*chīz*): "He should go into the jungle, slaughter a sheep, and leave it there. The 'thing' stays there and won't return." The pīr called this treatment *sadaqa* (sacrifice, charity). He described how he prescribes various forms of sadaqa as a cure for the distresses that he diagnoses in his patients/followers.

At that point, Akbar asked, "Is there ever a kind of sadaqa in which the patient gives a live sheep or goat to some poor person?" "Sadaqa" is an Arabic term for a central concept in Islam, but this pīr's concept of sadaqa was grounded in a frame of reference very different from that of the young man listening to him. This seemingly simple question was ideologically loaded: it highlighted the idea of sacrifice as charity.

The pīr, well aware of this point of view, assented and this time shifted his emphasis to the act of giving to the poor. He explained: "Some people give sadaqa to the poor, some to orphans." But as he elaborated, his stance, though explicitly linked with Islam in terminology at several points, became remarkably ambiguous: "One kind of sadaqa is that you cannot eat the meat of that goat. You slaughter it by yourself. You must dump all the blood down the drain to make it *halāl* [lawful — a concept in Islamic law]. Not a single drop of blood should remain in the house. You cut it in pieces and distribute it to the poor." He then described a sadaqa involving a live animal: "They take it out of the house, away from themselves, and leave it in the street. They can leave a chicken or a goat."

In this pīr's description, Islamic law, with its careful specification of how a sacrifice is to be performed, is intimately tied up with what other, more educated or reform-oriented, Muslims would call an ignorant superstition and even a manifestation of Hindu influence. Though his prescription for draining the blood of an animal to be sacrificed is consistent with Islamic prescriptions for any slaughter in order to make the meat lawful, the pīr's emphasis on getting every drop of blood out of the house suggests a concern with the potentially harmful effects of the blood itself, an idea that is grounded in a very different paradigm, one which the young man would not accept.

When the pīr described releasing the goat or cow in the street, Akbar asked, "Can any man catch it?" The pīr responded, "It just goes its own way. They take it out of the house, away from themselves and leave it." He then changed the subject entirely, effectively cutting off any further questions (a common strategy in the face of a challenge or inconsistency). Akbar was persistently concerned with charity and focused on the recipients of the animal, whereas the pīr was concerned with the removal of the animal from the presence of the person doing the sacrifice. Obviously, the pīr was here emphasizing the importance of ritually transferring a harmful influence to an animal and then removing the animal from one's presence. In his overtly Islamic prescription of sacrifice, which he formulated when challenged, his emphasis on removing every drop of blood implied that the influence of the malevolent "thing" goes down the drain along with the blood, which is thought to be highly impure by most Muslims. The poor may, therefore, eat the meat without being harmed, since the harmful influence is no longer in the meat.

In contrast, the principle that Akbar stressed is that God is always directly involved. He is the agent of cure, if there is to be a spiritual cure. The word of God and acts performed in accordance with the sharīʿat have the power to overcome harmful influences and transform them into "charity." From this point of view, a recipient cannot be harmed by a sacrifice: it is understood as an act of charity.[9] The blessing that derives from charity or sacrifice descends directly from God, overcomes any harmful forces or influences, and transforms the offering into something beneficial. What the pīr and young man were debating was whether an act such as sadaqa could be effective without God's direct intervention. The reformist position that the young man espoused was that the idea of spiritual efficacy without God's direct intervention was infidelity to God, tantamount to Hindu polytheism.[10]

It was evident that in the debate between Akbar and the pīr that they each had been through similar encounters before. The pīr had ready responses to Akbar's challenges. Nearly every pīr I talked to was very sensitive to the parameters that Islam imposes on their practice, a sensitivity that can be attributed to reformist pressure. One pīr, for example, read me a statement of the principles of Islam that he had carefully crafted in anticipation of my questions about his practice as a pīr. I was very familiar with these prescriptive statements—impersonal and abstracted from any specific practice—and after hearing these ideological formulations repeatedly, I tended to respond with carefully masked impatience and frustration, seeking to get past the ideology to what people were "really" doing, instead of appreciating the chance to experience the deployment of an ideology. What this practice of ideology suggests to me now, however, is that this pīr, like many others, was extremely self-conscious about his positioning with regard to an ideology of Islam that has great political significance in Pakistan. The principles of Islam, though presented by this pīr as the timeless Law laid out in the Quran and in the practice of the Prophet (*sunnat*), were in many respects the outcome of reformist objectifications, manifested in the practice of even those who are resistant to antipīr ideologies. The teachings of the Ahl-i Sunnat ul-Jamaʿat have provided both pīrs and those who visit pīrs seeking amulets with the vocabulary for generating an ideological response to reformist condemnations.

Despite their differences in age, which elicited overt deference in Akbar, Akbar spoke from a position of power — a power that reflects in part the sheer force of modernity. But Akbar's position was also buttressed by my presence: I represented the West and its power to observe. The dialogue had embedded within it a tension that in Pakistan is continually played out in arenas as diverse as national politics on the one hand and the status negotiations within the neighborhood on the other hand and even within the reform-oriented person himself.

A Dish of Blood

Embedded within my conversations with Aisha, Zahida, and the other people I met in Lahore are stories that reveal some of the complexity of the speaking subject's relationship to ideology. Identity constituted through the invariant ideological gaze — often manifested in those boring, ideological statements of position that made me fidget — stands in tension with a narrative self, a "self of stories."[11] Ideology constitutes an identity as sameness within a fixed structure of signs. The interpellated subject is the identity constituted through ideology, the occupier of a subject position, an ego that seeks to express fixed, unchanging truths about self and other and, therefore, hides or obliterates the inevitable slippage of its signifiers. The self as a character in a story, in contrast, has a dynamic trajectory and thus bears a structure entirely different from that constituted by ideology. Identity constituted within the context of narrative is fluid: "The person shares the condition of dynamic identity peculiar to the story recounted" (Ricoeur 1992:147). Narrative identity involves a dialectic complementarity of the elusive, mobile speaking subject and sameness, a dialectic of self and other than self. There is thus a fundamental tension between this narrative "self" and ideology. As Ricoeur has put it, story is a movement rather than sameness, a moment of identity being suspended between two poles.

In the case of the following story of Zahida's, the two poles are (at one interpretive level) modernity and tradition. In these conversations, attempts to claim a modern identity and to align one's actions in conformity with the constraints of the modern create a kind of alienation or splits in the subject. At the same time, such attempts also create certain satisfactions that come with successfully conforming to one's image of the modern, a kind of enjoyment associated with interpellation in a specific subject position (Allison 1993). But one's subjectivity is not fully determined by this alienating subject position. Narrative highlights and seeks to resolve the tensions between an ideological subject that cannot be fully encompassed by any single ideology and the experience of a subjectivity that escapes the Imaginary Order of ideologies.

One day I was talking with Zahida. We were talking about pīrs and superstitions in a kind of casual interview (she was cutting up vegetables for dinner while I took notes of our conversation, as I often did with her). Zahida recounted an experience of a trivial but puzzling incident that had made a strong impression on her. As she told the story, I could see that the act of narration gave her great enjoyment. I present the story here because she used the story as a paradigmatic articulation of her identity as a rational, modern Muslim woman, and this identity was a source of enjoyment.

> Now something happened one day. I was in the house. It was a winter day. When I had finished my work in the house, I filled a big clay pot with water and left it inside the house. I put a plate over the pot. Then I went outside, like this, to sit in the sun. When I came back inside a little later, I saw that the plate was full of blood.
>
> I was alone in the house. So I immediately thought, where could the blood have come from? I didn't get scared or worried—I didn't think anything like that. I just started to think like this: I just "tasted" the thought of where the blood could have come from. Because there was nobody in the house. "This is inside and nobody could have come this way, and I just now washed it and went out. And just now I came back." I thought and thought.
>
> Then I told myself that there are some sparrows around. If one was wounded, if someone tied it and spun it, by the throat—you don't know how here children tie string around their throats and play—so I thought, someone has hit many sparrows. They have been wounded. But then I thought, "How could there be so much blood?" So I said to myself that one was wounded. It drank some water. It was thirsty. It came inside. It sat on this plate. Its blood mixed with some water in the plate and the whole thing got dirty. And then it flew back outside. It drank some water and his blood mixed with it. Then it left. I knew immediately. If I hadn't thought, I would have shouted, just as the women do here. "Come, come, come. Tauña! Jādū [black magic]! Oh! Oh!" I told everyone. I told them how I solved this problem.

This subject as protagonist in this narrative moves from the unself-consciousness of everyday chores to a moment of confrontation: the world she has made orderly has been disrupted by a mysterious force, which she must combat. Who has filled the dish with blood? Is it black magic (jādū)? Is it the malicious act of an envious neighbor (taunā)? All the evidence suggests that it must have been jādū: nobody could have put blood in the dish in an ordinary fashion, since nobody could have been present. But the story does not take up the confrontation with a magician; rather, it shifts the confrontation to another level. The story became a reflexive clash between modern rationality and traditional superstition, a clash of explanatory modes. The self as modern Muslim is confronted with "proof" of the efficacy of jādū, and it is this proof which must be combated. Her weapons are her reasoning skills and her emotional control. Her antagonists are her imagined neighbors, who cling to tradition, the women who would have shouted out "taunā" and "jādū" without stopping to reason. Her reason saves her from becoming one of them. She vanquishes them and their explanations with an orderly series of hypotheses and proofs, thought experiments. Victorious, she tells the world her story. The story establishes her identity as heroine of the modern, torchbearer for the truth of a reformist Islam.

This brief story reminds me (but, I must emphasize, not Zahida) of the story of the mouth of Krishna, from the Puranas of Hindu tradition: a woman at her daily chores, a bit of dirt, and the structure of the universe is exposed.[12] The dish of blood, like the dirt in Krishna's mouth, created a rent in the mundane reality of Zahida's everyday life.[13] It catapulted her into a different type of consciousness, the position of self-reflexivity, or, in psychoanalytic parlance, the "observing ego." From this reflexive position, she repaired the hole with a skillful narrative suture. And with this suture (and many other similar sutures), she constructed an identity, a self constituted of stories.

This story begins in the sameness of everyday routine. Zahida even draws the moment of narration into the story: we are outside sitting in the sun, just as she was then. It is a bodily experience of continuity. Our own conversation has pushed her into a reflective, reflexive mode, just as the dish of blood had done. The detail of her reports of her thought processes in the story suggests two things: (1) the sight of the dish of blood not only caught her full attention but also made her self-consciously aware of her reactions at the time — she was observing herself as if through the gaze of another. The event ruptured the unselfconscious flow of daily experience. (2) Our conversation, including the setting, has triggered a reexperiencing of that reflexive moment, a "transference" of that past event to the present. I have become the gaze of the other — the rational scientist who will approve of her sutures of reality. The identity that she experiences under that particular "scientific" gaze has been reaffirmed in its continuity. There was undoubtedly a specific person who in her personal history was the original bearer of that gaze, a foundational "other," but for our purposes, what is of concern is not the particular configuration of personality traits and behaviors that characterized that other, but rather Zahida's relationship to an imagined other that represents a specific discursive ideology, who is reconstituted whenever Zahida invokes or is invoked by this ideology. This other is within her. At the moment of narration, it is between us.

The triumphant moment of knowing is analogous to Lacan's description of assumption of the mirror image — a fullness of mastery that is illusory. What is illusory is not the mastery, but rather the totality of the feeling of triumph and the apparently perfect fit between the image constituted in the gaze of the other and one's subjectivity. Triumph is fleeting, and then there is only the memory. But the experience confirms the whole ideological structure, fills in the gaps between the ideology and a reality that cannot be articulated.

Zahida's self-reflexivity was explicitly linked with a rational self. Critics of modernity have argued that the focus on the self as individual in modern discourse is associated with disciplinary practices that constitute the "self" as an experience of interiority and reflexivity (Foucault 1990b). This disciplinary constitution of a reflexive, interior self is exemplified in the doctrines of European Protestantism. It is possible to see Reformist versions of Islam operating in a similar fashion, producing a demystified, mechanistic world in which the only possible spiritual intervention is the rare act of God. But the fact that Zahida experiences self-reflexivity and a rationalist, mechanistic view of the world as linked does not mean that it is the peculiar characteristics of modernity per se that cause such reflexivity. The clash of discourses itself, apart from any specific content, is a more likely explanation: it puts people into the position of having to choose between realities, thereby exposing the agent that chooses. Subsequent chapters will support this argument by highlighting the cultural elaboration of such self-reflexivity in the Islamic tradition and by offering evidence for the presence of such self-conscious interiority apart from the specific influences of what is called modernity.

Aisha's Dream

To take the other side of the argument for the time being, it cannot be assumed that the ideological self-consciousness manifested in Zahida's and Aisha's stories of taunā and the dish of blood and in Akbar's debate with the pīr indicates a general transformation of consciousness brought about by the hegemonies of modernity. People live with inconsistency, failing to objectify certain of their own practices even when actively caught up in an ideological political movement that uses these very practices as a signifier.[14] The same individual may shift frames of reference from one context to another, even from one moment to the next, and may tolerate considerable inconsistency in his own beliefs and opinions, often without even realizing it (Ewing 1990a).

Pakistanis like Zahida and her family, who maintain a reformist orientation to Islam, are highly sensitive to issues of inconsistency because of the political and social implications of their beliefs and practices. Yet even in these very beliefs and practices that have been the focus of ideological elaboration, such as those associated with the rejection of the legitimacy of pīrs, they live with inconsistencies that they either fail to notice or seek to reconcile through stories.

Practices that have never been the focus of confrontation and objectification are enacted without self-consciousness. People are actually oblivious to inconsistency in their daily lives until situations of conflict arise or expectable routines break down. In such situations we are likely to see confusion, evasive maneuvers, and defensive strategies when participants strive to maintain a posture of consistency and to save face. There is no narrative in place that can account for the rupture; the habitation of a rationalist subject position is temporary.

The anthropologist may naively induce an episode of confrontation through seemingly innocent questioning. I did just this to Aisha, Zahida's daughter. When a juxtaposition suddenly makes an inconsistency evident, as may occur when the anthropologist thinks she is asking an innocent question, it is possible to see rapid defensive maneuvers that expose the process of synthesis and integration.

To illustrate: One day I observed Aisha preparing a plate of coins. Aisha had on other occasions been scornful of what she called her

neighbors' superstitious fears of harmful forces and malevolent intentions. On this occasion, she held her parents' hands on the plate of
money for a few moments, called the neighborhood children to the
door, and distributed the coins to them. Needless to say, I asked her
what she was doing.

She explained that she had had a disturbing dream about harm be-
falling her father, so she had decided to distribute some money to
beggars in order to ward off the harmful effects of her dream. She
explained to me that the money would have her parents' influence
(*asar*) in it: "I feel this," she said. "If something is wrong in their bodies
or spirits, if God is doing something to harm them, he won't do it after
this charity [sadaqa]." I asked her why she had put her parents' hands
on the plate. She replied, "Coming through their hands is the 'outlet'
for this badness." This explanation of sadaqa was virtually identical to
that of the neighborhood pīr who described sacrificing a goat as a way
of getting rid of harmful influences.

As I listened, Aisha's explanation reminded me of the practice of
"taunā," which she had previously described to me to illustrate the
extent to which her neighbors are mired in superstition. In taunā, as we
have seen, misfortune is thought to pass to the person who finds and
picks up a goat's head that has been thrown into the street. It seemed to
me that at that moment, while she was passing out the coins, Aisha's
orientation to such matters was not all that far from that of her "superstitious" neighbors. So I asked whether taunā works the same way.

Aisha hesitated (obviously assessing the implications of the question,
probably recalling, as I was, our shared history, including her vehement
denunciations of her neighbors for believing in such things). Then she
replied, "Yes. But it [taunā] is against humanity; it does harm to others.
All men are equal and shouldn't harm others. Also, taunā is food being
thrown, wasted. Food should be eaten. If we don't need it, we should
give it to others." She then changed the subject, as if to avoid having to
draw together the several stances she had taken over the course of a few
moments.

Though I induced this particular confrontation, similar confrontations (and frequently not as benign as this one was) often erupt in
Pakistan between adherents of a mediatory orientation (in which pīrs
are thought to mediate between God and the ordinary person) and
reformists, many of whom have little patience for what they feel are
corruptions of Islam that must be eliminated.

Some illustrative unpacking of this bit of dialogue, as the psycho-analyst might attend to it, with what psychoanalysts call the "third ear" can make explicit the conflicting stances and shifting subject positions manifested in this interchange. The psychoanalyst listens for the func-tions each utterance seems to serve, the effects it has in the immediate relationship between psychoanalyst and patient. Put more generally, or anthropologically, no utterance can be understood solely in terms of its overt content — participants in any dialogue are constantly (though not always consciously) monitoring why *this* was said *now* — what prag-matic functions the utterance served.

Attending to the pragmatic aspects of the interchange for the posi-tioning of the subject requires focusing on the implications of my ques-tion for our relationship, on how the question affected the representa-tions of self and other that were constituted in the dialogue, as an unfolding from our shared history.

The content and structure of her response suggest that she heard in my question the subtext "You are just like your superstitious neigh-bors," a predication or interpellation that she felt a need to defend herself against. Aisha maintained a rhetorical stance in opposition to taunā and in opposition to her neighbors who, as she had stated to me, practice taunā. The word "taunā" acted like a red flag that triggered her response. In earlier conversations with me, she had used the issue of taunā to distinguish her own family from her neighbors, asserting the ignorance and low status of her neighbors. When I had asked her on a previous occasion if she had any idea how the harmful influences in the goat's head could be transmitted from one person to another, she had said, "No, I really want to know, but I think that 85 percent of the people who believe it wouldn't be able to tell us why." (In this case, the grammatical structure of the response — in particular, the "us" — indi-cated that she had drawn me into an alliance and set up her neighbors as "other," forming an identification with my stance as an inquirer into the strange customs of the natives.) Her statement, with its use of statistics and an expression of the desire to "know," also echoed the social scientific tradition of inquiry that I represented and reinforced her identification with my "modern" scientific orientation.

On the present occasion, however, I had unintentionally pushed her into a defensive stance. She saw me identifying her with those neigh-bors, the natives to be studied. She attempted several defensive maneu-vers, culminating in an effort to redefine the situation altogether by changing the subject. It was evident to both of us that her responses were mutually inconsistent and that our alliance had to be reestablished on other grounds. In this situation she actively avoided juxtaposing two thoughts that she did not want to recognize as inconsistent, keeping each firmly embedded within its own carefully delimited context. In a psychoanalytic situation, the analyst might make the juxtaposition explicit and difficult to avoid. In my role as anthropologist, I spared Aisha this juxtaposition, as people commonly do in polite society. Like most of us, Aisha's ideological views of the world are situation-specific. When confronted with what is to her an obvious "superstition" like a goat's head at the door, she rejects it with a series of rationalist and Islamic reformist arguments. Explicit discussion of pīrs brings forth a similar ideological positioning, replete with accusations of fraud and corruption. But such positionings have little relevance when it comes to reactions to the immediacies of everyday life. Practices such as warding off the ill effects of a bad dream are not objectified or rationalized. They are a part of the repertoire of activities that help make the world feel like a safe and familiar place.

The Shrine in the Corner

The accusation of fraud is a powerful way in which people locate themselves vis-à-vis competing ideologies. This was probably the most frequent accusation made by Pakistanis about a particular pīr, or about pīrs in general. When I told people about the topic of my research, the most common first question was whether I had met any genuine or true pīrs (the obverse of the fraud).[15] When asked if a pīr I had met was a fraud, I found that revealing interchanges occurred when I responded by asking, "How would I know if this pīr were a fraud?" The answers I received made explicit the criteria by which people judged the legitimacy of pīrs and often revealed nuances of ideological positioning. Variations in usage are associated with different positions in the struggle over interpretations of sharī'at. The issue of fraud thus makes explicit the ideological constitution of identity.

At the moment that an accusation of fraud is made, identity claims with regard to competing ideologies are articulated. The accusation is often closely linked with the idea that someone who believes in a pīr is irrational: fraudulent (i.e., rationally calculating) charlatans are out to dupe those mired in tradition by appealing to hopes and fears instead of reason. Within the context of this ideological arrangement of signifiers, identities that articulate the relationship of self and other out of absolute difference are constructed. The accusation of fraud thus articulates a social boundary and prescribes certain technologies and practices as illegitimate and irrational.

Aisha took me to meet and interview the mother of a school friend, whom I shall call Ilmaz. This woman told us about her own dealings with a pīr. In our presence, her accounts manifested an unresolvable tension between what she "knew" to be a fraudulent practice and a cure so efficacious that she had to embrace it. In this case, the woman experiencing the conflict also acknowledged that the pīr who had provided the solution to her conflict was a fraud. This was, therefore, one of those times when the individual simply cannot suture the gaps between positions. As a result, the subject's conflictual movement is repeatedly visible. Our obvious identities as Westerner and modern reformist Muslim undoubtedly made this issue more salient than it might otherwise have been. On the basis of their life situations and appearances these two women could be assigned nearly antithetical identities vis-à-vis modernity. Under thirty-five, yet a mother of five, Ilmaz was "uneducated" (her own self-description), to the extent of being unsure about how much education she had had — probably through the fifth grade. She veiled herself whenever she left the house. Aisha, in contrast, was unmarried, in her mid-twenties, and college educated. She wore only a white doctor's coat over her *shalwār* and *qamīs* (loose trousers and tunic) and the obligatory *dopatta*[16] when she moved through the city, emblem of her identity as a professional yet respectable woman. She was visibly "modern."

Near the end of a long meeting, the two women had the following interchange in which such positionings were explicit:

> Ilmaz: For your mother's sickness, you should get *dam*.[17]
> Aisha: There is no pious person in our neighborhood who could do dam. That pīr you talked about before used to work in my father's factory. When he couldn't make enough money, he became a pīr.
> Ilmaz: Pīrs are those people who have died. In these days no one is a pīr.

This conversation is typical of the kind of not-so-subtle sniping that goes on amongst neighbors in mixed urban neighborhoods. These women have drawn on what in the national arena are competing ideologies about modernity and Islam, and the interchange involved a negotiation of status and identity.

In this conversation, the younger woman stated an obviously if implicitly ideological position: all pīrs, or at least all living local pīrs, the people from whom one would obtain the blessing of dam, are fraudulent. In doing so, she opened the possibility of a breach in the conversation—claiming the upper hand by suggesting that what appeared to be friendly advice about getting dam was wrongheaded (though her accusation was tempered by the ambiguity that perhaps it is only in this neighborhood that there are no legitimate pīrs). The older woman yielded the point. Though she had at first advised her to visit a pīr, she shifted ground, thereby agreeing with and broadening Aisha's statement and repairing the breach. The younger woman did not contest the point that there are dead pīrs, and the interchange ended in ambiguity, with a moment of silence and a shift of topic. If pushed, Aisha would probably have argued that one shouldn't pray to any intermediaries to reach God, a point I had heard her make on other occasions. The outcome of the conversation suggests the power of modernity as a discourse, with its rejection of the traditional pīr and his practices pushing the older woman into an inconsistent position, undermining her "traditional" views.

We had gone to visit this woman because, Aisha had reported to me, she actually had a shrine in her home, where she lit candles every Thursday, the day when most people visit Sufi shrines. We had gone off to find out more about what was to Aisha a rather peculiar phenomenon because I was interested in the followers of Sufi saints. What we found was a woman who felt that her life had been transformed by a cure effected by a pīr whom she, nevertheless, accused of being a fraud.

This woman was the wife of a middle-class government servant. They, with their five children, lived in a recently built brick row house, one of many identical units in a large complex built for government servants. Her son, a friend of Aisha's brother, had told her to expect us. We were seated in the living room and given Cokes, standard summertime hospitality only for those who can afford the high cost. Ilmaz's mother-in-law and a neighbor were also there and observed the conversation, joining in with an occasional comment.

I initiated the conversation by telling Ilmaz that I was meeting with people in different neighborhoods, talking with them about their way of life and about what was important to them. We began with a discussion about her family background and got into a rather generalized discussion about variations in social practices associated with different castes and variations in religious practices associated with different sects. I asked her what sect her family was identified with, and she replied "Ahl-i Sunnat ul-Jama'at." She explained: "I go to many shrines, and in my house there is a shrine [the first mention of this shrine in the conversation]. I go to many shrines in Lahore: Data Sahib, Shāh Jamāl, Shāh Kamāl, Pīr Makkī, and sometimes shrines in Multan and Pakpattan." (Her mother-in-law, who was present, added, "I want to visit Pakpattan, but it is hot, and I can't go.") I asked her several general questions about pīrs, which prompted her to ask Aisha: "Don't you know about these things yourself?" Aisha responded that she did, but that I wanted to hear different people's ideas for myself. When I asked her whether she followed a living pīr, she answered, "No, and my husband doesn't, either." She thus drew a distinction between living pīrs and her acceptance of dead pīrs at this early point in the conversation — the same distinction she would make in her interchange with Aisha near the end of our meeting.

A moment later, she offered to show us the shrine in her home. The shrine itself was extremely simple. Hidden behind a green curtain were two small corner shelves, one above the other, about a foot off the floor, each only six inches across at its widest point, with evidence of many candles having been burnt on them. The shrine was located in an otherwise strikingly "modern" room: the center of the room was occupied by a large dining table surrounded by ten chairs. (By way of contrast, in the house I lived in, with a family of similar economic position, family members took turns eating meals squatting in the tiny cooking shed attached to the side of the house. When there were guests we ate on a cloth spread out on the floor of the living room.)

As we returned to the living room, she began to explain the origins of the shrine:

> When I first came to these quarters, this dining room was a veranda. My father's brother's daughters came to stay with us, and so I built this room for the girls. I put a bed along the wall. Two or three days after putting the bed there, I became ill. I was very sad, I had no peace. My husband is very nice, but we started to quarrel. My cousin thought, "It is because of me that they quarrel," be-

cause my husband used to take them to the bus. I said that it wasn't because of my cousin, but because I get upset. Then I told my neighbor [who was present at the time of this interview] that I get upset all the time. She suggested that I visit a pīr, so we went to Ichhra [a neighborhood adjacent to this neighborhood of government housing, about two miles away] to see a living pīr, whom she knew.

When we got there, I gave him one rupee twenty-five paise; he charged a fixed rate. He said, "You have a pīr in your house." Now I believe that he was a liar. Even at the time I didn't believe in taʿwīz. But when I got sick I said, "Someone did taʿwīz to make me sick." That living pīr called this pīr [the one whose shrine is now in her home]. This pīr said, "You must remove the bed from that room; you must give me a corner big enough for one person to sit."

My husband and son started to make fun of me, because they said it is impossible to leave a corner of the room for a pīr. But after a few days, my husband and son saw lightning in this room at midnight. Then they started to follow this pīr. Whenever I desire anything in my heart, it is fulfilled. I don't know if it is because of this pīr or Data Sahib or anyone else. Some neighbors also follow this pīr. I burn an oil lamp every Thursday. Two or three neighbors also follow this pīr, but we don't allow many people to come because this is not a *darbār* [public shrine]. [KPE: Do you know his name?] No. He hasn't told us about himself. Here there used to be a graveyard. So in some quarters people face problems; in others people have a good life. [KPE: Does the pīr ever communicate with you?] When I get sick sometimes, I have an *ishārat* [waking dream] in which he says I will get well. The government is offering us bigger quarters, but I don't want to move because of this pīr.

Ilmaz's narrative is shot through with gaps, uncertainties, and inconsistencies. The account of the shrine describes a discontinuity: it is a narrative effort to repair a breach between her identity as a modern woman and something she was unable to control, an irruption from elsewhere, a subjectivity not contained by the fixed signifiers that locate her in a specific subject position. The pīr in her dining room allowed her to repair the breach.

In order to elucidate the significance for Ilmaz's identity of the pīr who lives in her dining room, I construct an account of the steps that she appears to have gone through that lead up to her acceptance of the pīr, piecing together evidence from the gaps and inconsistencies in her narrative with additional material from our conversation.

Just before Ilmaz found her pīr, she was in a state of acute distress. Her symptoms revealed the truth of her situation, proclaiming the hollowness of an identity she was trying to live, revealing it to be empty. She and others in her environment sought to identify the source of this anxiety, in effect attaching signifiers to her symptoms to give them meaning, to bind the anxiety she was experiencing. The pīr successfully operated as such a signifier. An understanding of how and why it worked also clarifies how individuals articulate and contend with the discourse of modernity, providing evidence of how it operates and the extent of its hegemony.

Much of Ilmaz's difficulty seemed to be focused on her husband; specifically, how she saw herself constituted through her husband's gaze. She identified with the modernist orientation of her husband and attempted, unsuccessfully, to maintain a positive identity within this discourse. This struggle shaped her relationships with us in the interview situation, thereby making visible this hidden issue. Ilmaz expressed her relationship to "modernity" through a series of signifying practices and her positive evaluation of these practices: In our conversation, she explicitly discussed her approval of eliminating caste (zāt) as a basis for social identity and occupation, living in modern housing, throwing out old papers, having her husband in a government job, having modern furnishings, and being educated.

Many of Ilmaz's statements contrasted a social order based on caste with a new social order based on new sources of status. She spoke approvingly of the social order that arises from the sameness of their government housing: "People are known by the numbers of their quarters. No one cares for castes. Sometimes people hide their caste because they belong to a low caste and don't like insult." This rejection of caste extends to strategies for choosing marriage partners: "My husband doesn't care for castes. He says that originally we are human beings. We must show the girl to the boy and the boy to the girl before marriage because they have to pass their life together. Islam doesn't restrict people to arranged marriage within their own caste. I wouldn't care if she is high or low caste. I will ask if she is well-mannered or educated."

Here, in the shadow of an allusion to her husband's attitudes, Ilmaz confidently expresses her dedication to the "modern" way of arranging marriages. But earlier, in the context of her discussion of previous marriages among her relatives, she sounded more ambivalent: "My half brother is just like a father to me. He arranged the marriages of his brothers and sisters. [KPE: Were they of the same *birādarī* (brother-hood, kin group)?] Yes, same birādarī, same zāt. We don't arrange marriages outside of our birādarī and zāt. But maybe now I can't say I won't arrange the marriage of my children outside of the birādarī. But before it was not done."

When, later, I asked about the history of the zāt, she replied: "The elders have died. So we don't know about the history. We can't tell our children and their children. My *dādā* [grandfather] had some records about the history, but we couldn't read them because the papers were very old. They were thrown out; we didn't like old papers. New people like new things." This passage suggests a shifting subject position, from one emerging out of the context of family and zāt, based on an identification with her half brother and a regret about the broken ties to her family's past, to a modern orientation toward the new, tinged with bravado.

For Ilmaz, modernity has its most powerful manifestation in education. She is proud of her husband and his high-status occupation, which was made possible by his modern education. This education, like government housing, enables one to escape the stigma of a low caste: "Our zāt is Sandhu. In the old days, they were tailors, but now different people adopt different professions. Some still become tailors and barbers. But because my husband got an education, he is doing a government job. His brothers are also in government jobs. Now he is giving his children an education." Though Ilmaz can identify with the modernist project through her husband and her children, it is precisely this aspect of modernist discourse that interpellates her negatively, because of her lack of education. She has adopted the trappings of modernity in the furnishings of her home—a dining-room table to seat ten, a TV, a ceiling fan, but she herself embodies the old days: "Women were not allowed to work, but now they get an education and work outside the home. In the old days people didn't teach us because they didn't like it."

Her mother-in-law offered a clue to the difficult position this puts women like Ilmaz into. "I have one daughter, and my husband didn't allow her to study." Her son, Ilmaz's husband, is different and has encouraged his own daughter to study. But Ilmaz cannot assume this signifier of modernity for herself. Ilmaz is, by her own self-label, "uneducated," an identity that she adopted in self-deprecation in our conversation, in which both Aisha and I embodied the educated woman. If her husband approves of educated women, this offers a potential threat to the security of her marriage and a powerful source of jealousy. She perceives in herself a lack.

Modernity versus pīrs (tradition) is for her partly a contrast between male and female worlds. Women are being forced to enter a male world (working outside home), entangled in the nets of a subject position legitimated through rationality. The validity of female interests and bases of sociality are denied, delegitimated in the word "fraud," and those who believe are labeled irrational.

Ilmaz's belief in the pīr under her house operates according to another logic that is powerful not only for her but for everyone else in the room, even Aisha. This logic operates in the following terms: The housing project is built over a graveyard, and so every family will experience some influence from the souls of the dead persons they live closest to, especially if their house is built directly above a grave. The nature of that influence depends on the spiritual quality of the dead person: some families experience a good life and others experience difficulty. The dead pīr, being spiritually developed, can have a more direct and powerful influence on the living than can the graves of the ordinary dead. He communicates explicitly with another pīr, and he is able to make lightning appear in the room, a minor miracle. When he is treated with the proper respect, his *barakat* (blessing) becomes evident: the family feels his generalized auspicious influence, and for Ilmaz, "Whenever I desire anything in my heart, it is fulfilled." This is an expression that people frequently use when discussing the nature of barakat. The pīr now appears in her dreams, also a common pattern.

Despite the positive qualities of the dead pīr, qualities which the pīr described by Ilmaz clearly manifests, he may also act in a manner that resembles the actions of a bhūt or *jinn* (a nonhuman spiritual creature). When his grave is not shown the proper respect, he will afflict the living, just as does the jinn whose resting place is defiled. Ilmaz had thought that black magic had been worked on her: "Someone did ta'wīz to make me sick." "Ta'wīz" is the word normally used to refer to an amulet containing verses of the Quran, which a pīr will write for his followers as part of his curing and problem-solving techniques. In this case, she was thinking of a ta'wīz that had become *ultā*, perverted in form and in intent. Instead, she discovered that she was dealing directly with a spiritually powerful being. This woman's symptoms resembled a mild case of possession, in that she "had no peace." But whereas the jinn in a case of possession will be subjected to exorcism, the pīr is entitled to considerable respect, and in this case a shrine was built for him. The woman now performs a ritual of burning oil lamps for him every Thursday, just as she would at a public shrine. The grave's status as a shrine is further enhanced by the fact that neighbors also acknowledge the pīr's presence and pay their respect to him. He is now a positive force in this woman's life, a force that she would not want to abandon. The story of a pīr living in a woman's dining room, then, has characteristics that resemble two other cultural practices. Women may gather on Thursdays at a shrine to pay their respects and to pray for wondrous deeds from a dead pīr or, less commonly, they may gather, also on Thursdays, to hear the oracles of a possessed woman.[18] In both cases, women are actively articulating their relationship to spiritual forces in their environment. The delegitimization of this "traditional" practice is thus a form of disempowerment of women associated with reform. It can also be seen as an imposition of the "discipline" of rationality.[19]

The pīr enabled Ilmaz to transcend her immediate situation, in which a series of conflicts and contradictions in her life had reached crisis proportions, and to reestablish her life with a new focal point of organization and articulation. During our conversation she quite succinctly summarized at least some of the major sources of her conflict: the unacceptability to herself of her own reactions, and her inability to deal with them directly. She stated that her father's brother's daughters had come to stay with her. She had gone to a great deal of trouble to make space for them, converting the veranda into a room for them. This suggests that they were planning quite a prolonged stay, undoubtedly for their education. Kinship obligations to her father's brother would have made it mandatory for her to accommodate the girls, no matter how she felt about it. She could not say that she did not like having them in the house and could not convey a hint of it to them, for fear of making them feel unwelcome.

She also mentioned the problem of a potential involvement between one of her cousins and her husband. She states directly that her husband spent time with them alone every day, when he took them to the bus. They went out in public with him while she remained at home. She mentioned the issue of jealousy but attributed it to her cousin's misperception of the situation. She thus made her feelings of jealousy explicit while simultaneously denying that they existed.

Finally, she asserted that her husband is "nice" and thus, like her cousins, cannot be blamed for the anxiety she felt. Therefore, she could only blame herself for the quarrels they engaged in. She got upset "all the time" and undoubtedly saw herself as less satisfying company than her cousins appeared to be. She could not escape her sadness and anxiety and yet could not admit its cause.

These conflicts and tensions, and undoubtedly others that she did not directly mention in her conversation with me, became focused on the pīr. He was the source of her illness and loss of peace. Her relationship to God had been disturbed because of her improper treatment of one of his representatives, the pīr. It was the pīr who did not want to make room for the cousins; he punished her for putting a bed for them in his space. The situation of having her cousins move into her home thus became only the indirect source of her anxiety. Her problems were thus displaced onto and solved through the pīr.

The pīr also became the vehicle of the solution of her conflicts. Practically, the bed could not be placed where she had originally intended, thus making less space available to the girls in an already very small house. More fundamentally, the pīr became an identifiable, nameable cause of an otherwise unacceptable subjective experience that she could not acknowledge or signify. She could deal with her anxiety in part by performing the proper ritual actions in relationship to him. The pīr also restored the woman's central role in the family, which she felt she had lost when her cousins arrived. She had a special, direct relationship with the pīr, as she hoped to have with her husband. The pīr became a shared symbol, and hence a focus of religious devotion, when the husband and son recognized his presence, but the woman continued to maintain her special relationship with him. The pīr is still the vehicle that enables her to transcend the tensions in her life: "Whenever I desire anything in my heart, it is fulfilled."

Though this pīr is clearly important for her, so important that she will not move to a bigger house, she does reveal quite a bit of ambivalence and uncertainty in her beliefs. Some of the ambivalence was probably a function of the context in which she narrated the story: she did not want to appear ignorant and superstitious when talking to me, the anthropologist, and to Aisha, whom she perceived as "modern" in outlook. Thus, she denied that she believes in bad taʿwīz now, knowing that black magic is scorned by many, and at another point in the conversation she asserted that she did not believe in taʿwīz of any kind.

This position was reflected in her assertion that the living pīr who told her about the dead pīr in her house was a liar. She also suggested his doubtful reputation by mentioning that he demanded a fixed rate for his services. The true pīr does not charge money of his visitors. Instead visitors offer him voluntary offerings. The scandalous reputation of the pīr whom she had consulted was well known, and she stresses her sophistication by acknowledging this, yet she did not want to question the validity of his help in her particular situation. She had actually experienced a cure from him. She dealt with this situation by citing other evidence of the existence of her dead pīr: her husband, son, and neighbors believe in him. Her uncle, a pious and learned man, also made contact with the dead pīr and pronounced him "an impressive personality."

In another effort at dealing with her doubt or the possible skepticism of her audience, she used another, somewhat inconsistent strategy to account for her cure. At one point she broadened the locus of her emotional support to pīrs in general. She said, "I don't know if it is because of this pīr, or Data Sahib, or anyone else." Once she has experienced the transcendence of her daily life with one particular pīr, the generalized idea of the pīr is perhaps a sufficient vehicle for her religious devotion, though she doesn't appear to really test this possibility.

Ilmaz's private pīr is a signifier of the speaking subject, that which has not been captured by a discursively constituted subject position. This signifier bears a metonymical relationship to the subject, a relationship expressed by its lack of name or identity in the public sphere. It is marked only by a place, the corner of the dining room, the site of the conflict that could not be kept out of sight. But this unnameable subject has been labeled a pīr and, hence, located vis-à-vis a discourse of Islam and of modernity. This pīr is for her a stand-in for the unnameable, as the nation or progress is a stand-in for the diverse interests and concerns of a population in the discourse of modern nationalism. In religious ideology, the pīr often functions as this unnameable flux of desire and fear. Ilmaz located her conflict in a broader social order, in relationship to discourses being played out at the national level. The issue of "nation" is located not elsewhere, in a distant capital such as Islamabad, but in her very home and body. Her home is government housing. The government has inserted itself between herself and her pīr, her subjectivity: the house covers his grave. The walls and floor of her house constitute her as a subject. She takes her identity from the number on her house, not from the zāt of her ancestors; it interpellates her in the symbolic order of the nation-state.

The dead pīr irrupts into this measured, ordered government space. The symptoms express her truth. Her anxiety is bound through the symbol of the saint — but this saint is part of a different discourse.

Zahida and Data Ganj Bakhsh

Zahida, too, lives with inconsistencies in her practices concerning pīrs — a phenomenon that she maintains a well-articulated ideological position against. Traditional practice — fending off jādū (black magic) and taunā (scapegoating) with the help of pīrs and their amulets — plays the role of temptation in Zahida's stories, as we saw in the story of the sparrow's blood. In many of her stories, Zahida tells of a life filled with trials and distress. During the times of trial, the neighborhood pīr offers the false promise of relief, always at the urging of a misguided neighbor. In contrast, asserting that there are no intermediaries between God and humans puts her on her own, in a relationship with a seemingly distant and inaccessible other. The neighborhood pīr is much closer.

Though Zahida not only denied the possibility of magic and taunā but vehemently accused pīrs of being fraudulent, she openly admitted to having succumbed to temptation and visited several pīrs during a time of extreme distress. She described how during a difficult time in her life, when she was plagued by chronic illness, a neighbor who had been very kind to her convinced her to accompany her on a visit to a pīr:

> She brought me, but when I got there, I saw a shopkeeper. It was a store full of things for doing "fraud" [she used the English word]. People use them in some way. We people don't believe in this kind of thing, but I was so sick that I went.
>
> After I watched him for a while, I was very angry. The pīr became angry with me. I do not believe in that sort of thing at all. My belief is in God. I can see the world, how people become pīrs. There is no one bigger than God. "So look," I said to my neighbor, "You have taken me there? You showed me what nonsense this one did." It is all a lie.

In this account, as in the story of the sparrows, Zahida demonstrated that, despite a moment of temptation, when she succumbed to her neighbor's influence, she was able to maintain her devotion to God as a proper Muslim. In terms of her reformist understanding, this was another story that demonstrated her ability to maintain her reason in the face of trial and temptation.

Zahida not only told me about the anger that accompanied her moral condemnation of the fraudulent activities; she also reenacted the anger in her facial expression and tone of voice while reliving the scene. The feeling of anger reinforced her ideological position, and she obviously felt pleasure at reporting her outrage. Her anger was an assertion of power and control. She, in turn angered the pīr, whose credibility she sought to undermine, and she insulted her neighbor. Her aggressive assertion of identity as a proper Muslim was in response to the possibility of being assigned the identity of a woman who visits pīrs.

But her story did not end there. She told me how shortly after her visit to the fraudulent pīr, her husband was transferred to another city. Zahida remained behind because of her children's schooling, a common phenomenon in the main cities of Pakistan. Several of her children were still quite small, and she found the stress of managing the household on her own intolerable. A close friend, seeing her distress, urged her to accompany her to the shrine of Data Ganj Bakhsh. As she narrated the incident to me, she asserted that she still doesn't "believe in this thing." Her friend had convinced her that they would simply go to pray and come right back home:

> She took me to Data Sahib by force. OK. We went and she prayed. For me, for us. And I didn't offer any prayers. I just said the *fatiha* [the opening chapter of the Quran], just as one would do when visiting the tomb of any *buzurg* [elder]. Two tears fell, my tears. Then I just returned home.
>
> It was done by God. My husband submitted an application, to be sent to Lahore. Then it was granted. I—we were amazed. How could such an order have happened? I told my husband to take five rupees to Data Sahib's shrine, because my friend had told me to do that when my prayers were answered. I told many people about this thing, about Data Sahib.

She then described how, when her son fell seriously ill, she prayed, "Give him health from this illness, dear God. Then I will cook a *deg* [a very large pot of rice] and send it to Data Sahib." When her prayers were answered, she went to the shrine and fulfilled her promise.

The point is that many people say about Data Sahib, "We go there and do *pūjā* [Hindu prayer, i.e., worship of the saint]." Now to us he is only a buzurg. He is a buzurg if you go there and offer *du'ā* [Muslim prayer]. Just as now if we want to do any task — for example, I want to have you do some task. You know how to do it, this task of mine. You have this much "power." You don't heed my words. So I say to your daughter, "Julia. Daughter, tell your Mama to please do this task for me." [My own daughter, then age two, was with me.] In just this way I have thought about elders such as Data Sahib. Nothing more. People go and do pūjā at shrines. It is my opinion that if there are any people who are near God, it is those who have loved God very much. They have actually done this. So we can go to them to say fātiha and offer prayers, or we ask him to be our speaker, saying, "Please intercede for us."

So, there are many pīrs who sit in this neighborhood. I have heard of many and I saw them when I was so ill, too. And you have, too, I think. I have taken an amulet, too. Almost everyone does this. So we take all this to be wrong. But the things I have seen have been proven to me. I know them.

Zahida's stories are organized in terms of an ideology of modernist Islamic reform, in which an array of signifiers drawn from various sources have been "fixed" in specific relationships. Practices also constitute signifiers. The signifier "idolatry" (shirk) has a central place in the Quran and has been an important tool in the mobilization of Muslim community around specific practices. A central component of Zahida's ideological stance is her linking of the signifier "shirk" to the practice of visiting pīrs. Though she does not actually use the word in the above story, the signifier organizes much of what she said. In the second story, it lies behind the statement "There is no one bigger than God." In her story of Data Sahib, the signifier "shirk" is invoked through another signifier, "pūjā." Pūjā is the Hindu practice of praying before the image of a deity and is for the South Asian Muslim a signifier par excellence of idolatry. Zahida's discourse has thus linked the act of visiting a pīr with Hindu practice. Hindus are the enemy, the hated other. Avoiding idolatry is a central component of the discipline of being a proper Muslim, and worshiping pīrs is idolatry. The practices of the living pīr she visited are thus linked with the signifier "idolatry" in the structure of her ideological stance.

In the story of her visit to Data Sahib, Zahida expressed contrary positions simultaneously and attempted to resolve them. She still maintained the position that it is wrong to pray at shrines, an attitude that she was taught early in childhood. But her experience has forced her to adopt the position that it is proper to visit the shrines of certain highly respected saints, if one is careful not to pray to the saint as an independent agent who will grant one's request without God's help (what she called "doing pūjā"). In her formulation, she partially justified visiting the shrine by equating the visit with the kind of visit one would pay to the grave of one's own parents or other deceased elders.

Other members of the family had also visited the shrine of Data Sahib, but felt considerable conflict about doing so. When one of the daughters went to visit the shrine, I was told by another family member that she had gone to visit relatives. Someone else in the family told me privately that she had actually gone to the shrine. It was clear that visits to the shrine were not to be publicly acknowledged. Aisha, telling me about her own visits to the same shrine, emphasized that her mother does not believe in it: "She feels bad when I go, but she doesn't stop me." She carefully described the limits of her own belief: "I don't believe that his body is still there. It is a pious place because different pious people come there for prayers. We can see the sign that once a pious body was buried there. That's all. Otherwise his soul is in the house of God. It is a peaceful place."

In this family, a discrepancy has developed between their public attitude of rejection of pīrs as fraudulent and their carefully circumscribed relationship with one particular shrine. Intense ambivalence about visiting even this shrine creates complexities and discrepancies in the family's account of itself, and perhaps even in the communication process within the family. Adding to the complexity are the "political" implications of their ambivalence within the neighborhood and among those who share their reformist orientation. Family members have taken a certain stance on issues such as taunā and pīrs, which are important during the maintenance of identity, especially in interactions with neighbors. Even if Zahida and Aisha, as well as other family members, had been able to work out an entirely satisfactory position on the issue of visiting the shrine of Data Sahib, they were still concerned that their activities could be misinterpreted by others and used against them.

In her narratives about visiting the shrine of Data Sahib, Zahida struggled to resolve the tension between her modern, reformist identity, for which being a proper Muslim means avoiding shrines, with practices that are inconsistent with that position. Her experiences with Data Sahib contradicted her modernist view of reality. Yet she never tried to explain away the miracles brought about by Data Sahib, as she did with respect to the blood on the dish. This is because her image of the saint is of a powerfully significant other whose presence she has experienced in ways that defy explanation within the framework of a modern reformist ideology. Through the work of narrative, she seeks to protect only one pīr, Data Sahib, from the accusation of fraud. She is supported in this by his prominent role in state ideologies of national identity.

Conclusion

Many Pakistani Muslims display a self-consciousness about their identities as Muslims, which is manifested in the carefulness with which they articulate their ideas of what constitutes "proper" behavior as a Muslim. Much of this self-consciousness has been fostered by the relentless critique of traditional Islamic practices preached by adherents of the Islamic reform movements that have swept across South Asia. The Pakistanis whom I have presented here subscribe to rather diverse views concerning the limits of proper Muslim behavior and are quite articulate about their respective stances. Furthermore, for each of them there is much at stake beyond the consistency or correctness of their beliefs. Taking a particular ideological stance also means asserting one's social and even political position vis-à-vis one's neighbors and the wider society. The neighborhood pīr had a stake in maintaining a following that sought what had been branded traditionally based treatments, but he also felt a need to identify with a form of Sufism that follows prevailing interpretations of Islamic law (sharī'at). For Zahida's reform-oriented family, their position was closely linked with their negotiations of status in what they saw as a basically traditional neighborhood. Yet even these people, who were so self-conscious about their basic orientation and could draw upon the models provided by prominent religious leaders and politicians for articulating their positions, could not be contained by these subject positions.

Ideologically systematized reform movements have striven to make

Islam unambiguous. They stress that there may be no mediators between God and humans, and that all appeals for help must be made
directly to God through prayer. By redefining the limits of proper Islam,
reformists have severely narrowed the range of acceptable practice and
belief. Such an unambiguous stance is difficult for many Muslims to
maintain. New cultural forms are continually being generated in an
effort to integrate at least the most blatant inconsistencies. But even in
the absence of new cultural forms that serve as effective syntheses,
individuals have a remarkable capacity to cope with radical contradictions, in part by keeping only one frame of reference in mind at any
particular moment. As a result of such strategies, even those individuals
whose Islam appears to be fully objectified, expressible in systematic
ideology, also live other discourses — not repressed but contextually
delimited.

Fanon (1968) and Nandy (1983) characterized a split in the subject
induced by colonialism as creating a public side and a secret "traditional" side. Zahida, Aisha, and Ilmaz would seem to reflect the position of the postcolonial subject that is split between "two contradictory
beliefs, one official and one secret, one archaic and one progressive"
(Bhabha 1986a:168). This split is embodied in Ilmaz's dining room: the
official table and chairs, English-style, that mark her as modern, and
the secret shrine for a nameless pīr, hidden behind a curtain. But this
public-private dichotomy is misleading. It is more useful to think of
different discursive spaces, defined largely by whom the speaker imagines his or her interlocutor to be. It is more accurate to say that there are
different audiences, different discourses: Ilmaz communicates the existence of this saint in certain situations, and other ritual associated with
the shrine is, to a limited extent, public.

The experience of splits, of discrepant ways of talking about the
social world, is not limited to the postcolonial subject. A similar split
can be seen in situations in which the structure of difference cannot be
characterized in terms of "modernity" and "tradition." It appears, for
instance, in Bedouin women's poetry (Abu-Lughod 1986) and in the
songs that women in South Asia sing at the time of marriage, songs that
are a subversive mix of celebration and protest (Raheja and Gold
1994). Analyses of the content of these forms of poetry make it clear
that the legitimacy of male dominance is hegemonic only in the sense
that it shapes what people say and do in public spaces. In the carefully
delimited contexts where the poetry is recited or sung, women express a

very different set of ideas that are critical of their positioning with regard to men. These phenomena suggest that this split is not simply a product of recent historical circumstances. Closer scrutiny of the vicissitudes of the subject as the individual negotiates shifting subject positions and contexts will show that such splits occur whenever the subject enters into a social order and are particularly salient in a relationship of domination and subordination.

5

A *Pīr*'s Life Story

I began this book with a brief description of my first encounter with a Sufi pīr, Sufi Ghulam Rasul (Sufi Sahib). This encounter shaped the direction of my subsequent research, primarily because of its ambiguity. Because the neighborhood pīr has been a target of ideological strug-gle — a focus of intense devotion and bitter attacks — a pīr such as Sufi Sahib is a particularly fruitful locus for examining the relationship be-tween a discursively constituted subject and the complex nexus of meaning and motives embodied within the individual. In Sufi Sahib, I was confronted with a man whom I never felt that I knew, in the sense that I never felt that I could accurately describe his motives, goals, sig-nificance to others, and power. My categories, which were borrowed from the Pakistanis I knew and divided the world into "traditional" pīrs and "real" Sufis, did not adequately capture him. Nor did the stories and reactions of his associates, neighbors, followers, or enemies. In this chapter, I turn my attention to this ambiguity and its significance.

We can consider ideology to be a structure of signs that rests on metaphorical relationships: for example, the pīr is nothing but a "busi-nessman," Sufi Sahib *is* a khalīfa (spiritual successor) of Miān Sher Muhammad, who is his *murshid* (teacher). The subject is thereby iden-tified or fixed by these metaphors. Competing ideologies organize their metaphors, their identifications, differently: the pīr is a "friend of God," all pīrs are frauds. The individual's ego is a set of self-representations or identities based on such identifications. The subject thereby attempts to adopt a position within a metaphorical structure of signs. In the process the subject also negates other representations: In asserting "I am *not* a fraud," the pīr thereby takes up a subject-position vis-à-vis the negated proposition. But an identity based on metaphor is static — it is a subject *position* vis-à-vis a fixed set of signs. Narratives, in contrast, are capable of representing the movement of the subject — its failure to fully occupy an "identity." They are a basic way in which the person not only claims a specific identity and expresses an ideology that may be contested by others but also moves among identities and seeks to shape the relationships among them. Most narratives weave together multiple voices, so that there is a slippage in the positioning of the subject within the narrative.[1] In the process of narration, the speaker may also weave competing ideologies together within the narrative structure. Successfully doing this is often a source of power.

Sufi Sahib, like all of us, presented himself through narratives. Through his narratives, which *were* powerful, he negotiated, for a re-markably varied audience, these competing ideologies about the pīr and located himself within this contest as an individual with a unique history. By focusing on his narratives and the reactions to them, I articulate this process of negotiation and its power. I identify the ideological positionings of the subject, but my focus is on the moments of slippage, the points of ambiguity, where the subject cannot be identified with a single subject position.

Usually life histories are presented in a narrative sequence — either a sequence constructed by the narrator or by the author of the written text. But ethnographic texts intended to give voice to the informant are caught in an unresolvable bind, obscuring how the oral narrative is an outcome of the encounter itself, taking shape in the space between speaker and interlocutor. The textual re-creation of a narrative se-quence obscures precisely the ambiguities and fluidity of the encounter that I intend to focus on, reifying the subject in a fixed identity.[2]

In *The Interpretation of Dreams* (1955a), Freud developed an alternative strategy for interpreting a narrative. Virtually ignoring the dream's narrative sequence, he focused instead on another kind of se-quencing: the dreamer's chains of free associations to the various images in the dream. With this technique, Freud was able to present the dream subject's multivocal fluidity, its conflictual presence/absence within the manifest content of the dream narrative. Given that I, too, am trying to point to and highlight a subject that is not encompassed

and captured by my discourse, I have chosen to follow approximately
Freud's strategy. Though I don't, strictly speaking, have free associations to work with, I follow Freud in focusing on the images and their
ambiguities, on the disjunctions between narratives, on my own confu-
sions as a series of narratives were constructed between Sufi Sahib and
myself. Like the psychoanalyst seeking to make sense of an analysand's
fractured narrative, I focus on those aspects of our conversations that
left me pondering.

Freud recognized that dreams have images that prove to be nodal
points, from which meanings radiate out in all directions. Narratives,
when subjected to interpretation, often seem to have similar nodal
points. As I ponder the records of my first encounter with Sufi Sahib, I
find my reflections organized by a word that seemed to operate as a
nodal point for Sufi Sahib, drawing me into a complicated and conflictual web of meanings that conflated the categories through which I
sought to understand him. The word is *mu'akkal*.

In our first meeting, which was an unplanned surprise for both of us,
I asked Sufi Sahib, "How did you become a pīr?" After tending to the
needs of his followers for several minutes, he replied:

> *Pīri* is nothing. There is just permission from God. I had a strong
> desire to know how man and other creatures came to exist. . . . I
> was fond of prophets. I wanted to know the method of seeing
> them. I made a connection with an elder, Miān Sher Muhammad,
> who was a saint. I did *bai'at* [an oath of allegiance] with him.
> According to the Sufi way, he looked after me. He told me certain
> methods. I started to perform these *'amal* [actions], as he had told
> me to do. I acquired a mu'akkal, which is now present in me.

I had never heard the word "mu'akkal" before, nor had Yasmin, the
young Pakistani woman accompanying me. From the context it seemed
to be some kind of spiritual entity. My Urdu-English dictionary, which I
consulted that evening, defined *muwakkil*, "(vulg. *mu'akkal*)," as one
to whom power is delegated, deputy, viceregent, substitute (Platts
1967:1092), but with no mention of the use of the word in a spiritual
context. I wondered whether Sufi Sahib was talking about some kind of
possession experience. Or was the mu'akkal simply a spiritual force, an
aspect of his teacher, or of God directly?

During our second meeting, Sufi Sahib discussed mu'akkals more extensively, in response to Yasmin's direct question, "What are mu'ak-

kals?" There are serious ambiguities at crucial points in the translations we made of the tape recordings of that second session, points at which Yasmin, a native speaker who grew up in Sufi Sahib's neighborhood, seems to have misunderstood or failed to recognize common Urdu/ Punjabi words that I can now identify readily (with the benefit of hindsight). Only as I studied the records of this conversation did I realize how confused we had been about Sufi Sahib's use of the word "mu'akkal."

It could be argued that my own confusion can be unproblematically accounted for — I was simply unfamiliar with the subtleties of the language and was trying to learn about Sufism as if inscribing on a blank slate whatever I heard and saw. But I am led into a network of significances by asking why Yasmin was so confused by the word "mu'akkal" and failed to comprehend the common words that Sufi Sahib used to describe mu'akkals. How could she have misunderstood?

Oversimply put, she was interpreting Sufi Sahib's utterances through a grid of antipīr stereotypes that created certain expectations about how Sufi Sahib would present himself. Yasmin and Sufi Sahib held different beliefs, components of competing ideologies striving for political and social hegemony: Yasmin's orientation led her to misinterpret systematically several of Sufi Sahib's utterances, as I will demonstrate. But the vortex of competing meanings does not simply lie in the space between Sufi Sahib and Yasmin: my presence and what I represented added additional significances to Sufi Sahib's utterances, as did the presence of Sufi Sahib's followers and other visitors. Beyond that, multiple vortices of significance can be identified within each of us. My confusion arose out of my effort at the time to map onto an organized conceptual grid a string of utterances enshrouded in ambiguities. Alternative interpretations constituted divergent realities. I had fallen unawares into the midst of the multiple competing ideologies about the legitimacy of pīrs.

Sufi Sahib lived simultaneously in a world of local neighborhood politics and in nationally based Sufi and political networks, where his alignments required a different accounting of himself. The mu'akkal as a sign rests at a node where multiple inconsistent strands of Sufi Sahib's life met in uneasy juxtaposition. Like Freud's dream symbols, the mu'akkal simultaneously hides and reveals the tensions embedded in Sufi Sahib's narratives. Sufi Sahib's mu'akkal retains the traces of his past: adolescent rebellion, attempts to acquire status and money, the roots of an identity as a member of the Arain agricultural caste, his political maneuvering at the kinship and neighborhood level, his concern for the expectations of followers of diverse backgrounds and beliefs, his engagement in Pakistani political discourse, the moral and practical constraints of being a pīr, and the Sufi tradition with its literary models for the life of a saint. But, because of its ideological and political ramifications, the mu'akkal as a sign has been an uneasy vehicle at best for the resolution of conflicts that arose as he built a life and took a stance. By unpacking the layers of significance and specifying the array of interlocutors addressed whenever Sufi Sahib called upon this image, we can see how identity is constituted out of narrative—how the narrative quilts together the elusive desiring subject and the reifications out of which identities or self-representations are constructed, the nexus of meanings that constitute the ego within multiple discourses.

The brief, unplanned personal narrative Sufi Sahib told me at our first meeting included all of what he considered the essential elements of his identity as a pīr. This was the skeleton or condensation of his life story, encapsulated in a set of central signs that a stranger could make sense of, but only by reading into the narrative a wide range of background knowledge, that is, by fitting the account into certain commonsense interpretations and shared cultural understandings. I thought I had a coherent picture, but as the details were filled in over the subsequent three months of meetings with him, I had to reinterpret radically many of the elements of the story. In fact, I never did pin down all of what would constitute the facts, or even essential elements of Sufi Sahib's identity in the eyes of others.

I will now unpack ambiguities encoded in these apparently coherent narratives. Based on what I learned in my subsequent interactions with him and with others who knew him, I will point to (but fail to capture) the multiple voices with which he spoke, the complexities of his subject positioning, and the elusiveness of his subjectivity.

The Mu'akkals

As Sufi Sahib's narrative continued on that first day, he described how he became a pīr, a successor to Miān Sher Muhammad. The story continued:

> I acquired a mu'akkal, which is now present in me. I began ascetic exercises [*riyāzat*], which one does over and over for many hours.

While doing these practices over and over, I cried in the wilderness, and then I got a "law degree": I am the lawyer; God is the judge. Then God ordered me, "Pray for the people I send to you." My spirit is working. God accepts my every prayer.

By performing ascetic exercises (which he called both ʿamal and riyāzat) prescribed by his pīr, he acquired something, which he described first as a "muʾakkal" and subsequently as a "law degree," perhaps restating his point in different terms to be sure I understood what he was talking about. Or was he saying that he did two different things, "ʿamal" and "riyāzat," and acquired two distinct things? Clearly, the signs "muʾakkal" and "law degree" have different referents. "Law degree" is obviously a metaphor; muʾakkal was probably not intended to be.

Sufi Sahib used the image "law degree" knowing that it would be readily comprehensible to me, that it articulated an aspect of our relationship. Since I was at the time pursuing a doctorate, Sufi Sahib's use of this image suggests that he was establishing our relationship on common ground: I was not yet a Ph.D., and he already had his "law degree." The image also evoked issues of our encounter in a postcolonial environment, where the power and authority of the Sufi pīr has been shaped in part by the competing power and authority of those with credentials from an educational system created by the British in a context of colonial domination. These are pragmatic components of the sign, contextual meanings based on his usage in this dialogue.

Clarifying the significance of the term "muʾakkal" is more difficult. Sufi Sahib's claim to have performed certain actions (ʿamal) to acquire a muʾakkal coincides well with the prescriptions contained in popular manuals of Sufi practice. Instructions for such practice are readily available in Urdu to anyone who is literate. In the book bazaar in Lahore, for instance, I found books such as *Ta ʿwizat-o-ʿAmaliyat Sufiyya* (Sufi Amulets and Spells), translated from Arabic into Urdu (ʿAziz al-Rahman n.d.[a]). Such popular books are based on a system of practice laid out in earlier works, especially the book *Jawāhir-i Khamsa* (The Five Jewels), the work of a sixteenth-century Gujarati, Muhammad Ghaus Gwaliori (d. 1562), the main representative of the Shattāriyya Sufi order (see Schimmel 1975:355), which is also available in Urdu. The *Jawāhir-i Khamsa* presents a table that links each of the twenty-eight letters of the Arabic alphabet with an attribute of God. Both a jinn and a muʾakkal (which the English writer Thomas Hughes translated as "guardian angel" in his *Dictionary of Islam*) are identified with each letter of the alphabet.[3] Another Indian Muslim source describes these mu'akkals as being like low-status angels (Nizam-ud-Din 1914:267).

As I interpreted him, Sufi Sahib had told me that he had learned how to perform the type of rituals ('amal) that can be found in popular texts and that, he claimed, Miān Sher Muhammad had taught him.

At this point, then, it appears that Sufi Sahib meant the same thing by "mu'akkal" and "law degree." A mu'akkal associated with *nūri 'ilm* ("luminous knowledge") is an angel that is somehow linked to one of God's attributes.[4] By drawing on the power of this mu'akkal, Sufi Sahib was drawing on God himself.

There is some ambiguity in all this, however,[5] ambiguity that became evident in our second meeting two days later. When, in our second meeting, Yasmin asked directly, "What is a mu'akkal?" Sufi Sahib launched into a monologue that lasted well over thirty minutes. Though his narration at first clarified what he had been talking about earlier, both Yasmin and I eventually became confused. This occurred at the point when he stated that his pīr Miān Sher Muhammad had forbidden him to call on mu'akkals because it was against sharī'at. His response to the initial question "What is a mu'akkal" was rather indirect: in a rhetorical style often used by Pakistani Muslims, he began his answer with a story taken from the Quran, the creation of Adam. In the story he described the origins of the relationship among humans, angels, and jinn. He thereby provided a kind of conceptual map, locating mu'akkals within a system of signs. Sufi Sahib's story established the reality of such phenomena by drawing on the absolute source of authority, the Quran. His account is thus reminiscent of the *Jawāhir-i Khamsa*.

Sufi Sahib then turned without interruption to his personal involvement with mu'akkals:

> When I grew up I became conscious and I began to wonder where all these things came from. Then I started to search for resources. Some people told me about Quranic verses. Doing spiritual exercises [riyāzat], I put my life in danger, I took no food. I was very enthusiastic about finding these things. In the Quran God mentioned angels of light; it means mu'akkals. I have seen those mu'akkals. I can get work from those mu'akkals. There is nūri 'ilm [luminous knowledge], and the mu'akkals of this are angels. There is another, *kālā 'ilm* [black knowledge], whose mu'akkals are jinn.

So God said that jinn-mu'akkals are your inferior. I have done some "research," but *I didn't do any 'amal* [emphasis mine; this contradicts what he told me at our first meeting], because I knew that when I can practice nūri 'ilm, there is no need of kālā 'ilm. Angels are superior to jinn. . . . By this means, I used to know things before people told me about them. I used to tell people what they want, what they have. I reached my goal.

Most people who accept the legitimacy of pīrs would generally agree with Sufi Sahib's division of the knowledge of spiritual things into nūri 'ilm and kālā 'ilm (see Ewing 1982). Angels, jinn, and humans are all created beings possessed of intelligence. Angels are created of light, jinn of smokeless fire, and humans of clay.⁶ According to Sufi Sahib, "mu'akkal" is a term that encompasses both angels and jinn.⁷ In this context "'ilm" means a set of techniques and formulas which, when used properly, draw upon specific spiritual beings or forces and bring them under the control of the practitioner. Nūri 'ilm is based on verses of the Quran and draws upon the power of the names of God and their associated spirits or deputies (mu'akkal). Kālā 'ilm, in contrast, draws upon Satan, Hindu deities, the jinn, ghosts, in other words, any spiritual being other than those directly under God's control. It is on this basis that pīrs are distinguished from magicians (*jādūgar*). Pīrs approach the ideal of the "perfect man" who is close to God; they draw only upon his power. This power must somehow include angels, but not jinn. Magicians, on the other hand, are wicked idolators who draw on sources of power other than God, including jinn. Sufi Sahib had aligned himself on the side of nūri 'ilm.

He did not, however, mention his Sufi teacher Miān Sher Muhammad as the source of his knowledge about mu'akkals this time, in contrast to his statements during our first meeting. Instead, he vaguely alluded to "some people," who had told him about Quranic verses. He had also done "some research" on these topics, especially with respect to black magic. By research he probably meant that he read some books on the subject, like those I had found in the book bazaar.

Having drawn these conclusions as I listened, I became confused, unsure of what I was hearing, as Sufi Sahib continued his answer to Yasmin's question about mu'akkals. I will indicate the points of confusion in the translation:

Now you would ask, "What is *'ishq* [passionate love], what is *tasawwur* [visualization]?"⁸ [Needless to say, it would never have occurred to me to ask this question at this point — it was quite a leap as far as I was concerned. But " 'ishq" and "tassawur" are basic Sufi terms.] I began to find that I needed more resources. I started to perform service for auliyā [saints] and buzurg [elders]. They told me to do riyāzat. They told me the Quranic verses and tarīqat [the Sufi path]. Then at last I received a visualization. Who did I make a connection with? Miān Sher Muhammad; he came in my visualization. He wasn't present here, but while I was sitting, I began to receive his orders. Spiritually, I heard. After that, there was nothing in the world I couldn't see. I also had the visualization of the Prophet, after that of my murshid. I drowned in this visualization. I forgot all spectacles, worldly games, and visualization of mu'akkals [tassawur mu'akkal ka].

Here the translation I worked out with my research assistant is, I now think, wrong. What we worked out was: "I forgot all spectacles, and worldly games, and what was left was the visualization of the mu'akkal [tassawur tha mu'akkal ka]," the opposite of my present interpretation.

I am talking with you while my soul is working with the original soul. In my visualization is my murshid. Through my murshid, I can see your face. . . . Whenever I wished, I saw my God. Then I knew that I had received that lawyer's certificate. Now I can present that certificate. My murshid gave me orders, saying, "You don't have to go anywhere. Keep sitting, keep uttering Allāh ka zikr [God's name]. Present any person who comes to you in the house of God." This was the order of my murshid. He presented me this salt, for illness, financial problems, frustration, for any kind of person. Whoever has problems of the heart, spiritual problems, I give this water, to stop the confusion of the heart. He gave me a reward.

My murshid followed all the principles of Islam according to sharī'at. So I do as my murshid did. Maybe sometimes I can't do as he used to do, but I try. So when I began to hear from people that they had recovered because of the water or salt I had given them, it meant that it had started to work. With the order of God, I can remove any trouble you come with. I had gotten the mu'akkal with nūri 'ilm. If we have good practices, then its angel would be nūri mu'akkal. But my murshid, because he used to follow all the orders of sharī'at, stopped me from telling people about nari [fiery, hellish] mu'akkals.

"Nari" is what Yasmin heard on the tape. This is plausible in the context as she interpreted it, but, given what follows, it is more likely that he said "nūri" (light), which would not have made sense in terms of our understanding at the time. By now we were becoming hopelessly confused as we worked to translate from the tape recording.

> My murshid said, "If you tell people about nūri [nari?] mu'akkals, this is against the sharī'at. Give it up." Twelve years ago mu'akkals used to work for me, give me massages, everything I asked, but my murshid stopped me. He said, "You are comparing mu'akkals and God, and this is against sharī'at." At that time I had such power that I could call them again and again, but this was against the orders of my murshid. Mu'akkals are jinn, mu'akkals are angels. After doing riyāzat, these mu'akkals are all *ma taht* [inferior].

Yasmin did not recognize "ma taht" at all in this context, probably because she misunderstood what he was trying to tell us.

> These mu'akkals can recognize the person who does riyāzat.
> After that there is 'ishq [passionate love], which was like a sea, and I jumped into that sea of 'ishq. There was a storm, problems everywhere. My resource was Miān Sher Muhammad. He held me, and I went under water. Under that water was the whole of creation. My murshid said, "You just watch. You can't tell people. If you tell, you will be punished, as people were punished before."

Though, according to Yasmin, he said that his murshid stopped him from talking about "fiery" mu'akkals, he also said that mu'akkals used to work for him twelve years ago, but that now they don't. In light of Sufi Sahib's statement, that he studied about kālā 'ilm but never practiced it, it could be concluded that the practice he gave up was that of nūri 'ilm, if we assume that his various statements all hang together. Does this make any sense to suggest that Sufi Sahib gave up nūri 'ilm? Isn't nūri 'ilm what I had seen him practicing when he licked salt and blew some Quranic verses on it? Isn't this what pīrs do?

Sufi Sahib made the status of mu'akkals clearer in his next utterance:

> I know what you want. [My thought: What could I want? To bring mu'akkals under my control?] Indirectly I will tell you because I can't break the order of my murshid. So when a person does riyāzat, 'amal, then jinn become subservient to man. The

mu'akkal is limited power. This is just a resource which is very low in God's affection. Mu'akkals can make mistakes, but the *rūh* [spirit] cannot make mistakes.

As I go over the stories of other men who mentioned mu'akkals, a similar ambivalence about mu'akkals seems to be the prevailing message. Such ambivalence is evident, for example, in Jaffur Shurreef's *Qanoon-e-Islam*, a detailed account of the local practices of Deccani (South Indian) Muslims written in 1832 by a Deccani Muslim who was employed by the British as a teacher of Urdu (Shurreef 1973). Why the apparent ambivalence about mu'akkals?

Here is a moment where the mu'akkal is operating as a nodal point at which competing discourses intersect. The mu'akkal takes on an opposite valance within each discourse. In our first meeting, Sufi Sahib was operating within one discursive frame. In our second meeting, he took up quite a different subject position and was operating within a different discursive frame. By highlighting the mu'akkal in our questions during the second meeting, Yasmin and I had unintentionally (though perhaps Yasmin knew perfectly well what she was doing) highlighted a slippage that Sufi Sahib himself sought to obscure.

A Shift of Audience, a Shift in Subject Position

Though I have described the general context in which Sufi Sahib told me about mu'akkals, I have neglected to specify what is perhaps the most important component of any social context: precisely who else was present and listening. Something had shifted from one meeting to the next. Yasmin and I were not Sufi Sahib's sole interlocutors. He was also speaking to and for his followers and other visitors. Our conversations about mu'akkals took place over two days. It was during our first meeting that he said, "I acquired a mu'akkal, which is now present in me." Yasmin and I had not been expected; the other people present were an everyday sort of clientele. Our second meeting, two days later, was prearranged. It is probably not by coincidence (though I could not figure out a way to ask politely) that several of Sufi Sahib's socially important followers were also present. We were served an elaborate lunch, for which these "important" followers also stayed (after several of his other followers had left). Furthermore, I had, with Sufi Sahib's permission, brought a tape recorder, which was running when he talked of mu'akkals.

This was obviously a very different social context from that of our first meeting. With the tape recorder on, one would expect Sufi Sahib to be more circumspect in his answers. (Yasmin, in fact commented on how careful he had been as she listened to a section of the tape.) The followers present, who were all men, were a highly educated group and included a brigadier general, professionals, businessmen, and a young man who had just returned from his university studies in England. Their understandings of Islam tended to be rather different from those of the people, mostly women, who had come to request salt and a blessing. These men accepted the legitimacy of Sufi pīrs, but they rejected many of the beliefs and practices associated with popular Islam. Theirs was essentially a reformist stance that reflected the developments in South Asian Muslim thought since the late nineteenth century.

Sufi Sahib's discussion of mu'akkals on this second day reflected a version of Islam characteristic of reformist Sufis, such as the 'ulamā trained at Deoband (see Metcalf 1982). The reformist stance is that there must be no intermediaries between oneself and God (even unprescribed rituals are condemned as intermediary), and certainly not another being, such as a "mu'akkal."

One of the clearest articulations of this reformist stance against popular custom was that of the nineteenth-century 'ālim (scholar of Islamic law) Maulana Thanawi (1864–1943). Writing during the height of British colonial rule, when Muslim leaders were still reacting to their loss of political control of the subcontinent, Thanawi and other reformers sought to strengthen the foundation Muslim community by reforming individual practice (Metcalf 1990:4). His book *Bihishti Zewar* was written specifically for women, who, he argued, were traditionally uneducated and, consequently, were mired in superstition and the practice of un-Islamic local customs that Thanawi regarded as being against sharī'at. Thanawi's position against unprescribed, unnecessary ritual is clear. He was against setting up a ritually clean space even for a Quranic reading for the dead, a practice very similar to one of the basic components of the rituals necessary to acquire a mu'akkal. "At the least, Thanawi warns, this is an unnecessary elaboration and a distraction from normative observances. At worst, it is intended not to transfer benefit to the dead but to invoke powerful figures, who transform the food, to come to one's aid. It suggests a magical efficacy, alien to normative Islamic rituals. All this is nothing less than *shirk*, the assigning of partners to God" (Metcalf 1990:84).

Nūri 'ilm, if defined as the enlisting of mu'akkals through the ritual use of Quranic verses, letters of the alphabet, and the names of God, is for reformists such as Thanawi a violation of sharī'at. The intentions of the 'āmil (the practitioner), whether for a purpose that helps others or harms them, are irrelevant. The basic issue is shirk. "You have heard about the spiritual power (tasir) in elders. It is this. Do not look for other kinds of power — for example, the power to say something and make it happen; or to remove sickness by breathing on someone; or to make a wish come true by preparing an amulet; or to make someone feel agitated through direction of the pir's attention (tawajjuh) toward that person. Never be deceived by these powers" (Metcalf 1990:200).

But Thanawi does not deny that such powers are real and exist: "Whoever is against the shari'at cannot be a friend of God. If anything amazing appears by the action of such a person, it is either magic or the work of that person's lower soul (nafs) and of Satan. It should be rejected" (Metcalf 1990:70). Thanawi also accepted the existence of angels and jinn. Most importantly (and this is what distinguishes his position from more fundamentalist attitudes as they have been expressed in the twentieth century by leaders such as Maulana Maudoodi), Thanawi accepted the importance and spiritual power of Sufi saints: "Many mysteries are made known to the saints either while they are awake or while they sleep; these are 'openings' (kashf) or 'illuminations' (ilham). Accept them as true if they are in accordance with the shari'at, and reject them if they are against the shari'at" (Metcalf 1990:70). The contrast that Thanawi drew between magic and illuminations, both of which may manifest themselves as otherwise unexplainable displays of spiritual power, is that the magician, through ritual actions, compels the mu'akkal to act according to the magician's wishes. Illuminations, in contrast, come unrequested from God.

This distinction had political implications: women were advised to follow only pīrs who were also 'ulamā, preferably those trained at Deoband. The authority claim in this advice can be tied to the issue of mobilizing the Muslim community in a colonial setting, which was one of Thanawi's central concerns.

Miān Sher Muhammad, whom Sufi Sahib claimed as his spiritual teacher, was also noted for his concern with eliminating folk practices from the practice of Sufis and for his direct political involvement in the shaping of the Muslim community in the late colonial period. Miān Sher Muhammad had close links to the political regime. His sons, who act as his successors, were involved in anti-Bhutto politics in 1976 when I visited the shrine. Sufi Sahib's father, who had actually visited Miān Sher Muhammad and had made the hajj (pilgrimage to Mecca), probably had also taught his family a reform-oriented version of Islam.

With the benefit of hindsight, I can now argue that when Sufi Sahib said that Miān Sher Muhammad had told him to give up mu'akkals, he did not mean "fiery" mu'akkals, that is, jinn, as Yasmin had understood him to say, but rather the angels associated with nūri 'ilm. Going back to my discussion of the law degree and the mu'akkal, as Sufi Sahib had used them in our first conversation, I now offer a reinterpretation. I had concluded that 'amal and riyāzat were merely synonyms in this context, as they are in popular practice. But now I would say no, that these were actually different things. His law degree was, rather, an "illumination" in Thanawi's sense, which is bestowed by God at his pleasure only to a Sufi who carefully adheres to sharī'at as defined by reformists such as the Deobandis (i.e., who follows the "laws"). Receiving such illumination does not depend on actions ('amal) such as setting up a ritually clean space, but on the riyāzat of the Sufi, the ascetic disciplines of meditation and prayer. Sufi Sahib, twelve years earlier, had given up his practices as an adept ('āmil). He gave up control and gave himself up to prayer. He drowned in the sea of 'ishq (love). When he had received illumination, he was told by God to become a pīr, to argue in God's court for the needs of his followers.

This reformist concern with distinguishing 'amal and riyāzat is particularly clear in Sufi Sahib's second account, given in the presence of his important guests. His overriding concern in this context is evident in his statement, "My murshid followed all the orders of the sharī'at." His murshid stopped him from using mu'akkals at all for precisely the reason that Thanawi had also used: "You are comparing mu'akkals and God, and that is against sharī'at."

On the basis of this interpretation, I can construct my own provisional biography of Sufi Sahib, focusing on his stories about mu'akkals: As a young man, Sufi Sahib read several books about acquiring spiritual power by performing certain ritual actions ('amal). These books contained instructions about both kālā 'ilm and nūri 'ilm, and he, therefore, learned about both of them. He was careful to perform only those that he considered lawful, in accordance with the sharī'at. These included only those prescriptions and incantations that involved reciting the names of God or certain verses of the Quran. But the names of God have both a jinn and an angel associated with them. Sufi Sahib invoked and learned to draw upon the power of an angel and avoided unlawful contact with the jinn.

Then twelve years before I met him, Sufi Sahib became dissatisfied with his accomplishments and established a new contact with the Sufi teacher Miān Sher Muhammad, who was reformist in his interpretation of the limits of sharī'at. Miān Sher Muhammad rejected as shirk Sufi Sahib's use of a mu'akkal acquired through nūri 'ilm, saying that Sufi Sahib was comparing the mu'akkal to God. Sufi Sahib, therefore, gave up his previous practices and plunged himself into prayers and meditation that were prescribed by Miān Sher Muhammad. He experienced the love of God directly, received illumination, and became a *walī* (a Sufi term meaning "friend of God"). Because of this closeness to God, his spirit is infused directly with the power and blessing of God, and he has no need of mu'akkals.

So it is possible to come up with a consistent story out of the narratives he gave us during our first two meetings, one that Sufi Sahib would have approved of, I suspect. But this story is no more stable than the original narratives.

Is Sufi Sahib "Really" What He Claims to Be? Divergent Views

Why did Sufi Sahib bring up the rhetorically controversial mu'akkals at all? Why didn't he simply avoid them in his narrative account of himself? One reason he didn't suppress mu'akkals altogether was because these are seen as a legitimate source of power by most of the people whom he sees on a day-to-day basis. These were the people who were present when I first asked Sufi Sahib for an account of himself. Many people knew Sufi Sahib. Though most of his devoted followers, especially the visitors of high social status who had come from other areas to visit him, had known him for only a few years, his neighbors and local followers had known him longer. They had a rather different view of him and were skeptical of his claims. They were also well aware of his activities with mu'akkals.

Sufi Sahib was undoubtedly well aware, at least in a general sense, of what people say about him. In any communication with me, these people were also, implicitly, his interlocutors, since he knew that I could and probably would talk with others about him. Putting together the reactions of various people, then, it is possible to identify several reasons why Sufi Sahib's stories of his life were so ambiguous.

The issue of the truth of Sufi Sahib's stories loomed particularly large in the minds of many of those who have had contact with him. His story was contested on many different grounds. These were people of a wide range of backgrounds, and their reactions to him reflect correspondingly diverse concerns. Their reactions give us a dizzying array of constructions or interpretations of this individual life, structured by various ideologies and transected by the discursive structure of modernity.

At our first meeting, Sufi Sahib had begun conversing with us by saying, "Pīrī is nothing. There is just permission from God." I saw in this comment Sufi Sahib's reaction to the way his wife had introduced us as "students interested in studying pīrs." He was acknowledging that the word "pīr" is often used in a derogatory sense. He was concerned that we would have this sense of "pīr" in mind and might even hold such an attitude ourselves, as obvious representatives of a modernist discourse. His strategy for handling this potential criticism was to agree with us that those pīrs who prey on the masses are corrupt. He thus separated himself from those pīrs and asserted that what is really at issue is not one's following or appearance but one's actual relationship with God.

Sufi Sahib also stressed his adherence to the principles of Islam, distinguishing himself (1) from those pīrs who believe that as Sufis they can ignore Islamic law because of their esoteric practices and pure spiritual state (the disreputable qalandars or malangs) and (2) from those pīrs who exploit their position for worldly gain. Pīrs who fall into each of these categories are typically labeled corrupt or fraudulent by middle-class, urban Pakistanis.

But his effort to distinguish himself from ordinary, corrupt pīrs did not succeed with everyone. As we left his house after that first meeting, Yasmin and I encountered a woman who knew Yasmin. Having observed where we had been, this woman remarked, "Sufi Sahib used to feed my buffalo. He is a fraud." This woman may have been denying his legitimacy on the basis of his caste identity as Arain, an agricultural caste. For some people, only a *sayyid* (a descendant of the Prophet) can be a pīr. But several days later we met this woman's daughter among the women seated before Sufi Sahib.

For some of Sufi Sahib's critics, primarily other Sufis, the central issue was the nature of his initiation into a Sufi order, which is marked by the ceremony of bai'at. Sufi Sahib foregrounded his act of taking bai'at with Miān Sher Muhammad in his conversations with me, yet the issue of bai'at in Sufi Sahib's narratives was nearly as ambiguous and elusive as was the *mu'akkal*. It would be possible to represent Sufi Sahib's life organized in terms of bai'at as a nodal point. In a body of Sufi literature known as *tazkarat,* the history of the Sufi orders is told in terms of the lives of its prominent saints, who are linked through a chain of spiritual succession. Through the ceremony of bai'at the disciple swears allegiance and devotion to the spiritual guide, the pīr. If the follower becomes sufficiently developed spiritually during the course of his training under his pīr, the pīr may at some point designate him to be one of his successors (khalīfas) in another ritual. While hearing his first account of this experience of bai'at, I assumed that Sufi Sahib had gone through the ceremony in the usual ritual way. In his first, brief account of his life, Sufi Sahib had said, "I made a connection with an elder, Miān Sher Muhammad, who was a saint. I did bai'at with him." Given the tazkarat literature as a frame of reference, Sufi Sahib seemed to be saying that, following the Sufi tradition, he had visited the famous teacher and Sufi Miān Sher Muhammad, had undertaken the ceremony of bai'at with him while still a child, had studied intensively under him, and had eventually become one of his designated successors (khalīfa).

It became clearer only in one of our later meetings that he had received this initiation and the khilāfat from Miān Sher Muhammad in a dream. Thus, he had not gone through the turban-tying ceremony by which a pīr typically designates a successor, as I had assumed. I had come to realize only after several meetings with Sufi Sahib that, except for his visit to Miān Sher Muhammad when he was ten years old, all of his meetings with Miān Sher Muhammad had been in dreams and visions. In fact, Miān Sher Muhammad had died when Sufi Sahib was still a child. Sufi Sahib received some of his instruction while praying and sleeping at his shrine. This is a practice characteristic of the Naqshbandī Sufi order, to which Miān Sher Muhammad belonged, but it is a claim to legitimacy that is, not surprisingly, often contested by successors who have gone through a public ritual. In the context of our conversation, he may have immediately surmised that as some kind of scientist I might not have recognized initiation through a dream as an event at all.

Few people, either detractors or followers, questioned his legitimacy on the basis of his relationship to the Naqshbandī Sufi order to which he claimed to belong or on how he had undergone the ritual of bai'at. Not surprisingly, one person who did so was a successor of Miān Sher Muhammad who had been given the khilāfat in a public ceremony. The sons of Miān Sher Muhammad, who were themselves rival sajjāda nishīns (successors to the responsibility of caring for his shrine and its activities), did not even know Sufi Sahib.[9]

Miān Sher Muhammad had also designated four khalīfas. One of these khalīfas, who was familiar with Sufi Sahib, lives in Lahore. When I talked with him about Sufi Sahib, he did not question the validity of Sufi Sahib's inner experience, but he did deny Sufi Sahib's claim to be a khalīfa. Miān Sher Muhammad's successor accepted the possibility that Sufi Sahib's experiences of Miān Sher Muhammad could have been caused by a spiritual connection between pīr and follower. He even gave a similar instance from his own experience. But he disagreed about the definition of khilāfat:

> Sufi Sahib has a misconception to think that he is a khalīfa. It came in a dream. When you think you have been blessed with khilāfat, it is a misconception. For example, I have a devoted follower. I want to pass my khilāfat to him. I saw in a dream that I was passing it to him. If he gets that dream, it does not mean that he has that khilāfat. Actually, I want him to come here and receive it in a ceremony, so everyone will know.
>
> One can get the *faiz* [blessing] of a saint after his death, under certain conditions. The person must have love and devotion for the saint, and he must copy his life. But that blessing will not make him fit to be a khalīfa. Khilāfat is actually a post, given only in the lifetime of the saint.

This pīr's definition of khilāfat rested entirely on issues of social order and legitimate succession. Inner experience must be affirmed in the external world. He stressed that the Sufi orders have a public institutional structure, including rituals that establish a chain of succession. He spoke in terms of an ideology that reinforced his own legitimacy and authority. Within the institutional structure supported by this ideology, Sufi Sahib was an outsider.

Some people denied the legitimacy of Sufi Sahib on the grounds that he is not a sayyid (a descendant of the Prophet Muhammad). He was a member of the Arain caste, a large agricultural group with a strong political identity and caste organization; he lived in what was known as an Arain neighborhood. This was not an identity that Sufi Sahib shrouded in ambiguity. Instead he repeated the story of a famous Arain Sufi saint, a story that I heard from many Arains:

Bābā Bullhē Shāh [one of the Punjab's most well-known saints] became a disciple of Hazrat 'Ināyat Shāh, even though Bullhē Shāh was a sayyid and 'Ināyat Shāh was Arain. When Bullhē Shāh returned to his own house, the women of his family condemned him for becoming the disciple of an Arain. Then he went again to 'Ināyat Shāh and told him that the women did not like this. 'Ināyat Shāh took all the light that he had given to his disciple. Then Bullhē Shāh went to a family of dancing girls and started to work as a servant. After twelve years, Bullhē Shāh went with one of the dancing girls to 'Ināyat Shāh for an 'urs where she was to dance. Bullhe Shah covered his face and started to dance in a state of *jali* [passionate love]. 'Ināyat Shāh asked, "Are you Bullhē?" He replied, "I am not Bullhē; I am *bhula* [forgetful, lost]." 'Ināyat Shāh embraced Bullhē Shāh. Bullhē Shāh once again received that light and returned to his family's village.[10]

Sayyids long ago lost the centuries-old contest between themselves and other groups for sole legitimacy as pīrs, though traces of the social domination of sayyids are still in evidence, especially in rural areas, where sayyid families often continue to control local shrines.

Sayyid Fazal Shah, another pīr who lived three streets away from Sufi Sahib, is a sayyid. His house is located beside a small shrine built for one of his ancestors 250 years ago. People in the neighborhood consider him a pīr because "my father had a beard and used to mention God and people used to come to him as a pīr. So now they come to me." He was very humble about his own spiritual accomplishments, his main concern being to demonstrate that he does not write amulets and accept followers as a business. His identity as a pīr was firmly established because of his lineage, and it was affirmed architecturally by the shrine next door.

Though himself a sayyid pīr, he did not deny Sufi Sahib's legitimacy on this basis. Sayyid Fazal Shah had visited Sufi Sahib two or three times himself for his own problems, because friends had told him that Sufi Sahib belonged to the same silsila [Sufi order]. He told me that Sufi Sahib was "OK" but that he had seen Sufi Sahib scold his son. "After that I didn't go there again because I didn't like the way he treated his son." He was willing to acknowledge that it is possible to become the spiritual successor of a pīr solely on the basis of one's character. Though circumspect in his comments, he made it clear to me that he felt that Sufi Sahib's character was questionable, and thus it was not likely that he was really Miān Sher Muhammad's successor.

Some of Sufi Sahib's neighbors, personally familiar with his past, presented conflicting images of Sufi Sahib. The most direct criticism of Sufi Sahib made by a neighbor was that "his father was really a good man, but this Sufi has a business. He gets things from people. He has opened a shop" (i.e., he makes money from being a pīr).

Another woman who respected Sufi Sahib said: "He gives water and salt. He doesn't do any ta'wīz. People are cured with just water and salt." For these people, as for many Pakistanis, the writing of a ta'wīz is a sign that a man is conducting "business," charging money for the ta'wīz. Sufi Sahib, his followers, and detractors all contrasted the piety of a true pīr with the "business" concerns of a fraud. For many, Sufi Sahib's identity as a legitimate pīr or as a fraud rested on whether his motivation for being a pīr was based on making a profit.

Those whom I met at his baithak (reception hall) who were seeking a solution to specific problems were also concerned with this issue but focused on his ability to work miracles. These people told story after story of his ability to perceive hidden illnesses and to cure them with his prayers and with salt over which he had prayed. Most individuals said that they were followers of Sufi Sahib because he solved their problems, he doesn't charge money, and he knows about Islam.

One woman whom I spoke with in her home, for instance, was extremely critical of most pīrs. In recent years her husband had squandered most of his earnings seeking a cure from one pīr after another. According to her description, her husband, normally a sensible, intelligent man, had fits during which he was convinced that someone was working some kind of black magic on him. She described several different pīrs, some of whom charged large sums of money to exorcise whatever was possessing him. They had visited Sufi Sahib two or three times: "He didn't take money. He said, 'He has no jinn, just weakness of the brain. I'll give you salt. Bring me oil to pray over.'" Like most visitors who go to Sufi Sahib for a specific problem, she knew nothing of his background and was not concerned about it. She respected him because he gave what she considered a plausible diagnosis and did not charge for his service.

Despite their criticisms, Sufi Sahib's neighbors regularly attended the monthly rituals in honor of 'Abdu'l-Qādir Gīlānī[11] which Sufi Sahib sponsored. According to my observations (which may, of course, have suffered from the distortion of my presence), it is only at these rituals that Sufi Sahib collected money, in the form of donations made while the follower was in a state of ecstasy. One young man, the son of a follower, focused his criticism of Sufi Sahib on the fact that Sufi Sahib took money and food from people at these rituals and suggested that it was for this reason that he held the ritual so frequently. But to Sufi Sahib and to many of his followers, there was a profound difference between charging a rupee or two for an amulet and accepting freely given donations that are independent of specific acts on the part of the pīr. Such donations have always been an important part of the pīr-follower relationship in Pakistan and are a sign of devotion on the part of the follower. His detractors focused only on the fact that he takes money.

These neighbors and local followers were frequently joined by people from other parts of Lahore and beyond. Sufi Sahib had a number of highly educated followers, including high-ranking army officers, a doctor trained in England, and a professor at a local college, to name a few whom I met. For them, his identity as a pīr rested on his ability to answer their questions about Islam, not as an educated scholar, which he was not, but as a Sufi whose inner experience made such education unnecessary. They tended to be less concerned with the details of his life, focusing more on an emotional connection between themselves and Sufi Sahib.

A high-ranking army officer from Islamabad whom I met at Sufi Sahib's baithak talked to me extensively about Sufism, and described the nature of the communion between a pīr and a devoted follower. He praised Sufi Sahib and told me stories that were evidence of Sufi Sahib's "ESP,"[12] by which he meant Sufi Sahib's ability to transport himself spiritually and appear to followers in distant places. Though not a murīd of Sufi Sahib's, the army officer had himself experienced Sufi Sahib's presence in this way several times. He focused primarily on the fact that Sufi Sahib had had a profound spiritual connection with his own Sufi teacher and thus had the strength to guide others through such an intense immersion.

A student whom I met at Punjab University had visited Sufi Sahib many times. He said that Sufi Sahib talks about Islam and seems to know something. He told me that he knew Sufi Sahib because his grandfather is one of his followers: "My grandfather reads the Quran and stays up at night saying prayers. He always wants to go to Sufi Sahib and hear him teach about Islam."

One devoted follower, a retired accountant who had worked for the American consulate, described an intense dream experience of his own that led him to Sufi Sahib.[13] He spent much of every day at Sufi Sahib's feet, tending his needs, performing "service" according to the pre-scribed Sufi model.

Redefining the Past

Neighbors who criticized Sufi Sahib tended to do so in terms of their knowledge of his past life. They refused to accept Sufi Sahib's rein-terpretation of his life in terms of his identity as a pīr. The neighbor who remembered how he used to feed her buffalos, for instance, did not accuse him of any activities that would disqualify him as a pīr; but she said that because of his background he was not of a status that she could respect. To her, he retains that identity.

In contrast to the sayyid pīr I spoke with, who had inherited his position from his father, becoming a pīr was a turning point in Sufi Sahib's life. This transition involved a reinterpretation of his past. But instead of hiding those aspects of his past that were incompatible with his identity as a pīr, Sufi Sahib focused on specific events and inter-preted them in terms of his present identity.

One day I talked with one of Sufi Sahib's neighbors who, as it hap-pened, was also his niece and knew a great deal about his past. Her description of how Sufi Sahib became a pīr gives us a very different view of him. Her story highlighted a traumatic episode, a rupture, in Sufi Sahib's life. By comparison, Sufi Sahib's narratives repaired this rup-ture. The niece told me the following:

> He used to work in a cinema and was a landlord. One day some-thing was stolen from his uncle's house. His uncle accused him of the theft. Sufi Sahib was summoned to the police station and was insulted there. He got distressed. Then he started to read the Quran. His murshid is Miān Sher Muhammad. He used to pray the whole night and read Quran. Again something was stolen from the house of his uncle. But his uncle discovered that his aunt steals things. From that time on he continued to say prayers all night long, and that's how he became a pīr. . . . Before he became a pīr he used to hang around with other young men. He was very different.

Sufi Sahib's niece's account of his life emphasized the impression he made on people before he became a pīr, when he was associated with the cinema, a favorite hangout of young men — a particularly worldly occupation. She focused on an external event which she identified as the stimulus which led to the change in Sufi Sahib's life. Though Sufi Sahib did not tell me about this event, their stories are not incompatible. This became clearer as I got to know him better. He never described the incident concerning his uncle and the police station directly, but he alluded to it. He also acknowledged that his relatives were not all convinced of his honesty, and he explained their skepticism in terms of a parallel experience in the life of the Prophet:

> People were against the Prophet. They thought, "He is from us, but he has gotten bigger than us." The same thing has happened with me. My relatives are against me. My relatives think that I am a thief, a criminal. If you were to tell me that someone was saying that I am a thief and a criminal and drink wine, they are right because I steal the love of God when everyone is sleeping. I drink wine, but that wine is different; it is the intoxication of religion. I don't mind, because they don't know what wine I drink. There are still some people who would respect me in my presence, but if you saw them, they would talk abusively about me. My father's real younger brother is like that.

When Sufi Sahib's niece focused on Sufi Sahib's activities in the days before he was a pīr, she was careful to avoid criticizing him directly. Her story of how he became a pīr was, like Sufi Sahib's own stories, ambiguous. She did not describe any inner transformation; she did not say whether he became a pīr only because his overt praying gave him the appearance of being a pīr or because of a real inner transformation facilitated by Miān Sher Muhammad. She did not say, for instance, that Sufi Sahib is a pious man; she merely described his actions. She left it to the listener to infer that he was inwardly too pious to be a thief. An alternative interpretation is that he was let off the hook, perhaps because of his prayers. He may even have used the power of the Quran to change his uncle's perception — invoking spiritual power for personal gain. (This is believed to be possible with a mu'akkal, as Sufi Sahib himself said: "Mu'akkals can make mistakes, but the rūh cannot.") In contrast, she described Miān Sher Muhammad as a pious man and Sufi Sahib's father as a good man. When asked directly her opinion of Sufi Sahib, she replied: "We are relatives. Many people from outside the neighborhood come to see him. We don't believe in him the way other people do. We just go to *gyarvin* [the monthly ritual held in honor of ʿAbduʾl-Qādir Gīlānī]. Some relatives think that he is a pīr. People from different places think that he is a pīr."

This statement is also ambiguous. She may have been denying his legitimacy as a pīr by saying that she doesn't believe as others do. Or she may have been criticizing the excessive ways in which some people follow pīrs, in violation of the principles of Islam. The message I received from her statements is that she was willing to reinforce the image of Sufi Sahib as a pīr, to keep up appearances, but that it may be that Sufi Sahib is a pīr in appearance only.

Another proposition that emerges from the account of Sufi Sahib's niece is the likelihood that Sufi Sahib was a rebellious young man. Her description of his activities as a youth reminded me of young men I had met who claimed to have dabbled in black magic. Their pursuit of power through muʾakkals had a quality of rebelliousness about it, including a lack of concern about whether a particular activity was within or beyond the bounds of proper Islam.

Young Men and Black Magic

In talking with other people, especially with college students, I learned that to use "muʾakkals," as Sufi Sahib had done, is characteristic of young men who do not regard themselves as especially pious. I met several college youths who had themselves pursued such interests, performing rituals and repeating prayers over and over, in order to acquire power over others. Several men reported that they had once practiced kālā ʿilm (black knowledge) but had given it up out of fear, typically after the birth of a child, whom they were afraid would be harmed by such practices.

Jaffur Shurreef, the author of *Qanoon-e-Islam* (1973), is an example of a young man who experimented with techniques intended to gain control of spiritual beings for his own ends. Though rather removed in time and place from Sufi Sahib (he was a nineteenth-century South Indian Muslim), aspects of their historical background are similar: they both participated in a South Asian Muslim culture based on an Urdu literary culture and on intimate exposure to British colonialism and bureaucratic institutions. In his discussion of exorcism, he expressed what seems to be a common motivation that prompts young men to explore both kālā ʿilm and nūri ʿilm: curiosity. In this description, as in the descriptions of several young men with whom I spoke, there is no element of piety, but rather the lure of something powerful and dangerous, with hints of resistance against adult authority.

> This teacher of the alphabet has for a long time cherished the greatest curiosity to dive into this mysterious science, and has, consequently, associated much with divines and devotees, exorcists and travellers from Arabia and Ujjum (every country in the world, save Arabia), by which he has acquired some knowledge of it; but all the advantage he has derived therefrom may be summed up in a well-known proverb, "Koh kundun; moosh girruftun." "To dig a mountain up, and find a mouse." (Shurreef 1973:202)

One might assume from this that Shurreef was declaring that there was not much truth in all of this magic, especially given the context of a book written for British administrators, written in a style of detached observation. Given this context, the following statement may even be tinged with a hint of sarcasm, written from a stance of alignment with his British employers and rulers: "In short, it is no easy matter to command the presence of genii and demons; and, in the present day, should these races of beings be near any one, so as to obey his calls, such a one would, no doubt, instantly be set down as a *wullee* (saint), or one endowed with the gift of miracles" (Shurreef 1973:214).

The following statement, however, belies this interpretation: "The author of the present sheets (lit. this teacher of the alphabet) has endeavored to prove the effects of the reading of two or three of these *isms;* but he found it a most difficult task to finish them; for he met with such strange sights and frightful objects as completely deterred him from concluding any one of them. Moreover, conceiving it labor lost, he relinquished the design altogether" (214). One comment indicates that Jaffur Shurreef was raised in a tradition in which knowledge of the formulas associated with the names of God was regarded as lawful, sacred knowledge (therefore, not in keeping with reformist prescriptions such as Thanawi's): "To this teacher of the A,B,C, through the grace of God and the favour and kindness of his tutors (including his own father), a great variety of powerful *isms* and select sentences of the *Qoran* have descended; but as they have been imparted to him as profound secrets, it would be improper for him to disclose them" (214).

The conclusions of young men in Lahore who had dabbled in this mysterious science were similar to Jaffur Shurreef's. Even among college students, not a single one that I spoke with rejected it as unscientific. Rather, those who rejected it did so on the grounds that calling on a being other than God is against Islam or, more pragmatically, the process is just too scary and dangerous to follow it through. Such students may position themselves as "modern" in many situations, or, in rejecting magic, may identify themselves as Islamic reformist. But the intensity of their reactions to the practice of magic reveals an aspect of consciousness that is not organized by these ideologies and their underlying discursive structure.

Magic is a discourse of resistance. It includes a rebellion against the ideological gulfs that divide adult communities. Several young men I knew in Lahore demonstrated resistance to the ideological gulf between Hinduism and Islam, ignoring social pressure to rule anything Hindu out of bounds. One Muslim young man told me about his past as a magician (jādūgar) who had acquired some of his knowledge of the subject from an ʿāmil and some from books on the subject. He called himself both an ʿāmil and jādūgar, and most of the words which he used to refer to his craft were Hindi. The particular aspect that he had studied was *mantar* (Hindu incantations), which he stressed was not kālā ʿilm but rather pure, like nūri ʿilm. Nevertheless, its results were fast, like kālā ʿilm. Types of magic are distinguished, not by the source of magical power (*the* crucial issue for most Muslims), but on the purpose for which the power was used. Mantar was a part of a different discourse that organized reality in a manner fundamentally different from the organizing ideas in Islam. His father, a *maulvī* (Islamic scholar), would undoubtedly have disagreed with and strongly disapproved of his way of categorizing things. As the son of a Muslim maulvī, he was well entrenched in the Muslim system, and he had learned jādū out of fascination for the illicit and dangerously powerful, with little fear for the future of his soul at that stage in his life. Like many young men, he didn't seem to care much about what God or his father thought about his activities, until he became a father himself. Upon marriage, he gave up the whole thing because of the dangers it posed for his family. He claims now to be a dutiful Muslim.

The perspective of youth was also evident in the comments of another young man, who was scornful of Sufi Sahib's current activities as a pīr (and who was himself often in trouble with his father): "Sufi Sahib used to have muʾakkals and could exorcise jinn, but twelve years ago he started to take money, fruit, and food from people. He bought land with the money. He is very clever. He collected money and gave it to his son to make a movie. It was very cheap and full of bad songs that played on the radio. The film was banned by the government about four or five years ago. Now Sufi Sahib has lost his mu'akkals because of these activities." It is striking that both Sufi Sahib and this youth agreed that twelve years ago Sufi Sahib stopped controlling mu'akkals, a view that is itself an interpretation of a change in Sufi Sahib's behavior; yet they disagreed radically about the reason why. This young man did not reject Sufi Sahib's claim to have had control over mu'akkals. He thus accepted the interpretive frame used by Sufi Sahib: that jinn and mu'akkals exist and that Sufi Sahib did have power to perceive and control them. His criticism was not that Sufi Sahib illegitimately claimed the identity of pīr but that he subsequently became corrupt because of his power and thus lost control over mu'akkals.

Many young men seem to view the taming of mu'akkals as an avenue to power at a time in their lives when they are otherwise relatively powerless and subordinate to their fathers. The structure of incantations and rituals itself makes very little distinction between good and evil, or between power from God or from other sources, and young men downplay distinctions that could be made. Obedience and piety do not seem to be the primary concern of one who is seeking mu'akkals, despite Sufi Sahib's claim that he was careful to enlist the aid only of angels through nūri 'ilm.

Sayyid Fazal Hassan, the sayyid pīr who lived a few blocks from Sufi Sahib in a home adjacent to his family's ancestral shrine, also talked about mu'akkals. His story should help demonstrate how this idea of spiritual intermediaries is lived out by young men. While still a boy, he turned to the solitary pursuit of mu'akkals:

> I was ten years old when my father arranged a second marriage. I got upset. My second mother's behavior was very strange with me. I used to sit by the grave of my mother. Sometimes crying, I slept there. I used to sit in the mosque to get a specific *manzil* [destination, spiritual stage]. All my knowledge that I am telling you now I got while sitting in the mosque and at the grave, studying books. For instance, Hazrat Solomon was king of all the creatures. He had a minister whose name was Asif Bin Barkiya. Once there was a bird called *hudhud*. That bird came [Solomon understood the speech of animals]. The bird informed him that there was a woman named Balkīs governing over the area of Saba. Solomon

thought, "I must convert her to Islam." The jinn said, "We can bring her by 6 o'clock [in four hours]. But Asif Bin Barkiya winked his eye and the empire of Balkīs was before Solomon. So sometimes men can do more than jinn. I was trying to be the kind of person who winks and brings things. But I couldn't do that.

[KPE: Did you have any success at all?]

As men have four angels, in the same way jinn have four mu'akkals. Gabriel is a messenger. Azrā'īl controls life and death. Mīkā'īl controls floods, earthquakes, wars. Isrāfīl, when all the world is finished, will blow trumpet and people will get ready for judgment day. No, I was not successful. But I have seen mu'akkals, listened to them, seen their power.

His desire was unconstrained by "modernity" or "reform." The mu'akkal operated as a signifier for this desire. Interestingly, the story of Solomon that Fazal Sahib recounted was one in which a man is able to bring him into the presence of a powerful woman who lived at a great distance. It is probably no coincidence that Fazal Sahib focused on this story as he sat at his mother's grave, seeking a guide who would give him the same power.

Rearticulating a Rebellious Youth through Sufi Textual Discourse

Sufi Sahib used several rhetorical strategies to build a public identity as a pīr through narrative. Despite public evidence of a young adulthood that was in many eyes rebellious and corrupt, he highlighted continuities in his orientation to Islam instead of suppressing his past altogether. One of his strategies for reinterpreting the past was to create a contrast between his overt actions and his inner state. He projected two selves: an outer and an inner self, a distinction that is a basic concept in Sufi thought. Having made this contrast, he admitted that his activities as a young man had been worldly (as his neighbors testified). Nevertheless, he created an image of himself as having always been pious, as evidenced by his never having missed any prayers, despite the impression he created in the eyes of the world. He became a pīr when the connection between his inner and outer selves was reestablished, through the guidance of his spiritual teacher (murshid).

This process of projecting a pious identity draws power from the trajectory of his story's unfolding plot. In this plot, the continuity of the

pīr's essentially pious character — his stable "identity" — is asserted.
The movement of his life is a movement through "stages" as these are
articulated in Sufi manuals. Each stage is the tearing away of a veil. In
Sufi literature, the *malāmatī* (blameworthy) serves as the model for Sufi
Sahib's depiction of himself as a young man. It is an explicitly articulated subject position in which the actor draws blame on himself to help
kill his pride and self-involvement. Most Sufis see it as a lesser stage on
the Sufi path (see, e.g., Hujwīrī 1976:65–66).

In one of our later meetings, this malāmatī theme was affirmed in a
paradoxical story about an incident in the days before he became a pīr.
The story was intended to demonstrate his piety in performing an act
which appeared to reveal his lack of piety:

> Once my father was taking all the family on the pilgrimage to
> Mecca. I refused to go. He got angry, but he didn't understand why
> I wouldn't go. When I told him why I wouldn't go, he embraced
> and kissed me. I didn't go. At that time I was involved in business. I
> had no link with the Prophet. I was not able to go to Medina in
> that condition. But now I think, but I am not sure, that I would be
> able to go. When the Prophet calls me, then I will go.

By adding the comment that he is not sure if even now he is pious
enough, he enhanced the piety of the act of refusing to go to Mecca. He
emphasized that he does not do things for appearances, and in fact
demands far more of himself than do ordinary men, a characteristic
technique used in Sufi literature to demonstrate piety.

One of the reasons that Sufi Sahib's narratives were powerful and
appealed to an educated elite was the way in which they reproduced
existing Sufi literary genres, thereby positioning him as a Sufi pīr who
could be seen to embody the uncolonized memory of the past. Sufi
Sahib's narratives, like the discourses of many pīrs whom I met during
the course of my research, tended to resemble two forms: (1) discourses
on Islam, roughly resembling *malfūzāt* literature (sayings of the saints),
or (2) stories of their own involvement in Sufism and discipleship under
a Sufi saint and teacher, in a form characteristic of tazkarat literature
(biographies of the saints that often trace the chain of spiritual transmission from Sufi to disciple within a Sufi order). In my own project of
learning about Sufi Sahib, I found myself frustrated at times by Sufi
Sahib's accounts of his life, because I had to listen to hours of description of the principles of Islam when I wanted to hear more of what to
me constituted the particularities of his life. But Sufi Sahib's extensive

discourse on Islam followed the model of malfūzāt literature. This discourse is the everyday conversation from which a devoted disciple may cull sayings that encapsulate the Sufi master's spiritual experience (see, e.g., Maneri 1980).

Aware, too, of the genre of tazkarat literature, Sufi Sahib was already familiar with the idea of having someone write a biography about him when I met him and asked for a story of his life. One man who visited Sufi Sahib often was another Sufi who is a scholar and runs a small dispensary for homeopathic medicine in the neighborhood. He and Sufi Sahib were close friends. He began visiting Sufi Sahib to ask questions about religion. He said that he had visited many different auliyā (saints) but that only Sufi Sahib had been able to answer the questions he had asked. He was writing Sufi Sahib's biography: "In that biography, I am writing only what I see, not those things I just hear from people. If I just ask people who honestly believe in Sufi Sahib, they would hide any bad things. So I come here myself to see him and the people. I have been writing about the soul." Though I never saw the biography this man intended to produce, the genre is a living one, and I saw a number of published biographies of other living or recently deceased saints (e.g., Azimi 1983). In the tradition of this tazkarat literature, most of the events that Sufi Sahib described focused on his relationship with his murshid, on incidents that exemplified his piety and spiritual transformations, and on the miracles he has performed for his followers. For Sufi Sahib and his biographer, the essence of a life was the spiritual heart (*qalb*) and its relationship to God. Worldly events are significant only as they reveal the condition of the heart.

As Peacock has pointed out, particular religious traditions have an important shaping influence on the structure of life histories (Peacock 1984). In many Muslim hagiographies extraordinary spiritual strength and piety are present from birth. But the literature on the lives of Sufi saints is also replete with accounts of conversion and repentance, which is an important first step on the Sufi path and an important theme in many Sufi texts (see al-Ghazzālī n.d.; Maneri 1980). Farīd ud-Dīn ʿAttār's early-thirteenth-century account *Tadhkirat al-Auliyaʾ* (Memorial of the Saints), for instance, includes an account of Al-Fozail ibn Iyaz's (d. 803 CE) conversion to the ascetic life entitled "Fozail the Highwayman and How He Repented" (ʿAttār 1990:53).[14] This account bears a resemblance to Sufi Sahib's story of himself. Despite Fozail's practice of brigandage, he is depicted as having always been inclined to piety; for instance: "He would divide the loot among the bandits, keeping for himself what he fancied. He kept an inventory of everything, and never absented himself from the meetings of the gang" ('Attār 1990:53). "It is said that by nature he was chivalrous and high-minded"; "All his inclination was towards right doing" (55). This is 'Attār's account of his conversion and repentance: "One night a caravan was passing, and in the midst of the caravan a man was chanting the Koran. The following verse reached Fozail's ears: *Is it not time that the hearts of those who believe should be humbled to the remembrance of God?* It was as though an arrow pierced his soul, as though that verse had come out to challenge Fozail and say, 'O Fozail, how long will you waylay travellers? The time has come when We shall waylay you!'" ('Attār 1990:55). He then fled, proclaiming to all that he had repented and sought forgiveness of his adversaries. Piety and spiritual power were finally turned to their proper end.

We can see the shaping influence of this narrative structure in Sufi Sahib's life story. Certainly in the brief life history he gave me during our first meeting, he stressed continuities. He stressed his early interest in knowledge of and contact with prophets and saints. He did bai'at with his pīr Miān Sher Muhammad. Because of his spiritual exercises, he acquired spiritual power, a mu'akkal, which he still has. He did not emphasize any difference between that and his current activity, though the discerning listener who knew him could find an implied disjunction, between acquiring a mu'akkal and acquiring a "law degree."

Despite the unavoidable disjunction between his practices as a youth and his current position, he managed to stress the continuities in his personality. He stressed his early curiosity about spiritual matters, his ability to carry out extreme austerities, and his care to draw only on aspects of the Quran, rejecting kālā 'ilm. His success in acquiring a mu'akkal was a testimony to his innate spiritual strength and piety. His error was merely lack of guidance, which finally came to him in the form of Miān Sher Muhammad. In this narrative, then, the point of disjunction was the moment when he experienced a visualization of Miān Sher Muhammad.

The Power of Sufi Sahib's Narratives

On our way to visit Sufi Sahib the morning following our second visit, Yasmin told me that she planned to get some salt blessed by the saint for her brother, who had been ill, and her mother. I was surprised, since I knew that she had been taught that all of the activities in which pīrs engage are fraudulent and that their presumption to have some closer connection with God than ordinary people was a violation of the principles of Islam. She had defined Sufi Sahib as utterly different from herself at the outset and, therefore, saw anything he said about magic, supernatural beings, and spiritual power as merely information about the ways of the superstitious and the uneducated, as material she was collecting because I was interested in it. She had understood the distinction that Sufi Sahib had made between nūri 'ilm and kālā 'ilm as a familiar strategy that pīrs use to keep their practice within the bounds of Islam, a strategy that she personally rejected. She was, in effect, humoring him in his claims to legitimacy. She had not expected him to join her in rejecting mu'akkals altogether and, therefore, misheard him when he did just that. Is that why Yasmin was convinced by our second conversation with Sufi Sahib?

Sufi Sahib's long narrative about mu'akkals during our second meeting was an impressive performance. Far from being inhibiting, the presence of so many important people on that day seemed to make him expansive. He spoke extensively of his devotion and love for his pīr Miān Sher Muhammad. He talked of drowning in the sea of 'ishq. He was able to communicate this love of his pīr so effectively that Yasmin had been convinced. At one point she went so far as to say, "I will follow this pīr, too. I won't go to him after you leave, but I will consider him pious."

I took her to mean that she had been convinced that he was being straightforward, that he had actually done the spiritual exercises he had claimed to have done, had actually had the experiences of Miān Sher Muhammad that he reported, and was able to infuse barakat (God's blessing) into a piece of salt.

I think Yasmin's own strategy for social positioning by rejecting pīrs was disrupted when she met so many high-status, well-educated men in Sufi Sahib's presence. When she encountered members of the social elite who accepted Sufi Sahib, it violated her existing understandings of the relationships among pīrs, the teachings of Islam, and social status, understandings that had been appropriate in her interactions with many of her neighbors, whom she regarded as socially and intellectually inferior to her. Confronted with this new situation, she was willing to negotiate a new reality. The power of a discourse to convince is played out in just such moments and is in large part generated by the social position of the bearers of that discourse. Her temporary "conversion" is an example of the fluidity of the hegemonic process and its direct link to the power of social status to convince in specific social contexts.

I myself was still unquestioning of my position and saw myself as operating from the ethnographer's subject position as neither the "village atheist" nor the "village priest" (in the Geertzian sense [1973b:123]). Nevertheless, Sufi Sahib had begun to have an effect on me, too. At one point during our first meeting, Sufi Sahib had told me explicitly that he would come to me while I was sleeping. He also told me that he could reach me, come to me, in America. It sounded rather like boasting, but a couple of his followers who had studied abroad reported that they had received communications, including help on exams, from him. At that point, I eagerly recorded everything they told me, thinking, as the interpretive relativist I had been trained to be, about the implications of such beliefs for Pakistani concepts of self and person. But these pronouncements did not touch me, their evidence was not evidence for me. Privately, I translated their experiences into Freudian-like interpretive schemas and labeled them "magical thinking." I appropriated their experience as knowledge, infantalizing its richness and alterity in true Orientalist fashion.

But Sufi Sahib did as he had promised. At the time, I was living with Yasmin's family. That night I awoke in the middle of the night, so startled from a dream that I sat upright.[15] My awakening woke Yasmin, who was sleeping on a cot next to mine. I told her the dream, in which I had seen a white horse approach me. In the dream, I had the clear sensation of something touching my thumb, which startled me awake. Yasmin declared that it had been the saint, just as he had promised. I marveled aloud about the power of suggestion, thereby placing the phenomenon immediately within a psychological interpretive scheme (i.e., that dreams come only from the dreamer's internal states) but was haunted by the odd sensation of the touch. A feeling of what Freud (1955b) described as the "uncanny" washed over me.

During the course of my fieldwork, I mentioned this dream several times to people. My having had that dream was significant not only for Yasmin but for people of all backgrounds, a fact that repeatedly reinforced the powerful impression that the dream had made on me. But early in my fieldwork, such social reinforcements, though offering temptations to believe, were not serious challenges to my own orienta-

The shrine of Sufi Ghulam Rasul under construction

The shrine of Sufi Ghulam Rasul's father in Miānī Sahib graveyard, Lahore

tion and identity. To accept such beliefs would have meant entering a social world that was beyond the pale for me personally: I could not imagine taking on what I saw as beliefs characteristic of an uneducated Pakistani woman. I imagined that I was learning the beliefs of those whose parochialisms had not yet been eroded by the realities of modern life. I was studying the wholly other.

The challenge to my reality became more serious when my research expanded beyond the urban village where I was living. Casually, I once reported the dream to a Pakistani psychiatrist who had spent several years in England. After a formal discussion about the ways in which some of his highly disturbed patients experience their beliefs in pīrs, he invited me to lunch with his family at his home, which adjoined his office. He asked me to tell him more about my research. At some point, almost jokingly, I mentioned the dream, and he suddenly became very serious and wanted to know more about that pīr. I found this shift of orientation on the part of a colleague even more jolting than the dream experience itself — I was being socialized into the significance of dreams by a Pakistani whom I had thought shared my interpretive, scientific world, a man whom I regarded as an authority.

The power that Sufi Sahib had displayed by sending me, the Western scientist, a dream, also reinforced Yasmin's reaction and operated as a significant, if perhaps transient, factor in her self-positioning. She apparently regarded my dream as authoritative and was at least temporarily convinced of the saint's spirituality and power because of the dream. I began to understand what Sufi Sahib's elite followers had found in him.

I first encountered Sufi Sahib in the ritual context of the baithak, seated before his followers. In this context, he occupied a subject position that is difficult to live up to: the exemplary figure of the pīr. But when I returned to visit Sufi Sahib nine years later, I was dismayed to learn that he had died a month before my arrival. One of his followers took me to visit his grave. I saw a not-yet-completed shrine covering the grave, built out of donations from his followers. It was then, too, that I saw for the first time the shrine that Sufi Sahib had himself built for his father. The two adjacent shrines were to be nearly identical. The ruptures and discontinuities of Sufi Sahib's youth and background had been obliterated. An unbroken chain of spiritual descent from the Prophet Muhammad had been affirmed in stone.

6

Stories of Desire: Reclaiming the Forgotten *Pīr*

I have shown in chapter 5 how Sufi Sahib's narratives were replete with metaphorical self-representations that located him with respect to certain ideologies and distanced him from a negative positioning by others as he sought to inhabit an identity as a Sufi pīr: he was the advocate who represents his followers to God; he was the teacher and healer; he was the misunderstood but dutiful son. Points of discrepancy between representations were obscured through ambiguity, gaps were sutured with new metaphors as Sufi Sahib negotiated his way through diverse positionings and strategically located himself in a powerful identity. Many highly educated Pakistanis who regard themselves as modern, rational, and professional are also caught between ideologies, inconsistent in their self-representations, uncertain about how to articulate their relationships to Islam and to modernity. Many are drawn to Sufism and yet avoid identifying themselves as Sufis. Their conversations about Sufism display ambivalence and show evidence of intense conflict. It is in the midst of such conflict that the movement of the experiencing subject reveals itself.

I now turn my attention directly to this elusive subject, to that aspect of the individual that evades capture by an ideology, yet erupts into narrative, then hides within the narrative's flow. If, with Foucault, we suppose that the individual is transected by multiple discourses, it would be expected that the subject inhabits these discourses in diverse ways. As Benveniste (1971) has argued, the subject is captured in speech, but there is always a discontinuity between the "me" of discourse that is captured through metaphorical identity and what Lacan would call the subject of the Real, the speaking subject, the elusive "I."[1] However, it is not the case that the speaking subject is simply not present in speech. Rather, its presence flows through speech. It leaves its traces through a simultaneous presence/absence. It is linked metonymically to the signifiers used to express it, meaning that the signifier, instead of representing the subject, merely points to it and marks its fleeting presence. What is it that manifests itself so fleetingly, disrupting speech with its passage? In Lacanian thought this presence has been labeled "desire," specifically, the desire for recognition by another subject. Its obverse is fear. The presence/absence of the elusive subject is, from this perspective, manifested most obviously as desire and fear.[2]

Desire and fear are also central concerns within Sufi discourse. The stories that Pakistani Sufis gave me, stories of the search for a pīr, have at their heart the experience of desire. Desire ('ishq) draws the Sufi ever closer to God. Desire moves many contemporary Pakistani Sufis into a search for a spiritual guide, a pīr. In conversation with a Sufi or a seeker, I felt its power wash over me when the seeker began to speak of it—a palpable presence. One businessman told me about his first encounter with his pīr: "When I looked at him, I knew that this was my pīr. He looked at me and smiled. Then I felt my life start to ebb out of me, starting from my toes. I felt I was going to die." As I focus on the issue of desire, I thus begin to move toward the questions that Sufis themselves have asked about the relationship of the subject to the world and to another subject and of the ability of language to capture that relationship.

Specifically, I examine the process of "conversion" to Sufi practice or discipleship, which typically means accepting someone as one's pīr. In conversion narratives the subject, through a process of identification, allows itself to be structured by a specific ideology, to be located within a specific arrangement of signs. In the converted, we see (among other things) the triumph of a particular religious ideology and accompanying shifts in social practices, relations, and self-experience. We hear stories of the converted because they are meant to be heard. Sufi Sahib is a good example: his stories were a means by which he identified with a subject position and located himself vis-à-vis a complex community. Reflecting the structure of these public narratives, our common understanding of conversion is of an all-or-nothing process, in which the converted individual takes on a new identity articulated through a religious ideology.

But a focus on conversion as a process, especially among the tempted but not converted, highlights the moment before closure and reveals how the individual is transected by ideologies, moves through competing discourses, and is activated by desire and fear. The elusive and ambivalent subject is startlingly visible in the conflicted narratives of the not-yet-converted.

The speaking subject can be recognized only in relationship to an other. The project of representing the subject in a written text is, therefore, paradoxical, since the subject will always elude my representations. My goal here is, therefore, to articulate a strategy for highlighting the effects of the elusive subject, by metonymically pointing to the subject's movement through speech. I can best do this by examining speech in which I am part of the conversation, in which I am the other for my interlocutor, focusing on the relationship created by my conversations with another. In the terminology of Freudian psychoanalytic practice, what I am doing in these interpretive analyses is following the "transferences" of desire and fear as they were experienced in significant relationships with others in the past into the immediate relationship constituted by our conversation. I also attend to my own countertransferences as they develop in my interactions with another. I use these instances of relationship as a source of insight into the conflicts of the subject.

Lest it appear that I, as anthropologist, am an objective observer located above (or beneath) such desire and conflict, this discussion will move uncomfortably (for me) close to my own experience of Sufism. In the first section, I focus on a Pakistani man living in North Carolina who was drawn to Sufism because his father had become a devoted Sufi late in life. In our conversations, he displayed conflicts about getting too involved in Sufi practice. In the second case, I focus on my own relationship — my desire for and fear of recognition and relationship — with a practicing Sufi. In each case, my analysis turns away from the focus on content that an analysis of ideologies, even competing ones, allows, to a focus on the relationship that was created by my conversation with another. Finally, I turn to a state that in Sufi thought is closely associated with desire but distinguished from it: *muhabbat* (love). I explore the relationships among desire, fear, and love, considering how they are conceptualized, distinguished, and experienced by Sufis.

Sufi Desire and Western Discourse

Several Pakistanis have shown me how suddenly and intensely desire may manifest itself in casual conversation. This is particularly evident in a context in which the speaker moves from a subject position as a secularized professional who shares my frame of reference as a (social) scientist to the position of a seeker. In my discussion of Sufi Sahib in chapter 5, for instance, I described what happened when I told a psychiatrist recently returned from England my dream about Sufi Sahib: his gaze betrayed a sudden, apparently intense desire to meet Sufi Sahib, an abrupt shift from the stance of professional, scientific psychiatrist. I saw a similar recalling of desire in another man, a Muslim from north India, a professor at a major university in India whom I met while he was a visiting scholar in the United States. Both men illustrate the movement of desire as it transects the individual.

One difficulty with examining the issue is that the expression of desire is always relational. The presumed identity of an interlocutor, or of the expected audience for a text, mediates this desire. When I am present, for instance, the imagined "West" is always present. The effects of the Western gaze, which bears the weight of an Orientalist past, shape all of my encounters with the desire of the Sufi. I see a rupture when the topic of conversation turns to Sufism. There is a perceptible split between the face the psychiatrist or the professor or the businessman turns to someone like me — the subject position they assume regarding a modern discourse — and themselves as the subject of another discourse. In our conversations, because I am present, the "West" is necessarily present.

The subject position of the postcolonial professional with respect to the face to be turned to a Western stranger in public conversation is often remarkably easy to disrupt. The English-trained psychiatrist practiced modern medicine. His psychiatry was thoroughly grounded in biology and the physiological causes of psychiatric disorders. Knowing that I was researching pīrs, he maintained a distance toward the practices associated with pīrs, and he expressed the stance of the scientific observer: if those of his patients who have visited pīrs have been helped, it is because of their traditional worldview and the placebo effect. So when I mentioned that I had visited a pīr who seemed to have sent me a dream, his shift was an abrupt slide across discourses, the manifestation of a desire previously not present in the interaction.

I saw a similar abrupt slide in my interaction with the professor, who heard me give a talk on pīrs at an evening colloquium. As we stood chatting over cocktails following my talk, I described my research interests. He began discussing the extent to which masses of people are mired in ignorance and will flock to the shrine of a fourteenth-century saint for his 'urs — so gullible that a travel agency has been making a hefty profit arranging a kind of pilgrimage, transporting customers around on a three-shrine circuit. As he described it: "People from miles around are followers of Sabir. There are two 'urses a year. Now there are tour agencies who have developed this — they have created a pilgrimage circuit, like the Hindus. Poor people who could never afford to go to Mecca. So they go to Sabir's shrine, then on to Delhi to pay their respects to Nizām ud-Dīn. They've created a new thing. In the old days, people would visit just one shrine." As he spoke, he implicitly located himself vis-à-vis this practice, his subjectivity occupying a tone of voice that said that this phenomenon was proof of postcolonial rupture and inauthenticity: in the old days they only would have visited one shrine, but now their practice has been penetrated by capitalism, which reveals the underlying meaninglessness of the practice, as something that could be engineered for profit — or exploited politically. He spoke from the position of the social scientist looking at local north Indian Muslim culture.

But when I queried his assumption that the traditional way was somehow more real, he paused. Speaking as a fellow academic, I suggested that the intervention of a travel agency might not necessarily mediate the relationship between the pilgrims and the shrine. With my question modern technology and profit were for the moment abruptly deprived of the power they had had to uniquely create meaning.

His position shifted as his perspective on my attitudes changed. When he got back to India, he would visit the shrine his father had taken him to as a child, he said. He had in the past arranged Sufi gatherings for his colleagues at the university, and maybe he would do so again, he revealed. But he also expressed concern that his more "hardheaded" colleagues would think that such goings-on were strange. He conveyed to me a longing, a desire, that his positioning within the modern had no place for.

Our conversation had a certain structure, and our encounter revealed the movement of desire through a postcolonial subject. As professors, as colleagues, we operated within an imaginary order in which the "professor" is constituted and each of us is self-consciously fixed. "Professor" is a metaphorical characterization of our elusive subjectivities, an identity that we share but that neither of us fully inhabits. But the topic of our conversation, his cultural "traditions," potentially divided us with respect to this Western academic discourse. When I disrupted his constitution of me as a representative of Western academia by disagreeing with him, the discourse shifted, the "I" and "you" as signifiers slid (for each of us) within a social order in which we embody a certain power relationship, and we entered a different imaginary. When he revealed his own desire as potentially identical with that of a denigrated other (one of the ignorant "traditional" masses who seeks a pīr) in the discourse of modernity, he risked being fixed as an object, recognized as subordinate. By querying him about his modernizing assumptions, was I saying, in effect, that I do not participate in that particular discourse of modernity and therefore do not denigrate that other? Or, as a modern subject do I (as his other) desire an other that is not a modern subject, thereby exoticizing him? There is always a risk.

We met again over lunch for the dual purpose of discussing issues pertaining to his own research where my expertise as an anthropologist was relevant and of continuing our discussion of his experience of Sufism. As our conversation evolved, the traces of his desire became more visible. He described the feeling that comes over him whenever he hears qawwālī (songs) sung in honor of Sabir, the fourteenth-century saint he had mentioned after the colloquium, who has been an object of devotion in his family for many generations.

> Whenever I hear a song for Sabir, I feel this emotion—I put my head down and start to cry. So I felt a very strong connection to this old saint through my father and grandfather. I haven't visited the shrine since I was a little boy, but I will when I go back to India. Faqīrs living at the shrine would travel, and they would stay at our house—hundreds of miles from the shrine—because they knew my father was a "man of heart." And it was a big house. They would stay for a night or two. They carried books, poems about the saint in their bags. They would read the same books over and over—a kind of devotion. They were literate people.
>
> [KPE: Would you go to a living descendant?] No, just to the shrine, to pay my respects, like "checking in" [laughs]. [He is very careful about his positioning here in response to my "inter-

Dancing in a trance state

viewer's" question.] There are probably several of them — with court cases, fighting over land. But there is probably one who has received the pure spirituality of his ancestor. That's the way it works. If I found one like that, I might go and listen to him.

My father used to go to the shrine. He would tell his problems, and he would come home feeling much better, having been in the presence of such a spiritual man.

I just remember the *sam'a* [a gathering for listening to Sufi music and poetry]. It made such an impression on me. When I organized a sam'a, I invited some *qawwāls* [singers of Sufi music]. They told me that they had been to the house when my father was alive. [His father had died when he was a young man.] I didn't know I had invited the very same people. When I heard the song for Sabir, I just cried. I don't know, there is something about that saint. Other people experienced *kaifīyat* [a state of ecstasy] — their arms kept shooting out as they danced around. I could have danced, but I had more control than that. They were closer to the saint.

Every time I hear the song for him, I cry, just like that. All the poems that have been written about him — in Persian, local languages, they are so beautiful. The content isn't much — they just praise him, but the connection is there.

Though under the circumstances of our informal conversations on the subject I did not have the opportunity to elicit any clarifications about his feeling of "connection" with the pīr, his affect when describing his experience seemed very similar to that communicated by others who described their state of longing — a kind of desire that is reactivated on the telling. It is a desire that transcends the constraints of secularism or science. But it is a desire that is quickly replaced by fear and evasion as soon as it becomes a potential basis for a public identity as a Sufi in the gaze of a Western other.

A Narrative of One Who Is Not a Sufi

Ahmed (not his real name), a young Pakistani professional now living in North Carolina, is another who has been tempted by Sufism. He is basically secular in orientation, though Muslim by upbringing. Several years ago, his father, who himself had earned a doctorate in economics from a British university and had worked in international banking, went through an experience of conversion and became a Sufi after many years as a nonpracticing Muslim. At his death, his new identity was engraved on his tombstone, in the form of the spiritual genealogy of his Sufi order. Ahmed's father's conversion had a significant effect on Ahmed but did not lead to his own overt adoption of a Sufi identity. His struggle over conversion, reenacted in my university office, offers another concrete instance of how multiple ideologies interact in a specific sociopolitical milieu and demonstrates how the subject moves through these ideologies as it constructs a narrative disrupted by traces of its own desire and fear.

My strategy for exploring Ahmed's struggle with conversion is to observe how he enacted conflicts surrounding conversion in our conversations. Ahmed showed me that he is tempted by conversion, a temptation that also stimulated anxiety. His utterances and my responses shaped our evolving relationship in ways that can be traced and interpreted. I attend not simply to the content of his utterances as expressions of different ideologies, but to the moments of slippage and their implications for our relationship and for the movement of the subject. I will present portions of the interview, analyzing it from the perspective of how agency manifests itself in conflictual speech.[3]

Ahmed began the interview expecting to talk about his father's Sufi guide, Qazi Sahib. We had already begun to do so at a previous meeting, and he seemed to enjoy reconstructing a detailed sequence of events at a typical *mahfil* (Sufi gathering) as he had experienced it in Pakistan. He began with an experience-distant description, as if given from the stance of a video camera. This stance, induced partly by the specific question I asked to get things started, created a safe distance between himself and the material, providing him the power and control that comes from a seemingly objective gaze. It also set up an alliance between us, with him functioning as my eyes. Ahmed maintained and projected the subject position of a modern scientifically oriented professional, a colleague of mine.

Nevertheless, he showed many signs of conflict, of a struggle between this identity and an interest in Sufism that was powerfully charged with memories of his now-deceased father. In his talk of the Sufi pīr, desire for something unreachable seemed to manifest itself.

This narrative demonstrates how the speaking subject is constituted linguistically in relationship to an interlocutor. It reveals the operation of desire as something that dislocates the subject and disrupts its identifications with specific subject positions. It also shows the fragmentary nature of the subject, which does not fully succeed in its effort to stabilize itself through narrative. This instability, the elusiveness of the subject in relationship to the interlocutor, is particularly evident in the use of pronouns: in how the subject constituted as "I" stands in relationship to the "you" of the speaking situation.

The pronouns "I" and "you" are instances of what linguists call indexicals. Indexicals are signifiers that have no stable signifieds but assume meaning in relationship to the subject of discourse, even potentially shifting referents within a single utterance.[4] As Benveniste argued, "Language is possible only because each speaker sets himself up as a *subject* by referring to himself as *I* in his discourse" (Benveniste 1971:225) and, conversely, language is the basis of subjectivity. The "I" constitutes the speaker as a person in relationship to a "you," the interlocutor, and establishes a relationship to that which is spoken, what Benveniste calls a "testimony to the identity of the subject" (Benveniste 1971:226). Consciousness of "I" comes about because the speaking "I" contrasts itself to a "you" that is exterior to it.

I focus here on the use of the indexical "I" as a stylistic device,[5] as a marker of the relationship of the subject to the discourse. More accurately, I focus on a process of substitution, in which the speaking "I" is in certain contexts replaced by other pronouns. These substitutions reveal the discontinuities in the subject and the conflicted nature of the subject's desire. In this case, interpretation of Ahmed's pronoun use also requires attention to his use of verbal tense markers, another indexical feature of language, because it is through the creation of distinct temporal spaces that Ahmed located himself in relation to the narrative and to me.

Focusing on certain portions of the dialogue that I interpreted as being particularly conflictual for Ahmed, I will demonstrate that it is precisely this conflict that is indexed through his use of pronouns. Ahmed did not know where to locate himself within the narrative that he constructed for me. Though he constituted himself as the speaking subject by calling himself "I" in the usual way opposite the "you" who was his audience (i.e., me), he generally avoided using "I" within his narrative. In other words, the subject who was present with me in the interview kept sliding away from the subject who had been present at the mahfil, avoiding identifications with that remembered self and its experiences in the room with the pīr. The subject struggled to evade representation in the narrative. It did this through rapid shifts in the use of pronouns.

After some informal conversation, I framed the interview with an initial question: "Can you just lay out some of the steps of the format of the mahfil?" In his response to this question, he spoke for approximately thirty minutes, interrupted only by my occasional request for clarification. The occurrences of "I" or "me" in Ahmed's near-monologue are few and far between. As he began his description, it occurred only in the context of verbs in the present tense or in the polite imperative. These occurrences establish, mark, and maintain the present relationship between the speaker and the interlocutor, the interviewer. So in response to my initial question, he began: "OK, Let me reconstruct, try to reconstruct something here." This utterance established a specific project that the subject is embarking upon.

After this initial framing of his project, he began his description, and first-person pronouns disappeared, replaced by a distancing third person "they" and "it" (the latter giving agency to the mahfil itself) and the second-person "you," which suggests that he saw himself functioning as a facilitator so that I could imagine myself in the situation:

> To begin with, almost inevitably it started after sunset prayers. . . .
> You'd arrive there at the location to be part of the sunset prayers.

> You would offer the prayers together and then everyone would sit together in—on the floor, in the chosen room. And they would begin by a lecture. So—[pause]—like, the leader, if you will, would first give a lecture on a topic of relevance, or the topic he or she has chosen to speak on that day. So, it would be a very short and concrete lecture.

The next instances of the use of "I" were scattered through the description, and all appeared within the context of metacommentaries on the narrative. For example, "After the lecture, there used to be a—what I might call, a short recess." In this instance, he has commented on the narrative itself and on how he is shaping it for this specific audience. By his choice of the word "recess" he has imported an English term not normally used in the context of a mahfil but rather in contexts that he would expect me to be familiar with, thus drawing on something he presumes we share. This "I" thus locates him as a speaking subject, clearly anchoring the "I" in the here and now. Another occurrence functioned in the same way: "I'm now forgetting the exact sequence here," alluding to the act of narration itself.

A subsequent use of "I" is a bit more complex and indicates that he was beginning to inhabit the narrative in a new way. "After that people were offered to drink and eat part of the food, if they so wished. The water used to go very quickly, I remember that [laughs]. There was usually only one glass." It is still metacommentary, with the "I" referring solely to the narrator, yet it is a narrator who "remembers" and, therefore, was present. Furthermore, his emotional reactions, evident in his laugh, are beginning to enter the narrative. I suspect that he was reproducing in the room with me an experience he had at the mahfil, when he observed that there was never enough water to meet the demand. This reproduction was possible because he had at the moment of observing the disappearance of the water been in a kind of observational mode similar to the one he was in with me, a similar subject position.

It was immediately after this moment that Ahmed's use of pronouns, and, thus, the framing of subject positions began to shift:

> Then—this is like we're talking up to now from the beginning, we're talking probably an hour altogether. Again, the timing and the format vary from one mahfil to another, but approximately. Then would come the part where we would go into this trance that

> I was talking about. And the way it would begin is that someone
> would turn the lights off, keeping perhaps one light in the back on.
> And everyone would gather as near to the murīd as possible. And
> the murīd would then say a prayer.

Here he used "we" in two different ways. In the first sentence, the first
"we" is ambiguously either the "royal we" or the speaker and interlocutor allied in the common project of reconstruction. But the second "we"
marks the moment of slide; it straddles the "we" of narration" and the
"we" of participation in a manner reminiscent of the auto mechanic
who says, "We're talking about an hour" as an estimate of how long it
will take to fix your car: it's not the talking but the fixing that takes an
hour. By the next sentence, the speaking subject has for the first time
fully identified with the "we" of the mahfil participants. The speaker at
that moment began to inhabit the dialogue in a new way, breaking a
frame that he had previously drawn around his "reconstruction" project. Previously the "I" of the present speaker had been firmly marked
off from the "they" (or slightly less firmly "you") of the mahfil.[6] The use
of "I was" in the same sentence marks a move to recover his analytic
observing stance, a move back into our interaction. It is a kind of
"looking back," analogous to the child whom Lacan describes as entering his own mirror image but then immediately looking behind his
shoulder to see his mother's approving gaze.

From this point in the narrative Ahmed increasingly betrayed his
ambivalence about the phenomenon he was describing — specifically,
trance. His inconsistent use of pronouns became particularly evident as
his description got closer to the moment when people began going into
trance. These pronouns were a shifting index of the extent to which he
felt himself identified with the process of experiencing trance and God's
immediate presence. After sliding into the narrative with "we," he
jumped back out and shifted to "they," before returning to the more
ambiguous "you."

> Everyone is sitting now and sort of facing the murīd. And nearer
> to the murīd than they were before. So, like if they were spread out
> all over the carpet and the murīd was here, then they would sort of
> move in a little bit, to be nearer the murīd. The murīd would then
> say a prayer and start chanting "Allah." Now, that is in this par-
> ticular case. I have also attended other mahfils by other murīds,
> and they chant something else. And their formats are vastly dif-

ferent. I mean, this particular murīd used to chant "Allah hu," and theoretically, if you're a pious and religious and whatnot, you can get yourself so intoxicated with that, or so engrossed in it, that you can actually begin to feel yourself saying, "Allah hu," without even saying it.

It was almost as if, as Qazi Sahib used to tell us, you know that there comes a stage when you just begin to say it even though you're not saying it. It's subconsciously in there, and your tongue starts moving and your heart starts beating. And one thing that you would guarantee is that if you were doing it sincerely and if it was working for you, you—your heartbeat would shoot up. Very, very strong heartbeat.

It was during this stage, and the main reason for the people to sort of gather round him rather than stay away from him, is that he would receive what is called "Allah ka nūr," or light, guidance. And, what he had to do was: he would then, one by one, choose all the people that were around him and sort of touch them at the place of their heart, just with one of his fingers. And, as he explained it to me, that would redirect some of the nūr that he was receiving to his disciples or followers, or whatever you want to call it, and increase the intensity of the people that were present or were participating.

Then he raised the sensitive issue of his personal experience directly, shifting to the first-person pronoun. The speaking subject suddenly appears prolifically in the utterance, but it is in order to reestablish a relationship of collaboration with me as interlocutor through an act of denial that severed his connection with the phenomenon he had just described:

> I used to say to—I can tell you very categorically that I never achieved that state where I would say that I had totally lost my time or place or any of those senses. Uh—but [stress], I can also tell you that in most of these mahfils that I attended, there were people there who used to go through a stage—I would say about ten to fifteen minutes—into this [pause] activity. But I feel that they would just sort of lose their sense of time and place and [pause] their senses. Start moving around or just go on and on. And then it used to be the murīd who used to, like, make a judgment as to when it had gone long enough or perhaps in some cases,

far enough that maybe it had become dangerous to continue for some people. He would, at that time, very, very slowly stop the proceedings and then they would offer a prayer of thanks and all that. But the way he would stop the proceedings . . . he would not just: "Allah hu, and stop now" [laughs]. It used to be — he would start saying other verses. And that was an indication to everyone to relax and come back to reality. And then, towards the end of his finishing up, someone would switch on the lights.

After his description of the mahfil, Ahmed made more explicit some of his anxieties surrounding the issue of trance and his own position in relationship to it, anxieties that he had experienced within the mahfil itself. He told me a story of confronting the pīr directly with these anxieties. In contrast to his description of the mahfil, where the spoken "I" of the present conversation had no comfortable locus in the past, this story created an identity between the remembered "I" and the speaking "I:" "Some people had gone through a major trance. Other people had not. Which made me wonder what the story was. So, I asked him one day, right. Categorically."

Not only is the "I" who spoke to the pīr identified by the same signifier as the "I" who is presently speaking; Ahmed also reproduced in our conversation some of the reflections on his action that probably anticipated his question of the pīr: "right. Categorically." He then re-produced the question itself, reliving the moment with me. It is itself a full moment, when he has the full attention and acceptance of the pīr. In this moment of love he can describe his own lack, the gap he feels between himself and his image of the real Sufi.

There are people there I see who become so, let's say, intense, that they start dancing round and round and all that. And there are other people like myself who, at all times, know exactly what's going on, even though our eyes are closed and we are concentrat-ing, or at least trying to concentrate as much as the others. And my question to him was, "Is this an indication to you of who's more religious or less religious?" And he gave me an answer that again strengthened my faith in him. He said, "No, no. It's not that. It's not that he's more religious or you're more religious. None of us — none of us humans can make a judgment about another one. Maybe what you're doing is right. Maybe the fact that you keep your senses all the time is right. Maybe those people are wrong. I don't know." He said, "All I can say is, the fact is that all of these people are participating and they are going to benefit from it. This is all I can say." To me, that was a very nice answer, you know. He could have said, "Yah, he's more religious. Tough luck. You gotta work harder on your morals," or something [laughs]. But he didn't [pause]. I liked his answer very much. That was a nice answer.

He described a contrast between what he expected as an answer — a kind of superego response, an interpellation of the "Hey, you" variety, which stimulates guilt (" 'You gotta work harder on your morals,' or something") and is embedded in conflict and rivalry, and the response he got, which was an unconditional acceptance.

Later in the conversation, Ahmed returned to a position from which his own subjectivity began again to slip away from signification as he identified the criticisms that he imagines his Pakistani friends living in the United States might level against Sufi practice. "There are two extremes. There are two levels of criticism. One is 'too religious,' another is 'simply wacky.' What I'm saying is, the person who considers himself to be Muslim may identify the process as wacky or too religious. We're not even talking about the people who do not consider themselves to be practicing Muslims. That would be another category." He reiterated several times that he has avoided talking to anyone about the subject directly, thus making it clear that he is imagining these criticisms. This is the other created by the subject. The subject is then interpellated vis-à-vis this other as "wacky," or "too religious."

As he continued, he projected onto the other his own fear, creating a kind of doubled other. "I get the feeling (I don't know why I get the feeling), I get the feeling that they would be afraid. I'm not sure, afraid of what? Afraid of the process maybe, or afraid of turning to fundamentalism — afraid of being branded a fundamentalist. I'm not sure what afraid of." The other is itself constrained by fear of an other, resulting in an effect analogous to a hall of mirrors, in which there are infinite images reflecting off each other. This is an effect of his position as a postcolonial subject living as a minority in a diaspora community. He displays a fear of an Orientalizing discourse constituted out of the categories that he can see being used by the Western media when they describe Muslims. It creates an identity that he and his Pakistani friends seek to evade, a condition of being Muslim that is penetrated by the derogatory label "fundamentalist," closely associated with the alien, the foreign, even the violent, the terrorist. It forces him into a marginalized position, to which he responds by silently conforming to the demands of that doubled other.[7]

It is within the context of this Orientalist discourse that the notion of science gets caught up in an ideology in which "science" as a signifier is associated with logic and rationality and contrasted with that which is foreign and irrational, Oriental. Given our respective relationships to this discourse, on apparently opposite sides of the Orientalist divide, it might be expected that at this moment in our dialogue, our relationship would have shifted. But Ahmed located himself in a peculiar position — in a form of symbolic identification with my gaze as a representative of the other. This shift is evident, once again, in his use of pronouns. He speaks of the "foreigners" who are subjected to this discourse as "they": "Here's the problem, here's the problem. The issue, I think comes down to the way foreigners from developing nations behave when they come down to what is typically known as the developed nation. And they come to the United States and they come to England and they see, they hear a lot about two things: logic and science, logic and science." But his subject position immediately shifts in his next utterance: "And I can tell you very categorically that Islam is against neither of them." He is once again present as subject, as the "I" instructing me, for the moment occupying the subject position of Muslim and arguing for the synthetic capacity of Islam. In this context, he is the Muslim communicating to the non-Muslim, and we are on opposite sides of the Orientalist divide, which he is challenging as a Muslim. But he cannot sustain this position for long and finds himself unwillingly drawn into the Orientalist position because of his identification with a scientific ideology.

> But the problem becomes that, for example, how logically can you explain to someone the fact that, if you are quote committed and in connection with Allah, with an appropriate setting like the mahfil and with an appropriate guide, your murīd, you may actually be able to receive some guidance from Allah through him?
>
> I have said this statement. You've heard it. But if I sat down here and tried to put it in some logical framework, I can't. Other than religion. OK, that's the problem. The problem would be: how would some of these people who are always talking about logic and science and be doing the right thing and making sense out of everything they do and all that — they may find it difficult that —

How can we explain this phenomenon? How can that person go into trance?

KPE: Right, so it's too immediate. It brings religion right down into everyday.

Ahmed had ostensibly put the problem in cognitive terms, as an issue of belief, as if science and religion were incommensurable paradigms. Though he posed the issue in terms of a tension between Western science and the idea of the infusion of an experience of God into daily life, he said several times that Islam can readily encompass the limited perspectives of scientific discourse. Even the question he finally got to with so much affect, "How can a person go into trance?" is readily answerable in ideological terms. And he has the empirical evidence to show that people do, in fact, go into trance. He is even convinced by their extraordinary perceptual powers in this state: at one point he movingly recounted how, at the moment his father was fatally injured in an automobile accident, his fellow Sufis, still in a meditative state, had felt the disaster. The cognitive aspects of conversion are thus not really problematic, judging from Ahmed's statements.

This cognitive emphasis is masking a different order of phenomenon, which could better be characterized in terms of desire and fear. That I intuitively recognized that the issue was not a cognitive one is suggested by my response to his question "How can we explain this phenomenon? How can that person go into trance?" I responded by highlighting the issue of the personal immediacy of the experience and its relevance for everyday experience. At the time, the conflict—the fear versus the temptation—was becoming manifest in our conversation, and we could both feel its immediacy and intensity.

This fear and intensity is reflected in his next utterances, when pronoun shifts became rapid as he brought the subject into the room and, ultimately, to himself: "I think *you're* afraid of that. I don't know what *it's* afraid of but there is something that may inhibit *people* from participating. *I* would say *I* was one of *them, you* know. *I* am still confused about how is it possible?" (My emphasis.) In this last sentence, he started with an indirect question, then converted it to a direct question midsentence, as if wanting to ask me directly to help him out with this.

A: I can understand, I can visualize a person getting so much into religion that he can then begin to receive some of that guidance from Allah.

KPE: Because you've seen?

A: Now, keeping in mind that guidance is not some sort of [inaudible]: here's what you should do and here's what you shouldn't do. It's just some nūr, as you say, some light. Some unconscious light that you feel you have received that makes you a better person, makes you a better religious person, in any case.

KPE: But it somehow changes the way you are as a person?

A: It does, it does. And that brings to mind another thing that people often get concerned with here, foreigners who have come here, is about the difference between morals — moral education and religious education.

This last statement was an adroit conversational move that took us away from the conflictual issue of his temptation to conversion to the issue of teaching Sunday school to the Westernized children of the Muslim population. It continues the theme of Islam in a foreign land, but focuses on the less personal, the common ground of the Muslim community in America, protecting its heritage in the face of secular and Christian pressures. This shift was facilitated by my question, which instead of aiming at feelings as it should have, pushed him into intellectualized concepts.

Vestiges of his confrontation with a personal conflict continued to be evident in this conversation. Though he had shifted to an apparently straightforward topic, his utterances were very confused and difficult to follow. He wound down by saying, "It's very confusing. Some of these people that we're talking about may bring some point up, too. About the whole religious concept to begin with, and the mahfil in particular." He thus acknowledged his confused state, but attributed it to the intellectual issue of morals and religion. Once he had recovered himself, he brought the topic back to the Sufi gathering.

In the above dialogue, he expressed inchoate fears that his social relationships with friends, family, colleagues, would alter or be undermined. The problem, as Ahmed expressed it, was the possibility of confrontation with people who are skeptical or critical of Sufi practice. These people are Pakistanis, but they are Pakistanis in an American environment. For Ahmed, the projection of a "professional" identity is not incompatible with a Sufi identity, as his Sufi master has skillfully demonstrated (a point I will discuss below). But in America, this professional identity is refracted through his imagined construction of the generalized gaze of the American, which threatens to marginalize him.

Despite this inhibiting gaze, Qazi Sahib, his father's Sufi guide, is a strong draw for Ahmed, a focus of his desire for recognition. Ahmed had seen a dramatic shift in his father's behavior and a facilitation of their relationship as a result of his involvement in Sufism. "In the last two or three years of his life, he changed very dramatically." This was the period in which his father had become a follower of Qazi Sahib.

> I was here, in the United States. I did my bachelor's here, my master's, and then I was going to do my Ph.D. He was guiding me on what I should do for my Ph.D., and I was disagreeing with him. And the last time I met him before he died, we disagreed, but that was it. There was no anger in him, and therefore I did not feel threatened about disagreeing with him. You know. "You shouldn't do this. This is my advice, blah, blah, blah." Which again, to me, was a very strong indication that he was converging to Sufism or whatnot, where one of the main characteristics is that you present your viewpoint and then let the people figure out what they need to do.

Not only did Ahmed recognize the beneficial impact that Qazi Sahib had had on his father; he sees Qazi Sahib as a powerful role model for himself. One of the things that Ahmed admires about Qazi Sahib, who also held an important position in Pakistan's government, is his successful integration of his religion and his practical life, something that Ahmed has not fully achieved for himself. As Ahmed said, "It's just amazing to me that he can bring them together so neatly and, at the same time, keep them apart," meaning that he can synthesize the two perspectives while contextualizing and compartmentalizing his relationships. Ahmed has had contact with him both in his capacity as a high-ranking government official and at Sufi gatherings. Ahmed himself found it difficult dealing with him in such different settings. Ahmed has not yet achieved an integration he is comfortable with, though the examples of both his father and Qazi Sahib offer him powerful models to follow.

Such a model is powerful because it offers not only an experience of community but an alternative to the dichotomy between science and religion that locates Pakistan on the global periphery and creates for the Pakistani professional a marginalized identity as subordinate to his Western colleagues. In contrast, a Sufi identity is represented through a history — the Sufi lineage — and supported through a relationship —

with the Sufi master—who has himself successfully transcended his own experience of inconsistent or marginalized identities and is near the center of political power and prestige, even by international standards.

But in an American environment, the process of "conversion" carries with it more uncertainty. The threat of marginalization is more immediate, a part of daily experience. One's identity as professional is, consequently, more crucial but also more precarious. Ahmed's narrative suggests that in this situation his identity is constituted, not by his ability to come to a satisfying synthesis of science and Islam, but by a complex sequence of mirrorings: he is constituted by his imagined construction of the community of fellow expatriate Pakistanis in North Carolina, who in turn are imagining their own identities with regard to their construction of how their American colleagues perceive and locate them.

The Sufi identity offers the opportunity for a more centered identity—grounded not only in an imagined image of God reflecting back one's identity, nor primarily in relationship with a dominant other, the Sufi master, but in the immediate, bodily experience of trance.

Yet this opportunity is particularly risky in an American environment perceived as rational and restrained. There is the danger that his Pakistani friends will label him as "wacky" or "fundamentalist" in order to distance themselves from a signifier that threatens to marginalize them further.

When we examine the process of conversion as it is played out within the individual, we see that it is not simply one of competition and struggle between incommensurable perspectives, as it may look when articulated in a public arena. There is a difference between public rhetoric and the perspectives and experience of the individual whose soul—identity and loyalty—is hanging in the balance. Kuhn's (1970) idea of paradigm notwithstanding, changes in belief can be a gradual, synthetic process. In Ahmed's case, the human capacity to synthesize and to integrate is manifested in a version of Islam where science and God comfortably coexist. Even the idea of direct infusion of the "light" of God into immediate experience—the trance—would be unproblematic if it weren't for affectively powerful relational issues associated with that experience, relations that locate the actor in a political universe. Taking on a new identity is a socially disorienting process. It requires a break and a leap that is less a matter of belief than of relationship and the courage to shatter a labyrinthian hall of mirrors. An identity change is a risk and a rupture. It is the last, public stage of a gradual, deniable process of conversion. At the moment of rupture, the materiality and physicality of ecstasy are linked to the world of discourse, and the individual goes public with a conversion narrative that, in a political act, highlights the rupture and labels the convert's new identity.

The Fear

For many of those who are tempted by Sufism in today's postcolonial world, the barriers to immersion in Sufi practice are framed cognitively in terms of a clash between a Western secularist, scientific discourse and Islam. But when their ambivalence is examined closely, the problem appears to be less one of plausibility in the face of the power of Western discourse than of a fear that accompanies the intense desire that pervades Sufi accounts of themselves and their relationship to a murshid. What is the fear? Perhaps its source can be located in the following story, narrated to me by a Lahore businessman who is also the disciple of a pīr. In this story, the merger of the personalities of the disciple and the pīr is given vivid cultural expression. The subject is collapsed into the other, resulting in ecstatic annihilation:

> When a murshid is about to die, he may decide to pass on his spirituality to someone. He calls this person, takes his face between his hands, puts his lips on the lips of that person, inserts his tongue into this person's mouth, and embraces him. It happens so quickly — it changes a person completely. All veils are lifted completely and spiritual enlightenment comes. Whatever a shaikh has, this person has it, too. For example, my *dādā* murshid [literally, "grandfather teacher," i.e., the pīr of one's pīr], had a disciple, not a learned person, but a man who served him faithfully, giving him his water pipe, getting groceries, sweeping the floor. He served with the utmost devotion for several years. One day the murshid was in a kind mood and promised to pray to God to give him anything he wanted. The disciple asked, "Honored master, make me like yourself." When he said that, an expression of sorrow flitted across the murshid's face, and he said, "Don't ask me for this." But the disciple held him to his promise, so they went alone into a room. My murshid and *pīr-bhā'īs* [literally "pīr-brothers," disciples of the same pīr] waited outside for fifteen minutes. Sud-

denly the door opened. We thought that our murshid was standing in the doorway, but we looked closely and found that it was the disciple. But there was a radiance about him — he looked like our murshid. He stepped across the threshold, and then he heaved one long sigh and fell dead. We ran to pick him up, but he was dead. The murshid said, "I tried to dissuade him. I told him he wasn't ready for it. But he wouldn't listen, so I put myself into him, and he couldn't bear it." This is what happens; this is how a transfer takes place. So before he transfers this spirituality, the pīr prepares the person for it.

This is a story of the structure of desire in Sufi terms. It graphically depicts the impossibility of desire: the moth desires the flame but is burnt, annihilated when it flies too close. The subject, which is founded on separation, collapses unless the person is "prepared." Preparation involves developing the personality through the inculcation of discipline.

The moral of this particular story was that the process of identification with the Sufi master involves a slow, gradual transmission — a structuring of the personality over many years. This structuring involves a play of distance and closeness that is often frustrating for the disciple and exacerbates the experience of longing desire for that which is absent. A story told by the famous Sufi Jalāl ud-Dīn Rūmī about his murshid exemplifies this process:

> It seems that one day Rumi went to his murshid's house. But when he arrived, he found that Tabrizi had just left. Rumi quickly looked down the narrow streets and saw the coattails of his master as he turned into an alley. He followed his murshid. Yet whenever he got near, Tabrizi went into another house, and Rumi followed him in. But once inside he did not see his master anywhere, so he went up on the flat roof. But he did not see him on the roof, either.
>
> So he jumped off, and his murshid caught him in his arms.[8]

Desire is only possible when the murshid retains the wall of separation, resisting the disciple's fantasy of merger. Anxiety arises out of a fear that the wall will collapse, threatening that the impossible desire will be fulfilled. The disciple must be able to trust the murshid to be there when needed and, as importantly, to be absent, when that is necessary for the disciple's development.

The subject, writes Kristeva, is founded on a necessary emptiness — on a fundamental recognition that the infant is not the mother's ultimate object of desire, that what the mother of infancy ultimately wants is "not-I." It is the infant's realization of difference. A space opens up between the child and mother, a painful separation that must be maintained if the ego is to emerge (Kristeva 1986b:257).[9] Narcissism is a defense against the emptiness of that necessary separation, a structure on which the subject builds its imaginary representations of itself. Desire — or at least one form of desire — is born out of the loss of that primal undifferentiated state. It is a desire for that which has no meaning because it precedes meaning, which is itself founded on difference. The subject as reified, nameable entity is founded in separation and undergoes a further alienation with its entry into the structure of language (Lacan's Symbolic Order): "The subject exists because it belongs to the Other, and it is in proceeding from that symbolic belonging that causes him to be subject to love and death that he will be able to set up for himself imaginary objects of desire" (Kristeva 1986b:253).

The story of the lowly devotee is a story of the collapse of the structure of desire. The painful separation has been overcome, and thus the ego collapses. The subject ceases to be. Though by plunging into the flame, the devotee willingly suffered his own extinction, many people experience intense anxiety in the face of such a threat and throw up defenses to ward it off. The professor and Ahmed expressed concerns about the incompatibility of their secular, scientific identities with Sufi practice. But the focus of their anxiety centered around their fear of giving up "control," fear of letting go in the moment of ecstatic trance, fear of the collapse of the fixed boundaries of an Imaginary subject position.

My Desire

Sufi literature is replete with depictions of the state of longing. For the past ten centuries it has been fashionable among Sufis to speak of passionate love ('ishq) or desire (shauq) for God, following the example of the tenth-century Sufi Nūrī, who wrote of his passionate love for God (see Ernst 1985:98). But others have been scandalized by the idea. Ghulām Khalīl, an opponent of Nūrī, considered those who speak of "desire" and "love" in any context to be no better than adulterers (Ernst 1985:97), thereby making an association with sexual desire explicit. But Nūrī's usage entered Sufi thought and became a common means for Sufis to express their relationship with God and even with the human spiritual guide, the pīr. It is out of these relationships that the Sufi experience of self emerges, annihilated and reconstituted in the experience of God. Though most expressions of longing are stated in terms of a desire for union with God, devotion to one's Sufi master is often expressed in similar terms. As Seyyed Nasr explains a verse of the Persian Sufi poet Tabriz, "To behold the perfect master is to regain the ecstasy and joy of the spring of life and to be separated from the master is to experience the sorrow of old age" (Nasr 1977:58).

While investigating the relationship between the Sufi and his guide, I was constantly challenged by Sufis to experience that relationship. I found this challenge tempting and dangerous, like the call of the sirens. This experience helped me recognize that for many Pakistanis, too, the draw of the Sufi is highly conflictual: desire and fear are closely intertwined.

Psychoanalytic understanding relies heavily on the experience of a relationship in which the patient "transfers," and thereby reenacts, unconscious conflicts in a relationship with the psychoanalyst. The psychoanalyst in turn experiences the reenactment of his/her own conflicts in the form of "countertransferences." Reflection on these countertransferences enables the analyst to apprehend the patient's conflicts. Anthropologists, though espousing the principle of participant observation, have not traditionally used their own affective reactions as a research tool (but see Devereux 1967; Ewing 1987). Since my informants made it clear that I could not simply understand Sufism as an outside observer, I follow the same principle in assuming that I cannot, in turn, begin to represent Sufi practice without conveying at least some aspects of the way in which I was drawn into this powerful discourse (see Ewing 1994).

As in the psychotherapeutic encounter, that which is most difficult to discuss is usually that which is linked to the heart of the matter at hand. I follow the same principle in trying to communicate an aspect of my own experience of Sufism. I, therefore, focus on a point where desire and fear were intensely present, on an episode where I have difficulty remaining present as a subject, just as Ahmed had difficulty remaining present in his discussion of trance in the mahfil.

This fear has many components, but one of the ways in which it manifests itself in Sufi practice is in a tension between spiritual desire and sexuality. The close links between the desire for God and sexual passion is something of an open secret: the primary criticism that is made of certain classes of Sufis who are viewed as corrupt is that they engage in activities that when specified sound like the sexual fantasies of the critic (see chapter 8).

Near the end of my first round of research in Pakistan, I explained to a Sufi who was also a High Court justice that I had not gotten involved in Sufism myself. He commented, "It's like having coke instead of champagne" (a comment whose significance is complicated by the Islamic prohibition against alcohol, making it a forbidden pleasure). What I did not admit to him then was that, though in overt behavior and conversation I always played the part of the anthropologist — observing, taking notes, interviewing — my own subject position had been severely challenged by the power of Sufi discourse. And what I experienced in these very uncomfortable moments forms the foundation from which I now interpret. I describe and analyze the experiences these Sufis described — the longing, the love, the feeling of death — from my own, first-person perspective. My goal is to demonstrate, by making explicit who I was to the people I talked to and vice versa, how they constituted me as other and how I constituted them as other. I aim to show just how love and desire — that which I and most anthropologists have systematically expunged from our "work" — shape the Sufi project. Only in this way is it possible to move beyond the categories of Western discourse into a position that is structured in other terms.

I focus here on what was for me a traumatic encounter that I had with a Sufi about ten months into fieldwork. I offer an interpretation of my confused musings as I recorded them in a series of journal entries that narrated the story of this particular encounter. It is not the "best" or most "spiritual" encounter I had during my fieldwork, were I to judge my experiences in such terms. The man I will be describing is by no means the perfect Sufi. I met many other Sufis who were much closer to at least my fantasy of what a Sufi should be, and others on the Sufi path subsequently made veiled allusions to the shortcomings of this man. But this encounter revealed to me the complex workings of desire, subjectivity, and power and helped me to understand the fear that often tinged the desire expressed by many of the people I talked with.

My encounter occurred during a period in which the "natural" separation I had made between my "field notes" and my "journal" — my "work" and my "self" — had begun to break down. The episode I recount was a moment when the barrier dropped. One meeting was recorded in my journal, the next in my field notes, and the next in my journal. There was no longer any separation about what I thought and felt in my "spare time" and my research. My work was beginning to shape not only my experience of Pakistan but even my subjective experience of me. To put it in Lacanian terms, signifiers began slipping in an alarming fashion as my own desire began to intrude, disrupting my identity as observing anthropologist.

I include a preamble taken from my journal — my meeting with the man who introduced me to the Sufi I will be focusing on — because it indicates the way in which I was subtly being drawn into the tissue of Sufi reality. I had met a television writer who was involved in Sufism — who seemed to be on the kind of longing quest I had heard of from many others. Our conversation had occurred in his office, and I felt the power of his longing as he talked of Sufism. I recorded the following in my journal, because it seemed at the time to have more to do with me than with fieldwork, since it was explicitly about me and my supposedly inner or private states:

> [He said,] "Sufism is not practice, because practice is work, and work produces sweat and exhaustion. It's all in plans. Don't get caught up in plans. Just accept what comes, accept what comes from God." His hypnotic voice trailed off, and I suppose he was looking at me, but I don't know. I suppose I was looking at him. But what I felt was the sinking of my awareness to its source, a resting in the planless moment. Then quietly, almost abstractedly, he said, "Ah, you will learn many, many things." Then he made what felt like a violent leap and asked me if I had seen the wedding customs, the henna put on the bride's hand, the decorations. I returned to academic repartee and told him some more about my research among pīrs and the customs I had observed. I said nothing about the moment I had experienced. As we concluded the meeting, he promised to help me with my research by taking me to meet his pīr a few days later.

Two days later, I recorded in my journal that after our meeting, a mutual acquaintance reported to me that he had seen the television writer, who had said that I was a "real Sufi, a faqīr." I was taken aback, since I had said nothing of that moment I had experienced.

A few days later, the television writer and his wife took me to meet his pīr. This was a part of my "work," and so I recorded the event as field notes. I was quite impressed with the setting. It was the first "real" *khānaqāh* I had seen — a compound where Sufis actually lived together with their teacher, just as I had read about in the old Sufi texts. After I had spent some time in a gathering with the pīr and the couple who had brought me, I was introduced to a tall man in his thirties, a doctor, and was told that he would answer any questions that I had. With a black beard, fur Jinnah cap, and slightly tinted glasses, he was an imposing figure. He spoke fluent English, and so I felt comfortable talking with him, able to express and understand subtleties that were beyond my capabilities in Urdu. At that first meeting, we talked for about two hours. According to my field notes, our conversation began in the following way:

> The doctor asked me about my research. Another bearded, older man, whom I didn't notice at first, sat with us. I suppose I assumed that he couldn't follow our conversation, but eventually I realized that he would agree at certain points and clearly knew English well. The doctor briefly summarized my research for him in his own style: "She is studying pīri-murīdi. The phenomenon of simple people wanting to be fleeced by pīrs." When I protested that this was not how I would have phrased it, he said, "He knows what I mean," and they gave each other a knowing look, as though his words had a double significance — as though maybe it was a good thing for people to want to be fleeced by a pīr.
>
> The doctor asked me how I was going to distinguish simple people from nonsimple people. I protested at the rigid categories but proceeded to differentiate between people with a well thought out and consistent worldview and those who are more "simple," i.e., whose beliefs tend toward magic and whose ideas are not consistent with each other. He then proceeded to describe to me the simple person: "The simple person is simple in speech, in behavior, in knowledge, and in sincerity. The man who is simple in behavior tries to understand a situation and take the most direct actions. For example, that man held out a dish in our direction. This man here thought that the dish contained edibles. And so it does. He thought that since edibles are meant to be consumed, the intention was to put the plate before you, since you would seem to be the person to consume them. Actually he misunderstood, because the intention was that the edibles be put in the sun to dry. That is simple behavior. Do you have any questions?

At that point, always the anthropologist, I asked him about his own experiences, trying to be in charge at some level, to move away from what I saw as abstract discussions that I had heard before, into the concrete data of life stories and personal narratives, as I often did in interviews. He willingly obliged. He began by admitting, "I used to be a very rigid man. It was inherited. My grandfather was a rigid man, my father is a rigid man." He then told me how he had come to be a Sufi — how he had been "stopped dead" by an experience while he was in medical school and then began his search for a murshid. When he met his pīr, he stayed. He had been living with his pīr for fourteen years, writing commentaries on the Quran.

After our conversation, we arranged to meet again in four days. I recorded that next meeting in my journal, rather than in my field notes, because it shook me up. I felt that I was writing about me, and I interspersed the narrative of our conversation with my thoughts about life, society, and my reactions to the Western authors I was reading in my spare time.

> Another strange experience today — embarrassing to write down, maybe because I am so confused. Sometimes waking can sink to dreaming, until there is no reality left.
>
> I went today to the khānaqāh of Hazrat Fazal Shah and talked again with the doctor. I was nervous as I entered, I think because I have a desire to accept a guide, find a "perfect man" [*insān-i kāmal*], or at least someone who is wiser than I. Yet I am torn, afraid of the danger of getting carried away into falseness, carried away from my own truth. I felt that I should act the anthropologist, and I knew that I was putting too much of myself on the line. But to understand a Sufi, mustn't one be a Sufi?
>
> We began to talk as though the conversation had been broken off just five minutes before. He said that one must have certain equipment to tread the world over, the equipment being those things he told me last time, about looking for sincerity in a person. He gave me a very good answer to my question, "What if your murshid orders you to go against sharī'at?" As he answered it, I realized that I hadn't even understood the question I was asking — it was purely hypothetical, but the completeness and immediacy of his answer made me realize that he had probably himself been through the experience of his murshid having ordered him to vio-

late the sharī'at. As he put it, "If someone becomes so rigid, this diversion from the doctrine of sharī'at is needed," and "rigid" is precisely how he had described himself in the past. But he still has a long way to go, though I don't think he realizes that himself.

When I began to throw out hints of my own view of reality, we began to have difficulty. He didn't understand my questions, partly because I didn't phrase them well. . . .

[two pages of conversation omitted]

The doctor's speech was hypnotic, but I think he hypnotized himself as much as he did me, or maybe he was being deliberately manipulative. He penetrated my eyes, and I felt a contact whenever I was looking into his as he talked. At those times, he would talk circles around an idea, repeating it over and over again in slightly varying ways, making the words into a kind of mantra, echoing through my mind. He seemed to be trying to control my mind, and then suggestions kept bombarding me. Words began standing out — "lips" — "the body"; his words were no longer answering my question about the direction of society changing. His speech flowed from all heading toward God Almighty to the destruction caused by making contacts, attachments with things. A man holding onto a buffalo by wrapping a chain around his hand was killed because the buffalo started to run, and the man couldn't free his hand. All is changing, all dies.

But then the argument lost its coherence, as the sexual allusions multiplied. He distinguished cells of the body — genetic cells from somatic cells. Somatic cells die, but genetic cells are passed on. "Are your parents alive?" They are passed on from your parents to you, and from you to your children. The genetic cells are concerned with your rūh [spirit] because they do not die. The cells which die are not connected with your rūh.

Now, this sounds like an interesting theory — and could certainly be a key to explaining the spiritual power of hereditary pīrs, but my impression was that he was talking nonsense, just free-associating. He drifted on to sperm and ova uniting to form a zygote ("You must have heard these words"). When he actually mentioned "copulation," I looked genuinely shocked and disapproving; the whole idea is so out of place in mixed company in Pakistan. But I had heard many stories about the inevitability of seduction whenever a man finds himself alone with a woman. His reaction to my shock was to say that these were "deep matters" and that nothing must be blocked. I am a little fuzzy about the exact conversation at this point, but when he asked me if he had answered my question, I said "No." I tried to get back to the direction of society, but he remained on his previous wavelength. He threw in the word "sex," though in its more neutral context: "If the sex of the child is male, the child at birth has no temperament, if female, it has a temperament." He then expounded on the differences between men and women: "A woman is a part of the male individual. She is not a self-suffering total, but is only one part of that individual."

In my journal I reported quite a bit more of this and of my increasingly negative opinion of his answers. I went to pay my respects to the pīr, and then returned to the doctor, who began the "assault" again.

He told me that my shalwar [loose Pakistani pants] was not good. When I asked him why, he said that it was synthetic and that synthetics are bad for the body. "Wear only cotton clothes. I can help you." I thought he was going to say he could give me cloth, but he immediately asked me if I needed money. Once again I was as taken aback and confused as I had been when he mentioned copulation. He went on into what I then perceived as a contradictory discussion about monetary relations, saying that they prove a relation real: the material you possess must be shared.

In bringing up money, he pinpointed a thought that had flashed through my mind while I was in the assembly hall sitting by his murshid. When I was getting up to go over to the murshid, I had started to pick up my notes and purse. The doctor stopped me, saying, "Leave your notes here." So when I was sitting apart from my bag, I thought, involuntarily, "What if he steals my money?" and immediately answered myself, "Oh, well, it's only a hundred rupees or so." So he managed to bring up the thought by offering me money. He also tied the money to a spiritual link — which I saw as contradictory at the time.

But what had first struck me as absurd in our earlier conversation, the tie between genetic cells and rūh, was precisely the same kind of equation. He was not making a rigid distinction between spiritual and material, as I was. . . .

So now I don't know what to think. Was he just giving me a hard test today, or was he dehumanizing me, as I thought at the time? I think he is telling me that two things I have to face first, and now, are precisely sex and money and the way they define my ties to others. . . .

He good-humoredly allowed me to jump to the level of superficial questions like how many buildings were in the compound, growing more concrete with each answer.

My most serious doubts surround the belief structure he is presenting to me — surely he can't expect me to believe his statements about women. I hear hints of his rigidity, but maybe he has his reasons for telling me what he does — gives me a framework to disrupt the remnants of my certainties. But he also threw in encouragements for me to remember (if I ever doubt) that I am welcome back. He told me that he liked my personality because I don't just agree with everything he says; I stop him and tell him I don't understand. At one point he talked about the will of God in my coming to Pakistan, in coming to him and his murshid.

Looking back after many years (on what I can't resist pointing out was a much younger, less mature "me"), another memory comes back to me. There were several prayer rugs set out in the compound, right by the main doorway of the khānaqāh. The doctor was just beginning his prayers when I left the compound. As I walked past him, he interrupted himself, almost careened off the rug, and strode into the interior of the compound. I never saw him again. When I returned for another visit a few days later, I was told that he had temporarily left town with his pīr, and no one knew when he would be back.

I mulled over this meeting in several subsequent journal entries, as in the following, written four days later:

I should try to write honestly about my reactions to the doctor. I think about him the way I mull over someone I am really attracted to, but I know he tried to trick me into such an attraction. But I still have a doubt — he may not be entirely sincere, but maybe he really can read people and understand what life is all about better than I can. He must have learned something in fourteen years. I have to talk with him some more so I can get behind him and see what he is. Was he deliberately trying to hypnotize and corrupt me or was this such a new situation for him that his intentions got sidetracked? Is he thoroughly deceitful or just naively desirous? Then,

of course, there is the remote possibility that he speaks from the
rarified atmosphere of wisdom and deliberately pinpointed my
central issues, as I convinced myself into believing at the time. I
don't have enough data to decide among these different realities.

I still don't have enough data, but the issues I see in the encounter are
somewhat different from the questions I asked at the time. What I see
now is that for each of us, the meeting was not a simple conversation,
but a contact in which we both experienced serious disjunctions that
disrupted the subject positions from which we were attempting to negotiate the encounter, the fantasies we were trying to actualize. I went
into the meeting primed for a repetition of the experience I had had
briefly with the television writer in his office—a shift of consciousness,
a kind of trance state, to put it bluntly, using a highly charged term that
is difficult for me to own.

Phenomenologically, was my experience with the television writer a
trance state? It had been a feeling perhaps close to that experienced by
the man who described the first meeting with his pīr as a kind of dying.
And I suppose—though I cannot know for certain, since I did not ask
him—that it was a mutual state, since the television writer later reported to a friend that I was a Sufi, a faqīr, solely on the basis of
our otherwise ordinary conversation. From this evidence alone, my
assumption that this was a private, inner state of mine must be questioned. Something happened in the space between us. It was not by any
means a loss of consciousness or awareness of my surroundings. Freud
wrote rather disparagingly and imprecisely of the "oceanic feeling"
associated with mysticism. The experience could perhaps be more accurately described as an altered relationship to language and to self.

I experienced a similar state again with the doctor, but it was also
dramatically different. As soon as I started to give up my usual orientation toward the world, my usual mode of listening, the doctor's language began to change. Signifiers began to stand out, detached from
their linguistic contexts, starting a metonymic slide, constituting a desire that I was not willing to acknowledge. My subjectivity began to
dissolve into the space between us. I had maintained an ego or subject
position grounded on an imaginary fantasy (shared by many Pakistanis) in which the Sufi has transcended sexuality by blocking it out,
denying its relevance, as if I could interact with these men without
having the reality of sexuality "intrude." I had taken on what I experi-

enced as middle-class Pakistani attitudes toward sexuality and corruption, as a kind of imaginary fantasy, grafted onto my own WASP ways. I had made the mistake of equating asceticism with the blocking out of sexuality and desire. But in a doubled mirroring, I also imagined myself as an other in the doctor's fantasy of the American woman, who is sexually promiscuous and unsubmissive. I felt intuitively that his fantasy was one of domination, and our interaction became one of struggling for control, as I metaphorically "fixed" him into a new configuration informed by psychoanalytic concepts and gradually came to see him, not as the powerful authority in whom I was tempted to invest an ego ideal in a transference relationship, but as a man struggling with overly rigid ego boundaries and a powerful desire that interrupted and overwhelmed his ego. The only evidence I have for the interruption, however, is the way he "interrupted" his prayers when I walked by.

Looking back now, this encounter feels like an interaction that is well described in terms of the Hegelian struggle for recognition and domination. This experience raises the question of whether the disciple who submits to a Sufi pīr becomes a pawn under the control of a dominating leader — precisely the kind of relationship that Muhammad Iqbal excoriated in his criticism of the traditional pīr-disciple relationship. But we must not assume that there are only dichotomous possibilities, autonomous self-control or passive submission to a dominating leader.

Muhabbat

What is expected of the relationship between pīr and disciple? Maneri, a fifteenth-century Bihari (north Indian) Sufi, repeats a familiar Sufi image: "It is indispensable for a Disciple to put off his desires and protests, and place himself before the Teacher as a dead body before the washer of the dead, so that He may deal with him as He likes" (Maneri 1980:38). In other words, the disciple is expected to be accepting and unquestioning of his pīr. Pakistani disciples struggle with this expectation. I was terrified of it, afraid of the domination that could so easily develop within such a relationship. But Sufis kept pointing to something more, something different. Something they called "muhabbat" (love).

Ahmed's description of the change in his father that came about as he became a Sufi and adopted the ways of his pīr demonstrates how the experience seemed to involve the antithesis of control. Ahmed's father had ceased trying to control him, allowing their relationship to develop in a positive way. Similarly, the pīr himself refrained from trying to control others in his professional capacity. Kristeva sees as one aspect of the culmination of the psychoanalytic process a renunciation of the will to dominate (Kristeva 1987:62). Renunciation of desire (*taw-wakul*) is a preliminary step on the Sufi path. It is safe to trust only a Sufi pīr who has himself renounced a desire for control of others. The institutional structure of Sufism, with its formal transmission of authority to the khalīfa, is regarded as a safeguard to protect the unwary disciple. The institutional structure of psychoanalysis is intended to operate in precisely the same way.

One professional man, a former accountant who had worked for an American government office in Lahore, discussed his own failure to achieve this accepting state in his relationship with Sufi Sahib in terms of his own prior immersion in Western ways of thinking: "You see, my only fault was that I always tried to analyze what he said. I don't know why. Because you see, I had been a student of science also. I studied; I have a master of sciences, a master of social sciences also. He treated me as his confidential secretary. But I had my shortcomings. I questioned some of his acts. I tried to differ with him. These were my faults." Though this disciple expressed his inability in terms of a tension between his Sufi and professional orientations, he did not see "science" as a threat to a Sufi frame of reference, but rather as a device that he, in his weakness, had used to distance himself from his pīr.

The disciple brings intense desire to the relationship with the pīr. And the pīr who is truly a murshid responds with love. What is this love? A moment of it can be seen in Ahmed's story, when he asked the question of his father's pīr whether a trance state was proof of religiosity and felt that he received nonjudgmental acceptance in response. Frances Trix, in a thoughtful study of her interactions with an Albanian Bektashi Sufi over many years, characterized this muhabbat as a kind of attunement (Trix 1993:145). The teaching relationship between murshid and disciple is characterized by moments of revelation in which the disciple suddenly understands something in a new light. The moment of revelation is a moment of relational awareness. This kind of attunement is only possible if the disciple does not come to the interaction with a rigid framework already in place, into which he or she seeks to insert knowledge.[10] It was this kind of rigid framework that Sufi Sahib's disciple felt had formed a barrier between himself and his pīr.

"Attunement" is a subtle meshing of interaction behavior. Trix describes a long, slow process in which the disciple learns the nuances of the murshid's utterances, the resonances associated with reciting a piece of poetry that come from a shared history of conversation stretching beyond this murshid-disciple relationship to that of the murshid's with his murshid, and so on back in a chain of transmission extending over generations.

There are also psychoanalysts who have attempted to capture and describe what I think is precisely this modality of relationship, though the stress is on the psychoanalyst becoming attuned with the analysand rather than the other way around. Gedo describes learning the patient's idiosyncratic language so that the psychoanalyst's interpretations resonate with the patient in such a way that they feel like the patient's own (Gedo 1984:135–37).

Crucial to this process of attunement is an attitude of play. Kristeva has stated that "the more fortunate analysand terminates with a renewed desire to question all received truths; as in the time of Heraclitus, he becomes capable once again of acting like a child, of playing" (1987:58). It is through play that we reflect on and escape the discourses that contain us. As I sat in the khānaqāh of the doctor's murshid, I was impressed by the doctor's seriousness. I should have paid more attention to another man, half blind, who had deep smile wrinkles around his eyes. While the doctor and I were engaged in our "deep" conversation, our struggle over recognition, he emerged from a back room where he had obviously been bathing. He playfully "snapped" his towel at the doctor as he walked by, disrupting our concentration. It was a touch of the qalandar.

With the idea of muhabbat we come around to a perspective on the issue of whether a struggle for recognition within the framework of a hegemonic discourse (the Lacanian Symbolic Order) is an adequate way to describe the experiencing subject. The notion of play is crucial to our understanding of the subject of the Real and its relationship to discursively constituted subject positions, including those positions constituted by a dominant political and economic order.[11] Kristeva sees the prediscursive as a source of creativity and a potential locus of subversion of the Symbolic Order and its categories of meaning. I see the experiencing subject as moving among different modalities and an array of desires.

Modern Respectability and Antinomian Desire

7

The *Qalandar* Confronts the Proper Muslim

It is the 'urs of Data Ganj Bakhsh, whose Lahore shrine is one of the most important pilgrimage sites in Pakistan. On a field behind the shrine, set apart from the crushing crowds and the qawwālī (Sufi devotional singing) at the front of the shrine, men cluster around campfires, protected from the hot sun and cold nights by makeshift tents. Some wander with dazed looks, in long orange gowns, their hair in knotted masses; others wear dirty, tattered green gowns and gaudy necklaces. Several dance with bells on their ankles. One man sits nearly naked, wearing nothing but a loin cloth and several chains, heavy enough to lock up a motorcycle, draped across his chest and around his waist. These are the *malangs* and qalandars, religious mendicants who wander from shrine to shrine, following the "call" of long-dead Sufi saints. They are called by some the most exalted of Sufis, but they are also the most despised.

Within the social circles I usually traveled, qalandars are considered beyond the social pale. They are shunned for their reliance on hashish and their rejection of the outer, visible aspects of Muslim law. The middle-class urban Pakistani typically draws a sharp distinction between the pīr whom my neighbor might visit for an amulet or a bit of advice — and the "malang," who is to be carefully avoided or, if he comes to the door begging, is given a few coins or a bit of bread and sent quickly on his way.

The qalandar (as the so-called malang usually calls himself)[1] has

Malangs under a makeshift tent

Malangs dancing through the
streets of Lahore

appeared in Sufi discourse since at least the eleventh century, when the term appeared in the work of Persian Sufis such as Abū Saʿīd ibn Abūʾl-Khayr (967–1049 CE) and ʿAbdullāh-i Ansārī of Herat (1005–1089 CE) (see Karamustafa 1994:32–33). The term signifies one who resists the conventions of the prevailing social order,[2] the dress and etiquette of polite society. Typically, those who are identified as qalandars live in violation of sharīʿat openly and publicly.

Today's criticisms of the qalandars who are to be seen wandering through town or sleeping at a shrine are echoes of complaints that have been voiced through the centuries. Data Ganj Bakhsh himself would not have approved of the malangs and qalandars who gather at his shrine nine hundred years later and are obviously antinomian. Though in his extant writings he did not mention the qalandars by name, he castigated those who draw blame upon themselves by violating Islamic law,[3] characterizing it as a form of corruption:

> He who abandons the law and commits an irreligious act, and says that he is following the rule of "blame," is guilty of manifest wrong and wickedness and self-indulgence. There are many in the present age who seek popularity by this means, forgetting that one must already have gained popularity before deliberately acting in such a way as to make the people reject him; otherwise, his making himself unpopular is a mere pretext for winning popularity. . . . Whoever claims to be guided by the Truth must give some proof of his assertion, and the proof consists in observing the *Sunna* [Ordinances of the Prophet]. You make this claim, and yet I see that you have failed to perform an obligatory religious duty. Your conduct puts you outside the pale of Islam. (Hujwīrī 1976:65–66)

These accusations could have been made in today's Lahore.

The rhetoric of scorn from both sides — scorn for the apparent lawlessness of the qalandar on the one hand, and the qalandar's scorn for the misdeeds and corruption of pious "worldly" people — has a timeless quality that seems to transcend particular ideological and political struggles. Islamic law is deliberately violated. It is not a matter of disagreement over particulars of the law or its administrators, though this is common enough in Muslim circles. No matter what the law, the qalandar would violate it, deliberately and ostentatiously. This timelessness suggests that the qalandar is potentially more than (or something other than) just another ideological actor with a political agenda.

Portrait of a *malang*

The qalandar as sign bears a complex relationship to the qalandar as a living presence. The qalandar's oppositional mode of being in the world is expressed bodily — in dress, tonsure, personal spaces — and through practices that explicitly violate Islamic law. It is a richly articulated vocabulary of resistance that has developed through centuries of Sufi writings and practice. The qalandar breaks down the sharp distinction between public and private that organizes Muslim social space and visibly violates basic social codes. The living qalandar, by bringing into the realm of praxis violations of the basics of social order that for most people are limited to their private fantasies and secret thoughts, mobilizes simultaneously a powerful desire and fear. An individual who appears to be a qalandar may be characterized as criminal, poverty-stricken, mentally ill, depending on what the observer knows of that individual's circumstances, thereby neutralizing the power of the qalandar. As a signifier, the qalandar represents a fantasy of resistance for the middle-class subject that is threatening because it has roots in the cultural constitution of the ego itself.

The person who becomes a qalandar takes up (or falls into) this position as stigmatized other, as the abject, operating as a phantasm within his or her own society. Yet the living qalandar, like each of us, is a complex multipositioned individual, bearing traces of multiple histories, engaged in multiple projects, and identified with specific ide-ologies. The discourse of the qalandar is based on a Dionysian rejection of social forms, yet to live such a life — especially in the company of other qalandars — entails contradiction as social forms continually re-establish themselves.[4]

In this chapter, I examine the interplay between ideology and fantasy in the constitution of the qalandar as a historical subject. I look at how individuals who claim the identity of qalandar engage in specific con-frontations that locate them as historical subjects shaped by a domi-nant ideological discourse. As individuals each is uniquely situated. Like all individuals, they both adapt to and resist the distinctive prac-tices and controls of a historical era. In previous chapters, I discussed how urban neighbors' disagreements about the legitimacy of pīrs are often the medium through which ideological positions are taken. I articulated the explicit relationship of specific practices to the con-struction and negotiation of identity. The qalandar, too, may embody an ideology — often manifesting a subaltern resistance to a dominant social and political order. The image of the qalandar may become a vehicle for social protest at a specific historical moment.[5] They are shaped in some respects by the dominant ideologies and forms of social control of their times, but they are also shaped by their adoption of the peculiar identity of qalandar, constituted by a discourse that in certain respects transcends the practices of their time.

As my description at the beginning of this chapter suggests, qalan-dars continue to be an active and highly visible presence in Pakistan. As in narratives gleaned from Sufis writing more than five hundred years ago, my meetings with qalandars occasionally became confrontational, at times even scary. On the other hand, there were more qalandars who were friendly, even pleased to talk with me. But even in these situations, confrontations occasionally developed, instigated by bystanders who were upset that a Western researcher would be getting a wrong im-pression of Islam from such corrupt people. In one incident at one of Lahore's major shrines, a man who identified himself as a member of the Jama'at-i Islami actively sought to prevent a man who identified himself as a qalandar from talking with me, declaring that if I wanted to learn about Islam, I should go talk with the head of the Jama'at-i Islami, Maulana Maudoodi (which I had, in fact, done). In this case, the qalandar availed himself of the power of the state and summoned a policeman.

Some of the confrontations I experienced developed when I was in the company of a young man, a university student whom I shall call Mumtaz. I met quite a few malangs in Mumtaz's company. He was a graduate student at Punjab University, where I had a research affiliation. I had been warned by people at the university that these malangs are a dangerous lot, and that I shouldn't risk talking with them on my own. None of the women who often accompanied me when I ventured out into new places would go with me, because they feared for their reputations and their safety. For my safety, Mumtaz had been assigned as my research assistant. Our encounters at times devolved into a confrontation between Mumtaz and the qalandar—just the sort of situation in which ideologies make their appearance and identities are explicitly and agonistically reflected in the gaze of another.

The Qalandar and the Bureaucratic State

Though Mumtaz maintained his identity as university student and researcher when he was with me, talking with these people made him anxious. In reaction to his anxiety he deployed an ideology of modernization and called upon the protective mantle of the bureaucratic state to maintain his everyday reality. The more anxious he got, the more he took the initiative in asking questions—questions that generated a bizarre juxtaposition of seemingly incongruous worlds that at times became a confrontation. The specific contours of these confrontations reflect the contours of power in the modern nation-state as these shape the middle-class subject. Those contours also shape but do not determine the qalandar's identity and the forms of his or her resistance.

One time, seated before an intoxicated man with matted hair, dressed in little more than iron chains, Mumtaz asked, before I realized what he was doing and could change the topic of conversation, "If the government were to give you education and housing, would you accept it?" Though such questions, of course, did little to establish rapport, the question and the response were unambiguous instances of a clash of discourses, as Mumtaz relentlessly worked to maintain the hegemony of his middle-class values in the face of someone who challenged what are usually unexamined givens of everyday life—the need to wear clothes and comb one's hair, the custom of marking one's gender in unambiguous ways that are established by prevailing fashion codes. Mumtaz's anxiety produced a rigidity of perspective, with the conse-

A *nanga bābā* at the shrine of Miān Mīr in Lahore

quence that the hegemonic order that Mumtaz and others in his so-cial world strive to maintain became painfully obvious when he was plunged into situations that he normally would have avoided.

Among my own associations at the moment Mumtaz posed his ques-tion about government housing to the near-naked man seated before us was the image of Chicago's vast and disastrous public housing projects: high-rises such as Cabrini Green, with its drug-filled elevators and des-olate open spaces, a no-man's-land where not even a qalandar could survive. I thought, too, of the tidy blocks of brick quarters for govern-ment servants on the outskirts of Lahore. A qalandar-type did live near the even rows of houses, but his residence was a tiny shrine under a gnarled old tree, and the neighbors whispered about his red-rimmed eyes and the smell of hashish.

These were my thoughts. But what were the positions from which Mumtaz and the qalandar spoke? What happened in that moment when Mumtaz confronted the qalandar with a question about public housing? Can we trace the roots of this confrontation in the history of the discourses from which they operated?

Mumtaz apparently embraced some form of a modernist vision of progress that had no room for wandering mendicants but was consis-tent with his indoctrination as a sociologist. As incongruous as the question seemed to me at the time, Mumtaz's concerns were echoed in government projects of that period, projects that embraced even the qalandar. At the shrine of Lāl Shahbāz Qalandar in Sind, one of Pakistan's major shrines and a particular focus of pilgrimage for qalandars, the government of Zulfikar Ali Bhutto was busy constructing housing, as a government-sponsored pamphlet proudly reported:

> The environment of the mausoleum of Qalandar Lal Shahbaz is not in keeping with the dignity of the great saint. . . .
> The Government has now sponsored a development plan, the foundation stone of which was laid by the prime minister Mr. Z.A. Bhutto on 27th January 1974. . . .
> The scheme envisages construction of a housing colony consisting of 150 quarters to rehabilitate the persons displaced by development around the mausoleum.
> A number of plots, each measuring 240 sq. yards, have been developed on which two room houses are being constructed with space left for addition of more rooms. *Other shelterless people are being given one-room quarters on 80 sq. yd. plots.* (My emphasis; Sind Information Department n.d.:23)

In Mumtaz's discourse, echoing government policy, the qalandar has been assimilated to the category "shelterless." It is the pride of a modern government and social order to be able to provide for such unfortunates.

By his question, Mumtaz took the qalandar's culturally articulated resistance to a hegemonic order and redefined it as mere destitution, brought about through lack of education and gainful employment. Mumtaz located this qalandar in a specific social space, attaching to him signifiers that marginalized him and rendered him harmless. The qalandar's response to this maneuver was annoyance — a refusal to be objectified in that way. Mumtaz interpreted this resistance as evidence that the qalandar deserved his destitute condition: the qalandar would not take advantage of an opportunity to seek gainful employment, and so Mumtaz was justified in his moral condemnation.

The government, then, has an agenda that impinges on the life of the qalandar. Newspaper articles express concern with the "dignity" of the saint Lāl Shahbāz Qalandar as a way of projecting the benign power of the government.[6] But far from being a "shelterless person" who would be grateful for a small house and a fixed, carefully measured plot of land to call his own, this qalandar, a *nanga bābā* (naked holy man), articulated a very different notion of personal and social space. He had been at the shrine of Data Sahib, where we had met him, for four months. He was "sent" to the shrine by his pīr, Lāl Shahbāz Qalandar (the same saint whose shrine the government was actively developing). He planned to stay here as long as he continued to receive favor from Data Sahib. When he receives a sign — a dream — telling him to move on, he will go. He called what he is doing — the chains and the nudity — a chillā (a ritual ordeal), and he does it so that he can achieve a link with God. The chillā is a central part of the Sufi tradition and constitutes a noteworthy event in the hagiographies of many Sufi saints.[7]

Our social encounter — my efforts to create a common space in which we could reveal images of ourselves to each other — was unusual. This particular meeting was an artifact of my research: Mumtaz would normally have avoided any kind of social contact with this "other." The nanga bābā may or may not be exposed very often to a discourse of modernity and of middle-class respectability through encounters with people like Mumtaz. As a malang, he expects a certain type of reaction from visitors to the shrine: primarily to be ignored, or to be quickly handed money or food. Our meeting generated a direct juxtaposition of the qalandar's self-perception as operating under the orders of a dead pīr with the bureaucratic perspective of the socially marginal who suffers for lack of decent housing. As long as the government does not directly constrain the activities of such wanderers, qalandars continue to move through space as their spiritual ancestors did, operating outside or at the margins of a modernizing discourse.

A Female Malang

About two weeks into our work, Mumtaz told me that he knew of a female malang — quite an unusual phenomenon — who lived at a small shrine in the graveyard adjacent to his own neighborhood. But he warned me that these people were "criminal types" and had a really bad reputation in the neighborhood. So one afternoon, both of us apprehensive, we pulled up beside the shrine on Mumtaz's scooter. I noticed about ten sets of shoes at the threshold and was rather surprised at the indications of such a large gathering at the small shrine. An old woman with long matted hair wrapped around her head was walking about outside the shrine. Mumtaz said to me, "There's a lady malang."

A small shrine in Miānī Sahib
Graveyard, Lahore

I asked her if I could talk with her, and she gestured inside, saying that we should talk to her *sarkār* (master, chief). As I crossed the threshold, I could see that the tomb itself was in a small room on the left, and on the right was a dark, smoke-filled room in which the owners of all the shoes sat. The "sarkār" was seated against the south wall, next to a water pipe and an oven-like fire, serving a curry and chapātīs to at least some of those present. The sarkār did not offer us any.

The gender of this person was not immediately obvious to me: the word "sarkār" had led me to expect a man, and the voice was correspondingly husky. But I saw the same matted hair that I had seen on the woman outside. This person wore women's clothes: a white sweater over an unremarkable green printed qamīs (tunic) and black shalwār (trousers), a double strand of large black beads that looked like costume jewelry around her neck, and four assorted glass bangles on her right wrist. I had observed transvestites dancing at respectable weddings, people who in other contexts were students or job-holding young men. That had been one of my first experiences of the fact that gender is a contextualized social construct and that veiled women need hide themselves only from "men" who are so designated at the moment. So by the time I got to this little graveyard shrine, I was cautious about assuming any correspondence between bodily equipment and clothing.

Not surprisingly, these "malangs," as Mumtaz called them, were suspicious of us and overtly hostile when we entered. Our efforts at interviewing were not readily accepted. They were particularly suspicious of my project of writing a book, which I mentioned in my efforts to introduce myself. It was obvious in the first moments of our encounter that these people explicitly saw me as an enemy to be resisted. The discourses they saw me representing, however, were multiple. I was, first and foremost, a Westerner, and one of her followers who spoke English fluently inserted himself as a mediator between the sarkār (who called herself Bava Sahib) and myself, answering her questions for her. But his first utterance was an accusation: "You will write a pamphlet against us." Pamphlet-writing is a common expression of political infighting amongst adherents of the various orientations to Islam in Pakistan; it is also one of the strategies used by the government to wipe out what they regard as false pīrs who prey on ignorant people—usually in the form of a blitz of newspaper articles when a corrupt pīr engaging in illegal activities is found out. Though the terms of the debate have in many respects been shaped by the postcolonial situation Pakistan finds itself in, the debate is not at this point primarily between Westerners and Muslims, but rather among Muslims of various persuasions.

But Bava Sahib herself immediately brought the clash between Islam and the secular West into sharper focus. Before I had a chance to ask her anything, she said, "We are under the order of a pīr-murshid. Some people get by with science, some people don't believe in God. We call such a person an atheist."

To align myself on the side of religion (despite my "scientific" research), I replied that I was interested in finding a teacher and asked how she had searched for a murshid. Her response: "I am prevented from giving answers. The Quran says not to divulge the murshid's secret." She had drawn on the Quran for legitimacy, but, primed by Mumtaz's warnings about these people, the secrecy suggested to me either illicit, criminal activity, or perhaps black magic. I tried again: "When did you come here?" She replied, "Thirty-five years ago. The English had gotten hold of the letters of the *huzūr* [a person of high authority; Mumtaz later interpreted this to mean the Prophet Muhammad], and they were able to rule here with an army for one hundred years." I didn't understand what she had said (and Mumtaz was puzzled, too). The English-speaking man added, "God is no where. This is the belief of the atheists. God is now here. He is looking, listening, seeing, talking."

The British are associated with atheism and military domination. With the benefit of hindsight, I see that I might have been able to shift the alignments by drawing her into a conversation about her experiences under the British, thereby explicitly distancing myself from her colonial oppressors; but I was not so savvy. In his fear, Mumtaz clung tenaciously to the scientific interviewer model, which Bava Sahib had just objected to. Ignoring what now seem like obvious protests against a repetition of the exploitation and oppression that accompanied colonialism, he persisted with questions about a murshid. He fired a series of questions: "Who is your murshid?" The English-speaking man replied, "Muhammad Latīf Shāh Bukhārī." Bava Sahib corrected him, "No, Naqshbandī, not Bukhārī." "Is he living now?" "No, this is his shrine." "When did he die?" "When the Khaksar movement had just clashed, in 1919,[8] my murshid died. Six months before death, he said he would die. He died in April."

Though overtly answering our questions about her presence at the shrine and about her murshid, her utterances about the British say at least as much about how she perceived the interaction we were engaged in as they do about the British. The English had come in and stolen Muslim writings, just as I was trying to pry her secrets out of her and put them into writing. The English had succeeded in dominating for a hundred years, and I was trying to do the same thing now. When she described the death of her murshid, she alluded to the Khaksar rebellion, a moment of active resistance to colonial domination. Her next utterances became progressively more overt and active statements of resistance, culminating in an active threat of retaliation. She made what must have been to her an unambiguous expression of resistance: "What is your trouble that you are asking these questions?" I missed the significance of her question (which is more obvious in this translation than it was in her utterance—I thought she had asked why I was going to the trouble to ask her all these questions). I gave the wrong response: "I want specific information for a book." She had complained about what she saw as our hegemonic efforts to put her in a bad light—to write pamphlets about her, and she finally resorted to a direct metapragmatic statement about our discourse and a confrontation: "You two are trying to make everyone follow the same path. Stop it. Stop this, or otherwise someone who really has a connection with God will punish you, so stop this."

Given the presence of several large, dangerous-looking men, this threat was alarming. Earlier Mumtaz had warned me that these people were "criminals." I began to wonder if our safety was genuinely at risk. I was ready simply to leave. We had, after all, intruded upon and disrupted whatever activity these people were engaged in. Though I didn't have the power in that situation to disrupt the paradigm of research as domination — largely because of my own anxiety and because of Mumtaz's tendency to make rather rigid efforts at maintaining control when under stress — we prevailed. In what seemed like an almost miraculous rescue, another of the men surrounding Bava Sahib intervened, and we managed to get them to talk more freely with us for over an hour. They even allowed us to capture their words on tape.

This man must have been sensitive to the tension between Mumtaz and myself and to my awkward and failed efforts to place myself on Bava Sahib's side. He was also aware that this encounter was likely to end in a total social rupture. I was surprised when he suddenly intervened on my behalf, saying to the sarkār, "They want to know why you are here, why you became like this." This was exactly what I wanted to know, and, even more surprisingly, she responded with an extended account of herself:

> When I came here thirty-five years ago, there was no constructed area here. This human being received an order from God. I took up the way of my pīr-murshid. He is my bodyguard. Here you see this atmosphere, this environment — only a wicked man or an honorable man could stay here, but I have stayed here for thirty years. Can you imagine a woman staying here, even at night, in a graveyard? That shows that I am a faqīr. You should study the *tazkirat al-auliyā* [lives of the saints; see 'Attār 1990]. In this graveyard, the pure men of God are sleeping. When someone is burned with the song of tauhid [unity], everything will appear to him. Everybody knows me in Samnabad, Chauburgi, Islamia Park [the neighborhoods surrounding the graveyard, including Mumtaz's]. The predecessor of my predecessor. . . . Just as a father of a father is a grandfather, in the same way there was the predecessor of my predecessor. My predecessor was here, Bābā Malin Shāh. He was sent to another place. I was appointed here. He was of the silsila [chain of spiritual descent] Qādirī Qalandarī. There are so many silsilas — Qādirī, Qalandarī, Naqshbandī. As Dr. Iqbal said, "Sitaron ke age jahan aur bhi hen, othe nange faqīr nun Qādir Qalan-

dar kehnde ne" [a mix of Urdu and Punjabi: Beyond the stars there are other worlds; there are naked faqīrs, Qādir Qalandar has said]. We, being naked, are sitting there [asin nange ho kar, baithe hen]. There was a big murshid, Hazrat Ghaus-i Aʿzim [ʿAbduʾl-Qādir Gīlānī, the founder of the Qādirī order]. Then before him was the pure Prophet.

Though Mumtaz may well be right about the criminal aspects of the sarkār's day-to-day activities, this story suggests that these people are not merely criminals hiding under the garb and superficial practices of the qalandar. She and her followers do not simply use their identities as qalandars as some kind of deceitful cover for debauchery, as centuries of Muslim and British discourse about the common malang or qalandar would have it. This particular qalandar, at least, had a clearly articulated place within a silsila, with named ties to three generations of teachers (the sarkār herself, her teacher, and her teacher's teacher). She expressed links not only to the be-sharʿ (in violation of sharīʿat) Qalandarī order, but also to the bā-sharʿ (in accordance with sharīʿat) Qādirī order and its founder. Like other Sufis, she traced her spiritual descent back to the Prophet Muhammad himself. But the sarkār's story is not merely a mechanical recitation of the standard claims to legitimacy as a Sufi; it is itself a tazkarat (a biographical memoir), a weaving of a life with fragments of poetry.

Her story begins as the stories of many qalandars do, with an order from God to settle at a particular shrine. This story is the mark of a qalandar. I asked many faqīrs who live at small roadside shrines, as well as those who have set up temporary-looking shelters of blankets and boards at some of the larger shrines in Lahore, how they decided to come to that particular shrine, and most answered, "It was an order from God."

The qalandar considers his life to be regulated and guided by such orders. These orders come either directly from God or from a dead saint who requires the service of the qalandar. The dead pīr orders the qalandar to devote himself in service to his shrine. In many cases, the shrine, perhaps only a grave, has long been neglected. Once the qalandar arrives, it is his duty to keep the shrine clean, light oil lamps, and accept the offerings of neighbors. If no proper shrine has been built, he may be ordered by the pīr to collect funds and build one (Ewing 1984b:360).[9]

To allow the orders of God to structure one's life, the qalandar must completely abandon the social and material world of ordinary people. He thus becomes utterly exterior vis-à-vis the social world in order to enter the inner, spiritual world. Ordinary people must follow the sharī'at, which regulates the external, visible aspects of daily life, in order to demonstrate their submission to God. The qalandar, in contrast, is concerned only with the interior life. Having rejected the external world, he need not worry about or adhere to the sharī'at. His relationship to God need not be mediated by external rules. Rather, every action involves a direct infusion of the power and spirit of God into everyday life, through direct communication with God or a saint. The order often comes in a dream or in a state of intoxication brought on by the use of hashish. When we first entered, Bava Sahib had been speaking to two men, apparently explaining why she had settled at this shrine. I overheard her say, "I had no intention of doing faqīrī. But I came here and felt an attraction from this murshid, so I stayed." The qalandar, however, never knows how long he will stay in one place. Many pass their time traveling from one shrine to another, following the will of God and the order of whatever pīr may call him to come and serve. As in the sarkār's story, it is often difficult to determine if the order or attraction came from a living pīr, as I often and mistakenly assumed during our conversations, or from one who has already died. She went on to talk about her pīr: "I took up the way of my pīr-murshid." He had died in 1919; her communication with him is presumably through dreams and visions.

She went on to demonstrate her familiarity with Sufism, not just in its popular manifestations that are subject to condemnation by the government and the 'ulamā, but to the Sufi literary tradition: she advised me to study the *Tazkirat al-Auliyā*. The *Tazkirat al-Auliyā* is a compendium of biographies of Sufi saints written by the twelfth-century Persian Sufi poet Farīd ud-Dīn 'Attār (d. 1220), one of the classics of Sufi literature ('Attār 1990).

I noted at the beginning of this account that it was unusual to find a female malang living in a graveyard like this. Given the prevailing organization of gender in Pakistan, few women's life trajectories extend in that direction. After studying the narrative of this woman's life, I have concluded that the situation in which she found herself in old age, dwelling in a graveyard on the margins of middle-class society, was an outcome of resistance to colonial rule, an example of the ways in which individuals move among discourses and the way in which the discourse of qalandarī can be taken up at a specific historical moment as an element in a political struggle.

Her speech is laced with vestiges of colonial memories that, when properly located in their colonial context, not only explain some odd statements and her unusual situation, but also highlight the aspects of qalandar identity that were salient for colonial administrators and gave shape to qalandar resistance in that era. Following up her mention of the "Khaksar clash," I began to make sense of the peculiarities of her situation, including her male titles, as vestiges of a social movement that had taken shape during the height of the anticolonial and communal agitation that ultimately led to the Partition of India.[10] The Khaksars protested the formation of Pakistan in its current form, seeking instead a Muslim state stretching across north India. History was an important aspect of Bava Sahib's identity. She and her followers saw themselves as resisters. If I had been able to talk about their "criminal" activities, I expect that they would have interpreted them as acts of resistance to the current order.

Identifying the group's Khaksar roots also makes sense of the statement that had puzzled both Mumtaz and me, when Bava Sahib described the British taking letters of the "huzūr," which means royal presence or the person of the monarch or any high functionary (Platts 1967:478). The headquarters of the Khaksar movement had been in Ichhra, the section of Lahore where this graveyard where we sat was located. In 1940, there was a violent confrontation between the Khaksars and the colonial government. The government raided the Khaksar headquarters, confiscated important documents and records, and declared the movement illegal. This was the "Khaksar clash" that one of the sarkār's followers had alluded to when specifying the date of her murshid's death.

But Bava Sahib had been remarkably specific about the date of the murshid's death — April 1919 — long before the emergence of the Khaksar movement. During this month in 1919, there were major uprisings against the British throughout the Punjab. A strike was staged in Amritsar, and in retaliation, martial law was imposed in the Punjab. The administration of martial law in Lahore was particularly oppressive (*Report on the Punjab Disturbances, April 1919* 1919:86).

These malangs had used the dating of the murshid's death to allude to colonial oppression, telescoping two acts of oppression and resistance into a single event (see Taussig 1992a:40–48 for a discussion of this type of "historiography"). Bava Sahib was describing a Sufi teacher who died fighting, resisting colonial rule. These qalandars have been shaped by the historical moment in which they live. The colonial encounter continues to operate as an emotionally powerful sign that shapes today's encounters with representatives of a growing middle class.

The Qalandar as the Abject

The qalandar is transected by traces of what Gramsci called old hegemonies, which can be identified in today's practices. Nevertheless, for the middle-class subject, the qalandar is not a multifaceted, historically situated individual, but is rather a sign marking a subject position, a difference between "self" and "other." The qalandar operates as an "other" within a Muslim discourse of community. As sign the qalandar is a bearer of difference that explicitly challenges the naturalness of the prevailing social order from within.

The qalandar articulates the arbitrariness of order itself and potentially calls into question the implicit understandings on which it rests. Neighbors engage in ideological argument over the reality of a threat posed by finding a goat's head in front of one's door or the legitimacy of one pīr or another; in contrast, they generally agree without question that one should brush one's hair every day. But the qalandar challenges even practices that fall within this realm of habit: the qalandar might not brush his hair; he might not be obviously male or female; he might not even wear any clothes to speak of. The qalandar thus disrupts even the most basic unexamined habits, the established hegemonies, of everyday life. By operating as an inverted mirror that challenges the background understandings of daily life, the qalandar potentially exposes to scrutiny basic issues of subjective experience for the ordinary person. Paradoxically, by operating as a mirror in this fashion, the qalandar functions as a foundation on which the lawful Muslim subject rests.

Just as a community creates solidarity and a stable identity by drawing some kind of boundary around itself and distinguishing self and other through some kind of membership criteria marking difference, the subject builds an ego that is experienced as stable and whole by separating itself from and rejecting that which is not-self.[11] That which is rejected thereby functions as the ground or border on which a self-representation or subject position is founded. The rejected becomes what Kristeva has labeled the "abject" (Kristeva 1982). Originally a movement of separation from the maternal matrix, the process of abjection becomes attached to specific signifiers. The selection of what in particular is to function as the abject is a process that is shaped by participation in a culturally and historically specific discourse. To the extent that an individual founds an identity on the respectability of being a proper Muslim and is constituted through that discourse, the qalandar functions as an abject. The qalandar is explicitly be-shārʿ, without Law. As a sign, the qalandar is the antithesis of one who is "subject" to the sharīʿat. The qalandar is "not-Me."

An illustration of the function of the qalandar in the process of abjection comes from a Nepali Hindu, a young man for whom my mention of qalandars stimulated the following childhood memory: "We had to change trains at a junction near our home. People we called qalandars would be hanging around the station. Passengers would buy snacks served on leaves. The qalandars picked up the used leaves and licked the remaining food off of them." For Hindus, social boundaries are clearly drawn and an identity constituted through strict rules governing food consumption. Eating the leavings of others maximizes one's pollution. Contemplation of such an act produces disgust in the socially positioned subject. Sharing food in this manner, however, is also a sign of intimacy. It marks a lack of separation between self and other, as in the mother-child relationship.

In functioning as an abject, the qalandar must operate at the periphery, at the fringes of everyday life. The living qalandar as an individual is inevitably both more and less than the abject: he is more because the individual is a complex, historically contingent composite. He is less because a real person cannot fully occupy the position of an impossible, contradictory object, with which the subject both desires to merge and from which the subject must maintain a separation. To the extent that the qalandar actually functions as the abject in the maintenance of a law-abiding (bā-shārʿ) Muslim subject position, direct social engagement with the qalandar in any but an established ritualized manner is highly threatening. The presence of the abject arouses disgust and anxiety.[12] The qalandar always has the potential to bring the discursively constituted subject face to face with the contradiction-riven constitution of subjectivity itself and to throw the arbitrariness of its foundations into relief.

To illustrate the association of the qalandar or malang with abjection in popular imagination, I now focus on the fantasies and anxieties that the meeting with Bava Sahib stimulated in Mumtaz. Before we began our research together, I had asked Mumtaz to be the subject of an interview so that he would have some idea of the kinds of things I was trying to find out about and some experience with my interviewing style. At this point, the idea of our conducting research among qalandars was quite abstract for him. I began the "formal" interview with him (in English) by asking if his family ever visited pīrs. He replied, "Yes, they go to some — Data Sahib. Actually, my family is Shia. The pīrs are mostly Shia. Shias believe that Hazrat Ali was the first khalīfa, and pīrs also respect Hazrat Ali." In this safe context of what was actually a rather extended, generalized discussion of pīrs, he brought up the issue of malangs in a standard way:

> There are two branches of pīrs. One kind are those who get all their knowledge from the Quran Sharif. They believe that all occultism is from the Quran and do not use black magic. Pious people like Data Sahib are pious pīrs who draw their knowledge only from the Quran. The Quran says that kālā 'ilm exists but that those who practice it are *kāfir*.
>
> Pīrism, Sufism, malangism are all about the same thing. But malangs are sometimes different. People go to some malangs, but not all. People say that these persons are semi-mad, very near God.[13] Some malangs, though, are just beggars. . . . Sometimes malangs go from one shrine to another. But some people have made it a business. They pretend they are malangs and get money from people. In Pakistan and India now it is a very complicated system, because most of those who practice it do it as a business.

At this point, before his immersion in our research among the malangs, Mumtaz had already taken the stance of researcher reporting on "people's" beliefs, rather than on his own beliefs. These beliefs included an ambivalence about the malang. His first statements about malangs — on their alleged spirituality, their closeness to God, their semimadness — emphasized how they escape the ordinary bounds of human order and meaning. This perspective is immediately countered by statements about the corruption of most malangs. The copresence of these two attitudes highlights the ambivalence with which malangs are regarded. Though a target of contempt, they are also a potential stimulus for an experience of the sublime.

A respectable, socially elite young woman, for example, once told me that she sometimes imagines giving up everything for the life of the qalandar, becoming by this means a true Muslim. She mentioned a qalandar she had seen that morning camped out on the banks of the Ravi River. A glimpse of this man seemed to have triggered some kind of momentary fantasy, an opening into impossible possibilities.

In our encounter with Bava Sahib in the graveyard at the edge of his neighborhood, Mumtaz moved from a defensive position that focused on her criminality to a position of fear, which focused on the possible threat of black magic. Discernible through the contempt and the fear, however, was temptation. Mumtaz's unconscious fantasies appear in the interstices of his efforts to keep the malang at bay as a criminal. There is a movement between revulsion and temptation, passing through anxiety. In my presence, however, he firmly protected himself against any overt experience of the sublime.

Setting Boundaries around the Malang

I didn't realize at the time the social and psychological gulf I was asking Mumtaz to cross in my company as we visited and talked with what he called "the malangs."[14] He approached these interviews with malangs in the subject position of researcher: he identified himself with a "scientific" perspective on the world, a view which valued technology and the power of modern social institutions. But after our visit with the female malang, he mentioned to me more than once that his parents had told him not to go near the malangs in the graveyard. Were they only concerned with shielding him from the corrupting influences and the physical dangers the malangs might have presented? Perhaps. But other conversations with Mumtaz suggested that the fears and perceived danger went deeper than that.

Mumtaz, like other urban middle-class Muslims I knew, had been taught to avoid engaging with malangs as people. The malangs are a common enough sight in a lower- or middle-class neighborhood: some "malang" or "faqīr" is likely to knock at one's door begging at any time. Typically, a family member will hand him some change and he'll be on his way. Or they might give him a plate of food, which he will hastily eat while squatting in a corner of the courtyard. To me, of course, the malang, in exotic dress, was an object of great curiosity. But to the family I lived with, a donation was an easy way to keep a safe distance, a separation between the malang and oneself. The qalandar or malang is easily dismissed: he is probably corrupt and irreligious, and it is best to appease him to avoid trouble. Watching Mumtaz's reactions to the qalandars we met in our work gave me a window into why it was important to appease the malang. They occupied the interstices of urban space, present but avoided, outside the boundary of a middle-class social order, yet lurking nearby. Allowing anything but the most routine interchange opened up something dangerous.

The female malang known as Bava Sahib certainly disrupted the boundaries that organized social space. To me, trained in the anthropology of Mary Douglas (1966) and Victor Turner (1977), this person was an embodiment of liminality, an anomaly, betwixt and between the dichotomous categories that organize much of the everyday world: Was she a man or a woman? A saint or a criminal? The sublime or the abominable? And, with her home in a graveyard, was she of the living or of the powerfully dead, whose ghosts threaten to lure passersby to their doom? Not only could her identity not be firmly fixed; it was difficult to know how to begin, how to locate myself with respect to "her."

As I reflect back now on Mumtaz's reactions to engaging with malangs in conversation, it is clear to me that the "malang" who seems to the outside observer to be a nearby ubiquitous part of the backdrop of daily life was for Mumtaz something very dangerous, representing a danger that went way beyond any direct threat to his physical safety. The nature of the threat, the dissolution of the subject, is prediscursive. The primary evidence for it, therefore, cannot be what the subject says about it directly, but the defensive maneuvers the subject uses to protect itself. "The abject shatters the wall of repression and its judgements" (Kristeva 1982:15).

The evidence for the depth of the danger is the intensity of Mumtaz's response to it. Mumtaz responded to this danger by protecting himself. As I indicated at the beginning of this chapter, his initial reaction to anxiety was to take charge, to become his idea of what a professional social scientist should be—a competent administrator of questionnaires. When I asked few standardized questions, he jumped into the silences and supplied his own. At the time, Mumtaz struck me as having rigid middle-class blinders, and, watching him in action, I felt that he repeatedly tried to impose his prejudices on the malangs and qalandars we engaged in conversation, pushing a modernist agenda of education, housing, and social reform that seemed highly incongruous.[15] By asking a near-naked malang dressed in little more than chains about his interest in government housing, for instance, he had aligned himself with the state as a powerful protective force. In this context, the trope of modernity was a safety net, a defense. The modern is associated with the government, the authority of the state. By preaching development and reform, Mumtaz took on the gaze of the dominant other as represented in the state. At a psychological level, his superego was mobilized and he sought protection from the abject through identification with that other.

Having mentioned the corruption of most malangs in our preliminary interview, Mumtaz went on to describe a magician or pīr whose arrest had recently been featured prominently in local newspapers. I myself had seen his shop, which bore a prominent sign depicting a threatening face, on the main road running past my neighborhood. "Bengali Baba was a fraud. He was caught by the police for taking money from people." Mumtaz had actually met this "criminal." Bengali Baba had come to talk at Punjab University a few days earlier, and Mumtaz had been present, protected by the official setting of the university:

> We asked him if he knew magic, and he said, "I don't know black magic, I just know the alternative to it. I just tell people how to wash the black magic off." He said that the arrest was a scheme against him. He was dressed in a black suit and his skin was really black. One girl asked him if he could wash the black off himself. We arranged a function to ask him questions. He was very anxious to come to the university, and he dressed up for the occasion. Educated people don't believe so much in pīrs as uneducated people do.

Though Mumtaz is of the educated, and though he had easily labeled Bengali Baba a fraud and made fun of him, Mumtaz did not claim lack of belief, a point I will return to.

The link between the government and protection from the dangers of the malang showed up in this discussion of Bengali Baba. By arresting Bengali Baba, the government had demonstrated its power over a possibly dangerous force. The "magic" of the state[16] and its power to create order stands in opposition to the threatening power of the corrupt pīr and, by extension, the malang. The students had gotten this magician onto their own university turf — where he had unsuccessfully

Bengali Bābā's shop

attempted to impress them with his Western clothing. Within the safety of the university, a student had dared a racial taunt. Mumtaz in his account of the incident constructed a linguistic parallel that equated Bengali Baba's black skin, black magic, and dirt to be "washed." His reproduction of a woman's racial comment suggests that the situation was anxiety-provoking for the students, stimulating regression into what Freud labeled primary-process thinking. Mumtaz, for example, was struck by the incongruity of this "black" creature of the night wearing a Western suit, clothes that signify rationality, science, and respectability. Bengali Baba was actively being abjected, turned into a target of revulsion and derision.[17]

This experience of interviewing Bengali Baba, soon to become an arrested criminal, provided Mumtaz with a model that he could use to anticipate his work with me among the malangs. I represented the university: if the students could safely and respectably come into contact with Bengali Baba, then we could go off to meet with the malangs.

The Criminal, the Magician

Mumtaz's first line of defense, his way of drawing a boundary between himself and the malang, was to accuse the malang of being a "criminal." The criminal is, of course, one who transgresses regulations imposed by the state. After we left the shrine of Bava Sahib, Mumtaz gave me the neighborhood gossip and his own views about her:

> People didn't consider her a good woman. The commissioner ordered her house to be destroyed. It was called a house of corrupt things, like bhang [a form of hemp] and wine. Jaga Gujar was living there. He was a corrupt man, a bad-ma'āsh. He was a famous, wicked man. He had a gun. He had a house, but he would come to her because she was corrupt. Other corrupt men also came. She was taken to court, too. He's dead now. Three or four years ago, people couldn't go along this road at night because of robberies, and the neighbors thought the people at this shrine did it.

But some of Mumtaz's strategies for reacting to and denouncing the malangs did not fall within the range of his identity as a research scientist or as a representative of modernist state ideology. At one point during our interview with Bava Sahib, she threatened that "someone with a connection to God" would punish us. As we went over the tape later, Mumtaz denied her connection with God. This is the accusation of a Muslim: he is condemning her to the status of kāfir, locating her outside the boundary of the Muslim community.

But he did not deny that she could harm us. The kāfir is closely associated with black magic. When talking about his own background and experience, Mumtaz had said explicitly: "The Quran says that kālā 'ilm exists but that those who practice it are kāfir." The kāfir's black magic cannot be dismissed as something not true, since it is mentioned as real even in the Quran. It is, therefore, a real threat to us. The threat to punish us might well go beyond the physical danger we were in if we antagonized the men surrounding us in that small room. And such spiritual punishment would not be constrained by God's justice.

As a future social scientist, would Mumtaz take seriously such a threat? During my interview with Mumtaz, he had identified himself as a Shia. From his perspective, Shias are closely connected with the occult, meaning that they have sources of spiritual power that are hidden and, therefore, not accessible to all. The notion of things hidden is a particularly charged signifier for Shias: two major themes in Shiism are the hidden imām and the practice of hiding one's identity as Shia during times of persecution. Mumtaz wasn't merely a disinterested observer of hidden things. I asked him what he himself knew about the occult, and he replied:

People consult with me to learn about the future. I do palmistry. I read about it in books. I talked to pīrs, but they wouldn't tell me what they know. I went to professional palmists. I went and didn't tell them that I also knew how to do it. When I told them afterward, they were angry and said, "Why didn't you tell at first?" I know more than they knew about it. My grandfather had a book about it. Some people, my friends and such, say that I inherited the knowledge, but actually I read books. One of my uncles (my father's younger brother) taught me some things, but mostly he gave me books to read. He was the one who got me interested in it. But there was one special book he wouldn't give me, and he wouldn't tell me how to do it. He kept postponing it, saying, "Next week, next month."

At some level he took seriously the power and danger that Bava Sahib's liminality represented: he could not fully dismiss the possibility that she was more than just one of the living, a corrupt criminal. It seemed that she might possibly have actual connections with the dead who surrounded her in the graveyard and might well have control over the spiritual forces that are said to threaten passersby in the night. His reactions to her as we listened to the tape indicated that he did at least entertain the possibility that she was actually the saint that she claimed to be before rejecting it. When listening to the tape of the encounter, he focused his attention on looking for evidence that she did not actually have a connection either with God or with any other spiritual power.

Mumtaz's experience of black magic was not limited to the modern medium of printed books supplied by his uncle, who was an engineer, or to the contact he had had in an academic setting with Bengali Baba, who had been thoroughly discredited and humiliated. Earlier, he had had personal contact with at least one practitioner of black magic through his uncle. In this case, his uncle had called on the magician's expertise to help him with a problem.

These people [Mumtaz was referring to those who practice black magic] are usually those who do the dirtiest jobs, like sweepers. Sweepers know black magic, but are not called pīrs. They won't tell anyone how they do it. I knew one man, a sweeper, who wouldn't tell me about black magic. He had learned it from his teacher, who was also a sweeper.

[KPE: How did you meet this man?]

My uncle [father's younger brother] wanted help for a problem and called him. I watched what he did. For part of it, he took the head of a goat, used some flour and other things. He told my uncle to put the goat in the crossroads in front of the graveyard and to come back the next day. He told me that to learn this knowledge he had to learn the dirtiest types of jobs.

Mumtaz's two stories about his father's younger brother both involved activities that the uncle had simultaneously exposed him to and hidden from him. In this story, black magic is closely associated with dirt, people of low social status, and, significantly, graveyards (not to mention goat heads) (see Ewing 1982). His uncle's activities add further significance to his parents' warning to stay away from the graveyard and its malangs: people in his family clearly recognized the power and the threat of black magic. It was not merely something that other people — the lower class, the ignorant — did or experienced.

After we had left the graveyard and were back in the relative safety of my house, we went over our experiences together. At one point I asked Mumtaz about the people who were gathered around the female malang and why they go there if she has such a bad reputation. He replied, "Because they want help any way they can get it." He thought the visitors he had seen there looked "OK," but after thinking for a moment said, "The women I think come to get bad ta'wīz, ta'wīz for hurting others. He then added, "We shouldn't have gone inside. My parents don't allow me to go there. There is a room in the ground under the room we were sitting in, I have heard."

Mumtaz had been spooked by his contact with these malangs, about whom he had heard stories and rumors since childhood. He had tried to dismiss these people as corrupt frauds, mere criminals whom the government in the past had stepped in to control, dangerous only because they physically assault people on the road. But at some point his scientific research stance left him, perhaps at the moment when I myself felt a physical threat, and he realized that the university connection might not necessarily protect him. He was quite sure that they were not pious pīrs, not real malangs in that sense, though they did fit perfectly the paradigm of the black magician. His memories of stories of black magic, of the power of the hidden, were manifested in his mention of a secret room beneath us. It was not the protection of God that had allowed this woman to survive her thirty-five years in a dangerous graveyard, and not even her connection with the criminal underclass —

it was her hidden knowledge of black magic. And the threat of her power could follow us after we left — reaching beyond the graveyard, mysteriously disrupting our lives.

Temptation

Mumtaz suggested that such people take on the garb of the qalandar to hide their illegal activities — though it would seem that to someone looking at the world from Mumtaz's perspective, such garb would seem to be more of a flag advertising these activities than a disguise. The only reason that Bava Sahib was a malang, as far as Mumtaz was concerned, was in order to engage in sex and other crimes. He expressed the seemingly obvious, unexamined notion that sexuality, or at least the uncontrolled, unregulated expression of sexuality, especially female sexuality, is criminal. The presence of this malang produced a fear that was reproduced every time he passed along that street — a fear, but also a temptation.

The abject is an object of desire and temptation as well as revulsion.[18] But this temptation is threatening because it escapes the boundaries of order; the threat, and the malang who represents it, must be renounced, repulsed, kept at bay. The fear of passing by the graveyard at night, tinged with the temptation of illicit sex, echoes a popular theme among young men. A young man passes by a graveyard, where he encounters a beautiful young woman. She lures him into a sexual encounter, then reveals herself as a *churail* — a hag with her feet on backward. The churail is the ghost of a woman who has died while pregnant, in childbirth, or during the forty-day period of seclusion after the birth (the chillā).

British administrators collecting folktales and bits of ethnographic information from this area in the nineteenth century recorded such stories. Crooke, a member of the Bengal Civil Service in the late nineteenth century, wrote an account of the folklore of north India, *Punjab Notes and Queries,* in which decontextualized "facts" about popular belief are interspersed with analogous stories from Britain and other parts of Europe. But in his account of the churail he included a story he had heard firsthand from one of his servants. It was essentially the same story that I heard both first- and secondhand amongst young people nearly a century later: "I had a smart young butler at Etah, who once described to me vividly the narrow escape he had from the fascinations of a Churel, who lived on a Pipal tree near the cemetery. He saw her sitting on the wall in the dusk and entered into a conversation with her; but he fortunately observed her tell-tale feet and escaped. He would never go again by that road without an escort" (Crooke 1896, 1:271). At least two young men told me that they personally had seen such women in the graveyard and had fled, successfully escaping.

One young woman, who worked for me as a sweeper for a time, told me about a cousin of hers who had been lured by one of these creatures. According to her, he had actually set up household with the churail. He lived happily with her for several years — she cooked his meals and kept the house in order — until his relatives finally got an exorcist to banish her. He has been desolate ever since.[19]

One young man, with whom I had conducted extensive depth interviewing, revealed to me the preoccupations he often had while walking down a certain street near his home. Every time he passed on his way home from school, a certain woman would stand at her door and try to lure him into her house. Out of fear, he finally told his mother about it. This folktale pattern of the churail thus echoes the concerns of young men I talked with, perhaps shaping their experience of moving alone through the city, down familiar streets, in those empty times when nothing in particular is on one's mind. The churail theme links illicit sexuality, unsuccessful reproductivity, and death.[20] This malang in the graveyard seemed to represent such a figure for Mumtaz — an older woman whom he frequently passed by on his way home — a churail — a harbinger of sex and death. Not the sort of person with whom one would stop and have a harmless chat.

Conclusion

Studies of postcoloniality have suggested that the postcolonial subject has been severed from its past by the experience of the hegemonic domination of Western colonialism. Nandy and Fanon have both argued that this domination creates a rupture, producing a split between a public, Westernized self constituted by a Western gaze and a "secret," traditional self that has been retained by the colonial subject as a subterranean font of creativity.

Keeping in mind the significance of the qalandar, I would draw the fault lines that transect the individual differently. Here we can see alternative discourses operating. The ordinariness of everyday life and the positioning of the subject within it rest on a range of different foundations, depending upon the task at hand. In this confrontation with a female malang, secular, rational modernity was gradually displaced by another discourse—that of the proper, law-abiding Muslim, and the criteria for assessing "reality" also shifted accordingly. In both discourses, one's subject position may rest on an abjected "secret" self that has been projected onto another—and the other bearing each abjection may even be one and the same individual, but in each case, that individual is a different "other" and occupies a different subject position. In the case of the chain-covered nanga bābā, Mumtaz in his identity as social scientist abjected the qalandar in Western terms by locating him as one of the "homeless." Bava Sahib's position—and Mumtaz's—shifted several times over the course of our conversation. She was a criminal, a black magician, a temptress. She was also an oppressed colonial subject and a possible saint, but these positions escaped Mumtaz's gaze.

Those who have an interest in maintaining everyday life as unproblematic (and most of the middle class could probably be so described) would rather not peer into the mirror that the qalandar raises before them as proper Muslims. In heaping their scorn, the qalandar's interlocutors seek to maintain the silences that surround the hegemony of the everyday, averting their eyes from any hollowness that the qalandar might expose at the heart of conventional reality.

The qalandar is at the furthest extreme from the middle-class subject—the profoundly "not-Me." Yet the qalandar is painfully close, one of the grounds on which both everyday understandings and subjectivity itself rest. Serious engagement with the qalandar as a subject can be a terrifying experience. The qalandar lives at the border of social being, at the edge of the imaginary. The presence of the abject invites the subject to self-constitution through the exclusion of the abject as "not-Me." Yet the power of this signifier of abjection indicates that the middle-class individual, even one who is university educated and fully embedded in the "modern" world, is not fully "subject" to modern discourse. The folk tales that British colonial observers relegated to dying traditions continue to articulate the foundation of the experiencing subject, which rests on a flux of desire and fear.

8

The *Qalandar* as Trope

Expressing the negative side of the qalandar, a fifteenth-century poet at the court of Herat, Maulana ʿAbduʾr-Rahmān Jāmī (d. 1492 CE), wrote: "With regard to the kind of men we call *qalandari* today, who have pulled from their necks the bridle of Islam, these qualities of which we have just spoken are foreign to them, and one should rather name them *hashawiyya*" (a sect that Jāmī condemned) (Trimingham 1971:268). Jāmī, a member of the comparatively sober Naqshbandī Sufi order, contrasted the qalandar and malāmatī, who adheres to the duties incumbent on the Muslim and performs many supererogatory acts of piety but does them in secret, thereby appearing blameworthy in the public eye (Schimmel 1975:87).

In such condemnations, there is often a tension between the denunciation of the qalandars of one's own time, whom one may have personally encountered, and a view of the qalandar as a hidden saint, embodiment of the ideal of the perfect man (insān-i kāmal). This tension can be seen in texts spanning several centuries. Both Jāmī and his predecessor Suhrawardī, who lived three centuries apart, made the distinction between men of their own time "who took the dress of the *qalandar*s in order to indulge in debaucheries" and the true qalandar, whose spiritual concerns are genuine (Trimingham 1971:268; Schimmel 1975:88). The standard interpretation among scholars has been that the qalandars who are denounced are the ones whom one has personally encountered. But this assumption is questionable, since the denunciations are generally unspecific and have the structure of fantasy — they are the antithesis of an ideal of proper behavior.

In other literary contexts the qalandar's position is exalted, despite his often disreputable behavior. He seems to have escaped his abjection. The qalandar's exaltation is particularly evident in Persian Sufi poetry written in the eleventh through fifteenth centuries, though it continues as a theme even in the twentieth-century poetry of Muhammad Iqbal. Rūmī (d. 1273), for instance, wrote:

> Bazm-e sharab-o la'l-o kharabat-o kaferi
> molk-e qalandarast-o qalandar az-u bari
> guyi qalandaram man-o in del-pazir nist
> zira keh afarideh nabashad qalandari.

> Carousing and ruby-wine and ruins and unbelief,
> These are the kingdom of the qalandar, but he is detached from it.
> You say "I am a qalandar!" But that is not agreeable,
> Since qalandardom is uncreated.[1]

Why is the qalandar thus exalted? Is this qalandar a different being from the abject being who licks the leavings of others in a twentieth-century railway station?

The qalandar as a trope seems to play with two distinct modes of self-constitution: direct and indirect. Indirect constitution of the self through the exclusion of others — a theme that runs through Foucault's early studies of madness, psychiatry, and prisons (Martin et al. 1988:146) — is one way of characterizing the process of abjection, which puts the qalandar into a position similar to that of the criminal and the insane in the constitution of a discursive subject. There are clearly articulated devices for excluding this other within the Islamic tradition, most of which rest on ideas of orthopraxy — the qalandar's failure to conform to a proper Muslim life as articulated through Islamic law.

The Sufi tradition is also replete with books and manuals that prescribe techniques of direct self-constitution, some of them undoubtedly quite similar to the Greek and Christian texts discussed by Foucault in his later work *The History of Sexuality* (1990b), where he examined a range of texts and discursive practices that he argued played a role in "direct" self-constitution, operating as ideals to be emulated. Such books are filled with rules for proper conduct intended for novices on the Sufi path (e.g., Suhrawardī 1980). In this context, it is not surprising that the qalandar appears in his negative role, as an example of that which is to be avoided. But when we turn from the qalandar as a vehicle of indirect self-constitution, analogous to the Foucauldian criminal or insane, to the study of Muslim ethical techniques of direct self-constitution, it is perhaps odd that the qalandar reappears in a positive light, sometimes in the very text in which he is condemned.

Yet in the exalting of the qalandar there is something different from a simple direct self-constitution. As a signifier, the qalandar represents, instead, an opening into the sublime, an escape from order altogether. As Kristeva has suggested, "The abject is edged with the sublime" (1982:11); it offers the opportunity of losing oneself in joy (*jouissance*), in a flow that repeats the moment before the subject was separated out and alienated from itself. "The sublime triggers — it has always already triggered — a spree of perceptions and words that expands memory boundlessly" (12). In the eyes of others especially, qalandars are the repositories of deviance: they manifest sexuality, drunkenness, criminality, lack of moderation. Yet through their antinomianism they seek above all unconditioned subjectivity. Always caught in a paradoxical position, they are defined and objectified by their very acts of resistance. It is as if the image of the qalandar itself seeks to escape its bonds: it is a label for the deviant, a signifier for the unconstrained manifestations of unfettered love (as in the twelfth-century poet ʿAttār), an image of the selfless perfect man (the thirteenth-century Sufi Rāzī), an image of the uncolonized self (the twentieth-century poet Iqbal). The qalandar deconstructs selfhood. He obliterates identity. He seeks to become "not-Me" to himself.

As a signifier, then, the qalandar represents the negation of the socially constituted subject. The qalandar metonymically points to that moment when horror and the sublime are first separated out in the founding of the subject. This is both a social process, identified by Mary Douglas (1966) in her analysis of the close relationship between purity and pollution in the articulation of social order, and a psychological process, described by Kristeva (1982) in her development of the concept of abjection as the basis for the emergence of ego.

In the pages that follow, I explore how the qalandar as signifier marks a conceptual space that had opened in the worldview of many eleventh- and twelfth-century Persians: a reflexive awareness of the constructedness of all knowledge and the hollowness of everyday reality, which many thinkers today associate with the sweeping innovations of modernity. This space is associated with an awareness of the process of abjection and its close association with the sublime. I examine how, in their use of the qalandar as sign, Sufi thinkers of past centuries either explored this conceptual space or tried to render it invisible. Using the vehicle of the qalandar image, writers either problematized the process of identity formation or they sought to render the issue of subject position unproblematic. Their insights continue to serve as a possible basis for understanding the social and psychological constitution of the subject and are a part of the legacy of a still dynamic Sufi tradition. The living qalandars of today serve as an everyday reminder of this insight.

The Qalandar in Sufi Poetry

Scattered references to the qalandar appear in Persian literature in the eleventh century (see DeBruijn 1992; Karamustafa 1994:32–33). By the late eleventh and early twelfth centuries, the term is used as a literary trope in the writings of a number of Sufis and poets, including Ahmad Ghazzālī (brother of the renowned Abū Hāmid al-Ghazzālī), his disciple 'Aynu'l-Quzāt Hamadhānī (d. 1130), Sanā'ī (d. 1131), and Khāqānī (d. 1189).[2] In the thirteenth and fourteenth centuries, qalandari motifs were developed even further, particularly in the work of Sufi poets such as Farīd ud-Dīn 'Attār (see Ritter 1955), 'Irāqī (d. 1289), Sa'dī (d. 1292), Hāfiz (d. 1389), and Jalāl ud-Dīn Rūmī (d. 1273). At the same time, allusions to the qalandar began to appear in other types of texts, some of them critical of the antinomian activities of wandering qalandari bands, which apparently increased dramatically in number during this period.[3]

The qalandar as a trope in Muslim discourse emerged at a time when sharī'at, the law of religious community, was generally acknowledged to be the only basis for legitimizing social action but when the articulation of community and sharī'at was also being vigorously contested. Following the collapse of the Caliphate in Baghdad as a political center of the Islamic world in the mid–tenth century and a century-long rise and decline of Shia power, local centers of power and influence under Sunni Turkic rulers emerged in Persian-speaking areas. The political upheavals stimulated by the Turkish invasions led to a series of changes.[4] Old elites were displaced and replaced by a new upper class of religious leaders. These religious leaders, the 'ulamā, married into established families and took on the broader functions of a social elite, but, nevertheless, derived their authority from their reputation for Islamic learning and sanctity.

Before the eleventh century, Islam had been primarily the religion of elites in the eastern parts of the Muslim-dominated world. But with changes in the political order came mass conversions to Islam (Lapidus 1988:176). Religion became an important source of identity and in many cases replaced tribe or urban neighborhood as the primary basis for community. The schools of law and theology that had earlier been constituted of groups of scholars, judges, and their students became organized popular parties with mass support. As Sunni Islam rose to political dominance, communities bitterly debated which school of law (*mazhab*) was to be the basis of sharī'at. There was increasing pressure for conformity and considerable overt persecution (Hodgson 1974:192–93). Competing schools of law produced groups of vigilantes who attacked opponents and suppressed what they regarded as immoral activities (Lapidus 1988:176).

At the most obvious level, the qalandar represents the antithesis of these legalistic struggles and the pressure for conformity. The qalandar as sign expresses a particular social ordering of knowledge and subjectivity that crystallized between the eleventh and thirteenth centuries. It focuses on at least one intensively contested aspect of this social ordering of knowledge, power, and community: the antinomian, or that which violated sharī'at. The antinomian marked those aspects of subjective experience that were sharply bounded within the Sunni community so that they did not enter public discourse or practice. The focus of debate was on how to understand the significance and proper locus of the antinomian as either (1) an aspect of human experience and nature that is the antithesis of that which emanates from God and is thus to be externalized and extruded from the community, (2) something to be carefully bounded but explored within the private interior space of each individual as a path to God, or, finally, (3) a mode of resistance to be publicly enacted. Both of the two latter stances recognized the limited nature of the current hegemonic, as being public articulations of reality shaped by the existing structure of power. The qalandar marked a space within Persian Sufi discourse for cultural relativity. Furthermore, it provided a conceptual vehicle for articulating this debate about the status of sharī'at and violations of it.

The wisdom of the qalandars is often depicted as the antithesis of the legal disputation and sectarian fighting that many Sufis saw pulling the medieval Muslim world apart, as in the following lines attributed to the eleventh-century Sufi Abū Saʿīd ibn Abū'l-Khayr:

> Till Mosque and College fall 'neath ruins ban,
> And Doubt and Faith be interchanged in man,
> How can the Order of the *Qalandars*
> Prevail, and raise up one true Musulman? (Browne 1906, 2:265)

Broadly, the qalandar signified a counter to the excesses of formalism, where knowledge has been linked to social status and power. It was the antithesis of forms of knowledge that had, in their institutional manifestations, become distorted by a search for prestige, in which selfish goals have distorted community orientations.

The qalandar signifies the antithesis not only of reasoning, but of historical sources of authenticity as well. He has lost or abandoned the power of discrimination; he has given up useless disputations and rejected the intellect as a path to truth in favor of a loss of self in the direct experience of God. The image of the qalandar, shameless in his drunken stupor, effectively captures the loss of identity defined in competition with others that the Sufi seeks to experience in his love of God, as in a verse attributed to Abū Saʿīd ibn Abū'l-Khayr:

> Sir, blame me not if wine I drink, or spend
> My life in striving Wine and Love to blend;
> When sober I with rivals sit; but when
> Beside myself, I am beside the Friend. (Browne 1906, 2:265)

The qalandar had no pride. Pride is one of the "veils" that comes between the subject and the experience of God. Much Sufi literature is devoted to articulating this and other veils, the pitfalls that the apparently devout Muslim may encounter that become a barrier between the Muslim and God. (Many of these pitfalls are familiar to Western readers from Christian morality literature, which develops similar themes.) The issue of social pride is most directly addressed through the concept of the malāmatī, one who draws blame upon himself. As signifiers the malāmatī and qalandar are a criticism of the social process of constituting a positive self-representation or identity out of the gaze of the social other. They generate this critique by distinguishing the human gaze from that of God, the absolute other. The earliest mention of malāmatī, which predates the qalandar, is not of a specific Sufi order or other institution but of a certain class or type of person. The issue in early texts was less with identifying a particular social group than with spec-ifying the hidden characteristics of a class of people. Terms like "mal-āmatī" and "qalandar" are signifiers of aspects of social order.

For the most part, the literary image of the qalandar was used by Sufis who were themselves elite, who adhered to the social forms pre-scribed by Islamic law, and who had considerable prestige. When taken literally as an idealization of the wandering, antinomian mendicant who has rejected the pettiness, vanities, and corruption of the social order, the glorification of the qalandar would seem rather paradoxical or hypocritical coming from the pens of this intellectual elite. These literary Sufis asserted the importance of an ordered civil society based on adherence to the sharī'at. Yet the qalandar as trope bears an array of antinomian characteristics — explicit violations of sharī'at such as wine drinking, gaming, and the like, that these Sufis rejected in other con-texts. Some commentators on the use of qalandar imagery by these medieval Sufi poets suggested that Sufis such as the court poet Sanā'ī actually took up the life of the qalandar themselves, while others have seen no evidence for this in the historical record. This apparent incon-sistency between ideals expressed in poetry and practice has stimulated consideration of how this trope fits with other principles that are often expressed simultaneously, particularly the repeated admonition that the Sufi must not violate Islamic law.

Certainly in the writings of the thirteenth-century Sufi Najm al-Dīn Dāyā Rāzī (1177–1256), the figurative significance of the qalandar is explicit: "The *morid* must have the attribute of one who courts re-proach and the character of a qalandar, but not in the sense of con-travening the Law and imagining this to be the desired state. No indeed; such is the path and guidance of Satan, and it is by virtue of this error that the antinomians have been borne off to hell" (Razi 1982:263). By this time, Dāyā and other Sufi writers had found it necessary to ex-plicitly distinguish the qalandar as trope from the actual practice of antinomians, who had become an increasingly visible social presence.

The passage from Najm al-Dīn Dāyā Rāzī makes it clear that the qalandar and the antinomian, then, were understood in relationship to sharī'at, a principle for the ordering of society that focused on ortho-praxy. The Sufi poet Ansārī was such a passionate defender of the Hanbalite mazhab, one of what are now four schools of Islamic law, that he endured exile (in 1066) for his unyielding adherence to the strict principles of law represented by the Hanbalite cause. Yet a work attributed to him, the *Qalandarnāma*, begins with a story that demonstrates the dangers and vanity of scholarly knowledge:

> In a *madrasa* where young boys (including the writer himself) are absorbed in their theological studies, a *qalandar* suddenly appears. The stranger blames the boys for their vain ambition to become great scholars. Instead, they should show respect to the "elders" (that is: the Sufi *shaykhs*) who attend to their spiritual needs. The students become fascinated by these words and throw their books away, following the qalandar to a place called "the place of the chains" (*zanjirgah*), by which a madhouse is presumably meant. There he goes on to preach to Ansari personally, both in prose and verse. (DeBruijn 1992:78)

Whether or not this text was actually written by Ansārī, it is known that Ansārī was swept up into Sufi practice through his meeting as a young man with the aged mystic Kharaqānī, an illiterate peasant who himself had not been initiated by a living teacher, but by the spirit of another famous Sufi Bāyezīd Bistāmi (Schimmel 1975:89). Ansārī maintained a simultaneous attachment to a particular form of orthodoxy as the exoteric basis and foundation of community while at the same time stressing the importance of a spiritual experience of God that is not limited by theology or the community.

The qalandar is a vehicle of the message that God must be experienced directly. The "place of chains" clearly marks that which is beyond the social pale, the abject, that which has been extruded from the community. The author and the reader have been exhorted to give up the search for status and an identity based on social position by embracing the abject. But not simply abject — the place of chains suggests one who had no reason and is, therefore, the antithesis of the theologian. The qalandar is one who transcends the artificial limits of socially organized knowledge and reality.

One of the most influential articulations of the problem of the subject defined in relationship to knowledge and the social order in this period was the work of Abū Hāmid al-Ghazzālī (d. 1111). Though al-Ghazzālī himself did not develop the image of the qalandar in his work, there is a congruence between the development of his theorizing about knowledge and the literary florescence of the qalandar, both of which are manifestations of a historical formation that was coalescing at this time. Al-Ghazzālī's own life, as he depicts it in his autobiography, reads in some respects like an enactment of the call from the qalandar in Ansārī's *Qalandarnāma*.

A scholar from Khurasan, al-Ghazzālī is considered to have instigated a "fundamental revision of the foundations of Islamic thinking" (Hodgson 1974:180) and effected a synthesis of orthodox sharīʿat-minded thinking and Sufism that had a major impact on the development of Sufism as a social institution. His career attests to the growing power of Sufi discourse and practice at that time. Appointed at the age of thirty-three to the prestigious post of director of the Nizāmiyya Madrasa at Baghdad by the Seljuk visier Nizāmulmulk, al-Ghazzālī was an innovative and influential teacher and scholar of law and *kalām* (scholastic theology). He claimed to have read, understood, and critiqued every sect and school of thought available to him, until he reached a point when he realized that the intellect could not give him truth. Like Descartes several centuries later, he had reasoned himself into intellectual agnosticism, a point at which all knowledge was placed into doubt and all proofs were shown to be inadequate and refutable. He experienced this realization in the form of personal crisis, manifested as a physical and intellectual paralysis. Finally, he shocked his colleagues by abandoning his position and family. He took up the life of a wandering Sufi for more than ten years, an act that parallels the opening scene of Ansārī's *Qalandarnāma*.

After ten years of journeying as a Sufi, al-Ghazzālī returned to Nishapur, a city near his birthplace, where he resumed his public writing and teaching. It was at this point that he wrote an autobiographical work in which he recounted his intellectual crisis and articulated his position on knowledge and truth that he had developed during his years of Sufi practice (al-Ghazzālī 1980). He developed a new ideology that more adequately accounted for his experience. Al-Ghazzālī placed great emphasis on the maintenance of the Muslim community through the sharīʿat. The ideology he articulated justified and reinforced the legitimacy of the prevailing social order, with its strict emphasis on orthopraxy based on adherence to sharīʿat, which he acknowledged could not be justified rationally. At the same time his views gave him and others in a similar social position the space and freedom to explore their own inner experience without constraint.

Al-Ghazzālī provided a powerful articulation of a model of subjectivity in which there is a radical split between the exoteric and the esoteric. On the one hand, he emphasized the primary authority of a community modeled on the example of the Prophet (sunnat) to shape external behavior. As a state-appointed director of a new government-founded madrasa, he had been a central (though apparently ambivalent) mouthpiece of that authority. On the other hand, he exalted the individual, whose experience of an interior space potentially unconstrained by community law, tradition, or even language was the ultimate source of truth and reality (see Ernst 1985).

The Secret

The split between the exoteric and the esoteric, the public and private, was maintained by the secret. The idea of the secret is central to Sufi thought and is often found in conjunction with the trope of the qalandar. Al-Ghazzālī drew heavily on the principle of the secret in his own work. His personal use of this device in his own life is evident in his description of spiritual crisis. At the critical moment, when al-Ghazzālī was afflicted by what he called the "disease of doubt," he lived out a secret, hiding a discrepancy between his public identity and his inner state that was to characterize his later theorizing: "The disease was baffling, and lasted almost two months, during which I was a skeptic in fact though not in theory nor in outward expression" (Watt 1963:24). Even at the unavoidably public moment when he abandoned his teaching post, he maintained the disjuncture between his public identity and his real intentions: "I openly professed that I had resolved to set out for Mecca [i.e., to perform the public and socially expectable act of pilgrimage], while privately I made arrangements to travel to Syria" (Watt 1963:58).

Al-Ghazzālī's stress upon the secret as a way of maintaining a split between the exoteric and the esoteric reflected his convictions about the organization of knowledge as a basis for social order. The faith of the masses was to be scrupulously protected from error and doubt by carefully circumscribing their exposure not only to philosophical argument but also to the Sufi experience itself, which was likely to be erroneously interpreted by most people.

In describing the states he went through in his own inner experience, he wrote: "The first stage is characterized by the appearance of visions that have form and language: The mystics in their waking state now behold angels and the spirits of the prophets; they hear their speaking to them and are instructed by them. Later, a higher state is reached; instead of beholding forms and figures, they come to stages in the 'way' which it is hard to describe in language; if a man attempts to express these, his words inevitably contain what is clearly erroneous" (Watt 1963:61). What is erroneous is dangerous.

He was contemptuous of the reasoning abilities of the masses and felt that exposure to anything but simple doctrine might threaten their faith and, with that, the security of the community. He explained his position that the masses should not have access to philosophy, for instance, through the use of an analogy: "It is only the simple villager, not the experienced money-changer, who is made to abstain from dealings with the counterfeiter. . . . The majority of men, I maintain, are dominated by a high opinion of their own skill and accomplishments, especially the perfection of their intellects for distinguishing true from false and sure guidance from misleading suggestion. It is therefore necessary, I maintain, to shut the gate so as to keep the general public from reading the books of the misguided as far as possible" (Watt 1963:40).

In another work *Mishkāt al-Anwār* (The Niche for Lights), which sought to articulate the insights he had gained from his Sufi practice, al-Ghazzālī repeatedly resorted to the secret in his explications. In the following passage, he describes certain controversial Sufis' experiences of oneness with God:

> They were drowned in the absolute Unitude, and their intelligences were lost in Its abyss. . . . No capacity remained within them save to recall ALLAH; yea, not so much as the capacity to recall their own selves. . . . They became drunken with a drunkenness wherein the sway of their own intelligence disappeared; so that one [al-Hallāj] exclaimed, "I am The ONE REAL!" and another, "Glory be to ME! How great is MY glory!" [Abū Yazīd Bistāmī] and another, "Within this robe is nought but Allāh!" . . . But the word of Lovers Passionate in their intoxication and ecstasy . . . must be hidden away and not spoken of. (al-Ghazzālī 1952:106–7)

> In relation to the man immersed in this state, the state is called, in the language of metaphor, "Identity"; in the language of reality, "Unification." And beneath these verities also lie mysteries which we are not at liberty to discuss. (al-Ghazzālī 1952:108)

The experience of inward truth could not be permitted to displace outer law and doctrine, though al-Ghazzālī's privileging of inner experience raised the potential for this.

Hodgson has described the social implications of al-Ghazzālī's influence in these terms: "The work of Ghazzali may be said to have given a rationale to the spiritual structure that supported society under the decentralized political order, the order that resulted in part from the work of his patron Nizamulmulk" (Hodgson 1974:190). This structure presupposes a hierarchical religious life, with society graded into three classes: those who have unquestioned faith, those who learn the reasons for their beliefs (scholars), and those who directly experience truth, the Sufis. Al-Ghazzālī states explicitly that "every 'Perfect' man has three sets of opinions (*madhahib*), (a) those of his own environment, (b) those he teaches to inquirers according as they are able to receive them, and (c) those which he believes in secret between himself and Allah, and never mentions except to an inner circle of friends or students" (al-Ghazzālī 1952:19). He was concerned with articulating a form of Islam that was appropriate for the general population, and many of his books offer detailed guidance on how to live a proper Sunni Muslim life according to sharī'at, as in his extensive *Ihyā' 'ulūm ad-Dīn* (Revival of the Religious Sciences; al-Ghazzālī n.d.: 1975), but he also reinforced the place of a Sufi intellectual elite, those whose personal experience included some perception of ultimate truth itself. "Thus the Sufis were assigned a crucial role in supporting the historical Muslim community as a body, as well as in guiding personal lives" (Hodgson 1974:188). As al-Ghazzālī advised his readers: "Do not sit in company with the mob, but if you do, the correct behavior is to avoid engaging them in conversation, to pay little heed to their false-alarms, to ignore the bad language current among them, and to confine intercourse with them to the necessary minimum" (al-Ghazzālī 1975:91). In Hodgson's view, "Elitism in an extreme form was being superimposed on Islamic populism" (Hodgson 1974:192).

So what does all this have to do with the image of the qalandar? The sharp differentiation of public and private space and the authority of direct experience for the spiritually advanced gave the individual considerable license in the realm of the psyche. For al-Ghazzālī God is utterly unknowable through human language or concepts. There is a radical gap between the outer guidance provided by a discursive formation — whether that be the sharī'at, no matter how detailed, or even the images conjured up by the language of other Sufis — and the individual's actual inner experience, which may ultimately violate any doctrines, beliefs, and principles that the individual otherwise holds. The qalandar as a literary trope expresses precisely this sharp disjunction. The qalandar was focused above all on his own inner state, which was utterly unconstrained by any exterior law. It is probably no coincidence that Abū Hāmid al-Ghazzālī's brother, Ahmad Ghazzālī, was one of the lyrical Sufi poets who took up the trope of the qalandar in their writings as a way of expressing their exploration of this interior space.[5] For the publicly rationalist Abū Hāmid al-Ghazzālī, it was essential that such an antinomian inner force be tightly constrained by the constant guidance of an externally imposed order.

Perhaps his brother expressed what al-Ghazzālī himself avoided articulating publicly. Ahmad Ghazzālī used the qalandar image in his aphorisms of love, which focus on the mysteries of the relationship between lover and beloved, lost in mutual contemplation (Ghazzālī 1942:15). He "uses the image of the beggar (qalandar) and the ruins to illustrate the state of the lover who has subjected himself entirely to the demands of his love" (DeBruijn 1992:80). The orthodox of his time, however, were shocked by Ahmad Ghazzālī's theories of love. One of Ahmad Ghazzālī's disciples, ʿAynuʾl-Quzāt Hamadhānī, who also used the image of the qalandar in his poetry,[6] was executed for unorthodoxy in Baghdad in 1132. The divulging of secrets had very real political and personal consequences for these Sufis.

Sanāʾī of Ghazna (d. 1131), a Persian court poet who seems to have focused increasingly on Sufism as he aged, vividly developed the theme of the secret, so important in Abū Hāmid al-Ghazzālī's work, in connection with the theme of encounters with a qalandar guide. One of his poems describes a meeting between the poet and an old man. The secret is explicitly linked with unspecified debauchery. DeBruijn has summarized the basic story:

> [It is] a rather long poem about a meeting between the poet and a person described as "a shining figure, an ornament of old age" whom Sanaʾi sees coming down towards him from the mountain when he leaves his house "in all ignorance." The old man invites him to accompany him to a party. Together they go to a house which is beautiful, pure and without any sign of decay. However, the people inside are a bunch of rascals (*qawmi hama qallashan*) and *piran-i kharabati* who indulge in all sorts of debaucheries. When the poet is shocked by this scene, the old guide withholds him from a condemnation: "Do not regard their doctrine as sinful, but keep their secrets hidden from the people." (DeBruijn 1992:82)

In Sanāʾī's poem we see a maximal contrast between the outer and the inner, a pure house and an inner scene of debauchery. What are these debaucheries, and how could they not be sinful for the one who adheres to the example set by the Prophet Muhammad and the sharīʿat of the established Muslim community?

The poem is a graphic articulation of the ethical cultivation of the self as this is understood within the Sufi tradition. Venturing an interpretation of the poem, I suggest that Sanāʾī is describing a move along the Sufi path, from a stage of relative ignorance, marked by an exoteric awareness that is limited by strict adherence to sharīʿat, to a new stage. The old man is the Sufi guide. The house where the party is being held is the poet's body, which is clean, pure, and without decay due to his careful adherence to the law. The debauched (and in many other places Sanāʾī uses the term qalandar to express a similar type of character) are the poet's unfettered desires and thoughts, which do not obey the dictates of polite society. To condemn these desires would be to place an obstacle between the Sufi and the desire for God. To translate into Western psychoanalytic lingo, the repression barrier has been lifted and the guide, like the psychoanalyst, is telling the poet to look at what is there without condemning. (In this story, at least, the experience is limited to the specular, thus avoiding action.) Nevertheless, the pure house must be maintained and the secret kept. The debaucheries are known, experienced, and self-reflexively gazed upon, but are private. Therefore, in the poem they are not specified, being left to the private imagination of the reader/hearer.

The secret both marks and hides a discrepancy between outer order and an interior that violates that order. The order is not to be abolished: it is like the relationship between the signifier and the signified in contemporary poststructuralist discourse — the signified would not exist without the outer shell of the signifier to support it, to constitute it. The inner experience of the Sufi requires a Muslim society ordered according to the principles dictated by God. It is not that the interior is a reality that must be exposed at all costs. In contrast to the Cartesian notion that the inner self, the "I," is an entity more real, more essential than the phenomenal world and the body that houses that self, for these Sufis the inner experience is not an entity but a space that exists only within a properly constructed framework.

Unbounded Desire

The qalandar ideal — the realm of the secret — involved a certain relationship to pleasure. As Foucault argues in his *Use of Pleasure* (1990b), the control of pleasure has been a central aspect of the constitution of the self in the West, though attitudes toward pleasure have changed over the centuries; extirpation of pleasure, he claims, is the result of centuries of Christian theorizing. He argued that the ancient world was concerned with the control of pleasure through asceticism. As a counter to the Christian project of extirpation, Foucault drew on Plato's connection between erotic desire and pursuit of truth. Qalandar imagery suggests that an analogous relationship to pleasure developed in Muslim Sufi discourse. Due at least in part to the influence of al-Ghazzālī, this Sufi discourse penetrated mainstream Islam.

In Muslim discourse, pleasure has not been extirpated — it has been carefully bounded and contextualized, contained through orthopraxy. To be a proper Muslim is to follow the sunnat (the example of the Prophet) as interpreted through one or more schools of law. For the "mainstream" Sufi, the first step on the path is conformity of one's practice to sunnat. The pleasures of sex, for instance, are carefully hidden behind a veil, saved for lawful enjoyment in an explicitly defined time and place.

The power of the qalandar as an image in Sufi poetry comes in part because it plays with the significance of practice in articulating a relationship between the devotee and God. The qalandar is a trope for the fantasy of a basic violation of the principles that order pleasure, the self and society. The qalandar of Persian poetry explores not only the limits of knowledge, which had been al-Ghazzālī's preoccupation, but also the limits and secrets of fantasy and pleasure, which are explored in the writings of many Sufi poets. It is not a matter of avoiding excesses — excess within the imagination is, on the contrary, cultivated. ʿAttār, for instance, creates a detailed description of the beauty of a young boy (ʿAttār 1990:222). But excesses must be contained by keeping them secret and properly channeled. The pleasure of union with God is so great that ʿAttār may not reveal its secrets:

> But who can speak of this? I know if I betrayed my knowledge I would surely die; if it were lawful for me to relate such truths to those who have not reached this state, those gone before us would have made some sign; but no sign comes, and silence must be mine. Here eloquence can find no jewel but one, that silence when the longed-for goal is won. The greatest orator would here be made in love with silence and forget his trade, and I too cease: I have described the Way — Now, you must act — there is no more to say. (ʿAttār 1990:229)

Paradoxically, one of the core fantasies constituted by this discourse is that of eliminating the boundaries, removing the veil, mingling public and private. But these excesses of debauchery are themselves carefully bounded in graphic, but figurative language. As shaped by this discourse, subjectivity is, above all, created by the experience of boundaries, walls, "veils," and a core fantasy is of stripping away these veils, of experiencing an unbounded subjectivity.

The fantasy of flooding subjectivity with the unbounded experience of desire is accomplished by eliminating the faculty of intellectual discrimination. But discrimination and the setting of intellectual and legal limits, as I discussed above, was a core social issue and basis for conflict as political factions struggled over authoritative bases for knowledge and law. The issue of discrimination is central in the following verses, written by Sanā'ī, who used the trope of the qalandar extensively in his poetry:

> Sometimes I raise my cup in the middle of my devotions,
> Sometimes my cheek lies in the dust on the ground.
> Sometimes I cry out towards the heavens.
> Drunkenness has devastated me so much
> That I cannot discern words from their meanings.
> The minstrel is to me a muezzin;
> I cannot tell deceit from a sincere prayer. (DeBruijn 1992:81)

A "self" rooted in discernment and the ability to maintain conventional boundaries between the proper and the debased was to be abandoned (in fantasy) in favor of an ideal of social abjection and an unfettered, undistracted experience of unboundedness, articulated as obliteration of self in the love of God.

Living Qalandars: Ideology and Resistance

What has been a fantasy of the antinomian for the spiritually elite Sufis who were let in on the secret became for others a public way of life, a praxis. Though it is clear from many sources beginning in the thirteenth century that the qalandars as wandering bands of mendicants did constitute a visible and growing presence in the Muslim world, much of the power and significance of these living qalandars comes from their place within a discursive structure, as an enactment of the Imaginary in Lacan's sense. In a treatise against libertinism, al-Ghazzālī was extraordinarily harsh in his early-twelfth-century condemnation of those who, claiming to be Sufis, consider themselves exempt from prayer or the law against the drinking of wine. He articulated the danger in the following terms:

> There can be no doubt about the necessity of killing this man. . . . The execution of a man like this is better than the execution of a hundred infidels, for the harm done to religion is greater. With him is opened a door to license that cannot be closed. This man is more harmful than one who advocates libertinism for all. . . . This man tears down the law with the law, for he claims that he has not sinned except in that which is specifically for the general public. . . . Frequently he pretends that he has commerce with the world and commits sins only externally, while internally he is untouched by them. (Ernst 1985:119–20)

The antinomian in behavior is to be forcefully extruded from the community. The very harshness of al-Ghazzālī's position is evidence of the Imaginary function of the qalandar, analogous to the Jew in Nazi ideology. For Žižek: "A 'Jew,' for example, is in the last resort one who is stigmatized with the signifier 'Jew'; all the phantasmic richness of the traits supposed to characterize Jews (avidity, the spirit of intrigue, and so on) is here to conceal not the fact that 'Jews are really not like that,' not the empirical reality of Jews, but the fact that in the anti-Semitic construction of a 'Jew,' we are concerned with a purely structural function" (1989:99).

It is precisely the phantasmic structure of the qalandar's activities that appears in several sources that are critical of the qalandar.[7] Muhammad al-Khatīb, himself a stringent Muslim, wrote in 1284–85 a work devoted to castigating various heretical groups. Offering an account of the origin of the qalandars, he devoted considerable attention to the thirteenth-century qalandar Jamāl al-Dīn Sāvī and his followers. In this version of Jamāl al-Dīn Sāvī's life, that qalandar, having started out under the guidance of a Sufi noted for his strict conformity to the sunnat, leaves because of a "natural inclination" to laxity and heresy. He is joined in his seclusion by a beardless youth (by implication, the object of corrupt, homosexual desire) and several other disciples. They soon develop a large following. According to al-Khatīb, they frequently engage in illicit sexual relations, including sodomy, and consume wine and hashish (Turan 1953; Karamustafa 1994:6). This type of description of the qalandars appears repeatedly in sources throughout the centuries, through the colonial period in South Asia, and today in television dramas and everyday discourse. Frequently added to this characterization is the accusation that the qalandar secures a living through fraudulent practices, as in a thirteenth-century Arabic poem by Taqi al-Dīn ibn Maghribī of Baghdad.[8] These are the secret practices that the poet Sanā'ī gazed upon in his dream but was instructed not to condemn or reveal to the public.

The critics of the qalandar reveal the structure of their own desire and the shape of their own fears that are incited by that desire. Like the Freudian symptom, the criticisms of a strict law-abiding Muslim like al-Khaṭīb simultaneously reveal and conceal, repress and express al-Khaṭīb's own fantasies. These fantasies are the instantiation of desire as that desire has been structured by a dominant discourse of thirteenth-century Persia. It is a desire that has left its traces on individuals who live in Pakistan today.

This discursive structure emerged in a historical era when competing authorities struggled to control public articulations of "reality" in a clash of ideologies and discursive traditions (most notably, Arab and Persian). It not only organized desire and fear in terms of a rigid demarcation of an outer, public space and a discrepant inner reality; it also created an inner reality that was a self-reflexive subject position experienced as having infinite dimensions and power. The qalandar simultaneously represented this power and deconstructed the very dichotomy between inner and outer that it rested on. The qalandar was thereby a "line of flight" (Deleuze and Guattari 1987), escaping the discursive structure out of which it emerged.

Qalandars as Agents of Ideological Protest

Qalandars are not a particularly visible presence in the historical record. In the earliest references to them, in Sufi poetry and didactic texts, the qalandar has no concrete specificity as an individual and appears as little more than a vehicle for the desires and anxieties of the writer. But the phantasmic nature of the qalandar in many early Sufi sources — he is often portrayed, for instance, as the essence of debauchery — does not mean that living qalandars did not exist. The thinness of the historical record on qalandari as a way of life openly followed by specific individuals and groups in this earliest period is not surprising, given their antinomian rejection of status and its trappings: they are something that is best not seen. There are, however, somewhat later sources in which they resemble other Sufi orders, many of which were forming in this period, as part of the accelerating institutionalization of a mass participation in Islam (see Hodgson 1974).

The traveler Ibn Batuta, for instance, when passing through the town of Dimyat (Damietta) in Egypt in 1326, reported a *zāwiya* (residence) of qalandars, headed by a shaikh, just as he reported virtually every Sufi establishment he came into contact with. Though he had no words of praise for the shaikh (as he did have for many of the other shaikhs and zāwiyas he visited), he did not challenge the group's legitimacy or condemn their practice, but simply recorded without comment two miracle stories about their purported founder Jamāl al-Dīn Sāvī that he had heard (Ibn Batuta 1973, 1:37–38). This suggests that for Ibn Batuta, these qalandars were not abject representatives of the Imaginary, as they were for some of his contemporaries. It is evident that these were specific people he had encountered and engaged with socially.

According to Karamustafa, qalandars emerged as an identifiable social group in Syria and Egypt in the early thirteenth century (Karamustafa 1994:3), which is well after the emergence of the qalandar as a trope in Persian Sufi poetry. Karamustafa characterized them as "world-renouncing dervish groups" and as "radical protest movements that were directed against Islamic society at large" and more specifically, against the socially respectable institution of the tarīqat (Karamustafa 1994:100).[9]

The appearance of this particular Damascus group in the historical record is the result of institutionalization, a process that was characteristic of Sufi orders at that time. Members of this group are reported in several sources to follow certain distinctive practices, such as shaving the head, beard, and eyebrows, practices that clearly marked their identity as qalandar and as followers of the "founder" of the order, Jamāl al-Dīn Sāvī (d. 1253), who originated these practices.[10] These people, then, were paradoxically caught up in the social process of identity formation, establishing a position in the social order of Sufism. They formed zawiyahs or kanaqahs similar to those of other Sufi orders, organized around a leader (shaikh). They modeled themselves on the practice of the founding shaikh Jamāl al-Dīn, whose memory was perpetuated in anecdotal stories.

A hagiography devoted to Jamāl al-Dīn Sāvī was written (in Persian) by the disciple of a qalandari master in 1347–48 in Damascus.[11] The writing of the hagiography is itself a manifestation of this institutionalization process. It discusses extensively Sāvī's practice and his goals as a qalandar. Karamustafa has summarized the practices and goals attributed to Sāvī in this hagiography as follows:

> A Qalandar is one who frees himself from the two worlds through self-imposed death (*mawt-i irādī*) with the purpose of attaining continuous proximity to the Divine. The peculiarly Qalandarī habit of going naked with only leaves to cover the loins, removing all bodily hair, and sitting motionless and speechless on graves without any sleep or food except wild weeds are all viewed as direct consequences of this "premortem" death. . . . In brief, the Qalandar rejects society altogether and severs himself from both the rights and duties of social life. He spurns all kinds of social intercourse like gainful employment, marriage, and even friendship and devotes himself solely to God in complete seclusion. (Karamustafa 1994:41)

Within the hagiography itself, the contradiction between the antinomian path of the qalandar and the process of institutionalization is manifest, as Karamustafa has noted. Sāvī's three disciples attracted a large circle of converts to the cemetery where they resided. At first attempting to adapt his practice to collective life (by donning clothes and allowing followers to accept food offerings), Sāvī finally left Damascus and retreated to the isolation of another cemetery (Karamustafa 1994:42), leaving the order to be perpetuated by his disciples. But, of course, being part of an organized collective order, these disciples could not be precisely the qalandars of fantasy who reject the social themselves: they left that role to their idealized founder.

Though many of the qalandar groups of the medieval period may well have traced their origins to Jamāl al-Dīn Sāvī, it is likely that others did not. Clearly, he is not the source of inspiration for the qalandar poetry that was already well developed in Persia. It is interesting to note that according to Sāvī's hagiography, he began as a well-educated, mainstream Sufi from Sava in Persia before abandoning the world in Damascus. He may well have been acquainted with and inspired by existing qalandar poetry. By the same token, it is likely that others were similarly inspired and that still others, now invisible, may have been the models from which a poet wrote.

It is impossible at this point to trace an originary moment for an idea and a practice that had as a goal the evasion of the social order that would have recorded that origin. Jamāl al-Dīn Sāvī comes down to us because he was caught up in a social net, taken up into the ideology of a social movement that demanded an originary point. He thus stands as the "quilting point" of an ideology, to use Lacan's term as it has been taken up by Žižek.[12] He is the contradiction upon which the *qalandariyya* as a Sufi order was founded. To achieve identity as a historical subject Jamāl al-Dīn Sāvī had to alienate himself not only from himself, as any subject must to achieve self-identity, but from his identity as qalandar. This double movement suggests that, in taking up the signifier of the qalandar as an identity, the individual seeks to capture a subjectivity that is alienated through entry into a discursive subject position; the individual seeks an impossible object, a surplus of meaning that cannot be captured. The qalandar who succeeds in the goal of escaping signification also escapes from history.

Qalandars make their appearance in the historical record of Muslim India in the thirteenth and fourteenth centuries. There they are associated, not with Jamāl al-Dīn Sāvī,[13] but with two saints whose tombs continue to be prominent today: Lāl Shahbāz Qalandar (Shaikh 'Usmān Marwari [d. 1262]), who settled at Sehwan in Sind in today's Pakistan, and Abū 'Alī Qalandar of Panipat (d. 1323) in India. The qalandars of today in Pakistan continue to trace their spiritual genealogies to one or both of these saints. The shrine of Lāl Shahbāz Qalandar is an ideological focus and target of ideological struggles.

In texts spanning several centuries, there is a tension between the stance of viewing the qalandar as a hidden saint, embodiment of a world-renouncing ideal, and denouncing the qalandars of one's own time. The standard interpretation has been that the qalandars who are denounced are the ones whom one has personally encountered, but it strikes me that these denunciations are generally unspecific and have the structure of fantasy — the antithesis of the ideal. Both Suhrawardī and Jāmī, who lived three centuries apart, made the distinction between men of their own time "who took the dress of *qalandaris* in order to indulge in debaucheries" and the true qalandar, whose spiritual concerns are genuine (Trimingham 1971: 268; see also Schimmel 1975:88).

A prominent theme among Sufis of the thirteenth and fourteenth century in Delhi was a distinction between true qalandars and the criminal and dangerous. The distinction is framed in terms of the man who has renounced sharī'at and the social order because of his total absorption in God versus the man who uses the trappings of the qalandar as an excuse to engage in "debaucheries," simply indulging his worldly appetites.

The thirteenth-century Indian Sufi literature is replete with anecdotes of the *abdāl* (hidden saint), stories that hold in tension the ambiguity represented by the presence of a qalandar. Digby has noted several examples from Indian Sufi literature of the thirteenth and fourteenth centuries of anecdotes of saints (abdāls) concealed among the qalandars, including a story of Jamāl al-Dīn Sāvī himself (Digby 1984:34). As Digby retells it, the famous saint Bahā'al-Dīn Zakariya lodged one night in a mosque while traveling:

> Qalandars also arrived and took up lodging in a part of the mosque. During the night the Shaykh was awake at his devotions, he saw a Qalandar whose head was bathed with light from on high. . . . The Shaykh approached the Qalandar and said:
> "Oh Man of God, what are you doing in the midst of these?"
> "In order, Zakariyā', that you may know," the Qalandar replied, "that in the midst of every common gathering (*'ammī*) there is an especial person (*khāṣṣī*), on whose account the commonality may be forgiven."
> Naṣīr al-Dīn Maḥmūd then added that the Darwīsh in question was Muftī Jamāl al-Dīn of Sāva (. . . the founder of the Qalandariyya order). (Digby 1984:86)

A "common gathering" is a group of those who are uneducated, of low social status. The true qalandar of this story, in contrast, is a *muftī*, an authority on Islamic law, who is using his association with commoners, not to overthrow a hierarchical social order, but to demonstrate that one must look beyond dress in order to determine one's spiritual worth. It is certainly not a revolutionary story, but is rather an expression of the validity of the social order, since the superior spirituality of the educated shows through even the trappings of commonality. Jamāl al-Dīn Sāvī's identity has undergone considerable transformation.

Colonial administrators in the British period picked up Muslim fantasies about the qalandar as a dangerous phenomenon as they constructed their own discourse about the wandering beggar ascetic as a potential criminal or "profligate debaucher" (Ibbetson 1916:172), thereby translating a Muslim Imaginary into the British Imaginary of colonial India.

The qalandar of today is and is not the qalandar who makes fleeting appearances through centuries of Sufi texts. Despite continuities in the discourse of resistance, the twentieth-century qalandar is clearly not the qalandar who appears, for example, in texts of the Delhi Sultanate period and challenges the authority of an established pīr who enjoys royal patronage (see Digby 1984). The postcolonial social order that today's qalandar resists shapes him in ways undreamed of by the thirteenth-century qalandar who wandered into what we think of as India from Afghanistan or Iraq, across a then nonexistent border, and contested the practices and status of other, established Sufis who themselves were an important instrument of state authority. What the qalandars of Hujwīrī's time were resisting and what the qalandar now confronts — such as memories of colonialism, the welfare state's secularist discourse that constitutes the qalandar as homeless, and the Islamists' efforts to impose their modern interpretations of sharī'at on all members of the Muslim community — are very different, as are others' constructions of what the qalandar represents. Resistances cut across and remold in historically contingent ways.

On the other hand, old orders and old contradictions do not simply disappear with the coming of a new order; the break is not total. Echoes of the practices of the precolonial qalandars and the issues they contested remain in the practices of today's qalandars and their interlocutors. These echoes are heard through many filters — through the agendas of the established Sufis who wrote of the qalandars in the Delhi Sultanate period in texts that are still popular, through the concerns of British colonial administrators who marginalized the qalandar in their struggle to categorize and control, and even, occasionally, through their own hagiographers. The echoes of these old orders can be heard in today's positionings and confrontations.

9

The Subject, Desire, and Recognition

Desire is a flame that burns everything except the beloved, according to the thirteenth-century Persian Sufi poet Jalāl ud-Dīn Rūmī. The "self" is lost in the obliterating force of desire, like the moth in the flame (Rūmī 1925–40, 5:588). The significance of this desire has been all too easily reduced to the confines of the deterministic parameters of much of Western scientific psychology, where desire becomes a biological drive that has the parent as its primary object and is carefully channeled, sublimated, or repressed during the course of development.[1] When desire is reduced to the biological, its significance as a force that constitutes the subject within a political order is obscured. Desire has been privatized and located within the apolitical sphere of the medicalized psyche.

Sufism has undergone a similar fate of privatization under a Western gaze. For many Muslims, what had been a complex institutional structure was disrupted in the colonial period: Sufism was labeled the complement of "orthodox," public Islam and essentialized as a private, spiritual pursuit of the direct experience of God, and the institutionalized aspects of the pīr-disciple relationship were seen as historical accretions to what was assumed to have originally been a simple, pure experience. The linkages between spiritual authority and political influence were branded corruptions.[2]

But Islam is not easily encompassed within the category of "religion" that has been imposed upon it, and even Sufism, with its emphasis on inner experience, is not readily relegated to a private sphere. Sufis them-selves have recognized the important role of desire in the constitution of the political subject and the potential political significance of Sufism.

The early-twentieth-century Indian Muslim poet Muhammad Iqbal, whose speeches and writings were a powerful galvanizing force in the mobilization of the Indian Muslim community and the push for the formation of Pakistan, was scathing in his criticism of the passive long-ing for a pīr. Though writing as a resistant colonial subject, he accepted as true the Orientalist dichotomy that separated an active, technologi-cal West from a spiritual, slumbering East.[3] He focused much of his attention on certain forms of Sufism as a practice that had shaped the Muslim psyche and made it passive and dependent, as manifested in the relationship between pīr and disciple. The danger of Sufism for Iqbal was a political danger, that of being drawn into an authoritarian re-lationship with a spiritual leader, the pīr, in which the individual is trained to respond with passive acceptance to the appeals of any leader and to political domination.

Over the course of several centuries, the relationship between the disciple and the Sufi pīr had become formalized, institutionalized into Sufi orders (tarīqat). The practice of Sufism became so widespread that for many Muslims, one could not be a proper Muslim without having a relationship to a pīr. Just as institutions of the Catholic Church, such as confession, had the effect of constituting a historical subject, creating a discourse and a discipline that inserted itself between the subject and the human body (Foucault 1990a), the Sufi orders and the practices developed through these orders had created a discourse of desire and constituted a subject positioned within a specific social order. But-tressed by an elaborated discourse of "inner" experience, the subject was located within a hierarchical series in which one's status was deter-mined by one's level of spiritual development. The level of spiritual development could be known only by one who was more spiritually developed and who was attributed with the power of a unidirectional gaze. In this asymmetrical relationship the master had the power to recognize the subject but could not be completely seen in return.

Despite his criticism of the pīr and this one-way gaze, Iqbal actually drew on Sufism and its imagery to kindle a desire that would lead to a new kind of Muslim subject, one that would escape its colonial subor-dination and transcend the dichotomy between the Occidental and Oriental psyches. In his book-length poem *Asrar-I-Khudi* (Secrets of the self), Iqbal rearticulates the relationship between the self and God, reinterpreting the Sufi aim of desire in order to create a modern Muslim subject:

> The luminous point whose name is the Self
> Is the life-spark beneath our dust.
> By Love it is made more lasting,
> More living, more burning, more glowing. (Iqbal 1940:29)

and:

> When you make yourself strong with Self,
> You will destroy the world at your pleasure.
> If you would pass away, become free of Self;
> If you would live, become full of Self!
> . . .
> Advance from captivity to empire! (Iqbal 1940:99)

It would seem that Iqbal is simply giving the Western goal of developing the autonomous self a bit of Sufi window-dressing, contrasting his formulation with the traditional, passive Sufi goal of "becoming free of self." During his early adult years Iqbal had lived in Europe and immersed himself in the study of European philosophy. He was strongly influenced by Nietzsche's idea of the "overman." Yet his writing stirred the imagination and kindled the desire, not just of a Westernized Muslim elite, but of a people. His poetry is recited not just by lawyers and school children but by qalandars living in graveyards. Though Iqbal's focus on the self as an active force has passed through the filter of Western discourse about the self, he saw himself rearticulating a theme about self, desire, and consciousness already present within the Sufi tradition. The Orientalist lens, with its privileging of the autonomous, rational self, put a barrier between earlier Sufi writers and the modern world, a barrier that Iqbal sought to dismantle by recasting Sufi discourse into a language extolling the self.

Like many Muslim activists of the early twentieth century, Iqbal hoped to reformulate Islam by writing a foundational text, a kind of primer of Islam, alongside his poetry. In this work, *The Reconstruction of Religious Thought in Islam* (Iqbal 1971a), he attempted to clarify the status and validity of the type of religious experience that is at the heart of Sufism, juxtaposing the theories of several Western philosophers with those of Muslim thinkers, particularly Abū Hāmid al-Ghazzālī. Iqbal saw al-Ghazzālī as a pivotal figure—the Kant of the Islamic intellectual tradition, a thinker who recognized the limitations of human knowledge and rationality. In his writings Iqbal pointed to what he saw as al-Ghazzālī's insights into the centrality of desire to human action and its relationship to the constitution of the subject, insights that continued to be valid in the modern world. But he felt that al-Ghazzālī, unlike Kant, had erred in the prescriptions for human action that he educed from his insights on the limitations of reason. Al-Ghazzālī had declared that knowledge should be strictly controlled in order to maintain a stable social order.[4] One of Iqbal's goals was to recast al-Ghazzālī's thought into a more progressive framework by bringing it into relationship with European philosophy, and he did this by extolling the self.

The continuities between Iqbal's notion of desire and the subject and the way desire and the subject have been understood and deployed by earlier thinkers such as al-Ghazzālī are obscured by the Orientalist dichotomy between the Western and Oriental subjects. But poststructuralist deconstructions of Orientalism have brought the privileging of an autonomous self in Western discourse itself under scrutiny and have opened up an alternative starting point for assessing Iqbal's efforts to draw together past and present, an alternative lens for examining al-Ghazzālī's theory of the subject and desire and bringing his thought into contemporary discourse.

I will examine Sufi discourse about the subject without privileging the Western idea of the autonomous ego or self. One way to do this is by attempting to read al-Ghazzālī and, thence, Iqbal from the perspective of European theorists who set aside the idea of an autonomous ego and, from this stance, ask what kind of subject al-Ghazzālī posited. Only then will it be possible to characterize Iqbal's project for a modern Muslim subject without imposing on it at least that particular European assumption. This is in many respects the strategy that Geertz used in his programmatic paper "From the Native's Point of View" (1983). Geertz supposedly set aside the Western concept of self in order to better see the culturally specific categories through which members of three different cultures conceptualized selfhood. Geertz's approach to hermeneutic interpretation, however, obscured the extent to which he himself actively selected certain phenomena in order to construct *a* Balinese self or *a* Moroccan self. Though both my initial move of setting aside the lens of an autonomous ego and my interpretive goal are similar, I do not claim to be renouncing "experience-distant" concepts in favor of the native's "experience-near" (i.e., unreflexive and atheoretical) concepts, a claim that creates a hierarchical relationship between the observer and observed. I hope, instead, to set into relationship Lacan's and al-Ghazzālī's theoretical formulations, both of which are efforts to simultaneously capture and constitute the experience of the desiring subject.

The structure of Western discourse generates a dichotomy in which the autonomous, fully aware self defined primarily in terms of an interior individuality is held up as an ideal that stands in opposition to a dependency that is labeled pathology and associated with loss of self and lack of awareness or false consciousness. This ideology of an interior self is particularly well suited for the reproduction of a labor force that thinks itself free within the confines of a capitalist system. When deployed in the service of colonial domination, this ideology cast Sufi discourse and its expressed goal of obliterating the self or ego in the flame of desire in a negative light.

As I discussed in chapter 1, Freudian psychoanalytic theory, particularly in its earliest manifestations, was revolutionary in its decentering of the subject. Freud located agency in the unconscious: consciousness was a relatively superficial manifestation, the outcome of a struggle among conflicting forces in dynamic tension. Following Freud, Lacan set the divided subject, split by the entry into Language and a Symbolic Order and alienated from its own desire, at the heart of his work. I argue that a similar decentering of the subject also pervades al-Ghazzālī's work and at least certain strands of Sufi discourse. From the perspective of a Western gaze that has privileged an ideology of the autonomous, self-conscious individual, this Sufi discourse and its expressed goal of obliterating the self in the flame of desire has been interpreted as devaluing autonomy and fostering passivity, a judgment also reflected in Iqbal's writing. But these articulations about the self and its relationship to desire take on a different significance within the context of Lacanian theory, when it is freed of the evaluative lens of Western individualism. Desire for the Sufis, as for Lacan, is oriented toward an abyss. Exploring this parallel draws us closer to an understanding of Sufi experience and of the implications and limitations of Lacanian theory for an understanding of the constitution of subjectivity.

Al-Ghazzālī and Lacan

Al-Ghazzālī wrote that the closer the Sufi approaches to God, the beloved, "the more he apprehends the fathomless depth of His qualities, the abyss of His essence: therefore his longing to plumb deeper and more wonderful mysteries can never end" (Schimmel 1975:133). It is a limitless approach, a goal never to be reached. The self is obliterated in an intense, paradoxical desire, an essence that is also an abyss.

For al-Ghazzālī, as for Lacan, the speaking subject is founded on a void, a moment of separation, a lack. Though other Sufis have focused more intensely on desire and its imagery in their poetry,[5] al-Ghazzālī has written autobiographically of a profound interruption of his ego and its resolution in a way that finds resonances in Lacan's theory of desire and the subject. His work *Mishkāt al-Anwār* (1952), written after this interruption, is devoted to the inner experience of the approach to God. Specifically, in this text he made explicit the void upon which he saw the speaking subject to be founded.

Al-Ghazzālī's thinking, like Lacan's, includes a developmental perspective, tracing the emergence of the human subject out of an undifferentiated matrix of infancy. In contrast to much Western theorizing about the cohesive, autonomous self, including the developments in psychoanalytic thought that Lacan is so critical of, al-Ghazzālī wrote of the diverse "spirits" or faculties that constitute the subject.

In *Mishkāt al-Anwār* (1952), al-Ghazzālī recognized what he called gradations in the human spirit, which in modern parlance could be identified as cognitive processes. According to al-Ghazzālī, they emerge in a developmental sequence but are all copresent in the fully mature adult. He made a distinction between the "sensory spirit" and the "imaginative spirit" that is significant from a Lacanian perspective. The sensory spirit is the recipient of information brought in by the senses. It is to be found in the infant at the breast. The imaginative spirit, in contrast, is the recorder of information conveyed by the senses. Though present in some animals, it is not to be found in the infant, who forgets about an object that is out of sight. Al-Ghazzālī stressed that out of this second function — what we might call "object permanence" — emerges the conflict of desire that arises in the child's soul for something out of sight, based on the image preserved in the imagination, an absent presence. He noted the emergence of the image as a kind of split. In Freud and Lacan this split is linked to the separation of demand (a demand for love) from need (a physiological state satisfied by a physical object). This split produces a conflict as the child enters into the realm of the Imaginary (to put it in Lacanian terms). Al-Ghazzālī thus emphasized the development of the human being away from a reliance on a need-based input of the senses into a world in which signs shape perception rather than the reverse.

According to al-Ghazzālī, subsequent to the emergence of the imaginative spirit, the intelligential spirit and then discursive spirit develop. These are faculties not found in children. Adults are capable of apprehending ideas beyond the spheres of sense and imagination, and developing axioms of necessary and universal application. Intelligence is given precedence over the eye in determining causal explanations. The discursive spirit then takes data of pure reason, arranges them as premises, and deduces knowledge from them. This sort of reasoning has become detached from the "real" and bears many of the characteristics of what today would be called ideologies.

What is most highly developed in al-Ghazzālī's thinking and is significant for his theory of the subject is his view of the limitations of the higher modes of human understanding (intelligential and discursive reason) and the experience of subjectivity founded on this modality. Though not, of course, working from a Saussurean or Peircean theory of signs, he stressed the relational properties of the ideas we hold and their arbitrary relationship to "truth." He recognized the power of a cultural tradition in shaping the individual's reality: Christians believe Christianity to be the truth just as fully as Muslims believe in Islam. He concluded that our rational thought processes (ʿaql) on their own are unable to lead us any closer to "truth." Our cognitive processes alienate us from ourselves and our truth.

Al-Ghazzālī included one more "spirit" in his categorization of the spirits or faculties that appear during the course of human development: transcendental prophetic spirit. This spirit, in contrast to the others, is limited to only a few select individuals — prophets and some saints. It is based, not on the capacities of the conscious mind, but on an irruption from elsewhere. Access to truth requires an irruption, a disruption of the imaginary, of the ideologies, including the ideology of the "self" that place a screen or "veil" between us and truth. Without such an irruption, we are caught in a historically contingent discursive formation.

The affective significance of this irruption of prophetic spirit for al-Ghazzālī can be inferred from his discussion of the stages in the spiritual development of a certain relationship to God, tawwakul (reliance). The stages of tawwakul that the Sufi works toward reverse the developmental sequence of childhood (see al-Ghazzālī 1975). The lowest stage of tawwakul rests on the illusory image of the autonomous individual: the subject treats God like a competent, kind, and dependable lawyer to whom he entrusts his affairs. To describe the next stage of tawwakul, al-Ghazzālī used the analogy of the child's relationship to its mother, thereby making its psychological roots explicit: it is like the young child who knows only his mother and takes refuge in her whenever danger threatens. This child operates with the illusion of autonomy—the exultant child of Lacan's mirror stage, which imagines itself a whole in the presence of its specular image but is often reminded of its incompleteness, its fragmentary nature. The cognitive faculties, what he called the imaginative spirit, provide the basis for this illusory wholeness.

The final, highest form of tawwakul, reliance, draws on both the analogy of the infant and of the corpse, completing the circle of development. "Such a man lives before God in such a way as a dead man is kept before one who washes him" (al-Ghazzālī 1975:255). "He is like that child who knows that wherever he will stay, his mother will find him out. If he does not like to suckle his mother's breast, his mother will suckle him. Such a person gives up invocation as he trusts in His mercy and help and thinks that he will get more if he does not want than if he wants" (255). This is actually like the child in the womb; the point at which there is no separation and thus no need for demand at all. Implicit in this formulation is the understanding that any demand is a demand for love; it is a recognition that such a demand presupposes a gap between the mother and child. Al-Ghazzālī has captured that moment when demand, closely intertwined with need, first becomes separated from it. It is the moment when the demand to nurse is a demand to be recognized. The Sufi seeks to reclose that gap, to create a state of perpetual presence. Al-Ghazzālī recognized, however, that this state is impossible to maintain, that the gap always reopens. He stressed the difficulty of maintaining this stance: "Even if the second and third stages are attained, its lasting is still more difficult" (255). From a Lacanian perspective, the Sufi has, of course passed through the Symbolic Order, through the signifier, which has structured the unconscious. By focusing on the moment at which absence is no longer absence, one is confronting the paradoxical structure of the founding moment of the subject in absence, in lack. In Lacanian parlance, it is difficult to face constantly the divided nature of one's subjectivity, to hold in recognition the otherness of one's desire.

That al-Ghazzālī, like Lacan, recognized an absence at the heart of the subject is explicit in the following passage, in which al-Ghazzālī wrote of the relationship between God and created being: "Being is itself divided into that which has being in itself [i.e., God] and that which derives its being from not-itself. That being of this latter is borrowed, having no existence by itself. Nay, if it is regarded in and by itself, it is pure not-being" (al-Ghazzālī 1952:103).

For al-Ghazzālī, the Sufi as subject is the locus of an impossible desire. The subject is barred from the truth of its desire by seventy thousand veils, which are seventy thousand fantasies that the ego constructs to bridge the gap between the subject and the object of its desire. God, the object of desire, cannot be captured by metaphor, though humans are continually trying to do so. Al-Ghazzālī stresses this attribute of God over and over. He suggests that humans can properly attach signifiers to God only metonymically: in his words: "Now what is meant to be conveyed by this 'That Who' is the vaguest kind of indication, destitute of all relation of comparison, 'He transcends relation.' When Pharaoh demanded to know His essence, Moses merely indicated His works" (1952:128).

Kristeva in her development of Lacanian theory stressed the distinction between metaphor and metonym (Kristeva 1986b:246–48). Metaphors are by their very nature bounded, limited. They are the basis of fantasy, the structure of the Imaginary Order. The illusory ego is constructed out of and fixed by metaphor. In contrast, al-Ghazzālī's God, like the Lacanian other, can be indicated only by an unstable chain of signifiers that stand in a metonymic relationship to the subject.

One of Lacan's favorite metaphors for characterizing the constitution of the Imaginary ego and its relationship to the Symbolic Order is that of the mirror. The ego, the self, is the image in the mirror. The self is a metaphor, which the exultant child appropriates. The Symbolic Order, in contrast, is the frame of the mirror itself, that which is not seen. For al-Ghazzālī, the Sufi in a state of ecstasy may claim identity with God, just as the Lacanian child claims the image in the mirror as his own. Al-Ghazzālī, too, explained this phenomenon with a mirror analogy: "For it is possible for a man who has never seen a mirror in his life to be confronted suddenly by a mirror, to look into it, and to think that the form which he sees in the mirror *is* the form of the mirror itself, 'identical' with it" (al-Ghazzālī 1952:107). The Sufi, in other words, mistakes his own image in the mirror for God. In this case, the Sufi, in contrast to the child, has recognized the otherness of this specular image and feels himself to have been absorbed by this otherness — hence, the Sufi discourse about loss of self. But this is still fantasy, the fantasy of a merging of the self and other. Just as for Lacan, al-Ghazzālī says that the Other, God, the Symbolic Order, is not that specular image but rather the unseen form of the mirror itself. The gap can never be fully closed. The self of the Sufi is not God, but an existent not-being, illuminated only by a borrowed light.

It might be argued that it is actually the place of God in al-Ghazzālī's system that alienates the subject from itself, based on passages such as the following: "These gnostics, on their return from their ascent into the heaven of Reality, confess with one voice that they saw nought existent there save the One Real. They were drowned in the absolute Unitude, and their intelligences were lost in the abyss. No capacity remained within them save to recall Allah; yea not so much as the capacity to recall their own selves" (1952:106). Imagery such as the Sufi being a corpse in the hands of the washer or the nondemanding infant has commonly been interpreted from a Western perspective as the passivity of the Oriental. What kind of subject is it that offers itself up to God as the corpse in the hands of the washer, that loses the capacity to recall its own self?

We can answer this question by considering the result, according to al-Ghazzālī, of achieving total reliance (tawwakul) on God. What happens to the subject that imagines itself as a corpse or as an utterly passive infant? Al-Ghazzālī wrote: "He thinks that he moves similarly at the hand of his original fate. He is firm and steady. He thinks that the flow of his movements, strength, will, knowledge, and other attributes run through him compulsorily" (1975:255). The Sufi thus achieves power and steadiness of purpose. "The Prophet said: God says: A servant continues to come near Me by his optional divine services till I love him. When I love him I become his ear with which he hears, I become his eyes with which he sees, and I become his tongue with which he speaks. Here the force of pen is compelled to stop" (255). Al-Ghazzālī then lists heresies that develop out of this experience. In psychoanalytic parlance, this moment could be called the internalization of the other — or the recognition of the other who is already within us, who speaks through our desire. As Kristeva has written: "Analytic experience reveals that the discourse of the father, king, prince, or intellectual is *your discourse*. It is a logic that is within you, which you can domesticate but never dominate" (1987:55).

What is lost when the Sufi becomes the nondemanding infant or the corpse is the illusory ego, the series of illusory self-representations that we cling to to avoid having to face exposure as a fluid, changeable subject. Paradoxically, it is a position of owning one's desire, and not renouncing it, because to be in this state is also to be in a state of recognition that the "self" is nothing, that it is an illusory construction, an Imaginary fantasy. The Sufi who achieves the highest stage of reliance also questions all received truth, since reliance on such a truth is a turning away from God. This empowering relationship to God is possible only with the positing of God as an other that cannot be gazed upon, that cannot be named or interpellated. God is the object of an impossible desire, and the Sufi keeps the impossibility, the limitlessness, of this desire firmly before him.

Given al-Ghazzālī's intellectual milieu, the congruences between him and Lacan suggest that Lacan's theory is not strictly a modern Eurocentric one. Yet critics of Lacan have suggested that Lacan has reproduced many aspects of European discourse. Foucault argued that psychoanalysis is a discursive practice that contributes to the tightening control over individuals by constructing sexuality as a supposedly natural force, and locating it within the individual as something to be monitored and controlled. Lacan disrupted this naturalizing discourse, highlighting its arbitrariness and the power relations through which it is imposed. Al-Ghazzālī made a similar reflexive move. Yet both Lacan and al-Ghazzālī accepted the necessity of "normalizing" individuals by convincing them to submit to the dominant order, thereby controlling both practices and thoughts. Lacan assumed the universality and inevitability of a phallic Symbolic Order within which the subject must find a place, arguing that the alienation of the subject from its own desire is not the historically specific outcome of subjection to a repressive political or economic order but is, rather, the human condition, an inevitable consequence of the entry of the subject into language. Al-Ghazzālī, though his terminology is different, took a similar stance. For him, the maintenance of a "Symbolic Order," based on sharī'at and dictated by God, is a central part of a universal human project. He hinted at the arbitrariness of that order, the logic of which a human must not question because of its source in God. God is Order, to which the individual must submit, by which the subject must be interpellated. The ordinary person must be shielded from recognition of the arbitrariness of Order — that is, he must be controlled.

This discursive position also produces parallel forms of resistance within both al-Ghazzālī's world and Lacan's. The resistance takes the form of challenges to the necessity for all human experience to be channeled through a single Symbolic Order: it is a political challenge against claims for the naturalness of a hegemonic discourse. In European discourse, one manifestation of this resistance is the Nietzschean-Dionysian challenge to the kind of systematizing that is represented in the Hegelian tradition; in Islamic Sufi discourse, the systematizing of al-Ghazzālī finds an opponent in the qalandar.

In explicit criticism of Lacan, Deleuze and Guattari, for instance, advocate a Dionysian escape from a determining order (hence, their [1983] title "Anti-Oedipus"). They see desire as directly productive in its move toward and appropriation of an object. Though desire lacks a fixed subject, a centered self, it does not lack an object. The fixed subject emerges only as a product of a repressive social order. Deleuze and Guattari's is a political position, intended to be a subversive assault on this order. Their image of the human as a desiring machine, experiencing the world and others directly and desiring them with no gap, rejects the necessity of a Symbolic Order, rejects the idea that all desire is at its core a desire for the touch of the absent mother and the gaze of the judging father. Their model of the "schizo" is reminiscent of the qalandar in the Sufi tradition, the antinomian wandering begging ascetic who rejects the Law — who refuses even the gaze of respectability, who protects no self or ego, who, like a machine, moves through space because of the eruption of desire focused outward into the world. The qalandar, the nomad, acts without any "pressure" from consciousness, following the urgings of a Sufi saint experienced only in dream. The qalandar is the anti-Oedipus.

Deleuze and Guattari brand psychoanalysis, including the Lacanian variety, as a conservative tool of social control. Analogously, al-Ghazzālī was a conservative influence on the Muslim community. He developed a synthesis of philosophy, law, and Sufi thought that created a spiritual elite and excluded the masses from access to knowledge. He advocated that the ignorant not be informed of the locus and truth of their own desire for fear of its subversive power: like psychoanalysis, which is a therapy for the elite, the deepest insights of Sufi teaching and practice are only for a spiritual elite who have a personal investment in the existing social order. Persons who cannot restrain themselves from acting out their sexual desires need strict controls and punishments if they are not to constitute, like the qalandars, a dangerous, disruptive force. For the same reason, the ignorant masses should not be told that human knowledge is arbitrary and cannot encompass truth. Al-

Ghazzālī practiced what he preached, by cloaking his insights in the power of silence and secrecy.[6] Both Lacan and al-Ghazzālī must, therefore, be located as historical subjects whose insights are themselves manifestations of their positionings and interests within a dominant political order.

Nevertheless, insights such as al-Ghazzālī's should at least serve to undercut our own hubris about the unique power of our theories to penetrate the arbitrariness of social order and tradition. European discourse has tended to assume that cultures are experienced with a certain plenitude — that symbols actually succeed in confounding models of and models for reality, hiding the arbitrary precariousness of the human condition from those of us who have not yet been thrown into the modern and postmodern maelstrom of free-floating signs. Both Lacan's theory and al-Ghazzālī's highlight a fundamental gap in human systems of knowledge and a concomitant void on which the subject is founded.

By the same token, it would appear that, following the analogy I have constructed (Lacan:Deleuze and Guattari::al-Ghazzālī:the qalandar), the formative role of the social order in the shaping of desire and the creation of the alienated subject does not newly emerge within a capitalist order. Both Lacan and al-Ghazzālī posit an overarching Symbolic Order because they each stand in an ambivalent relationship to a discourse that is associated with a powerful politicoeconomic order and claims to be "reality," in a discursive field where other ideologies and other discourses make counterclaims. "Reality" is overtly and consciously contested in a dialogic process. It is this contest that opens up an interior space for self-reflexivity within the individual, a gap in which the plenitude of signs as transparently representative of reality is called into question.

Iqbal, Al-Ghazzālī, and the Qalandar

In his quest to reconstitute the Muslim subject as a powerful force in the face of European domination, Iqbal sought a middle path between al-Ghazzālī and the qalandar on the one hand and between Hegel and Nietzsche on the other. Iqbal recognized the brilliance of al-Ghazzālī's insights but felt that al-Ghazzālī's prescriptions for social order had led to the stagnation of the Muslim community. Specifically, like European political philosophers, he was critical of an order in which authority and power flow downward and outward from a political center, particularly when that center was a non-Muslim colonial power. Iqbal lived in a world where an ideology of order and authority legitimately flowing from the top of a social hierarchy was being replaced by the idea of authority emerging out of a popular mandate. Iqbal thus diverged from al-Ghazzālī because of changing historical circumstances: notions of political participation and the role of knowledge in the maintenance of political order had changed.

Iqbal drew both on Nietzsche and on qalandar imagery to express this new position that he envisioned the political subject taking within a modern Muslim community. Caught in the Orientalist degradation of Muslim culture, Iqbal found the image of the qalandar a powerful vehicle for escaping and transcending the East-West dichotomy that had penetrated his own self-constitution and that he felt rendered the Muslim powerless and degraded. But, like al-Ghazzālī, he was careful not to advocate antinomian rejection of order itself. He identified himself with both the qalandar and with Nietzsche while simultaneously denying them. One poem in particular manifests his way of handling specific thinkers, or positions, be it Nietzsche or the qalandar:

> I am one who has walked around
> The Haram with an idol under my arms.
> I am one who has shouted Allah's name
> When idols were in front of me.
> My heart still wants
> That I should go on seeking, though
> I have set foot
> On a path thinner than a hair. (Fragments 4; Iqbal 1971b:178)

Iqbal in his poetry repeatedly proclaimed that he himself is the qalandar:

> Come and join Iqbal's company,
> And share a drink or two with him.
> Although he does not shave his head,
> He knows qalandars' ways. (Iqbal 1971b:143)

Yet he also distinguished himself from the qalandar:

> Come, let us catch hold of
> The skirt of Iqbal's robe,
> For he is not one of the men who go about
> In patched-up dresses at saints' shrines. (Iqbal 1971b:151)

He rejected "Persian mysticism," yet extolled Persian Sufi poets. He claimed not to have been influenced by Nietzsche, yet he drew heavily on Nietzsche.[7] The qalandar represented for Iqbal the antinomian rejection of the idols of static social forms, but like the Persian Sufi poets of old, he rejected the concrete antisocial practices of historical qalandars. He was concerned, not with rooting out the fascisms of daily life,[8] but with creating a new sociopolitical order within the framework of the nation-state.

By recasting the Sufi goal as the cultivation of an active self, Iqbal sought to eliminate passive acceptance of colonial domination and of interpretations of Islamic law (sharī'at) issuing from a class of religious scholars that he and other modernists sought to displace. Iqbal's articulation of the Sufi goal was not the development of a Western-style autonomous ego, but rather realization that one is a subject who is guided by God. One should know this God, not through the passive acceptance of traditional ideologies or any prevailing hegemonic discourse but through a direct experience of one's true condition as a desiring subject. So that, like al-Ghazzālī's Sufi, one recognizes one's own desire and becomes the tongue with which God speaks.

Afterword

An alleged hadīth calls knowledge the "greatest veil" separating man from God (Schimmel 1975:140). The tension between rational knowledge and Sufi insight has always been a popular topic for Sufi poets. This juxtaposition of discourses and their struggle for hegemony is not new with the coming of Western secularist discourse. And Western discourse does not seem to have broken up Sufism as a "traditional" practice and recast it in Western terms. On the contrary, many Sufis recognize when science is used as a defensive veil or as a power strategy and have subordinated science to Sufi discourse without rejecting it altogether.

We too easily assume that modernity is a unique historical phenomenon that has created a new organization of subjective experience. Even Freud, who played a major role in recasting our notions of the human subject by dethroning consciousness and highlighting the universality of human desires beneath the veneer of civilization, assumed the possibility of progress toward a new form of rational, reflexive self-consciousness, to be engendered by the scientific technique of psychoanalysis. And anthropology posited a difference between the autonomous Western self and various traditional selves even as it promoted cultural relativism. The liberating potential of psychoanalysis has been challenged by those—such as Foucault and Deleuze and Guattari—who recognize this clinical technique as one of a range of increasingly invasive medical practices that, far from uncovering the hidden subject and its desires, create and control the subject by naming it. And anthropology has been jolted by critiques of its epistemological foundation into confusion about the very project of studying other cultures as if they were dying traditions.

The Muslim world is the antithesis of a static traditional society suddenly overrun by the West, though there are plenty of colonial and postcolonial sources that have portrayed it in such terms. It is, rather, an important part of the civilizational matrix that gave rise to the conjunction of forces that we now call the modern world. It could even be argued that the present questioning of Western Enlightenment ideas concerning the centered rational subject was itself stimulated by the new exposure to systems of thought such as Sufism that followed colonial expansion and the consequent dissipation of Europe's isolation from the rest of the world. Nevertheless, Muslim societies such as Pakistan were subject to a powerful colonial and scientific discourse that redefined local culture in many ways. My goal has been to articulate how this process of redefinition occurs and is experienced not only at a local level but within the individual.

It is not possible for an anthropologist to study the practice of Sufism with any sophistication without an adequate theory of the experiencing subject. Developing as an empirical social science, anthropology in its early years did not problematize the relationship between subject and object that its project of observation rested on and as a discipline has been ill-equipped to move beyond the disruption produced by poststructuralist critiques. Psychoanalysis brought the phenomenon of self-reflexivity into Western philosophical discourse in a new form. But anthropologists have generally not been particularly conversant with the subtleties of Western philosophical thought. During the heyday of cultural relativism, anthropology had little conceptual space for the universalizing associated with psychoanalytic approaches to the individual, and psychoanalysis was thoroughly unfashionable. But with the conceptual shift to a historical subject that is shaped by relations of power flowing through diverse discursive practices, anthropologists cannot avoid asking how individuals experience and manage themselves within the diverse networks of meaning and the mechanisms of constraint that characterize specific historical circumstances. The nature of the subject must be seriously engaged through the ethnographic project.

But why not just stick with Freud? Anthropologists who have taken a

psychoanalytic perspective in their work have until now virtually ignored Lacan and have had nothing to do with Deleuze and Guattari,
dismissing them as fancy theorists that have been taken up as a fad by
"the cultural studies people," asserting that these theories, while they
might offer an interesting new perspective on the analysis of cultural
productions such as novels and films, are not compatible with empirical research among real people of the sort that anthropologists study.
When anthropologists have engaged this body of theory, it has generally been associated with a shift of subject matter — to the study of
popular culture of a textual nature — media, comic books, and the like.

But Lacanian theory offers a powerful tool for explaining the power
of ideologies to stimulate desire and move people to action and submission without positing a cohesive ego as agent. It is this premise that
makes Lacanian theory powerful for analyzing cultural productions
such as ideologies and for examining how these ideologies operate in
specific social arenas. I agree that this premise also makes Lacanian
theory inadequate for explaining the complexities of daily life: Lacan
characterizes all of human interaction in terms of a single narcissistic
modality, the struggle for recognition. My use of Lacan may seem paradoxical, then, since I reject Lacan's fundamental premise that a Symbolic Order constitutes the speaking subject. I have opted instead for
the position that access to the world unmediated by language is not
only possible but constitutive of many aspects of subjective experience
and that a struggle for recognition is only one of the things humans seek
in their social relationships. The result is an individual who is a fragmentary flux of experience, only part of which is taken up into and
constituted by discursive subject positions. It is this aspect of experience that Lacanian theory illuminates.

Glossary

abdāl   saint, successor of the Prophet Muhammad

ʿamal   deed or act, incantation

ʿāmil   one who performs incantations

auqāf   bequests, religious or charitable endowments; singular waqf

bā-sharʿ   lawful, in accordance with sharīʿat

baiʿat   the act of swearing allegiance and obedience. Within the context of Sufism, initiation as the disciple of a Sufi guide or pīr

baithak   hall or reception area where a pīr receives visitors and disciples

barakat   blessing, auspiciousness

be-sharʿ   contrary to sharīʿat

bhang   a form of hemp

bhūt   a ghost or spirit that haunts graveyards and other dangerous places

burqaʿ   a garment designed to cover a woman and hide her from public view

buzurg   elder, ancestor, saint

chādar   a sheet or large shawl

chapātī   unleavened bread

chillā   a period of forty days spent in seclusion for fasting and prayer; a ritual ordeal. The forty-day period of seclusion after childbirth

chūhā   a mouse; a person afflicted with microcephaly

churail   ghost of a woman who dies during pregnancy or during the forty-day period of seclusion after childbirth

dādā   paternal grandfather

dam   literally, breath. A ritual in which a pīr bestows a blessing on someone by blowing on the person

faiz   favor, abundance

faqīr   a Muslim religious mendicant who has renounced worldly desires and possessions fātiha   the opening chapter of the Quran, which begins the recitation of prayer and is also offered as a prayer for the dead and at the shrines of saints

firishta   angel

gaddi   the seat of an eminent person

hadīth   tradition describing a saying or action of the Prophet Muhammad

hajj   pilgrimage to Mecca

imām   head of a mosque, leader of prayer

'ishq   passionate love

jādū   magic, usually black magic associated with Hindus

jādūgar   magician

jalālī   majestic and dangerously awe-inspiring

jinn   a being created by God from smokeless fire; mentioned in the Quran, along with angels and humans

kālā 'ilm   literally, black knowledge; magic that draws on power other than God's; it is often used to harm others

khalīfa   a spiritual successor of a Sufi shaikh or pīr

khānaqāh   a residence for Sufis

langar   a public kitchen or food distribution held at a shrine

madrasa   school for the study of the Quran and associated subjects

mahfil   an assembly or gathering

malāmatī   reprehensible; one who deliberately draws blame upon oneself

malang   an ascetic who wanders from shrine to shrine and is usually regarded as violating Islamic law

malfūzāt   sayings of a spiritual guide

mantar   a magical formula or incantation, associated with Hinduism

manzil   a destination or stage on the Sufi path of spiritual development

maulvī   an Islamic scholar

mazhab   one of the schools of Islamic law; a sect within Islam

mu'akkal   a deputy, one to whom power is delegated; a jinn or angel

muhabbat   love, affection

murīd   disciple of a Sufi shaikh or pīr

murshid   Sufi teacher and spiritual guide, who is also a shaikh and pīr

nanga bābā   a near-naked holy man

nūr   the light of God

nūri 'ilm   literally light knowledge: knowledge that comes from God

pīr   a Sufi master and spiritual guide; popularly, any Muslim healer

pīrī-murīdī   the institution of pīrs and their followers; this term is often used in a derogatory way

pīrzāda   son of a pīr

pūjā   a Hindu form of prayer; from the perspective of some Muslims it is the worship of gods and idols

qalandar   an antinomian Sufi, often a wandering mendicant

qawwāl   a musician who sings devotional music associated with Sufi saints

qawwālī   devotional singing associated with Sufi saints

riyāzat   training, a religious exercise

rūh   literally, breath; the spirit within a human being that links the person to God

sadaqa   voluntary charity, in contrast to zakāt, which is a compulsory tax

sādhu   a kind of Hindu mendicant

sajjāda nishīn   successor of a pīr, usually a biological descendant, who takes over responsibility for the shrine and followers of the pīr

sanyāsī   a Hindu term for one who has abandoned all possessions, an ascetic

sarkār   chief, master, lord

sayyid   descendant of the Prophet Muhammad

shaikh   head of a Sufi order, a pīr

shalwār   loose trousers gathered at the waist, worn by Pakistani men and women

sharī'at   Islamic law

shirk   blasphemy through idolatry, assigning partners to God

silsila   a line or chain of spiritual succession within a Sufi order

sunnat   a practice or saying of the Prophet Muhammad that serves as a model for behavior

tarīqat   a Sufi "path" or order

tasawwur   picturing a thing in one's mind; the practice of holding an image of one's pīr in mind as a form of spiritual exercise

taunā   a charm or spell; specifically, the practice of throwing a goat's head in the path of another to cause that person harm

ta'wīz   an amulet, usually written by a pīr, consisting of a Quranic verse that is put into a small case and worn around the neck for its protective and healing powers

tawwakul   replacing one's own desire with reliance on God

tazkarat   a biographical memoir or account of a Sufi pīr

'ulamā   scholars of Islamic law; singular 'ālim

'urs   anniversary of a saint's death, associated with an annual celebration, usually at the saint's shrine

walī   a friend of God, a saint; plural auliyā

zāt   tribe, caste

zawiyah   a residence for Sufis

Notes

Preface

1. I was in Pakistan for three months in 1974, for an extended stay between 1975 and 1977, and again for several months in 1984–85.
2. This was a complaint also expressed by Deleuze and Guattari (1983) and by Foucault, who began his intellectual career in the field of phenomenological psychology (see Foucault 1986) and who ultimately castigated psychoanalysis as a discursive practice that has medicalized and commodified the psyche.
3. As, for example, in the work of Silverman (1983) and Smith (1988).

Chapter 1: Hegemony, Consciousness, and the Postcolonial Subject

1. Early in my first fieldwork experience, I was following a network of friends and acquaintances in order to get to know people in the neighborhood. A neighbor introduced me to Sufi Sahib's wife, who couldn't figure out why I would be interested in talking with her when her renowned husband was receiving visitors in the next room.
2. At that time, very few people in that part of town had telephones.
3. As political ideology, certain versions of Islamism seek to escape Western hegemony by walling out anything Western — establishing and enforcing strict codes of behavior grounded in a particular interpretation of inherited tradition, marginalizing those who do not claim adherence to that particular interpretation. Scholars, however, have emphasized that various forms of Islamism are, in fact, thoroughly modern. It has been noted, for instance, how Islamist movements draw on Western innovations in political organization, communication, and technology (see Lawrence 1989). For an insightful discussion of the recent emergence of Islamist groups in Egypt, see Kepel 1993.

4. This point has been argued by Dirlik 1994. For several perspectives on postcolonial theory, see Williams and Chrisman 1994.

5. Appiah describes the significance of a painting *Yoruba Man with a Bicycle* in a way that captures this point: the cyclist does not ask how the bicycle entered his life; he just rides it to accomplish goals that did not necessarily change with his acquisition of the bicycle. "It is not there to be Other to the Yoruba Self; it is there because someone cared for its solidity; it is there because it will take us further than our feet will take us" (1992:157).

6. By local I mean those narratives intended primarily for a local rather than a national or international audience, admittedly not a distinction that can be firmly drawn.

7. Williams recognized the continuing presence of tradition but also stressed the unique transformative power of modernity — particularly in the modern metropolis.

8. But these "remnants" are not simply dead. They become contributions to public culture made by intellectual elites themselves, who play an important (though not exclusive) role in shaping popular culture. This process will be visible in my accounts of everyday experience.

9. This is an image reminiscent of James Clifford quoting William Carlos Williams in his discussion of the postmodern social trajectory: "No one to witness and adjust, no one to drive the car" (Clifford 1988:7).

10. In Pakistan, Punjabi has only recently begun to be used as a written language, beginning with a trickle of publications by the Punjabi Adabi Academy, which was founded with the aim of promoting and developing Punjabi language and literature. Punjabis, however, speak it among themselves in most contexts. Government policy has generally been to discourage the development of local languages in favor of the national language, Urdu, which only those who moved to Pakistan from north India at the time of Partition speak as a mother tongue.

11. The play's image of Lāl Shahbāz Qalandar dancing in chains echoes the dance of the tenth-century Sufi al-Hallāj to the gallows (see Massignon 1922).

12. Sehbai's objection to saint worship is also reminiscent of the poetry of Iqbal, who contributed to the guiding vision of many of those who argued for the formation of Pakistan (see chapter 3).

13. In making this point I agree with Aijaz Ahmad's criticism of the concept of the "postcolonial" as a subject shaped by colonialism. Subjectivities are constituted not by "moments" but by always accumulating processes of sedimentation and accretion: "The history of sedimentation which constitutes the Indian cultural formation includes much besides colonialism *per se*" (Ahmad 1992:172).

14. According to Raymond Williams, hegemony (as distinct from ideology) "is seen to depend for its hold not only on its expression of the interests of a ruling class but also on its acceptance as 'normal reality' or 'common sense' by those in practice subordinated to it" (1983:145).

15. See Young 1990 for a lucid account of this challenge to the Hegelian-Marxist notion of history as a progressive movement within the context of poststructuralism and theories of postcoloniality.

16. On the links between the Subaltern Studies group and poststructuralism see Said 1990 and Ahmad 1992:68.

17. Aijaz Ahmad had similarly criticized Said for this overpriviledging of the colonial (1992:172).

18. Homi Bhabha's project, for instance, has been to show us the colonial subject through the structure of colonial discourse: we see the colonial subject threatening the colonizer through devices such as mimicry (Bhabha 1984); we see resistance as an opportunity provided through the irresolution of the colonizers. While a creative demonstration of how psychoanalytic theory can provide new insights into how discursive formations operate, in this particular effort we see the colonized, not in terms of their own desires and fantasies, but in terms of the fantasies and fears of the colonizer.

19. For Foucault, for instance, a discursive formation emerges from a contingent conjunction of forces and practices that are the conditions of its possibility, but this discourse, in turn, stands between these forces and the constituted subject.

20. This difficulty has emerged as the central problematic for many theorists operating out of this poststructuralist paradigm, giving rise to provocative but convoluted efforts to account for resistance and agency, as in the work of Judith Butler (1990).

21. This was true, for instance, of Foucault's earlier writings, a limitation that Foucault sought to move beyond in his later focus on a Nietzschean view of power as a multiplicity of dispersed forces, with discourse being both one of these forces and a crystallization of forces.

22. Though this move is made in certain instances. See O'Hanlon 1988.

23. Guha (1983), for instance, posits a rebel consciousness that is primordial and autonomous, a move that Gupta (1985:9) criticizes as pure, Hegelian idealism but that O'Hanlon describes as part of a difficult strategy of deconstruction (1988:202).

24. These writers also from time to time slip into the tradition-modernity dichotomy that characterizes the hegemonic discourse that they are seeking to undermine when they simply reassert the power either of tradition or of a primordial resistant consciousness to resist the onslaught of a dominant discourse.

25. See Certeau 1984 for a critique.

26. The notion of the individual as a disunitary being has appeared in recent anthropological writing (Ewing 1990a; Kondo 1990; Murray 1993). Kondo's work, for example, is a significant improvement over earlier anthropological studies of the "self." Earlier studies ignored the phenomenon of disunity and inconsistency altogether and failed to problematize either the relationship between often inconsistent cultural constructs or the extent to which these constructs shape or determine subjective experience. Kondo presented the Japanese as continually negotiating selves through a range of shifting "subject positions." But she did not problematize the subject or agent who is strategizing through these shifting positions; nor did she problematize the motives she attributed to their strategizing. Instead of developing a theoretical apparatus that might locate the term "subject position" in either a theory of discourse or a theory of motive, she implicitly relied on an economic theory of rational choice, manifested in her repeated references to strategizing for power and advantage. The other has escaped from the bonds of cultural relativism only to fall into the trap of *Homo economicus,* a fate typical of those caught within anthropological theorizing, which has for so long relied on unexamined and, hence, over-

simplified theories of motivation and human nature. Bourdieu, for instance, himself admitted that he reduces human motivation to the single dimension of status competition (Bourdieu 1992). See Combs-Schilling 1989:28 and Eagleton 1991 for related critiques.

27. Most notably, Adorno, Horkheimer, Marcuse, and, more peripherally, Erik Erikson addressed this issue. See Arato and Gebhart 1978 on the Frankfurt School. With the exception of Anthony Wallace (1956, 1967), most anthropologists and psychoanalysts of a previous generation who were concerned with the relationship of culture and personality formulated their questions in terms of culture as a static entity that shaped the psyche toward the direction of a modal personality and did not address issues of dynamic social process and the subject as agent in their theories.

28. Ego psychology is a school of psychoanalysis developed by psychoanalysts such as Hartmann (1964), culminating in the work of Heinz Kohut (1977), who developed a "self psychology" that has come full circle to a centered, if threatened, self. For an overview of ego psychology, see Blanck and Blanck 1974.

29. Žižek (1989), following Althusser's example, has brought Lacan into a discussion of the constitution of the subject in relationship to ideologies, considering how successful ideologies mobilize a desire in the subject that is always deferred. In contrast to Althusser, he has systematically distinguished Lacan's Symbolic and Imaginary Orders, so that ideologies expressing the interests of specific social groups shape the subject at the level of the Imaginary, a theoretical move developed even further by Silverman (1992), who in her analysis of gender as a hegemonic system has highlighted this tension in Althusser's work. Silverman's strategy has been to negate the proposition that the Symbolic Order is organized in terms of the Phallus as a core signifier. Instead of giving up the Symbolic Order as a male domain or arguing for a nondiscursive subject that stands outside it, Silverman argues that the Symbolic Order as a structure of signs that organizes the unconscious has no specific content at all (returning in this to a position closer to Lévi-Strauss's structuralism, with its focus on difference), but is the structure of language as a play of differences. The Phallus as a signifier is an aspect of the Imaginary — merely one ideology (albeit a powerful one) among many, a specific instance of difference — through which the subject experiences the Symbolic, since the subject's access to the Symbolic is always mediated by specific ideologies and fantasies. The Phallus is a signifier within an ideology of male dominance. By making this distinction between a contentless Symbolic Order and the Phallic as an ideology, she is able to argue that the subject may resist a specific, hegemonic gendered discourse by resisting imaginary identifications with a gendered subject position while retaining a structured, nonpsychotic psyche. The woman or the homosexual can remain located within the Symbolic while rejecting the position of "other" within a phallocentric ideology. This formulation is also applicable to the theorization of the postcolonial subject, who is located as "other" to the Western self — often through the device of feminization (see, for example, Nandy 1983). It allows the postcolonial subject an alternative ideological positioning within metaphorical structurings of the Imaginary while remaining equally discursive.

30. This strategy of theorizing subversion and resistance through a turn to the non-discursive has its roots in Nietzsche's critique of the Hegelian view of history as the progressive development of reason; see Habermas 1987.
31. Ego psychologists such as Hartmann (1964), in positing a "conflict-free" sphere of the ego, have recognized a similar point, though Hartmann's formulations involve a reification of the ego, reintroducing some kind of cohesive, Cartesian subject.
32. They thereby distinguish their materialist theory of desire from Lacan's idealist position.
33. I will not go as far as Deleuze and Guattari, who generally avoid speaking of an individual by speaking instead of "desiring machines" in order to sustain their point about the absence of a subject.
34. It is also a theory that, as Kojève (whose interpretation of Hegel had a profound influence on postwar French thought) presents it, conflates two phenomena that Freud distinguished — oral incorporation and oedipal rivalry.
35. Only recently has there developed a recognition that there were significant influences that went the other way: the colonizers were also profoundly affected and their societies shaped by the colonial experience and by their colonial subjects (see, e.g., Freitag 1985; Parkes 1991).
36. Aggression, of course, may be experienced in a similar fashion.
37. His approach, however, downplays issues of domination, desire, and aggression from the side of those who have power over the child. In his model, social order is assumed to be basically benign, and his model becomes a normative prescription for the creation of an autonomous self in a "free" society, thereby reproducing a set of premises that moves away from Freud's idea of a decentered subject toward a Western liberal democratic ideal.

Chapter 2: Sādhus and Faqīrs: The Sufi Pīr as a Colonial Construct

1. Bhabha (1986a) has argued that Orientalist discourse is based on a simultaneous narcissistic and aggressive identification, manifest in the simultaneous existence of contradictory stereotypes linked with these two modes of identification. This structure can be seen in the violence of Davidson's compassion.
2. In a similar vein, Sir William W. Hunter in 1897 commented on the documents he had collected from district offices in Bengal: "We learn from these worm-eaten manuscripts that what we have been accustomed to regard as Indian history is a chronicle of events which hardly affected, and which were for the most part unknown to, the contemporary mass of the Indian people" (1897:7–8).
3. Within what was often for the British administrator an undifferentiated category of wandering, begging ascetic — indiscriminantly labeled *sādhu, faqīr, yogī, rishi, qalandar*, I focus in my own work on the Muslim Sufi — which encompasses the faqīr, pīr and qalandar — and on the practice and significance of the Sufi in contemporary Pakistan.
4. Emerging from administrative practices such as census-taking and the codification of law (see, e.g., Kozlowski 1985; Cohn 1987; Dirks 1987).

5. "The colonial policy redefined the Indian concept of the sacred according to British expectations of what religion should be about (in India, anyway). Temple rituals now concerned persons, families, and perhaps even castes; they were definitely no longer matters of state" (Fox 1989:100).

6. One of the specific effects of this move was to seek a separation of endowments (*auqāf*) intended to benefit primarily family members from those that served "public" needs, ruling the former invalid. This policy posed a serious threat to Muslim landowning families. See Kozlowski 1985 for a detailed account of this process and its culmination in the organization of various factions of the Muslim community against British policy concerning auqāf. To appease the Muslims, the colonial administration in 1913 passed the Waqf Validating Act, which had been sponsored by Mohammed Ali Jinnah, the Muslim leader who spearheaded the movement for Pakistan. For auqāf acts in twentieth-century India, see *Hand Book on the Waqf Act, 1954* (1985).

7. Asad (1993) has examined how the idea of religion as a historical category emerged in the West. He argued that the idea that religion has undergone a radical change since the Christian Reformation — from totalitarian and socially repressive to private and relatively benign — is a part of the story of secularization that is often invoked to explain and justify the liberal political worldview of modernity: it leads to the view that "politicized religions" threaten both reason and liberty.

8. This dichotomy echoes the terms of the debate between the romantics and utilitarians that began in the eighteenth century in reaction to the encroachments of industrialization in the north of England. The debate was then played out in the arena of empire (Ahmad 1992).

9. Among psychoanalysts, splitting is seen as a strategy for projecting undesirable aspects of the self onto an external object, the defensive character of which was stressed by Fairbairn (1952). Melanie Klein (1946; 1957:324–25) has written on the tendency of very young children to "split" the image of the caretaker into the "good" mother and the "bad" mother, associated with the subjective feelings of love and hate as a developmental phase.

10. See the fifty-volume series, *The Sacred Books of the East*, edited by Max Müller (1879–1900).

11. In this project, they embodied the dictum that knowledge is power by disrupting prior modes of transmission. This was probably more significant for Hindus and the authority of the Brahmans, which was based in part on privileged access to the Vedas. In fact, the Muslims had already begun this process of appropriating Brahmanical texts. It was, for instance, through a translation by the Muslim Sufi (and son of the Emperor Akbar) Dara Shikoh that Vedic texts first became available to a non-Brahman audience.

12. The introduction of printing itself created changes in the dissemination of Sufi texts — including those produced by Sufis — and, thus in the organization of Sufi practice (Ernst 1997).

13. The textual productions of living Sufis, which became voluminous as local printing presses were established, have continued to be dismissed as "ephemera" (and so

labeled by the Library of Congress PL 480 book acquisition program up to the present).

14. It should be noted, however, that the British were not the first to create a polarized image of the sādhu and faqīr. Muslim Sufi texts from the Delhi Sultanate period, for instance, are replete with images of the corrupt beggar in the guise of the Muslim faqīr and qalandar (see Digby 1984). From the eleventh century to the present, the Muslim world has produced qalandars who have challenged the naturalness of whatever paradigm of social order happened to be hegemonic at the time. Over the centuries "sultan and Sufi" have competed for authority, and accusations of corruption have flown in both directions. See Ahmad 1963 for an analysis of this complex relationship. Eaton (1978) suggests that the sultan who was struggling to consolidate his own authority typically enlisted the support of the Sufi, while the established sultan sought to minimize the influence of the Sufi.

15. This distinction has been reproduced in today's reformist Islamic discourse: I was frequently informed that pīrī-murīdī (the relationship between a spiritual preceptor and followers, a term with derogatory connotations of corruption and ignorance) has nothing to do with Sufism.

16. The nature of the threat of the holy man shifted over the centuries of colonial rule. In the earlier period, when British authority was itself less extensive, bands of religious mendicants did have considerable economic and religious clout (Hansen 1992:72; Bayly 1983:140–43; Lorenzen 1978:61–75). In the days of the East India Company, many wandering ascetics were organized in bands that were engaged in active rebellion against central authority or constituted an alternative source of authority in specific regions (Lorenzen 1978:72–73). This activity diminished in later periods. According to Bayly, the proportion of religious mendicants in the population had declined to 5 percent by 1880, having been considerably higher a century earlier (1983:126).

17. Writing in 1844, Burton alluded to this "contract system" and its effect on prices in Sind: "Under the Ameers, a Seer (2 lbs.) of Bhang [a form of hemp or marijuana] was always procurable for an Anna; now, under our contract system, it costs from five to six times that price" (1973:168). In 1893, a royal commission was established to study the problem of opium consumption in India. After two years of study, the commission determined that opium did not cause crime, disease, insanity, or death. Based on the commission's recommendation, the British Parliament declined to prohibit its use in India (Hunter 1907:239).

18. This information was later reproduced in Burton 1973.

19. The jalālī pīrs were one of several antinomian groups in the Muslim world.

20. Cohn was quoting from a copy of a letter from the president and council at Fort William in Bengal in their Secret Department, January 15, 1773, available in the India Office Library.

21. See Fani 1901, 2:225–26 for a description of this group.

22. Lorenzen (1978) notes that in the late eighteenth century there were large bands of sanyāsīs who operated as mercenaries for Hindus, Muslims, and the British.

23. This is Cohn's interpretation of British sources from this period (1964:176).

24. They did, however, eventually find themselves in the business of adjudicating cus-
    tomary law in the court system, particularly as it pertained to matters of inheritance,
    including the inheritance of rights to the income of shrines.

25. See Foucault (1973:43–45) on the establishment of workhouses.

26. For a number of years he worked as an accountant in the Indian Public Works
    Department before becoming a professor of natural science in the Government Col-
    lege, Lahore, until his retirement in 1897 (*Who's Who* 1908:1387).

27. The title of his revised edition of the 1889 volume is particularly revealing of his
    general orientation to the practices he recorded: *Cults, Customs and Superstitions of
    India: Comprising Studies and Sketches of Interesting Peculiarities in the Beliefs,
    Festivals, and Domestic Life of the Indian People; also of Witchcraft and Demonia-
    cal Possession, as known amongst them* (1908), complete with photographs and
    drawings supplied by his son, William C. Oman. My references will be to this 1908
    edition.

28. Oman's comments are consistent with E. P. Thompson's suggestion that in public
    perception, the real indigent were hidden, not visible on the streets so that the ones
    who were on the streets were tricksters: "By the 1840's many of the tricks of the
    imposters were known; unless he had the knowledge and humanity of Dickens or
    Mayhew, the middle-class man saw in every open palm the evidence of idleness and
    deceit" (Thompson 1966:266).

29. The phrase is to be found in the conclusion of his *Protestant Ethic and the Spirit of
    Capitalism* (1958), which was published in German in the same year (as a two-part
    article, in 1904, 1905) as Oman's book.

30. For an account of British Orientalism in the late eighteenth and early nineteenth
    centuries, see Kopf 1969.

31. The Theosophists were one of a number of movements opposing capitalist society
    and modern civilization that erupted during the late nineteenth century. Unitarians,
    for instance, perceived ancient India as embracing a monism that they also found
    attractive. Antimodernist Edward Carpenter (1914a:71–72, 82–83) found release
    from Western materialism in Indian spirituality. Many of these movements used the
    idea of Oriental spirituality, epitomized by the sādhu and faqīr, as a rallying point.
    The Theosophical Society had its roots in late-nineteenth-century American spir-
    itualism and Western occultism, which could be characterized in general terms as
    responses to the challenges that the empirical sciences and changing social order
    posed for established religions. Influential figures in the American spiritualist move-
    ment had themselves been members of the American Oriental Society and other
    scholarly organizations dedicated to the study of Pali, Sanskrit, and other ancient
    texts.

32. Though a useful counter to the mystification of what are actually contemporary
    issues and articulations, most arguments about the hegemony of colonial discourse
    exaggerate the extent to which colonized cultures were penetrated and distorted by
    ideologies spawned by colonialism. Even if economic transformations and displace-
    ments engendered by colonial practice were pervasive, it does not necessarily follow
    that these transformations were accompanied by or gave rise to analogously over-

whelming cultural understandings that would have resulted in a colonial mediation of identity and a penetrated colonial subject.

Chapter 3: The *Pīr*, the State, and the Modern Subject

1. For studies of this process of the building of a Muslim community, see Freitag 1988; Gilmartin 1988.
2. One Pakistani ruefully recalled the Hindu joke that the only things that distinguished the culture of the Muslims from other Indians was a particular cut of the pyjama.
3. As an example of this process, see Gilmartin 1984 for a discussion of the challenges to the moral authority of landed pīrs in the Punjab that developed in debates during the late nineteenth and early twentieth centuries.
4. It was not as though the British came into India with the Marxist line that religion is merely the opiate of the masses. Missionaries were a powerful presence, and many sought to argue that Christianity was somehow more rational and modern than Hinduism or Islam.
5. Much of the argument in this section is based on Ewing 1983.
6. It could be argued that the space for constituting a public discourse of Sufism was generated in part by the positive Orientalism and the example of activists such as Gandhi, who drew on Hindu sources made available to the Western-educated by the Orientalists. This raises the question of whether this Sufism emerged only across a rupture from the past into modernity. In chapter 9, where I focus more directly on the ties of Iqbal to Sufi discourse, I argue that it would be exaggerating the power of Western discourse to posit such a rupture, despite Iqbal's own extensive exposure to Western thinkers such as Nietzsche.
7. These are three of Pakistan's four current provinces.
8. This takeover was unsuccessfully contested before the Supreme Court in 1971 (*All Pakistan Legal Decisions* [PLD] 1971:401–25).
9. But small *madrasas* have mushroomed across the landscape of Pakistan in recent years. According to Muhammad Qasim Zaman, the number of madrasas rose from 137 at the time of Partition to 8,000 in 1995 (personal communication; see also Zaman forthcoming; Malik 1996).
10. I need hardly point out the incongruity of "Coke" representing Pakistani "tradition," though it only struck me after rereading this passage several times. A bit of the "modern" has been taken up into another discourse.
11. Data Ganj Bakhsh is the popular name for the well-known eleventh-century Sufi Hujwīrī. His only extant work is *Kashf al-Mahjūb* (1976), which in Nicholson's translation is subtitled *The Oldest Persian Treatise on Sufism*.

Chapter 4: Everyday Arguments

1. There has been little scholarship on the Ahl-i Hadith, aside from brief summaries in Metcalf 1982 and Malik 1996.
2. Studies of the Ahmadiyya include Lavan 1974; Friedmann 1989.

3. The Jama'at-i Islami temporarily had considerable say over government policy in Pakistan during the administration of Zia al-Haq in the late 1970s. Maudoodi's writings have had a formative influence on Islamist movements throughout the Muslim world (see Maudoodi 1963; Kepel 1993).

4. See Gilmartin 1988:60–62 for a discussion of the emergence and orientation of the Ahl-i Sunnat ul-Jama'at.

5. There is also a considerable literature that describes healing practices at shrines in other parts of the Muslim world. See, for example, Westermarck 1926; Crapanzano 1973.

6. Much of this new construction was made possible from earnings sent home by the many men who were employed as temporary workers in the Middle East in the 1970s and 1980s.

7. I have chosen to use pseudonyms to protect the identities of members of this family.

8. The maintenance of *parda* (the seclusion of women) is for many working- and middle-class families an important way of maintaining honor and status (see Vreede-de-Stuers 1968). Paradoxically, those even higher in status are typically less concerned with the maintenance of parda, and interpret Islamic law in different ways.

9. The tension between two views of the proper and effective ways for removing harmful influences is not limited to Muslims in a South Asian environment, despite the resemblance with Hindu practice. Even in early Jewish practice, the source of many Muslim practices, this tension existed. In one ritual among the Jews, the tension, interestingly enough, was explicitly enacted within the same ritual, split between two goats: "Two goats were presented by the people, one for God, one for 'Azazel.' The former was sacrificed to atone for the sins of the people; then the High Priest placed his hands on the latter, shifting to it the sins of the people. A man led it into the desert, after which he purified himself. In this way the sins of the community were driven off into the desert (the 'scapegoat')" (Perrin and Duling 1982:25).

10. This example of *sadaqa* resembles Hindu practice. When a person or animal sickens and dies, village Hindus in Uttar Pradesh may attribute the misfortune to the inauspiciousness of Kali (Raheja 1988). In such a case, the evil or inauspiciousness is transferred to a goat, which is then driven over the village boundary toward the next village. If someone should catch the goat and eat the meat, they would instantly die, because they would be recipients of that evil. From this Hindu perspective, whatever harmful influence had been transferred from the patient to the goat or chicken remains in the goat and is subsequently transferred to whoever catches it. The practice of *taunā* among Muslim women in Lahore is also similar to this Hindu practice of driving a goat out of one's village: a woman's misfortunes pass into the goat's head, and the person who walks over or picks up the goat's head will be harmed. Raheja's explanation of this Hindu practice is that Hindus separate out what is not compatible with oneself while opening oneself up to what is compatible, a concern very different from the concerns of Punjabi Muslims.

11. This analytic distinction was made and elaborated by Ricoeur (1992).

12. In the tale from the Puranas, the child god Krishna, behaving as any small child might, eats a bit of dirt in front of his friends. His mother, ready to reprimand him,

demands that her naughty child open up his mouth. When he does so, she is stopped short, for she sees within his mouth the whole universe. Immediately afterward, he returns her to the mundane reality of her everyday world, and the momentary rupture of her reality is closed (O'Flaherty 1975:218).

13. For an analogous phenomenon, see Geertz's description of his Javanese informants' intense fascination with an oversized mushroom (1973b).

14. In chapter 1, my reinterpretation of Geertz's episode of the Javanese uncle (Geertz 1973c) is an instance of this.

15. This was, incidently, true of people I met in the United States as well as in Pakistan.

16. The *dopatta* is a near-transparent scarf usually worn across the chest and shoulders by any woman who is also dressed in *shalwār* and *qamīs*. Virtually all women, including the most modern and elite, usually wear this form of dress.

17. Literally, "breath." In this context, it refers to water over which Quran verses are read and blown. The water is to be drunk by the afflicted person to effect a cure.

18. According to this logic, the line between possession by a jinn and contact with a pīr cannot be clearly drawn. There are many cases in which a woman may become possessed by a jinn yet not seek exorcism. Instead, she appeases the jinn by allowing herself to become possessed by it on a regular basis, often on Thursdays (see Steel 1884:126). In the one case of this activity that I heard of, a woman became possessed by a jinn regularly every Thursday on which she was "pure" (not menstruating). Other women would gather on these occasions to hear her oracles.

19. For a discussion of the Deobandi reformist effort as it focused on shaping the practice of women, see Metcalf 1990.

Chapter 5: A *Pīr's* Life Story

1. The narrative structure of a simple allegory, in contrast, is basically an ideology arranged in narrative sequence. Like an ideology it rests on a fixed set of metaphorical relationships, so that, for instance, the narrative subject *is* a pilgrim, life *is* a quest.

2. The difficulties of textually re-creating the fluidity of the encounter are well illustrated in Crapanzano 1980.

3. Two books available in English, Jaffur Shurreef's *Qanoon-e-Islam* (1973) and T. P. Hughes's *Dictionary of Islam* (1965), provide action-by-action descriptions of the rituals that must be performed in order to acquire a power over angels and jinn that are associated with particular Names of God. They include the word "muwakkil." Both Hughes's description and that of Shurreef are based on Gwaliori's *Jawāhir-i Khamsa*. In his entry "exorcism," Hughes printed in its entirety a chart taken from the *Jawāhir-i Khamsa* (1965:73). Other sources that discuss the theory of the Names of God are Schimmel (1975:177–78); and Khaja Khan's *Studies in Tasawwuf,* which includes a chart of created forms associated with each Name and a discussion of how a pīr writes an amulet using the Arabic letters associated with each Name (1923:46, 51–62).

4. God has ninety-nine names, each of which represents one of his attributes.

5. This ambiguity can be traced to the time of Muhammad himself. By some accounts,

"The Arabs presented the incantations [those used to ward off harm or evil] they knew to the Prophet who, one by one, accepted some and rejected others" (Glasse 1988:339), thus leaving ambiguous the moral status of such incantations in general.

6. "He created man of clay like the potter's, And the Jinn did He create of smokeless fire" (Quran, Sura 55:14–15).

7. Jinn, like humans, can be either good or evil, servants of God or of Satan.

8. *Tasawwur al-shaikh* is a form of meditation prescribed in certain Sufi orders, in which the disciple concentrates on forming a mental image of his spiritual teacher (shaikh) (see Trimingham 1971:213).

9. I visited one of these sons at the shrine and specifically asked him about Sufi Sahib.

10. For another version of this story, see Singh 1982:4–6. Bullhē Shāh died in 1752.

11. 'Abdu'l-Qādir Gīlānī (d. 1166), whose tomb is in Baghdad, is regarded as the founder of the Qādirī Sufi order. Though Sufi Sahib claimed affiliation with the Naqshbandī order, he also felt a close spiritual tie to 'Abdu'l-Qādir Gīlānī. The practice of holding a monthly ritual in his honor is a popular local practice.

12. His use of this word indicates his own efforts to align Sufi concepts with elements of Western thought.

13. See Ewing 1990b for an analysis of this man's dream experience and his relationship with Sufi Sahib.

14. Hujwīrī's *Kashf al-Mahjūb* (1976:97–100) also includes an account of Fozail, from which 'Attār drew some of his material.

15. See Ewing 1994 for further discussion of this incident and of the significance for fieldwork of the anthropologist's own beliefs and dreams.

Chapter 6: Stories of Desire: Reclaiming the Forgotten *Pīr*

1. As Lacan wrote, "I think where I am not, therefore I am where I do not think. . . . I am not wherever I am the plaything of my thought, I think of what I am where I do not think to think" (1977:166).

2. Speaking of "the subject" is itself a reification, a recentering. Nietzsche (1968) and, more recently, Deleuze and Guattari (1983, 1987) conceptualize instead a flux, a force: the subject *is* desire, *is* fear.

3. The interview was tape-recorded with his knowledge and consent.

4. Other examples of such indexicals include "here" and "there," and verb tenses, all of which are dependent of the positioning of the speaker for their significance (see Benveniste 1971; Silverstein 1976).

5. Benveniste suggests that there are certain typical procedures by which the subject manifests itself in discourse, what he calls the stylistic devices of discourse. He focuses particularly on the devices of metaphor, metonymy, and ellipsis (Benveniste 1971:75).

6. There was a single earlier use of "we" to refer to the participants of the *mahfil* performing a prayer. It was followed by an exaggerated concern with translation, so that I would understand the kind of prayer he meant, suggesting to me an anxious reaction to his use of "we," a fear of locating himself in the discourse of the mahfil,

his fear making me seem more alien and unfamiliar with what he was talking about than I actually was.

7. Nevertheless, this is not to say that the gaze of the doubled other is "hegemonic" in the sense of shaping his reality, his consciousness. Rather, the fear of this gaze leads him to compartmentalize his involvement in Sufism.

8. This story is quoted by Trix (1993) and is the version her murshid told her.

9. Freud conceptualized the child's archaic identifications, on which the ego is founded, as a process of oral assimilation (1964), in which the child becomes what it incorporates. In this Sufi story, the process of assimilation happened behind closed doors, but in other descriptions the oral-incorporative mode of transmission is explicit, concrete, and reminiscent of the archaic: the teacher inserts his tongue into the mouth of the successor.

10. Trix describes a professor who, in her presence, interviewed her murshid by imposing a framework of questions in a way that ignored the conversational cues that, when attended to with an openness to the relationship, lead to a subtle attunement.

11. In the game of Trobriand Cricket (Kildea 1975), for instance, there is a team "mascot" that disrupts the hegemony of the colonizer's gaze through playful mimicry, imitating the gawking tourist and his camera, thereby creating a reflexive commentary on the relationship between colonizer and colonized.

Chapter 7: The *Qalandar* Confronts the Proper Muslim

1. There have been several distinct antinomian, wandering groups that have traversed the Muslim world over the past several centuries. Karamustafa (1994) has presented the early history of several of them, including the qalandars. The malangs were apparently a more local group in the Punjab, but today the word "malang" is used by many people as a generic term for wandering beggar-ascetics and is often used interchangeably with qalandar. "Qalandar" has more explicit associations with Sufi practice; "malang" is the more commonly used term for labeling the people encountered at shrines and on the street.

2. The late-twelfth-century Sufi Shihābuddīn Abū Hafs 'Umar al-Suhrawardī (d. 1234) wrote of qalandars: "Much of their effort is in ruining customs and habits, and in loosening the bonds of rules of association" (Suhrawardī 1980:140). They are thus perceived as disrupting social order. Suhrawardī wrote *'Awārif-ul-Ma'ārif,* which has been popular as a guide for Sufis throughout the Muslim world, including South Asia.

3. Those who draw blame upon themselves, by appearing to be impious to the gaze of the general public, are called "malāmatī" and, though a distinct phenomenon, are closely associated with the qalandar in many Sufi texts. Suhrawardī explicitly compared the two: "Through the absence of hypocrisy, this crowd resembleth the malamatiya" (Suhrawardī 1980:140).

4. See Ewing 1984b for a discussion of the rules of community among malangs who travel from shrine to shrine.

5. Thus in Pakistan, Sindhis have waged a campaign against the dominant Punjabis

using the Sindhi saint Lāl Shahbāz Qalandar as their rallying cry. Similarly, the voices of an underclass occasionally find their way into precolonial Muslim texts. In thirteenth- and fourteenth-century India, for instance, stories about brick-slinging qalandars attacking established Sufis who enjoyed official patronage appear in a number of Sufi texts (see Digby 1984).

6. Bhutto was particularly interested in strengthening his own ties to his Sindhi roots, bringing Sind into greater prominence, linking the interests of the nation with those of Sind, and using the shrine of Lāl Shahbāz Qalandar as an object of national pride.

7. The Suhrawardī khalīfa I discussed in chapter 3 had mourned the fact that no one performs proper *chillās* anymore.

8. As I will discuss below, this is an anachronism, a telescoping of history.

9. Not all faqīrs who establish themselves in this way regard themselves as qalandars or are labeled malangs by their neighbors. One afternoon, for instance, I stopped at the shrine of Bābā Shāh Bhāg, a small shrine by the side of the main road that passed near my neighborhood. I spoke with the caretaker of the shrine, who explained that he stays at the shrine because he believes in this pīr, who died one hundred years ago. He identified two smaller graves beside the pīr's grave as followers who had lived at the same time, and he claimed to be their "pīr-bhā'ī" (pīr-brother). In a pattern similar to that followed by qalandars, he said that Bābā Shāh Bhāg had come to him in a dream and told him to do service at his grave. He explained that the grave had been only dirt, but that believers, including a rich movie actor and other neighbors, have spent a lot of money to make it *pakkā* ("finished," i.e., stone). (The shrine was still under construction when I paid my visit, and the extent of the improvements indicated that he had solicited considerable financial support.) When I asked him if any qalandars or malangs come to the shrine, he said that only "Sufi types" come, not malangs, thereby aligning himself with bā-shār' Sufism. He considered himself a Chishti.

10. The Khaksar movement was founded in 1931 by M. Inayatullah Khan (Allama Mashriqi), as a social movement dedicated to humanitarian service but with a military-like organization. *Khaksar* means "earthlike," and members were recruited from all classes. They wore khaki uniforms and bore shovels instead of guns as they drilled and paraded. The Khaksars used military titles and, a characteristic which was particularly unusual for this time and place, they trained women in the same manner as men. The title of the female malang I spoke with, "sarkār," would seem to echo this practice. My information on the Khaksar movement is taken from Muhammad 1973.

11. The ego as a process is founded through abjection, by which the subject separates from the maternal matrix. Abjection is a process closely parallel to Melanie Klein's (1946) elaboration of the concept of projection, in which the subject projects onto an external object that which is undesirable. I see abjection, not as a single act or unitary process that founds a coherent, bounded ego, but as a founding split that creates the possibility for reflexivity. Contextually specific self-representations develop on this foundation (see Ewing 1990a).

12. This is not to say that the qalandar inevitably stimulates these reactions in individuals. Abjection is an aspect of the discursive constitution of the subject, but it is not inevitable that the qalandar in particular functions as the abject for all individuals.

13. See McDaniel 1989 for a discussion of a similar phenomenon in Bengal.

14. In subsequent work among these people, I enlisted the aid of a research assistant who was considerably older and less firmly entrenched in the middle class: his personal contacts extended into this community, and his awareness of the perspectives and concerns of these qalandars as individuals was rich and nuanced. Unfortunately, he abruptly disappeared one day in the wake of serious allegations of illegal activity. But he was a superb researcher and a warm and kind person, a friend whom I very much regret losing track of.

15. I was very irritated with Mumtaz at the time, but when I look back, it becomes clear to me that my protective psychological umbrella did not cover Mumtaz. At that point in my fieldwork, I operated under the illusory protection of scholarly distance, which I also took to mean protection from rickshaw accidents and immunity from any serious consequences of the inevitable dysentery and amoebiasis I contracted by drinking mango milkshakes in local bazaars. Mumtaz must have been seriously threatened in these encounters with malangs. I, on the other hand, was in a state of chronic siege that I completely denied. A malang wasn't any more threatening than the careening rickshaws I rode in several times a day.

16. I am inspired here by Taussig's title, "The Magic of the State" (1992b).

17. The contribution of the man's identity as Bengali to this process of abjection should also be noted and placed within the broader context of the history of the two countries. This case illustrates the psychological dynamic of what it means to say that the Pakistanis and Bengalis were "two peoples" that were forced to act for a time as one nation. In another instance, a Punjabi woman said that her father's death in Bengal just before it became an independent country must have been caused by some Bengali putting poison in his soup. The Bengali was the threatening other.

18. The close connection between desire and revulsion was highlighted by Freud in his development of the concept of "reaction formation" (1953:238–39). Kristeva has developed this link in her concept of the link between the sublime and the abject (1982:11), a link that I discuss further in connection with qalandars in chapter 8.

19. Compare with Crapanzano's (1980) Tuhami, who had a similarly close relationship with a female spirit.

20. In Bangladesh, young Muslim men project a similar fear onto the Hindu women of Calcutta, whom they see as insatiable and aggressive (Jim Wilce, personal communication).

Chapter 8: The *Qalandar* as Trope

1. From *Kolliyat-e Divan-e Shams-e-Tabrizi,* ed. Foruzanfar, no. 175, 2 (Bürgel 1979: 47–48).

2. See Meier 1976:494–516 for a comprehensive survey of the use of the term; see also DeBruijn 1992 for a summary and analysis.

3. For information on qalandars in India during this period, see Digby 1984. On their rise in Anatolia, see Ocak 1993.

4. This summary is based on the overviews and analyses of Lapidus (1988) and Hodgson (1974).

5. According to Schimmel, al-Ghazzālī "is reported to have acknowledged his brother's superiority in the path of love" (Schimmel 1975:294).

6. His poetry was popular in thirteenth-century Delhi (Schimmel 1975:296).

7. Carl Ernst has also suggested that much of the supposed debauchery of the "libertines" lay in the imagination of their critics (Ernst 1985).

8. See Meier 1976 for a German translation.

9. Karamustafa (1994) has assembled evidence for the development and spread of qalandars as a Sufi order from the Fertile Crescent and Egypt to India and Asia Minor. He suggests that several antinomian and renunciatory movements arose in the non-Arab cultural spheres and that the early qalandars, though located in Arab regions, were ethnically Iranian and thus not of the cultural mainstream.

10. See Karamustafa 1994 for a detailed recounting of the stories of Sāvī as they appear in diverse historical sources and specifically 1994:18 n. 19, for a discussion of the date of his death. Karamustafa includes the text of several stories about Jamāl al-Dīn Sāvī as they were recorded over several centuries, by authors both sympathetic and antipathetic to the Qalandarī order.

11. This was written by Khatīb Fārisī of Shiraz in 1347–48. It is discussed and summarized in Karamustafa 1994.

12. Žižek has illustrated the process by which this ideological quilting takes place with the example of Coke or Marlboros as mass-media symbols of America. "Quilting" occurs when there is an inversion and "real" Americans start to identify themselves (in their ideological self-experience) with the image created by the Marlboro advertisement — until America itself is experienced as "Marlboro country." This technique of inversion creates a surplus of meaning that points to the unattainable object of desire on which the subject is founded (Žižek 1989:96–97).

13. Though anecdotes of Jamāl al-Dīn Sāvī do appear in several Sufi sources from the Delhi Sultanate period in India (see Digby 1984).

Chapter 9: The Subject, Desire, and Recognition

1. Though Freud himself struggled to encompass both causal explanations of psychical phenomena and a hermeneutic of the unconscious that sought to discover the meaningfulness of symptoms and other unconscious phenomena, this tension has often been lost in the application of psychoanalysis.

2. Western political discourse envisioned a new relationship between the state and the subject as citizen that inverted the authority relationship between ruler and subject, so that wisdom resided with the people and the elected official merely represented the will of the people.

3. In his efforts to "reconstruct" Islamic religious thought, he argued that "during the last five hundred years religious thought in Islam has been practically stationary" (Iqbal 1971a:7).

4. While agreeing with al-Ghazzālī's emphasis on mystical experience as the source of truth, Iqbal was critical of al-Ghazzālī's determination that language and rational thought could not progress, i.e., could not come to closer approximations of the truth because of their inherently finite nature. Iqbal identified al-Ghazzālī with the creation of a radical disjunction between religious experience and knowledge as a crucial turning point in Islamic thought, as the juncture when the rational tradition in Islam came to a halt, thereby causing "stagnation" and the ultimate weakness of the Islamic world vis-à-vis the West.

5. Including al-Ghazzālī's brother Ahmad Ghazzālī.

6. The same could perhaps be said of Lacan: he communicated in such a way that his insights were available only to the initiated.

7. See his essay "Nietzsche and Jalal ud-Din Rumi" (Iqbal 1979: 165).

8. See Foucault's preface to Deleuze and Guattari (Deleuze and Guattari 1983:xiii).

References

Abu-Lughod, Lila. 1986. *Veiled Sentiments: Honor and Poetry in a Bedouin Society.* Berkeley: University of California Press.

Ahmad, Aijaz. 1992. *In Theory: Classes, Nations, Literature.* London: Verso.

Ahmad, Aziz. 1963. "The Sufi and the Sultan in Pre-Mughal Muslim India." *Der Islam* 38:142–53.

All Pakistan Legal Decisions (PLD). 1959. "The West Pakistan Waqf Properties Ordinance of 1959." Vol. 11, pp. 202–5.

———. 1971. Supreme Court Case 401. Pir Rashid-ud-Din Daula v. The Chief Administrator of Auqaf. W. Pakistan Civil Appeal no. 13 of 1963.

———. 1976. "Auqaf (Federal Control Act of 1976)." Vol. 28, pp. 525–32.

Allison, Anne. 1993. "Hail Mother: Interpellation in Obstetrical Practices in Japan." Paper presented at the Biennial Meeting of the Society for Psychological Anthropology, Montreal, October.

Althusser, Louis. 1971. "Ideology and Ideological State Apparatuses (Notes towards an Investigation)." In *Lenin and Philosophy and Other Essays,* pp. 121–73. Ben Brewster, trans. (London: New Left Books). Reprinted in *Essays on Ideology* (London: Verso, 1984).

———. 1984. "Freud and Lacan." In *Essays on Ideology.* London: Verso.

Amin, Sheikh Parviz. 1979. "Baba Farid Shakar Ganj." *Pakistan Times,* November 26.

Anderson, Benedict. 1991. *Imagined Communities.* New York: Verso.

Ansari, Sarah F. D. 1992. *Sufi Saints and State Power: The Pirs of Sind, 1843–1947.* Cambridge: Cambridge University Press.

Appiah, Anthony. 1992. *In My Father's House: Africa in the Philosophy of Culture.* Oxford: Oxford University Press.

Arato, Andrew, and Eike Gebhardt, eds. 1978. *The Essential Frankfurt School Reader.* New York: Urizen Books.

Asad, Talal. 1993. *Genealogies of Religion: Discipline and Reasons of Power in Christianity and Islam.* Baltimore: Johns Hopkins University Press.

'Attār, Farid al-Din. 1990. *Muslim Saints and Mystics: Episodes from the Tadhkirat al-Auliya'* ("*Memorial of the Saints*"). A. J. Arberry, trans. London: Arkana.

Azimi, Khwāja Shamsuddīn. 1983. *Tazkarat-i Qalandar Bābā Auliya.* Karachi: Maktabha Taj Din Baba (Azimi Printers). (Urdu)

Bakhtin, M. M. 1981. *The Dialogic Imagination: Four Essays.* Michael Holquist, ed., Caryl Emerson and Michael Holquist, trans. Austin: University of Texas Press.

Bayly, C. A. 1983. *Rulers, Townsmen and Bazaars: North Indian Society in the Age of British Expansion, 1770–1870.* Cambridge: Cambridge University Press.

Benjamin, Jessica. 1988. *The Bonds of Love: Psychoanalysis, Feminism, and the Problem of Domination.* New York: Pantheon Books.

Benveniste, Emile. 1971. *Problems in General Linguistics.* Mary Elizabeth Meek, trans. Coral Gables: University of Miami Press.

Bhabha, Homi K. 1984. "Of Mimicry and Man: The Ambivalence of Colonial Discourse." *October* 28:125–33.

——. 1986a. "The Other Question: Difference, Discrimination, and the Discourse of Colonialism." In Francis Barker, Peter Hulme, Margaret Iverson, and Diana Loxley, eds., *Literature, Politics and Theory: Papers from the Essex Conference 1976–84,* pp. 148–72. London: Methuen.

——. 1986b. "Remembering Fanon: Self, Psyche and the Colonial Condition." Foreword to Frantz Fanon, *Black Skin, White Masks,* pp. vii–xxvi (London: Pluto Press). Reprinted in Patrick Williams and Laura Chrisman, eds., *Colonial Discourse and Post-Colonial Theory: A Reader* (New York: Columbia University Press, 1994).

——. 1990. "DissemiNation: Time, Narrative, and the Margins of the Modern Nation." In Homi K. Bhabha, ed., *Nation and Narration,* pp. 291–322. London: Routledge.

——. 1994. *The Location of Culture.* London: Routledge.

Blanck, Gertrude, and Rubin Blanck. 1974. *Ego Psychology: Theory and Practice.* New York: Columbia University Press.

Bourdieu, Pierre. 1977. *Outline of a Theory of Practice.* Richard Nice, trans. Cambridge: Cambridge University Press.

——. 1984. *Distinction.* Cambridge: Harvard University Press.

——. 1990. "Social Space and Symbolic Power." In *In Other Words: Essays Towards a Reflexive Sociology,* pp. 123–39. Matthew Adamson, trans. Stanford: Stanford University Press.

——. 1992. "In Conversation: Doxa and Common Life." *New Left Review* 191:111–21.

Browne, Edward G. 1906. *A Literary History of Persia from Firdawsi to Saedi.* 3 vols. London: T. Fisher Unwin.

Bürgel, Johann Christoph. 1979. "The Pious Rogue: A Study in the Meaning of *qalandar* and *rend* in the Poetry of Muhammad Iqbal." *Edebiyat* 4:43–64.

Burton, Richard F. 1973. *Sindh and the Races That Inhabit the Valley of the Indus.* 1851. Karachi: Oxford University Press.

Butler, Judith. 1990. *Gender Trouble: Feminism and the Subversion of Identity.* London: Routledge.

———. 1993. *Bodies That Matter: On the Discursive Limits of "Sex."* London: Routledge.

Calcutta Gazette. 1863. Calcutta: Government of India.

Campbell, Bruce F. 1980. *Ancient Wisdom Revived: A History of the Theosophical Movement.* Berkeley: University of California Press.

Carpenter, Edward. 1914a. *Never Again! A Protest and a Warning Addressed to the Peoples of Europe.* London: Allen and Unwin.

———. 1914b. *Intermediate Types among Primitive Folk: A Study in Social Evolution.* London: Allen.

Certeau, Michel de. 1984. *The Practice of Everyday Life.* Steven Rendall, trans. Berkeley: University of California Press.

———. 1986. *Heterologies: Discourse on the Other.* Brian Massumi, trans. Theory and History of Literature, no. 17. Minneapolis: University of Minnesota Press.

Chatterjee, Partha. 1986. *Nationalist Discourse and the Colonial World: A Derivative Discourse?* Delhi: Zed Books.

Chatterjee, Partha, and Gyandendra Pandey, eds. 1992. *Subaltern Studies VII: Writings on South Asian History and Society.* Delhi: Oxford University Press.

Clifford, James. 1988. *The Predicament of Culture: Twentieth-Century Ethnography, Literature, and Art.* Cambridge, Mass.: Harvard University Press.

Cohn, Bernard. 1964. "The Role of the Gosains in the Economy of Eighteenth- and Nineteenth-Century Upper India." *Indian Economic and Social History Review* 1:175–82.

———. 1987. "The Census, Social Structure, and Objectification in South Asia." In Bernard Cohn, ed., *An Anthropologist among Historians and other Essays,* pp. 224–54. Delhi: Oxford University Press.

Comaroff, Jean, and John L. Comaroff. 1991. *Of Revelation and Revolution: Christianity, Colonialism, and Consciousness in South Africa.* Vol. 1. Chicago: University of Chicago Press.

Comaroff, John L. 1989. "Images of Empire, Contests of Conscience: Models of Colonial Domination in South Africa." *American Ethnologist* 16:661–85.

Combs-Schilling, M. E. 1989. *Sacred Performances: Islam, Sexuality, and Sacrifice.* New York: Columbia University Press.

Crapanzano, Vincent. 1973. *The Hamadsha: A Study in Moroccan Ethnopsychiatry.* Berkeley: University of California Press.

———. 1980. *Tuhami: Portrait of a Moroccan.* Chicago: University of Chicago Press.

Crooke, W. 1896. *The Popular Religion and Folklore of Northern India.* 2 vols. London: Archibald Constable.

Davidson, Flora. 1946. "Shrines on a Northwest Frontier." *The Moslem World* 36:170–72.

DeBruijn, J. T. P. 1992. "The *Qalandariyyāt* in Persian Mystical Poetry, from Sanā'ī Onwards." In Leonard Lewisohn, ed., *The Legacy of Medieval Persian Sufism,* pp. 75–86. London: Khaniqahi Nimatullahi Publications.

De Saussure, Ferdinand. 1966. *Course in General Linguistics.* New York: McGraw-Hill.

Deleuze, Gilles, and Félix Guattari. 1983. *Anti-Oedipus: Capitalism and Schizophrenia.* Robert Hurley, Mark Seem, and Helen R. Lane, trans., Michel Foucault, preface. Minneapolis: University of Minnesota Press.

———. 1987. *A Thousand Plateaus: Capitalism and Schizophrenia.* Brian Massumi, trans. Minneapolis: University of Minnesota Press.

Devji, Faisal Fatehali. 1992. "Hindu/Muslim/Indian." *Public Culture* 5:1–18.

Devereux, George. 1967. *From Anxiety to Method in the Behavioral Sciences.* The Hague: Mouton.

Digby, Simon. 1984. "Qalandars and Related Groups: Elements of Social Deviance in the Religious Life of the Delhī Sultanate of the Thirteenth and Fourteenth Centuries." In Yohanan Friedmann, ed., *Islam in Asia.* Vol. 1, *South Asia,* pp. 60–108. Boulder, Colo.: Westview Press.

Dirks, Nicholas. 1987. *The Hollow Crown: Ethnohistory of an Indian Kingdom.* Cambridge: Cambridge University Press.

Dirlik, Arif. 1994. "The Postcolonial Aura: Third World Criticism in the Age of Global Capitalism." *Critical Inquiry* 20:328–56.

Douglas, Mary. 1966. *Purity and Danger: An Analysis of the Concepts of Pollution and Taboo.* London: Routledge and Kegan Paul.

Eagleton, Terry. 1991. *Ideology: An Introduction.* London: Verso.

Eaton, Richard M. 1978. *Sufis of Bijapur, 1300–1700: Social Roles of Sufis in Medieval India.* Princeton: Princeton University Press.

Elliott, Anthony. 1992. *Social Theory and Psychoanalysis in Transition: Self and Society from Freud to Kristeva.* Oxford: Blackwell.

Ernst, Carl W. 1985. *Words of Ecstasy in Sufism.* Albany: State University of New York Press.

———. 1997. *The Shambhala Guide to Sufism.* Boulder, Colo.: Shambhala Press.

Ewing, Katherine P. 1982. "Sufis and Adepts: Islamic and Hindu Sources of Spiritual Power among Punjabi Muslims and Christian Sweepers." In Steven Pastner and Louis Flam, eds., *Anthropology in Pakistan,* pp. 74–88. Ithaca: Cornell University South Asia Monograph Series.

———. 1983. "The Politics of Sufism: Redefining the Saints of Pakistan." *Journal of Asian Studies* 42:251–65. Reprinted in Akbar S. Ahmed, ed., *Pakistan: The Social Sciences' Perspective,* pp. 165–89 (Karachi: Oxford University Press, 1990).

———. 1984a. "The Sufi as Saint, Curer, and Exorcist in Modern Pakistan." *Contributions to Asian Studies* 18:106–14.

———. 1984b. "*Malangs* of the Punjab: Intoxication or *Adab* as the Path to God?" In Barbara Metcalf, ed., *Moral Conduct and Authority: The Place of Adab in South Asian Islam,* pp. 357–71. Berkeley: University of California Press.

———. 1987. "Clinical Psychoanalysis as an Ethnographic Tool." *Ethos* 15:16–39.

———. 1988. "Ambiguity and *Sharī'at:* A Perspective on the Problem of Moral Principles in Tension." In Katherine Ewing, ed., *Sharī'at and Ambiguity in South Asian Islam,* pp. 1–22. Berkeley: University of California Press.

———. 1990a. "The Illusion of Wholeness: 'Culture,' 'Self,' and the Experience of Inconsistency." *Ethos* 18:251–78.

———. 1990b. "The Dream of Spiritual Initiation and the Organization of Self Representations among Pakistani Sufis." *American Ethnologist* 17:56–74.

———. 1993. "The Modern Businessman and the Pakistani Saint: The Interpenetration of Worlds." In Grace M. Smith and Carl Ernst, eds., *Manifestations of Sainthood in Islam*, pp. 69–84. Istanbul: Isis Press.

———. 1994. "Dreams from a Saint: Anthropological Atheism and the Temptation to Believe." *American Anthropologist* 96:571–83.

Fairbairn, Ronald. 1952. *Psychoanalytic Studies of the Personality*. London: Routledge and Kegan Paul.

Fani, Mohsan. 1901. *The Dabistan; Or, School of Manners: The Religious Beliefs, Observances, Philosophic Opinions, and Social Customs of the Nations of the East.* 3 vols. David Shea and Anthony Troyer, trans. 1843. Washington: M. Walter Dunne.

Fanon, Franz. 1968. *Black Skin, White Masks*. Charles Lam Markmann, trans. New York: Grove Weidenfeld.

Flax, Jane. 1990. "Lacan and Winnicott: Splitting and Regression in Psychoanalytic Theory." In *Thinking Fragments: Psychoanalysis, Feminism, and Postmodernism in the Contemporary West*, pp. 89–132. Berkeley: University of California Press.

Foucault, Michel. 1973. *Madness and Civilization: A History of Insanity in the Age of Reason*. Richard Howard, trans. New York: Vintage Books.

———. 1977. *Discipline and Punish: The Birth of the Prison*. Alan Sheridan, trans. New York: Vintage Books.

———. 1986. "Dream, Imagination, Existence." Forrest Williams and Jacob Needleman, trans. *Review of Existential Psychology and Psychiatry* (special issue) 19:29–78.

———. 1990a. *The History of Sexuality: An Introduction*. Vol. 1. Robert Hurley, trans. New York: Vintage Books.

———. 1990b. *The Use of Pleasure*. Vol. 2 of *The History of Sexuality*. Robert Hurley, trans. New York: Vintage Books.

Fox, Richard G. 1989. *Gandhian Utopia: Experiments with Culture*. Boston: Beacon Press.

Freitag, Sandria B. 1985. "Collective Crime and Authority in North India." In A. A. Yang, ed., *Crime and Criminality in British India*, pp. 140–63. Tucson: University of Arizona Press.

———. 1988. "Ambiguous Public Arenas and Coherent Personal Practice: Kanpur Muslims, 1913–1931." In Katherine P. Ewing, ed., *Shari'at and Ambiguity in South Asian Islam*, pp. 143–63. Berkeley: University of California Press.

———. Forthcoming. "A Century of Visual Rhetoric: Theorising the Nexus between Creation, Consumption and Participation in the Public Sphere." In Rachel Dwyer and Christopher Pinney, eds., *Pleasure and the Nation: The History, Politics and Consumption of Popular Culture in India*.

Freud, Sigmund. 1953. "Three Essays on the Theory of Sexuality." James Strachey, trans. and ed. *Standard Edition*. Vol. 7, pp. 125–245. London: Hogarth Press.

———. 1955a. *The Interpretation of Dreams*. James Strachey, trans. and ed. *Standard Edition*. Vols. 4 and 5. London: Hogarth Press.

———. 1955b. "The Uncanny." James Strachey, trans. and ed. *Standard Edition*. Vol. 17, pp. 217–55. London: Hogarth Press.

———. 1957a. "On Narcissism: An Introduction." James Strachey, trans. and ed. *Standard Edition*. Vol. 14, pp. 67–102. London: Hogarth Press.

———. 1957b. "Mourning and Melancholia." James Strachey, trans. and ed. *Standard Edition*. Vol. 14, pp. 237–58. London: Hogarth Press.

———. 1964. "New Introductory Lectures." James Strachey, trans. and ed. *Standard Edition*. Vol. 22, pp. 5–182. London: Hogarth Press.

Friedmann, Yohanan. 1989. *Prophecy Continues: Aspects of Ahmadi Religious Thought and Its Medieval Background*. Berkeley: University of California Press.

Gedo, John. 1984. *Psychoanalysis and Its Discontents*. New York: Guilford Press.

Geertz, Clifford. 1960. *The Religion of Java*. New York: Free Press.

———. 1973a. *The Interpretation of Cultures*. New York: Basic Books.

———. 1973b. "Religion as a Cultural System." In *The Interpretation of Cultures*, pp. 87–125. New York: Basic Books.

———. 1973c. "Ritual and Social Change: A Javanese Example." In *The Interpretation of Cultures*, pp. 142–69. New York: Basic Books.

———. 1983. "From the Native's Point of View: On the Nature of Anthropological Understanding." In *Local Knowledge: Further Essays in Interpretive Anthropology*, pp. 55–70. New York: Basic Books.

al-Ghazzālī, Abu Hamid. 1952. *Al-Ghazzali's Mishkat Al-Anwar ("The Niche for Lights")*. W. H. T. Gairdner, trans. (Lahore: Sh. Mohammad Ashraf). Reprint of 1924 edition (Royal Asiatic Society).

———. 1975. *On the Duties of Brotherhood (al-Ghazzali's Ihya' 'Ulam Al-Din, Book 5)*. Muhtar Holland, trans. London: Latimer New Dimensions.

———. 1980. *Freedom and Fulfillment: An Annoted Translation of al-Ghazzali's Al-Munqidh min al-dalal and other Relevant Works of al-Ghazali*. Richard Joseph McCarthy, trans. Boston: Twayne Publishers.

———. n.d. *Imām Gazzali's Ihya Ulum-id-din*, bks. 3, 4. Fazal-ul-Karim, trans. Lahore: Sind Sagar Academy, 1978–79?

Ghazzali, Ahmad. 1942. *Savanih: Aphorism über die Liebe*. Hellmut Ritter, ed. Istanbul: Staatsdruckerei, Bibliotheca Islamica, Bd. 15.

Ghosh, J. M. 1930. *Sannyasi and Fakir Raiders in Bengal*. Calcutta: Bengal Secretariat Book Depot.

Gilmartin, David. 1979. "Religious Leadership and the Pakistan Movement in the Punjab." *Modern Asian Studies* 13:485–517.

———. 1984. "Shrines, Succession, and Sources of Moral Authority." In Barbara Metcalf, ed., *Moral Conduct and Authority: The Place of Adab in South Asian Islam*, pp. 221–40. Berkeley: University of California Press.

———. 1988. *Empire and Islam: Punjab and the Making of Pakistan*. Berkeley: University of California Press.

Glasse, Cyril. 1988. "Ruqyah." In *The Concise Encyclopedia of Islam*. Vol. 2, p. 339. San Francisco: Harper and Row.

Government of West Pakistan. 1961–62. *The West Pakistan Code*. Vol. 3, pp. 353–62.

Gramsci, Antonio. 1971. *Selections from the Prison Notebooks.* Quintin Hoare and Geoffrey Nowell Smith, eds. and trans. New York: International Publishers.

Guha, Ranajit. 1983. *Elementary Aspects of Peasant Insurgency in Colonial India.* Delhi: Oxford University Press.

Guha, Ranajit, ed. 1982–89. *Subaltern Studies: Writings on South Asian History and Society.* Vols. 1–6. Delhi: Oxford University Press.

Gupta, Dipankar. 1985. "On Altering the Ego in Peasant History: Paradoxes of the Ethnic Option." *Peasant Studies* 13:5–24.

Habermas, Jürgen. 1987. *The Philosophical Discourse of Modernity: Twelve Lectures.* Frederick G. Lawrence, trans. Cambridge, Mass.: MIT Press.

Hand Book on the Waqf Act, 1954. 1985. Delhi: Delhi Law House.

Hansen, Kathryn. 1992. *Grounds for Play: The Nauṭankī Theatre of North India.* Berkeley: University of California Press.

Hartmann, Heinz. 1964. *Essays in Ego Psychology.* New York: International Universities Press.

Harvey, David. 1989. *The Condition of Postmodernity.* Oxford: Basil Blackwell.

Hegel, G. W. F. 1979. *Phenomenology of the Spirit.* A. V. Miller, trans. Oxford: Oxford University Press.

The Herald (weekly magazine, Karachi, Pakistan). 1984a. "The Sufi Revival." September 1984, p. 42.

———. 1984b. "Waris Shah: When Will Official Recognition Come?" September 1984, pp. 57–58.

Hodgson, Marshall G. 1974. *The Venture of Islam: Conscience and History in a World Civilization.* Vol. 2. Chicago: University of Chicago Press.

Hughes, Thomas P. 1965. *A Dictionary of Islam; Being a Cyclopaedia of the Doctrines, Rites, Ceremonies and Customs, together with the Technical and Theological Terms of the Muhammadan Religion.* 1885. Lahore: Premier Book House.

al-Hujwīrī, ʿAlī bin ʿUthmān Sullābī. 1976. *Kashf al-Mahjūb: The Oldest Persian Treatise on Sufiism.* Reynold A. Nicholson, trans. 1911. Lahore: Islamic Book Foundation.

Hunter, William Wilson. 1897. *Annals of Rural Bengal.* London: Smith, Elder.

———. 1907. *A Brief History of the Indian Peoples.* Oxford: Clarendon Press.

Ibbetson, Denzil. 1974. *Punjab Castes.* Lahore: S. Mubarak Ali. 1883. Reprint of "The Races, Castes and Tribes of the People" from the Punjab Census Report of 1881. Lahore: Government Printing.

Ibn Batuta. 1973. *The Travels of Ibn Batuta, AD 1325–1354.* 3 vols. New Delhi: Munshiram Manoharlal.

Inden, Ronald. 1990. *Imagining India.* Oxford: Blackwell.

Iqbal, Javid. 1959. *The Ideology of Pakistan and Its Implementation.* Lahore: Ghulam Ali.

———. 1971. *The Ideology of Pakistan.* 2d ed. Karachi: Ferozsons.

Iqbal, Muhammad. 1940. *Secrets of the Self (Asrar-I-Khudi): A Philosophical Poem.* Reynold A. Nicholson, trans. and intro. 1920. Lahore: Sh. Muhammad Ashraf Press.

———. 1964a. "Islam and Mysticism." In Syed Abdul Vahid, ed., *Thoughts and Reflections of Iqbal,* pp. 80–83. Lahore: Sh. Muhammad Ashraf.

———. 1964b. "Islam as a Moral and Political Ideal." In Syed Abdul Vahid, ed., *Thoughts and Reflections of Iqbal*, pp. 29–55. Lahore: Sh. Muhammad Ashraf. Originally published in *Hindustan Review* 20 (1909).

———. 1964c. "Letter to Dr. Nicholson." In Syed Abdul Vahid, ed., *Thoughts and Reflections of Iqbal*, pp. 93–102. Lahore: Sh. Muhammad Ashraf.

———. 1964. *The Servant of Metaphysics in Persia: A Contribution to the History of Muslim Philosophy*. Lahore: Bazin-[i]-Iqbal.

———. 1971a. *The Reconstruction of Religious Thought in Islam*. Lahore: Sh. Muhammad Ashraf.

———. 1971b. *A Message from the East: A Translation of Iqbal's Payam-i-Mashriq into English Verse*. M. Hadi Hussain, trans. Lahore: Iqbal Academy.

———. 1979. *Discourses of Iqbal*. Shahid Hussain Razzaqi, ed. Lahore: Sh. Ghulam Ali and Sons.

Irigaray, Luce. 1985. *This Sex Which Is Not One*. Catherine Porter, trans. Ithaca: Cornell University Press.

Jafri, Rais Ahmad. 1966. *Ayub: Soldier and Statesman, Speeches and Statements (1958–65) of Field Marshall Muhammad Ayub Khan, President of Pakistan*. Lahore: Muhammad Ali Academy.

Jeffery, Patricia. 1979. *Frogs in a Well: Indian Women in Purdah*. London: Zed Press.

Karamustafa, Ahmet T. 1994. *God's Unruly Friends: Dervish Groups in the Islamic Later Middle Period, 1200–1550*. Salt Lake City: University of Utah Press.

Kepel, Gilles. 1993. *Muslim Extremism in Egypt: The Prophet and Pharaoh*. Jon Rothschild, trans. Berkeley: University of California Press.

Khalid, K. B. 1967. *Asar-i-Latif*. Hyderabad: Directorate of Information, Government of West Pakistan.

———. 1971. *Sachal Sarmast*. Karachi: Department of Public Relations, Government of Sind.

———. 1972. *The Poet of the People: A Miscellany of Articles to Commemorate the 220th Anniversary of Shah Abdul Latif of Bhit*. Karachi: Department of Public Relations, Government of Sind.

Khan, Ali. 1984. "Our Whole Culture Reeks of Sickening Nostalgia — Sarmand Sehbai." *The Herald*, October, pp. 78–80.

Khan, Khaja. 1923. *Studies in Tasawwuf*. Madras: Hogarth.

Kildea, Gary. 1975. *Trobriand Cricket: An Indigenous Response to Colonialism*. Berkeley: University of California Extension Center. Produced by Office of Information, Government of Papua, New Guinea. Film.

Klein, Melanie. 1946. "Notes on Some Schizoid Mechanisms." *International Journal of Psychoanalysis* 27:99–110.

———. 1957. *Envy and Gratitude*. New York: Basic Books.

Kohut, Heinz. 1977. *The Restoration of the Self*. New York: International Universities Press.

Kojève, Alexandre. 1969. *Introduction to the Reading of Hegel: Lectures on the Phenomenology of Spirit*. Allan Bloom, ed., James H. Nichols Jr., trans. New York: Basic Books.

Kondo, Dorinne K. 1990. *Crafting Selves: Power, Gender, and Discourses of Identity in a Japanese Workplace.* Chicago: University of Chicago Press.

Kopf, David. 1969. *British Orientalism and the Bengal Renaissance: The Dynamics of Indian Modernization, 1773–1835.* Berkeley: University of California Press.

Kozlowski, Gregory. 1985. *Muslim Endowments and Society in British India.* Cambridge: Cambridge University Press.

Kristeva, Julia. 1982. *Powers of Horror: An Essay on Abjection.* Leon S. Roudiez, trans. New York: Columbia University Press.

———. 1986a. "Revolution in Poetic Language." In Toril Moi, ed., *The Kristeva Reader,* pp. 89–136. New York: Columbia University Press.

———. 1986b. "Freud and Love: Treatment and Its Discontents." In Toril Moi, ed., *The Kristeva Reader,* pp. 238–71. New York: Columbia University Press.

———. 1987. *In the Beginning Was Love: Psychoanalysis and Faith.* Arthur Goldhammer, trans., Otto F. Kernberg, intro. New York: Columbia University Press.

Kuhn, Thomas S. 1970. *The Structure of Scientific Revolutions.* Chicago: University of Chicago Press.

Lacan, Jacques. 1977. *Écrits: A Selection.* Alan Sheridan, trans. New York: W. W. Norton.

Laclau, Ernesto, and Chantal Mouffe. 1985. *Hegemony and Socialist Strategy: Towards a Radical Democratic Politics.* London: Verso.

Lambrick, H. T., trans. and ed. 1972. *The Terrorist.* London: Ernest Benn.

Lapidus, Ira M. 1988. *A History of Islamic Society.* Cambridge: Cambridge University Press.

Lavan, Spencer. 1974. *The Ahmadiyyah Movement: A History and Perspective.* Delhi: Manohar Book Service.

Lawrence, Bruce. 1989. *Defenders of God: The Fundamentalist Revolt against the Modern Age.* San Francisco: Harper and Row.

Lears, T. J. Jackson. 1985. "The Concept of Cultural Hegemony: Problems and Possibilities." *American Historical Review* 9:567–93.

Lévi-Strauss, Claude. 1963. "The Structural Study of Myth." In *Structural Anthropology,* pp. 206–31. Claire Jacobson and Brooke G. Schoepf, trans. New York: Basic Books.

Lorenzen, David N. 1974. "La Rebelión de los Sannyāsīs." *Estudios Orientales* 9:2–13.

———. 1978. "Warrior Ascetics in Indian History." *Journal of the American Oriental Society* 98:61–75.

Lorraine, Tamsin E. 1990. *Gender, Identity, and the Production of Meaning: Feminist Theory and Politics.* Boulder, Colo.: Westview Press.

McDaniel, June. 1989. *The Madness of Saints: Ecstatic Religion in Bengal.* Chicago: University of Chicago Press.

Malamud, Margaret. 1994. "Sufi Organizations and Structures of Authority in Medieval Nishapur." *International Journal of Middle East Studies* 26:427–42.

Malik, Jamal. 1996. *Colonization of Islam: Dissolution of Traditional Institutions in Pakistan.* New Delhi: Manohar.

Manerī, Sharaf al-Dīn Ahmad ibn Yahyā. 1980. *Letters from a Sūfī Teacher: Shaikh*

Sharfuddîn Manerî or Makhdûm ul-Mulk. Baijnath Singh, trans. 1908. New York: Samuel Weiser.

Martin, Luther N., Nuck Gutman, and Patrick N. Nutter, eds. 1988. *Technologies of the Self: A Seminar with Michel Foucault*. Amherst: University of Massachusetts Press.

Massignon, Louis. 1922. *La Passion d'al-Hosayn ibn Mansour Al-Hallāj, martyr mystique de l'Islam exécuté à Bagdad le 26 Mars, 922: étude d'histoire religieuse*. 2 vols. Paris: Gallimard.

Maudoodi, Syed Abul 'Ala. 1963. *A Short History of the Revivalist Movement in Islam*. Al-Ash'ari, trans. Lahore: Islamic Publications.

Meier, Fritz. 1976. *Abū Saʿīd-i Abū l-Ḥayr (357–440/967–1049): Wirklichkeit und Legende*, Acta Iranica 11, pp. 494–516. Téhéran: Édition Bibliothèque Pahlavi.

Metcalf, Barbara D. 1982. *Islamic Revival in British India: Deoband, 1860–1900*. Princeton: Princeton University Press.

——. 1990. *Perfecting Women: Maulana Ashraf 'Ali Thanawi's "Bihishti Zewar."* Barbara Metcalf, trans. and commentator. Berkeley: University of California Press.

Mitchell, Timothy. 1991. *Colonizing Egypt*. Berkeley: University of California Press.

Mouffe, Chantal. 1979. "Hegemony and Ideology in Gramsci." In Chantal Mouffe, ed., *Gramsci and Marxist Theory*, pp. 168–204. London: Routledge and Kegan Paul.

Muhammad, Shah. 1973. *Khaksar Movement in India*. Meerut: Meenakshi Prakashar.

al-Mujahid, Sharif. 1974. *Ideology of Pakistan*. Lahore: Progressive Publishers.

Müller, Max Friedrich, ed. 1879–1900. *The Sacred Books of the East*. 50 vols. Oxford: Clarendon Press.

Murray, D. W. 1993. "What Is the Western Concept of the Self? On Forgetting David Hume." *Ethos* 23:3–23.

Nandy, Ashis. 1983. *The Intimate Enemy: Loss and Recovery of Self under Colonialism*. Delhi: Oxford University Press.

Nasr, Seyyed Hossein. 1977. *An Introduction to Islamic Cosmological Doctrines*. Boulder, Colo.: Shambhala Press.

Nietzsche, Friedrich. 1968. *The Will to Power*. Walter Kaufman and R. J. Hollingdale, trans. New York: Vintage Books.

Nizam-ud-Din, Syed. 1914. *'Aql-o-Shuur*. 1873. Lucknow: Newal Kishore Press. (Urdu)

Obeyesekere, Gananath. 1990. *The Work of Culture: Symbolic Transformation in Psychoanalysis and Anthropology*. Lewis Henry Morgan Lectures. Chicago: University of Chicago Press.

Ocak, A. Yaşar. 1993. "Kalenderi Dervishes and Ottoman Administration from the Fourteenth to the Sixteenth Centuries." In Grace M. Smith and Carl Ernst, eds., *Manifestations of Sainthood in Islam*, pp. 239–56. Istanbul: İsis Press.

O'Flaherty, Wendy Doniger, trans. and ed. 1975. *Hindu Myths: A Sourcebook Translated from the Sanskrit*. New York: Penguin Books.

O'Hanlon, Rosalind. 1988. "Recovering the Subject: *Subaltern Studies* and Histories of Resistance in Colonial South Asia." *Modern Asian Studies* 22:189–224.

Oman, J. Campbell. 1889. *Indian Life, Religious and Social*. London: T. Fisher Unwin.

——. 1905. *The Mystics, Ascetics and Saints of India: A Study of Sadhuism, with an*

Account of the Yogis, Sanyasis, Bairagis, and Other Strange Hindu Sectarians. London: T. Fisher Unwin.

———. 1908. *Cults, Customs, and Superstitions of India, Comprising Studies and Sketches of Interesting Peculiarities in the Beliefs, Festivals, and Domestic Life of the Indian People; also of Witchcraft and Demoniacal Possession, as known amongst them.* Rev. ed., Oman 1889. London: T. Fisher Unwin.

Pakistan Times (Lahore). 1959a. "Shah Latif 'urs' Begins at Bhitshah Today," August 20.

———. 1959b. "Governor's Address to Adabi Conference at Bhitshah," August 22.

———. 1969. "Fareed Academy to Be Set Up," June 11.

———. 1974a. "Data Ganj Bakhsh Urs on 13th," March 10.

———. 1974b. " 'Kindle Hearts with Divine Splendour': Madho Lal's Urs Begins," March 31.

———. 1977. "C.M. to Open Data's 'Urs'." February 7.

———. 1980a. "Details of Data's Urs Arrangements," January 6.

———. 1980b. "Data's Services to Islam Commemorated," December 29.

———. 1980c. "Thousands Visit Data's Shrine," December 29.

Parkes, Graham. 1991. *Nietzsche and Asian Thought.* Chicago: University of Chicago Press.

Peacock, James L. 1984. "Religion and Life History: An Exploration in Cultural Psychology." In Stuart Plattner and Edward M. Bruner, eds., *Text, Play, and Story: The Construction and Reconstruction of Self and Society,* pp. 94–116. Washington, D.C.: American Ethnological Society.

Perrin, Norman, and Dennis C. Duling. 1982. *The New Testament: An Introduction.* 2d ed. San Diego: Harcourt Brace Jovanovich.

Platts, John T. 1967. *A Dictionary of Urdu, Classical Hindi and English.* 1884. Delhi: Munshiram Manoharlal.

Population Census of Pakistan: Lahore District. 1961. *Census Report.* Part I. Karachi: Government of Pakistan.

Prakash, Gyan. 1990. "Writing Post-Orientalist Histories of the Third World: Perspectives from Indian Historiography." *Comparative Studies in Society and History* 32:383–408.

———. 1992. "Postcolonial Criticism and Indian Historiography." *Social Text,* nos. 31–32:8–19.

Prakash, Karat. 1973. *Language and Nationality Politics in India.* Bombay: Orient Longman.

Raheja, Gloria G. 1988. *The Poison in the Gift: Ritual, Prestation, and the Dominant Caste in a North Indian Village.* Chicago: University of Chicago Press.

Raheja, Gloria G., and Ann G. Gold. 1994. *Listen to the Heron's Words: Reimagining Gender and Kinship in North India.* Berkeley: University of California Press.

al-Rahmān, 'Aziz. n.d.(a). *Ta 'wizat-o-'Amaliyat Sufiyya.* Lahore: Allah-Wale ki Qaumi Dukan. (Urdu)

———. n.d.(b). *Ma 'dan al-Barakat fi 'Amal al-Salihal.* Lahore: Allah-Wale ki Qaumi Dukan. (Urdu)

Razi, Najim al-Din 'Abd Allah ibn Muhammad "Daya." 1982. *The Path of God's Bonds-*

men from Origin to Return: A Sufi Compendium. Hamid Algar, trans. Persian Heritage Series, no. 35. Delmar, N.Y.: Caravan Books.

Reddy, William. 1987. *Money and Liberty in Modern Europe: A Critique of Historical Understanding.* Cambridge: Cambridge University Press.

——. 1993. "Marriage, Honor, and the Public Sphere in Post-Revolutionary France: Separations de Corps, 1815–1848." *Journal of Modern History* 65:437–73.

Report of the Criminal Tribes Act Enquiry Committee. 1949–50. New Delhi: Government of India Press.

Report on the Punjab Disturbances, April 1919 (Confidential). 1919. October 11. Private collection of David Gilmartin.

Ricoeur, Paul. 1992. *Oneself as Another.* Kathleen Blamey, trans. Chicago: University of Chicago Press.

Ritter, Hellmut. 1955. *Das Meer der Seele: Mensch, Welt, und Gott in den Geschichten des Farīduddīn ʿAṭṭār.* Leiden: E. J. Brill.

Rosenthal, Franz. 1971. *The Herb: Hashish versus Medieval Muslim Society.* Leiden: E. J. Brill.

Rūmī, Jalāl ud-Dīn. 1925–40. *Mathnawī-i ma ʿnawī.* Reynold A. Nicholson, ed. and trans. 8 vols. London.

Sabri, Ehsan Qureshi. 1980. "Ulema and Saints of Sialkot." *Pakistan Times,* December 17.

Said, Edward W. 1979. *Orientalism.* New York: Vintage Press.

——. 1990. "Third World Intellectuals and the Metropolitan Culture." *Raritan* 9:27–54.

Sanyal, Usha. 1996. *Devotional Islam and Politics in British India: Ahmed Riza Khan Barelvi and His Movement, 1870–1920.* Delhi: Oxford University Press.

Sayeed, Khalid B. 1968. *Pakistan, the Formative Phase, 1857–1948.* London: Oxford University Press.

Schimmel, Annemarie. 1975. *Mystical Dimensions of Islam.* Chapel Hill: University of North Carolina Press.

Schwab, Raymond. 1984. *The Oriental Renaissance: Europe's Rediscovery of India and the East, 1680–1880.* Gene Patterson-Black and Victor Reinking, trans. New York: Columbia University Press.

Shibli, A. R. 1974. "Crusade against Social Injustice: Data Ganj Bakhsh." *Pakistan Times,* March 15.

Shurreef, Jaffur. 1973. *Qanoon-e-Islam; or, The Customs of the Mussalmans of India.* G. A. Hercklots, trans. 2d ed., Madras, 1883. Lahore: Al-Irshad.

Silverman, Kaja. 1983. *The Subject of Semiotics.* New York: Oxford University Press.

——. 1992. *Male Subjectivity at the Margins.* New York: Routledge.

Silverstein, Michael. 1976. "Shifters, Linguistic Categories, and Cultural Description." In Keith Basso and Henry Selby, eds., *Meaning in Anthropology,* pp. 11–55. Albuquerque: University of New Mexico Press.

Sind Directorate of Public Relations. 1971. *Qalandar Lal Shahbaz.* Karachi.

Sind Information Department. n.d. *Qalandar Lal Shahbaz.* Karachi.

Singh, Atam, trans. 1982. *Songs of Bullah.* 1940. Lahore: Panjabi Adabi Laihr.

Smith, Paul. 1988. *Discerning the Subject.* Theory and History of Literature, no. 55. John Mowitt, foreword. Minneapolis: University of Minnesota Press.

Somerville, Augustus. 1929. *Crime and Religious Beliefs in India*. Calcutta: The Criminologist.

Spivak, Gayatri C. 1988a. *In Other Worlds: Essays in Cultural Politics*. New York: Routledge.

——. 1988b. "Subaltern Studies: Deconstructing Historiography." In *In Other Worlds: Essays in Cultural Politics*, pp. 197–221. New York: Routledge.

Steel, F. A. 1884. "Possession — Saya." In R. C. Temple, ed., *Punjab Notes and Queries* 1(11): 126.

Suhrawardī, Shaikh Shahābu-d-Dīn 'Umar bin Muhammed-i-. 1980. *A Dervish Textbook from the 'Awarifu-l-Ma 'ārif*. H. Wilberforce Clarke, trans. Calcutta, 1891. London: Octagon Press.

Suleri, Sara. 1992. *The Rhetoric of English India*. Chicago: University of Chicago Press.

Talbot, Ian. 1988. *Punjab and the Raj, 1849–1947*. New Delhi: Manohar.

Taussig, Michael. 1992a. *The Nervous System*. London: Routledge.

——. 1992b. "The Magic of the State." *Public Culture* 5:63–66.

Thompson, E. P. 1966. *The Making of the English Working Class*. New York: Vintage Books.

Trimingham, John S. 1971. *The Sufi Orders in Islam*. Oxford: Clarendon Press.

Trix, Frances. 1993. *Spiritual Discourse: Learning with an Islamic Master*. Philadelphia: University of Pennsylvania Press.

Turan, Osman. 1953. "Selçuk Turkiyesi din tarihine dair bir kaynak: Fustāt ul-'adāle fī ḳavā'id is-salṭana." In *60. Doğum yili Münasebetiyle Fuad Köprülü Armağani*, pp. 531–64. Istanbul: Ankara Üniversitesi Dil re Tarih-Coğrafya Fakültesi.

Turner, Victor. 1967. "Symbols in Ndembu Ritual." In *The Forest of Symbols: Aspects of Ndembu Ritual*, pp. 19–47. Ithaca: Cornell University Press.

——. 1977. *The Ritual Process: Structure and Anti-Structure*. Ithaca: Cornell University Press.

Van der Veer, Peter. 1994. *Religious Nationalism: Hindus and Muslims in India*. Berkeley: University of California Press.

Vreede-de-Stuers, Cora. 1968. *Parda: A Study of Muslim Women's Life in North India*. New York: Humanities Press.

Wallace, Anthony. 1956. "Revitalization Movements." *American Anthropologist* 58: 264–81.

——. 1967. "Identity Processes in Personality and Culture." In Richard Jessor and Seymour Feshbach, eds., *Cognition, Personality and Clinical Psychology: A Symposium held at the University of Colorado*, pp. 62–89. San Francisco: Jossey-Bass.

Watt, William M. 1963. *Muslim Intellectual: A Study of Al-Ghazzali*. Edinburgh: University Press.

Weber, Max. 1958. *The Protestant Ethic and the Spirit of Capitalism: The Relationships between Religion and the Economic and Social Life in Modern Culture*. Talcott Parsons, trans. New York: Charles Scribner's Sons. First published in *Archiv für Sozialwissenschaft und Sozialpolitik* 1904, 1905; trans. 1930, George Allen and Unwin.

Westermarck, Edward. 1926. *Ritual and Belief in Morocco*. 2 vols. London: Macmillan.

Who's Who. 1908. London: A. and C. Black.

Wilce, James. 1994. "Repressed Eloquence: Patients as Subjects and Objects of Complaints in Matlab, Bangladesh." Ph.D. diss., University of California, Los Angeles.

Williams, Patrick, and Laura Chrisman, eds. 1994. *Colonial Discourse and Post-Colonial Theory: A Reader*. New York: Columbia University Press.

Williams, Raymond. 1977. *Marxism and Literature*. Oxford: Oxford University Press.

———. 1983. *Keywords*. New York: Oxford University Press.

———. 1989. "Metropolitan Perceptions and the Emergence of Modernism." In *The Politics of Modernism*, pp. 37–48. London: Verso.

Winnicott, D. W. 1965. "Ego Distortion in Terms of True and False Self." In *The Maturational Processes and the Facilitating Environment*, pp. 140–52. New York: International Universities Press.

———. 1971. "Mirror Role of Mother and Family in Child Development." In *Playing and Reality*. New York: Basic Books.

Wyschogrod, Edith, David Crownfield, and Carl A. Raschke, eds. 1989. *Lacan and Theological Discourse*. Albany: State University of New York Press.

Yazici, Tahsin. 1978. "Kalandar." In *Encyclopedia of Islam*, new ed., vol. 4, pp. 472–73. Leiden: E. J. Brill.

———. 1978. "Kalandariyya." In *Encyclopedia of Islam*, new ed., vol. 4, pp. 473–74. Leiden: E. J. Brill.

Young, Robert. 1990. *White Mythologies: Writing History and the West*. London: Routledge.

Zaman, Muhammad Qasim. Forthcoming. *Madrasas of Pakistan: Traditional Education and the Roots of Islamic Revival*.

Žižek, Slavoj. 1989. *The Sublime Object of Ideology*. London: Verso.

Index

sensory/imaginative spirit, 258–60;
transcendental prophetic spirit, 259
Ghazzālī, Ahmad, 242
Ghulam Khalīl, 185
Ghulam Rasul. *See* Sufi Ghulam Rasul
Gīlānī, 'Abdu'l-Qādir, 147, 151, 286
n.11
Goat's head. *See* Taunā: goat's head
Gramsci, Antonio, 21–26, 35–36, 217;
common sense, 22–23
Guattari, Félix. *See* Deleuze, Gilles, and
Félix Guattari
Gwaliori, Muhammad Ghaus: *Jawāhir-i
Khamsa*, 133

Hadīth. *See* Islam: Hadīth
Halāl, 101
Hallāj, al-Husayn ibn Mansur, 240, 276
n.11
Hamadhānī, 'Aynu'l-Quzāt, 242
Hartmann, Heinz, 279 n.31
Hashish. *See* Drug use
Hastings, Warren, 53
Hegel, G. W. F., 27, 264, 265; recognition,
33–35, 195
Hegemony, 1–37
Holy man, 47–50, 62–64
Hujwīrī. *See* Data Ganj Bakhsh
Humanism/Antihumanism, 17–18
Hurs, 49–50

Ibbetson, Denzil, 55–57
Ibn 'Arabī, Muhyīuddīn Muhammad, 72
Ibn Batuta, Abū 'Abdallāh Muhammad,
248
Idolatry. *See* Shirk
'Ilm (knowledge): kālā 'ilm (black magic),
135–42, 151–55, 158–59, 211, 219,
222, 224–27, 284 n.9 (see also Jādū);
nūrī 'ilm, 135–42, 151–54, 158–59
Imaginary Order. *See* Lacan: Imaginary
Order
Indian spirituality: as resistance, 61–64;
romantic poets, 61–62; Sanskrit texts,

61. *See also* Beggar-ascetic; Drug use;
Sufi; Wandering
Iqbal, Javid. *See* Iqbal, Muhammad: and
son Javid
Iqbal, Muhammad, 10, 195, 231, 232,
254–57, 265–67, 291 n.4; and son
Javid, 68–78
Irigaray, Luce, 34
'Ishq. *See* Sufi: desire
Islam: against, 96, 203; Hadīth, 83, 268,
272; Hanbalite mazhab, 236; hashawiyya, 230; -ism, 275; Orientalist view
of, 41–45; proper (Sunni), 96, 100,
125, 151, 218, 234, 244; rationalization of, 68–88; reformist orientation,
93–127, 140–42, 152–53; and science,
166–68, 179, 182–83, 196; Shia, 219,
224; as signifier, 65–67; -ic Socialism,
72; sunna, 203, 244; world of, 20–21.
See also Jama'at-i Islami; Pakistan;
Sharī'at; Shirk

Jādū, 121–25
Jama'at-i Islami, 76, 95, 205, 284 n.3
Jāmī, Maulana 'Abdu'r-Rahmān, 230,
250
Jinn, 117, 272, 285 n.18. *See also*
Mu'akkal
Jinnah, Mohammed Ali, 68, 280 n.6

Kālā 'ilm. *See* 'Ilm (knowledge): kālā 'ilm
(black magic)
Karamustafa, Ahmet T., 248, 287 n.1,
290 n.10
Khaksar movement, 212, 216, 288
n.10
Khalīfa, 144–45, 196, 272
Khan, Ayub, 70–77, 88–89
Khānaqāh, 189–93, 197
Khatīb, Muhammad al-, 246–47
Khilāfat, 85, 144–45
Klein, Melanie, 280 n.9, 288 n.11
Kondo, Dorinne K., 277 n.26
Kozlowski, Gregory, 280 n.6

Katherine Pratt Ewing is Associate Professor in the
Department of Cultural Anthropology at Duke University.

Library of Congress Cataloging-in-Publication Data
Ewing, Katherine Pratt.
Arguing sainthood : modernity, psychoanalysis, and Islam /
by Katherine Pratt Ewing.
p.   cm.
Includes bibliographical references (p.   ) and index.
ISBN 0-8223-2026-6 (alk. paper). —
ISBN 0-8223-2024-X (pbk. : alk. paper)
1. Sufism — Controversial literature.   2. Islam — 20th century.
I. Title.
BP189.36.E95   1997
297.4'09591 — dc21   97-14066   CIP

DATE DUE

#47-0108 Peel Off Pressure Sensitive